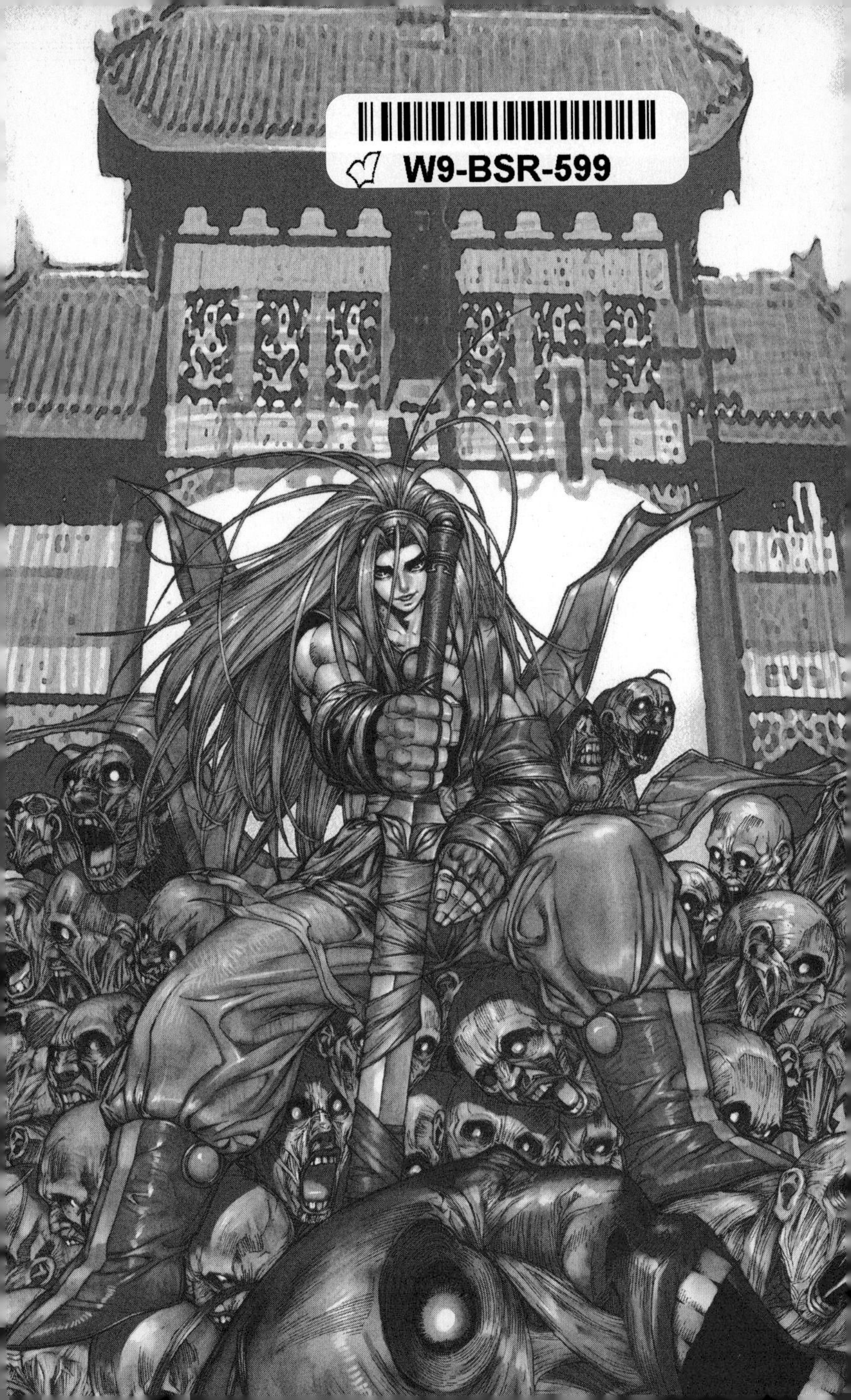

King of Hell Vol. 10
Written by Ra In-Soo
Illustrated by Kim Jae-Hwan

Translation - Lauren Na
English Adaptation - R.A. Jones
Copy Editor - Peter Ahlstrom and Chelsea Enea
Retouch and Lettering - Tom Misuraca
Production Artist - Jason Milligan
Cover Design - Seth Cable

Editor - Rob Tokar
Digital Imaging Manager - Chris Buford
Pre-Press Manager - Antonio DePietro
Production Managers - Jennifer Miller and Mutsumi Miyazaki
Art Director - Matt Alford
Managing Editor - Jill Freshney
VP of Production - Ron Klamert
Editor-in-Chief - Mike Kiley
President and C.O.O. - John Parker
Publisher and C.E.O. - Stuart Levy

A  Manga

TOKYOPOP Inc.
5900 Wilshire Blvd. Suite 2000
Los Angeles, CA 90036

E-mail: info@TOKYOPOP.com
Come visit us online at www.TOKYOPOP.com

ISBN: 1-59532-598-0

First TOKYOPOP printing: July 2005
10 9 8 7 6 5 4 3 2 1
Printed in the USA

KING OF HELL

VOLUME 10

BY
RA IN-SOO
&
KIM JAE-HWAN

HAMBURG // LONDON // LOS ANGELES // TOKYO

Who the Hell...?

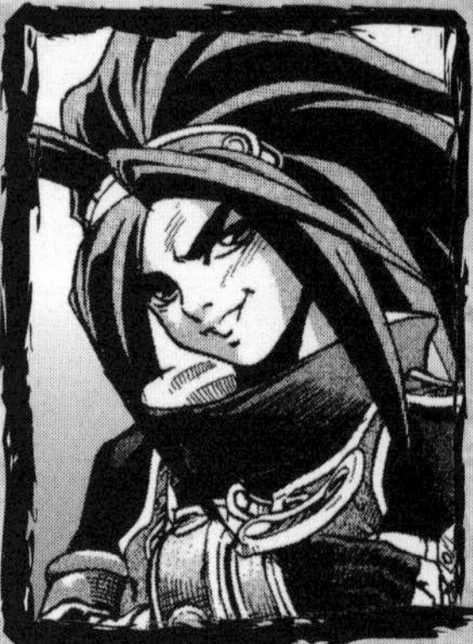

MAJEH:

When he was alive, Majeh was an extremely powerful and much-feared warrior. In death, Majeh was recruited to be a collector of souls for the King of Hell. Recently, Majeh was returned to his human form in order to destroy the escaped evil spirits for the King of Hell. There are two catches, however: Majeh's full powers are restrained by a mystical seal. His physical form is that of a teenage boy.

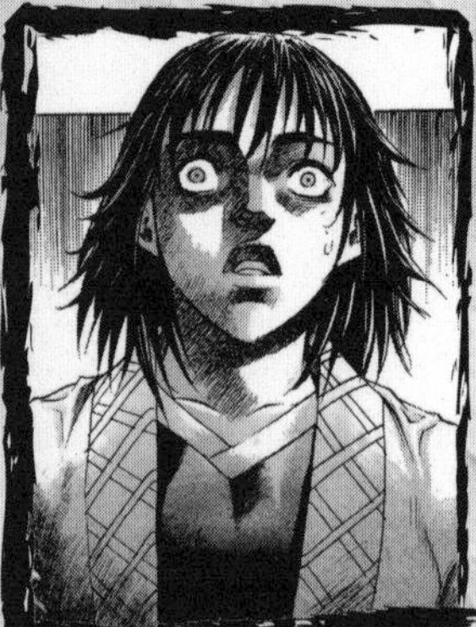

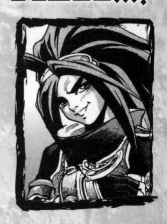

CHUNG POONG NAMGOONG:

A coward from a once-respected family, Chung Poong left home hoping to prove himself at the Martial Arts Tournament in Nakyang. Broke and desperate, Chung Poong tried to rob Majeh. In a very rare moment of pity, Majeh allowed Chung Poong to live...and to tag along with him to the tournament.

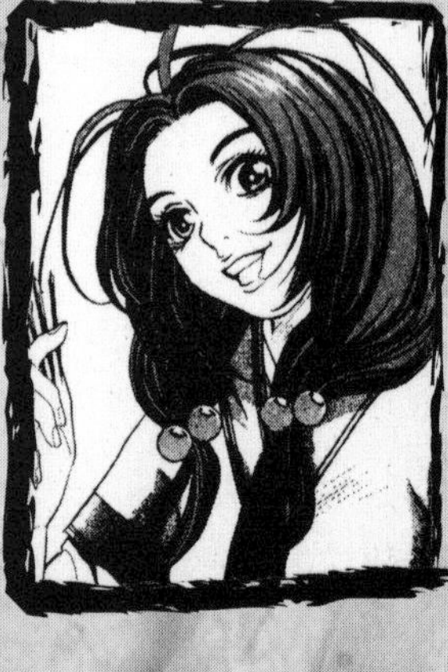

DOHWA BAIK:

A vivacious vixen whose weapons of choice are poisoned needles. After repeatedly humiliating the hapless trio known as the Insane Hounds, she joined Majeh and Chung Poong on the way to the tournament.

HUNTER:

A demon hunter of the Chung Myun Hhk Soo, little is known about Hunter (as he's known thus far) except that he's in his twenties, he's a little sensitive about his age, and he's an incredible fighter who's so afraid of bugs that he screams like a little girl.

MO YOUNG BAIK:

Self-described master of all the martial arts and host of the Nakyang Martial Arts Tournament. Though Mo Young has only a small understanding of Majeh's abilities, he has still placed his trust in Hell's cockiest envoy.

MR. SECRETARY:

Mo Young's subordinate, he has been pushing Mo Young and the White Sects towards war with the Black Sects.

YOUNG:

A 15-year-old sword-master, possessing incredible speed, he is affiliated with Mooyoung Moon--a clan of assassins, 500 strong. After seeing Majeh defeat the demon-possessed master at the martial arts tournament, Young admitted he has no interest in fighting Majeh...though Young's curiosity has driven the youthful assassin to accompany Majeh on his current mission.

BABY:

A 15-year-old from the infamous Blood Sect, Baby is several warriors in one...thanks to his multiple personality disorder. Baby is shy, gentle, and blushing; Hyur-ah is intense, unforgiving, and murderous; and Kwang is even scarier than Hyur-ah. The question remains: who--or what--else is also inside this young man?

What the Hell...?

Hell's worst inmates have escaped and fled to Earth. Seeking recently-deceased bodies to host their bitter souls, these malevolent master fighters are part of an evil scheme that could have dire consequences for both This World and the Next World. It is believed that the escaped fiends are hunting for bodies of martial arts experts, as only bodies trained in martial arts would be capable of properly employing their incredible skills.

To make matters even more difficult, the otherworldly energy emitted by the fugitives will dissipate within one month's time... after which, they will be indistinguishable from normal humans and undetectable to those from the Next World. The King of Hell has assigned Majeh to hunt down Hell's Most Wanted and return them to the Next World...but Majeh doesn't always do exactly what he's told.

Majeh was a master swordsman in life and, in death, he serves as an envoy for the King of Hell, escorting souls of the dead to the Next World. The King of Hell has reunited Majeh's spirit with his physical body, which was perfectly preserved for 300 years. Due to the influence of a Superhuman Strength Sealing Symbol (designed to keep the rebellious and powerful Majeh in check), Majeh's physical form has reverted to a teenaged state. Even with the seal in place, however, Majeh is still an extremely formidable warrior.

Along with the young, wannabe-warrior called Chung Poong Namgoong and a beautiful femme fatale named Dohwa Baik, Majeh made his way to the much-heralded Martial Arts Tournament at Nakyang--the most likely place for the warrior demons to make their appearance.

While Majeh fought in the tournament, the battle was suddenly interrupted. An elderly, one-armed, martial arts master--whose body was inhabited by one of the fugitive demons--forced his way into the arena and effortlessly killed two competitors. Despite his best efforts, Majeh also seemed on the verge of total defeat...though, as his life-force dissipated, the Superhuman Strength Sealing spell that limits his abilities was broken!

Freed from restraint, Majeh rose and easily obliterated his opponent. Though Majeh recovered very quickly from his battle injuries, he was still surprised to learn that, while he was out, his fellow contestants--including Chung Poong's older brother--were kidnapped.

While Chung Poong and Dohwa braved death in order to increase their martial arts abilities, Majeh and the Mooyoung Moon assassin known as Young searched for the missing martial arts prodigies and discovered a diabolical plot to transform the youthful fighters into zombies and start a war between the "black" and "white" sects. The architects of this evil plan appear to be the Sa Gok, a vicious, powerful group that almost brought down the entire martial arts world fifty years ago. Unfortunately, most of the sects believe the Sa Gok were utterly eradicated...which means they can only blame each other for their missing children.

After reporting their findings to Mo Young, Majeh and Young ventured to Devil Mountain to explore a tomb that had the town talking about treasure. At the entrance to the tomb, they found many warriors fighting to keep each other out. Eventually, many different groups entered and Majeh and Young followed the powerful fighter known as Hunter into the depths of the tomb. After fighting their way through many elaborate traps, all of the fighters found themselves in a central chamber, surrounded by animated corpses that kept rising no matter how severely they were wounded. Though Majeh and his companions are all incredibly formidable, it appeared that even they were eventually defeated by the zombie horde.

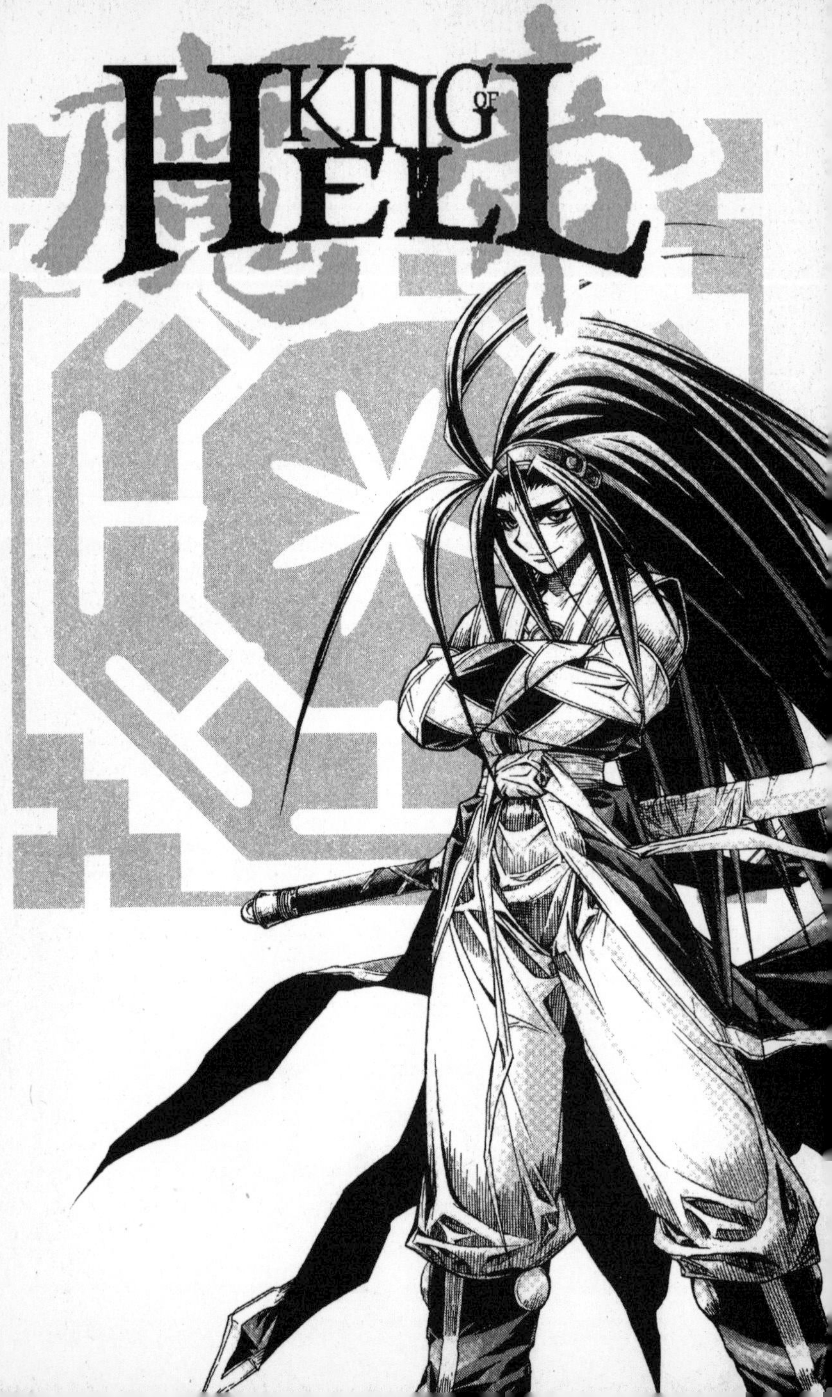
KING OF HELL

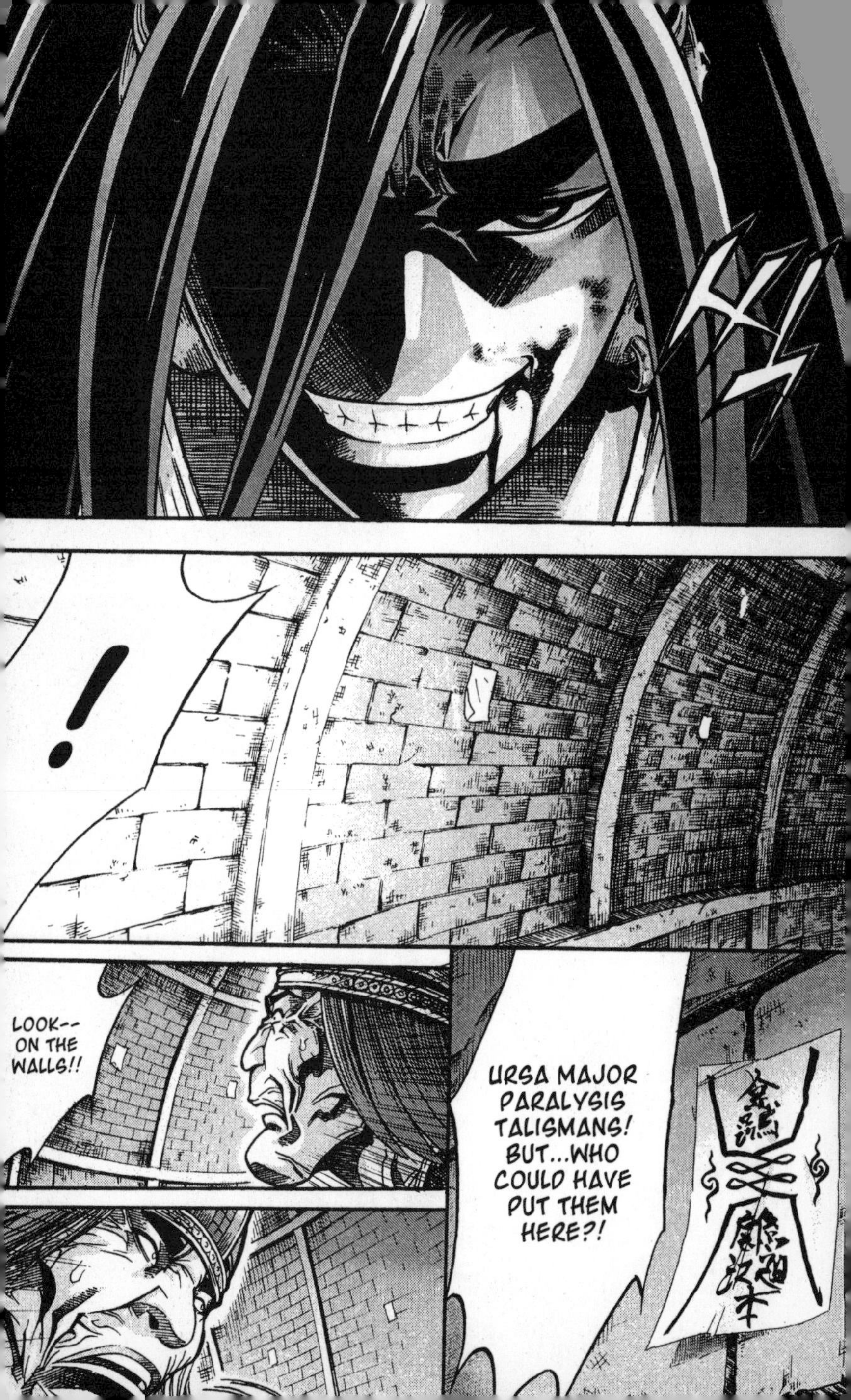

!
URSA MAJOR PARALYSIS TALISMANS! BUT...WHO COULD HAVE PUT THEM HERE?!
LOOK-- ON THE WALLS!!

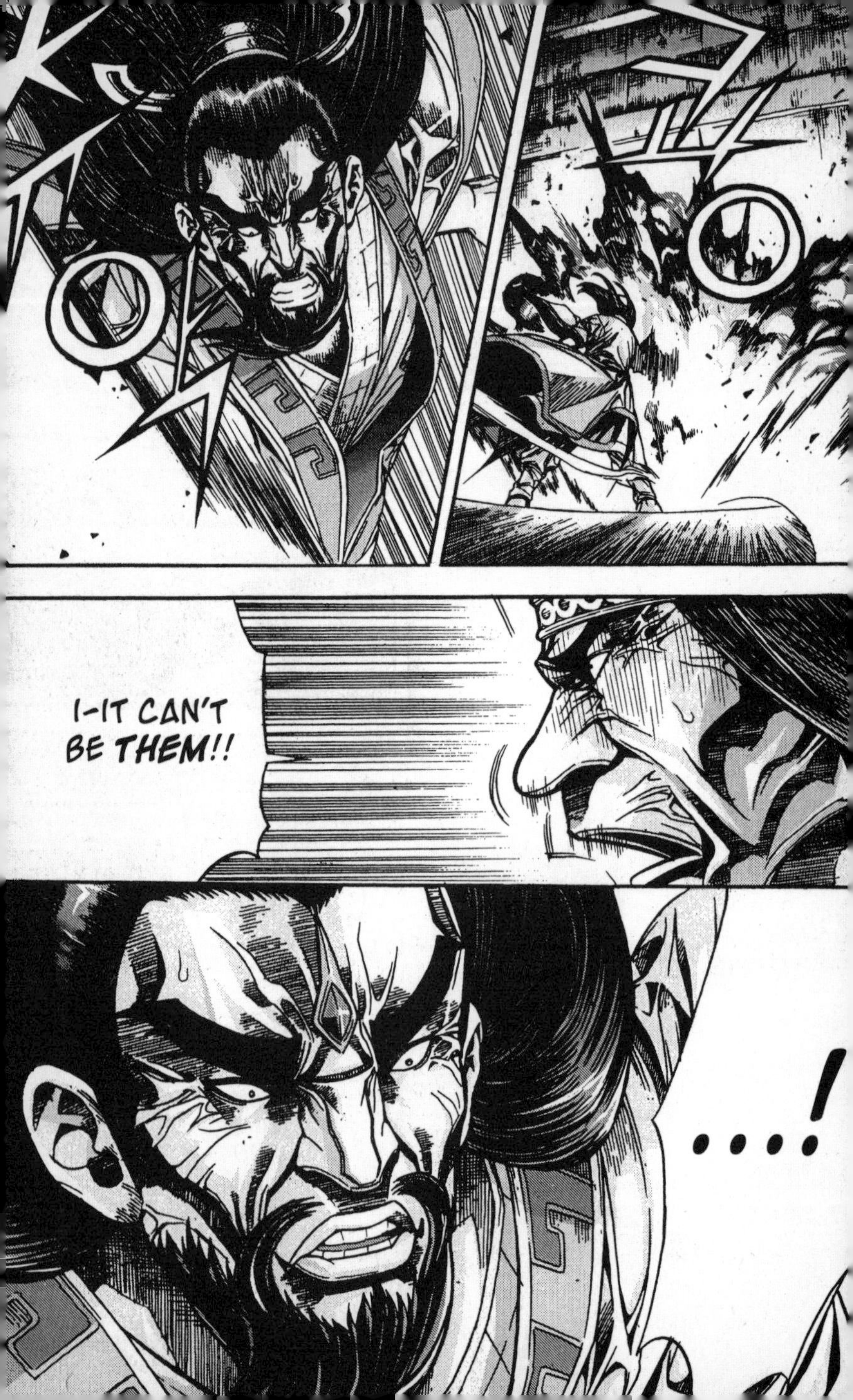
I-IT CAN'T BE THEM!!
...!

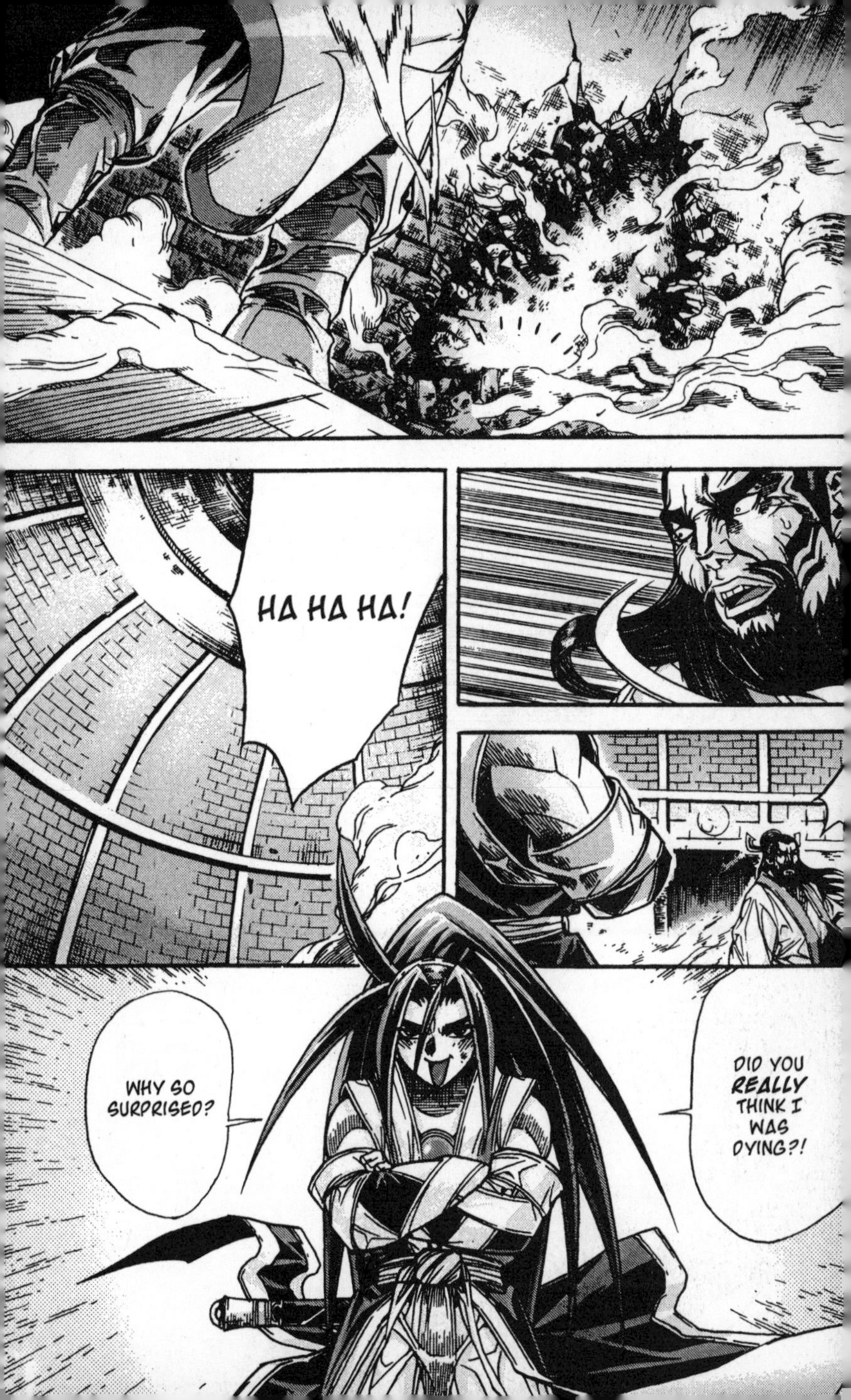
HA HA HA!
DID YOU REALLY THINK I WAS DYING?!
WHY SO SURPRISED?

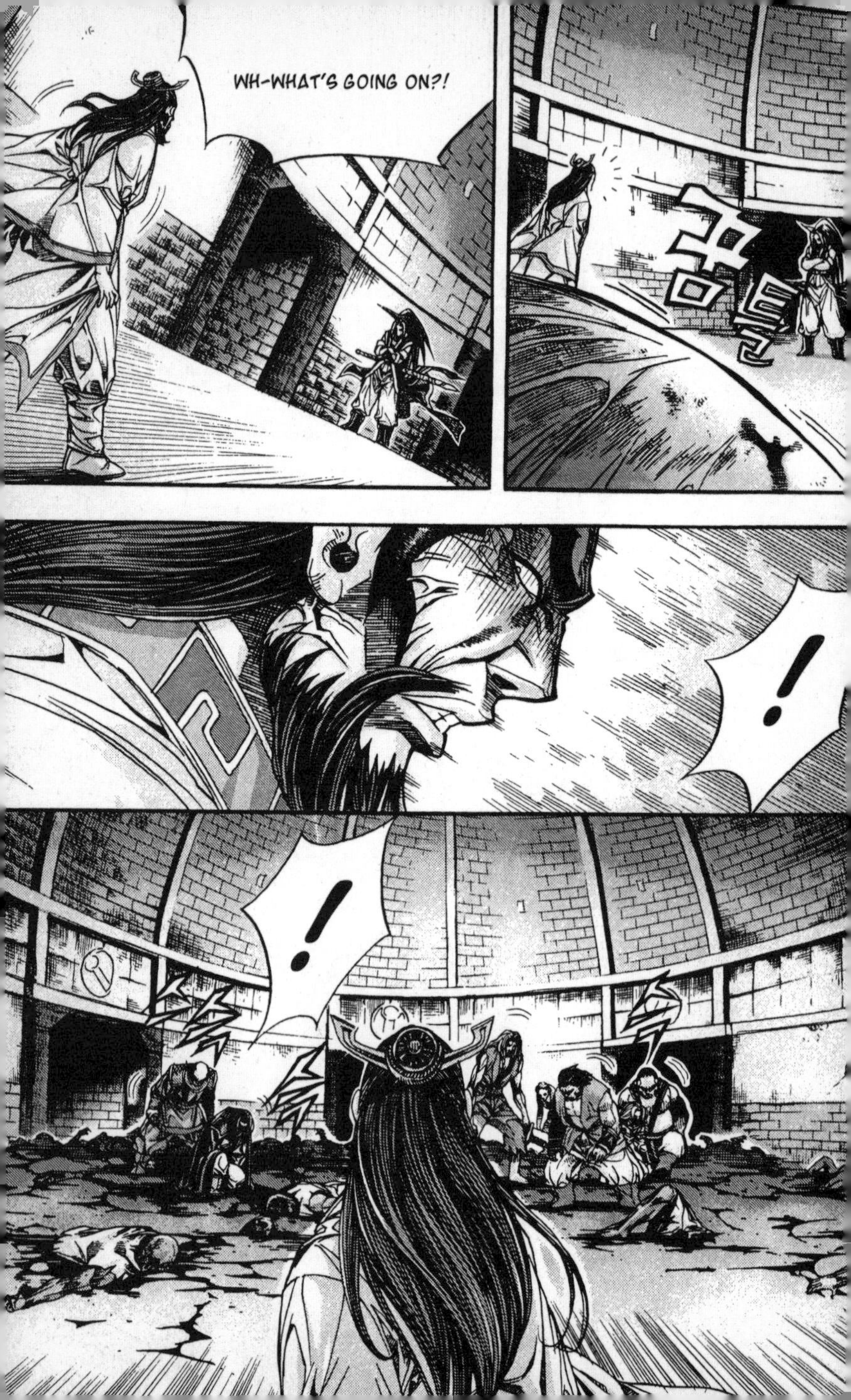
WH-WHAT'S GOING ON?!
!
!

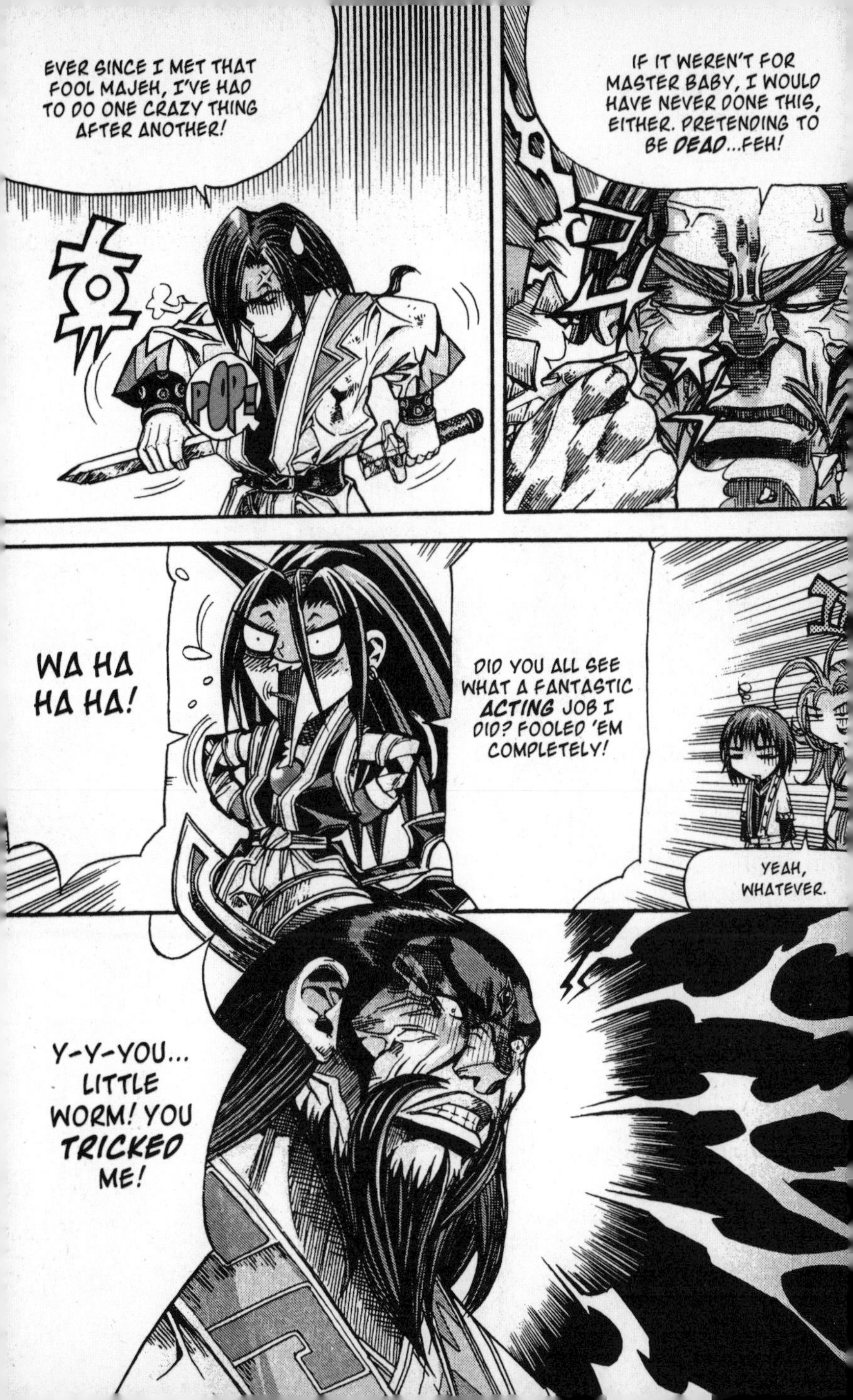
IF IT WEREN'T FOR MASTER BABY, I WOULD HAVE NEVER DONE THIS, EITHER. PRETENDING TO BE DEAD...FEH!
EVER SINCE I MET THAT FOOL MAJEH, I'VE HAD TO DO ONE CRAZY THING AFTER ANOTHER!
POP!
YEAH, WHATEVER.
DID YOU ALL SEE WHAT A FANTASTIC ACTING JOB I DID? FOOLED 'EM COMPLETELY!
WA HA HA HA!
Y-Y-YOU... LITTLE WORM! YOU TRICKED ME!

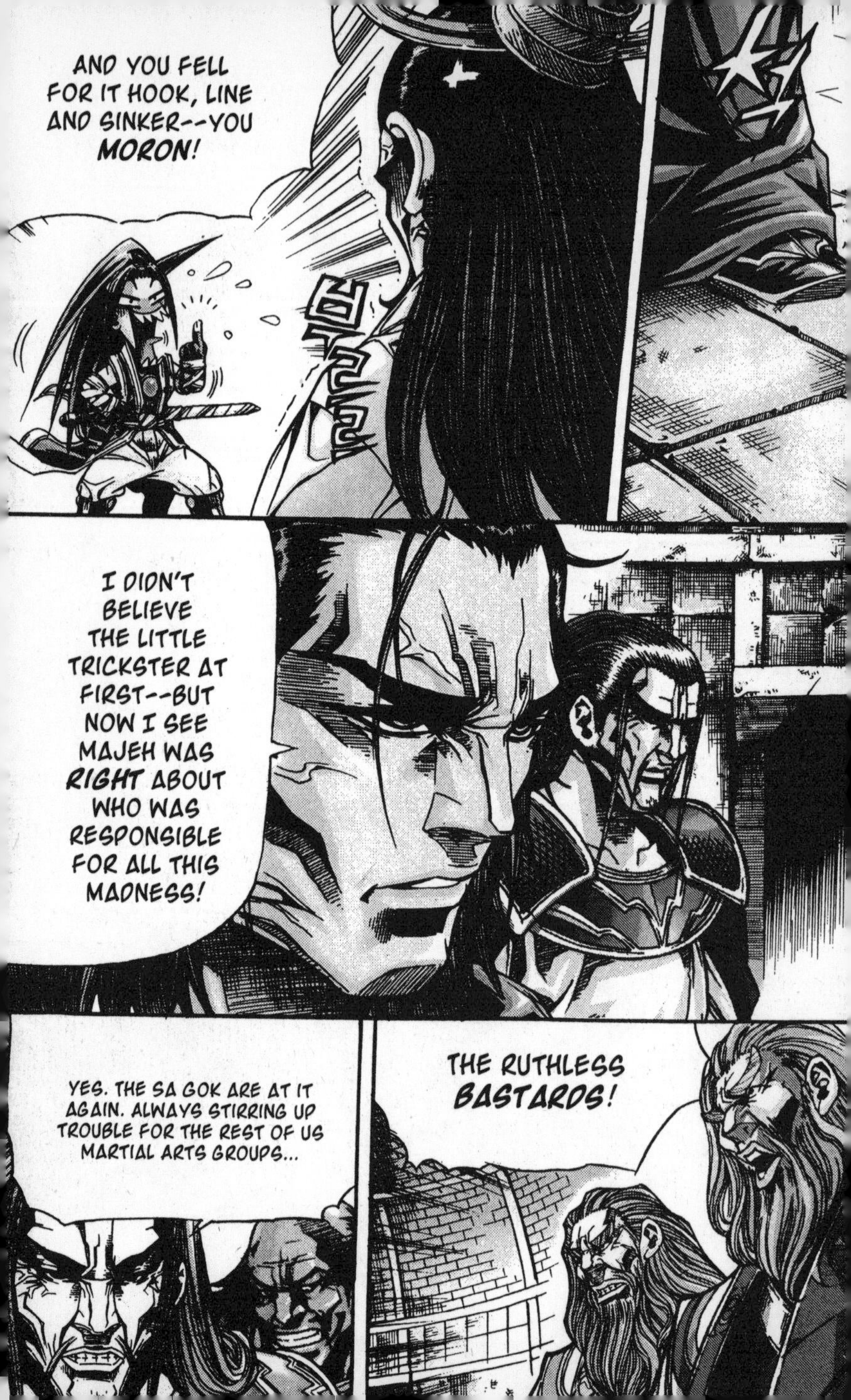
AND YOU FELL FOR IT HOOK, LINE AND SINKER--YOU MORON!
I DIDN'T BELIEVE THE LITTLE TRICKSTER AT FIRST--BUT NOW I SEE MAJEH WAS RIGHT ABOUT WHO WAS RESPONSIBLE FOR ALL THIS MADNESS!
YES. THE SA GOK ARE AT IT AGAIN. ALWAYS STIRRING UP TROUBLE FOR THE REST OF US MARTIAL ARTS GROUPS...
THE RUTHLESS BASTARDS!

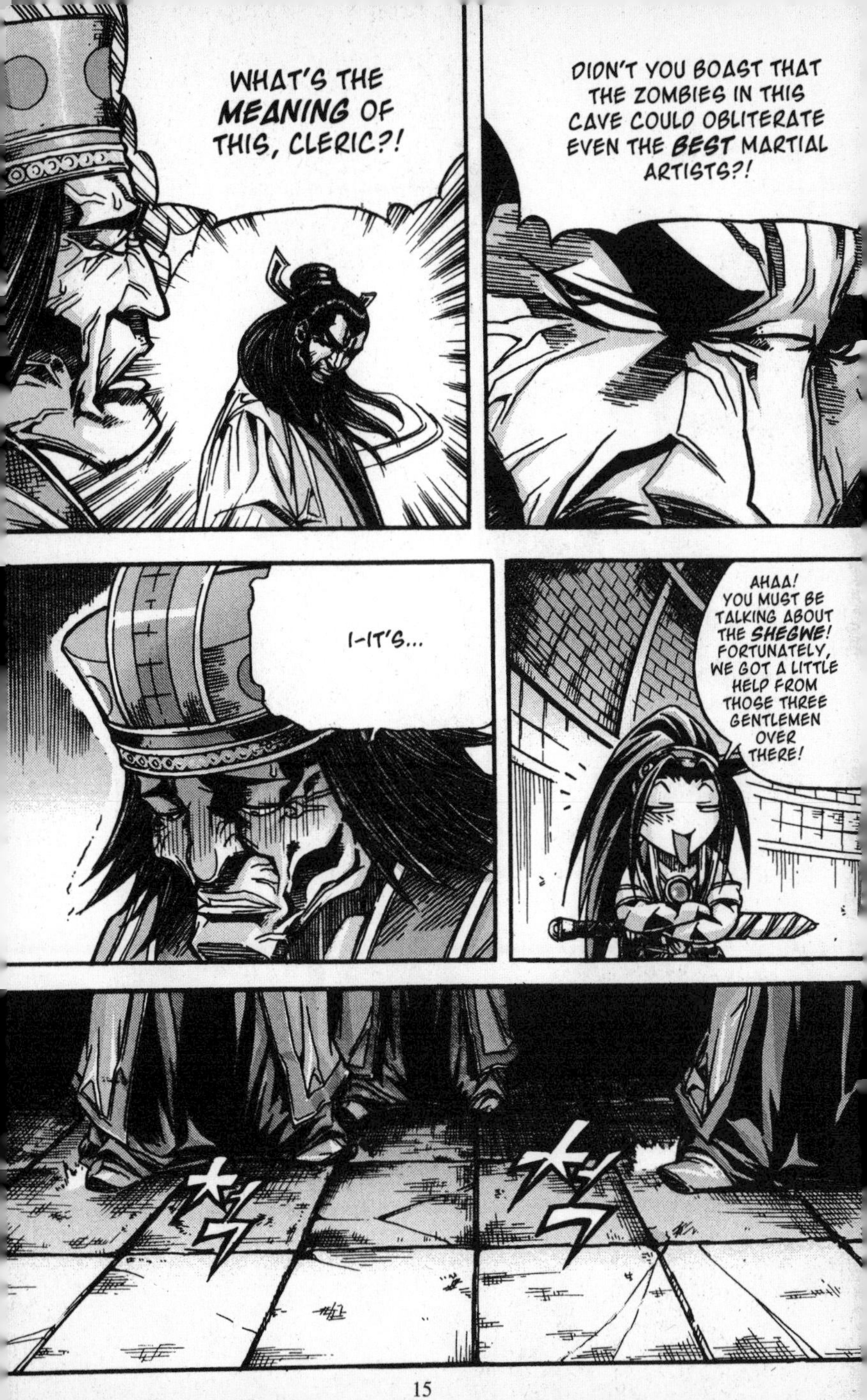
WHAT'S THE MEANING OF THIS, CLERIC?!
DIDN'T YOU BOAST THAT THE ZOMBIES IN THIS CAVE COULD OBLITERATE EVEN THE BEST MARTIAL ARTISTS?!
I-IT'S...
AHAA! YOU MUST BE TALKING ABOUT THE SHEGWE! FORTUNATELY, WE GOT A LITTLE HELP FROM THOSE THREE GENTLEMEN OVER THERE!

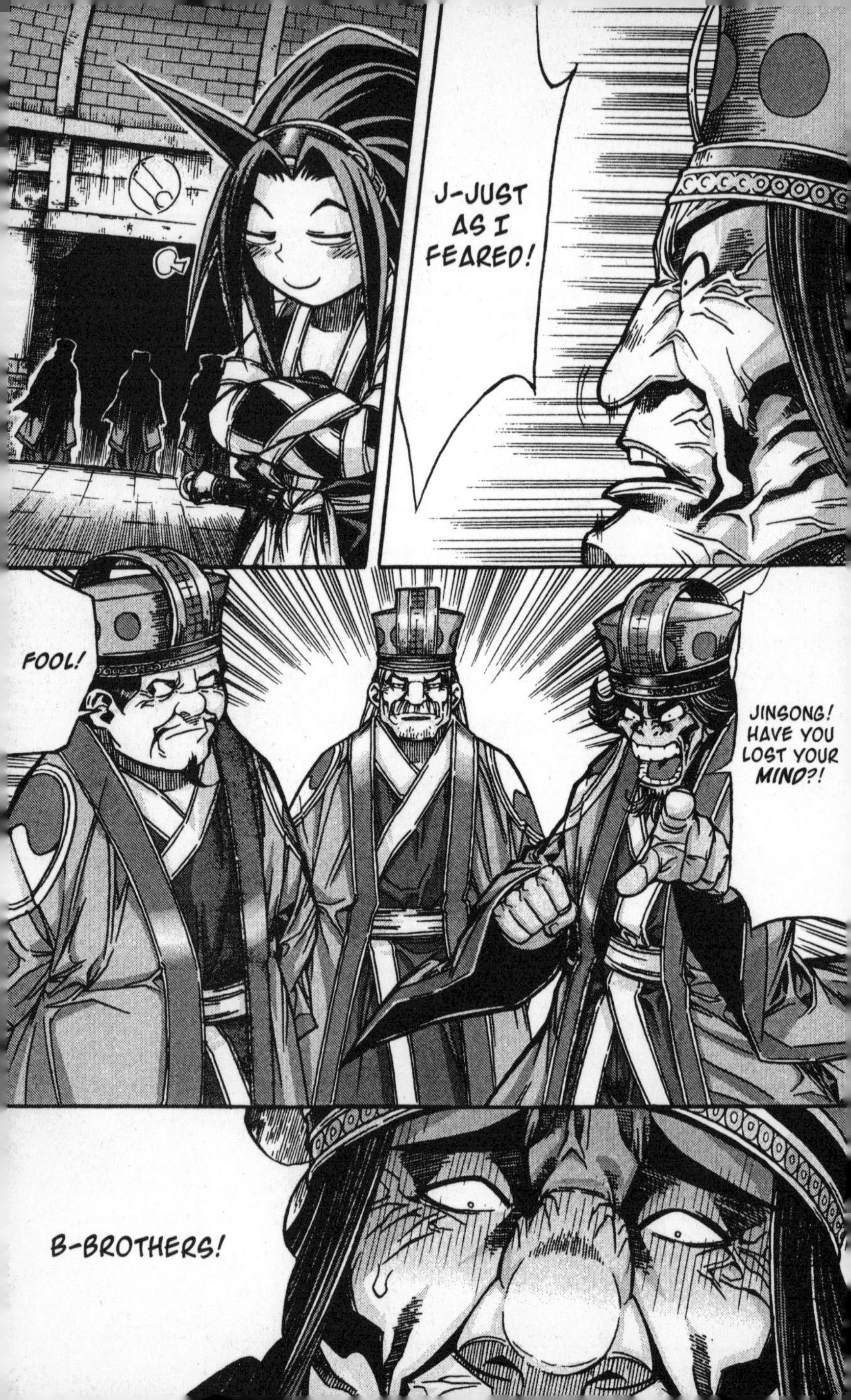
J-JUST AS I FEARED!
JINSONG! HAVE YOU LOST YOUR MIND?!
FOOL!
B-BROTHERS!

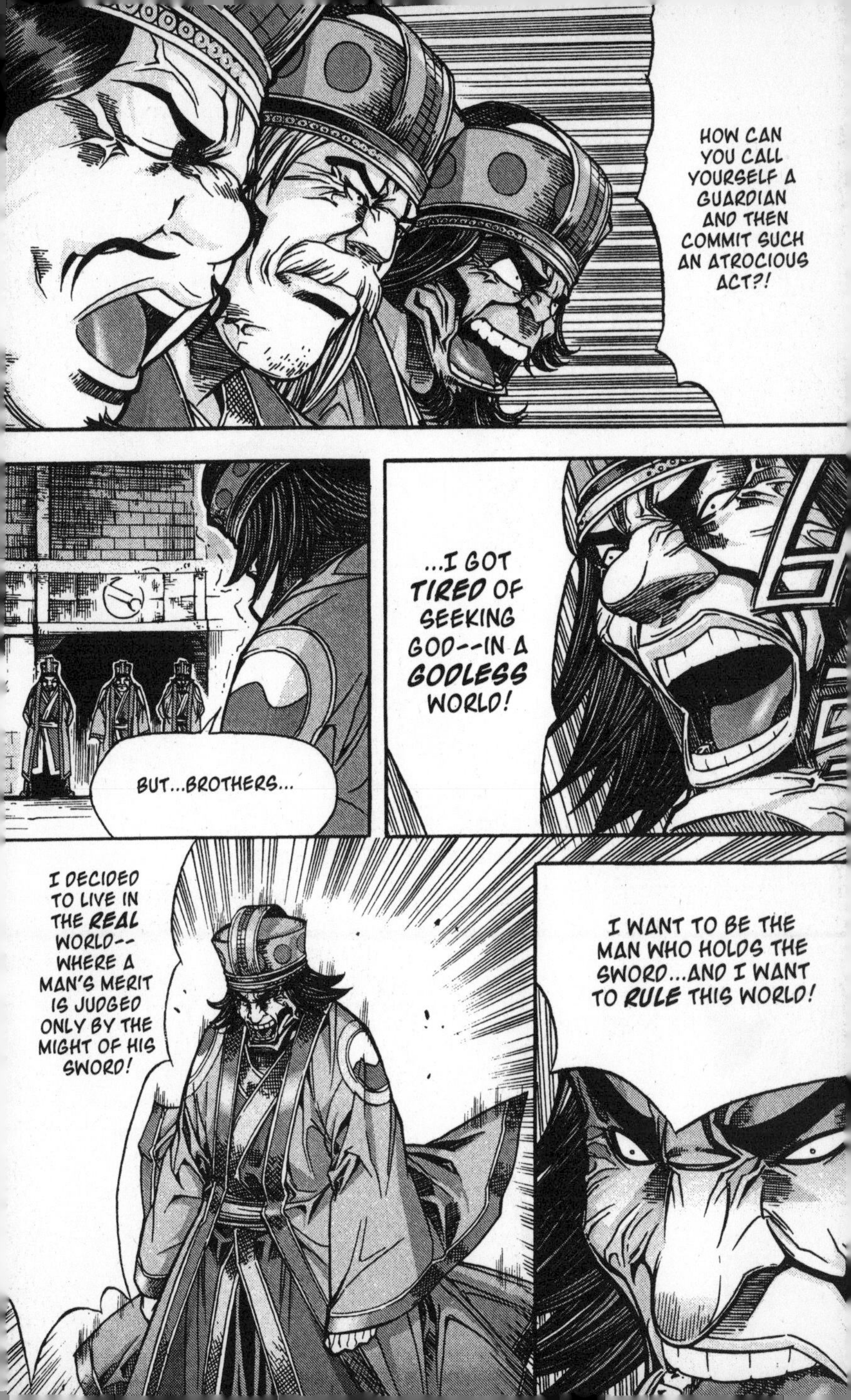
HOW CAN YOU CALL YOURSELF A GUARDIAN AND THEN COMMIT SUCH AN ATROCIOUS ACT?!
BUT...BROTHERS...
...I GOT TIRED OF SEEKING GOD--IN A GODLESS WORLD!
I DECIDED TO LIVE IN THE REAL WORLD--WHERE A MAN'S MERIT IS JUDGED ONLY BY THE MIGHT OF HIS SWORD!
I WANT TO BE THE MAN WHO HOLDS THE SWORD...AND I WANT TO RULE THIS WORLD!

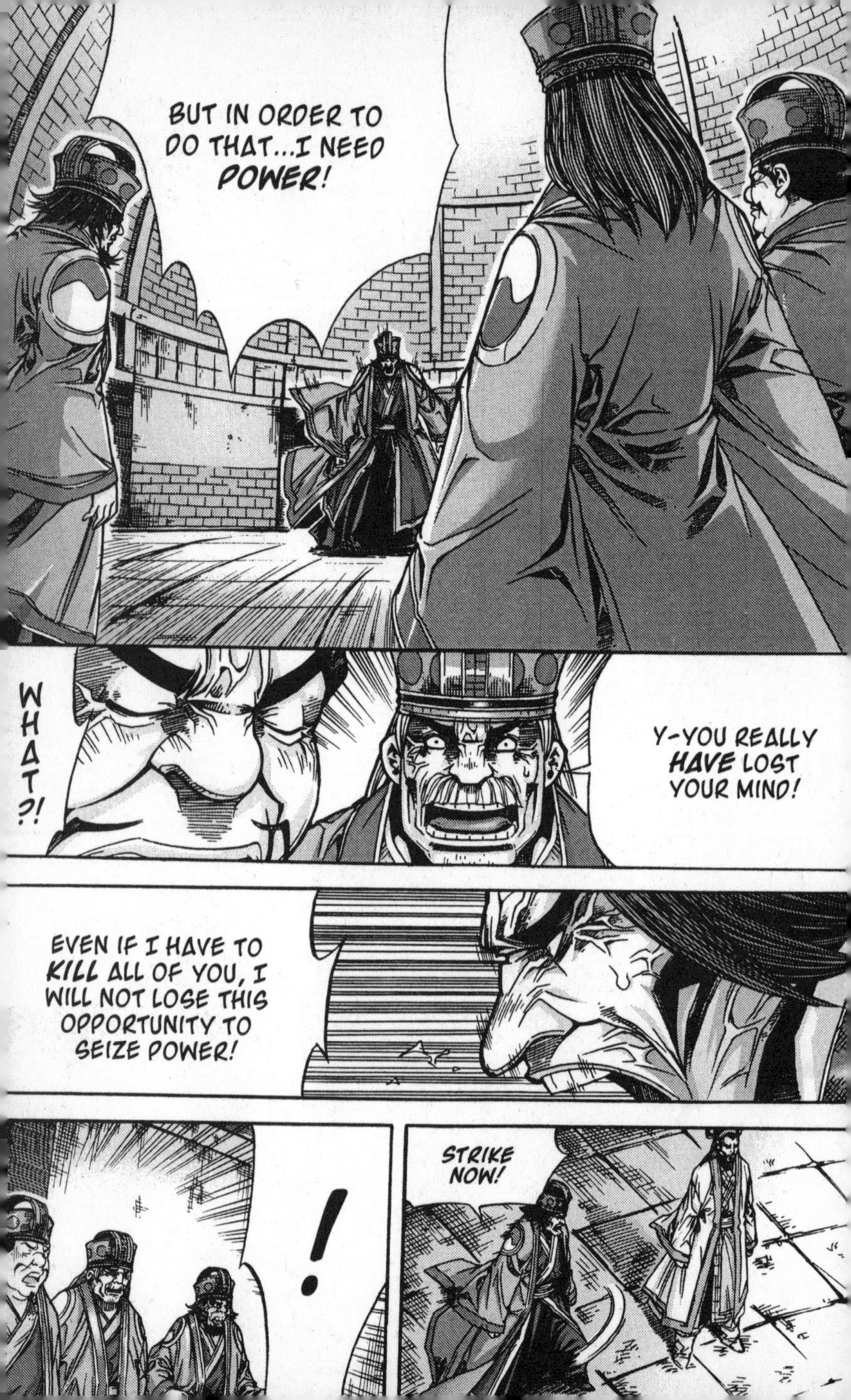
BUT IN ORDER TO DO THAT...I NEED POWER!
WHAT?!
Y-YOU REALLY HAVE LOST YOUR MIND!
EVEN IF I HAVE TO KILL ALL OF YOU, I WILL NOT LOSE THIS OPPORTUNITY TO SEIZE POWER!
!
STRIKE NOW!

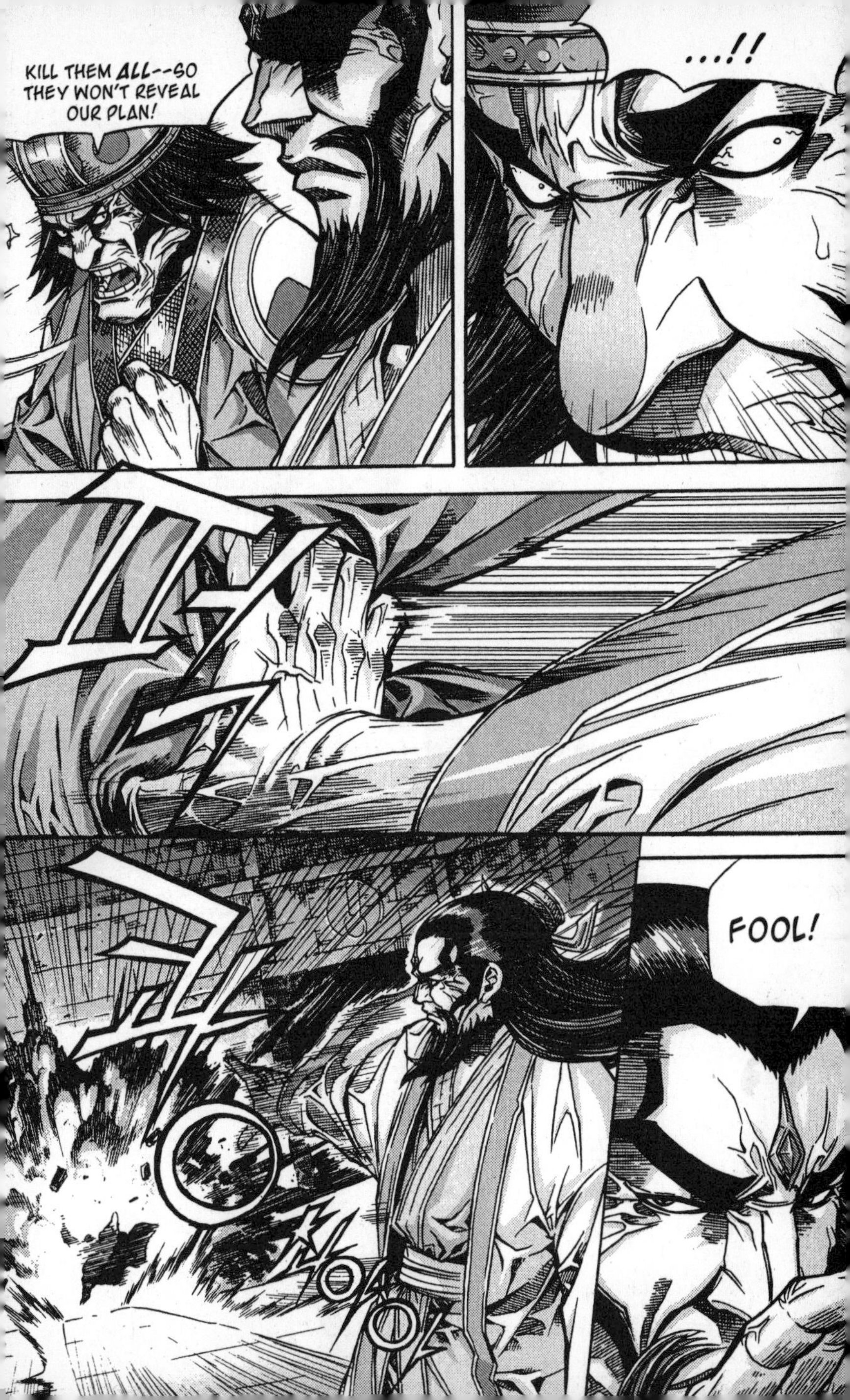

KILL THEM ALL--SO THEY WON'T REVEAL OUR PLAN!
...!!
FOOL!

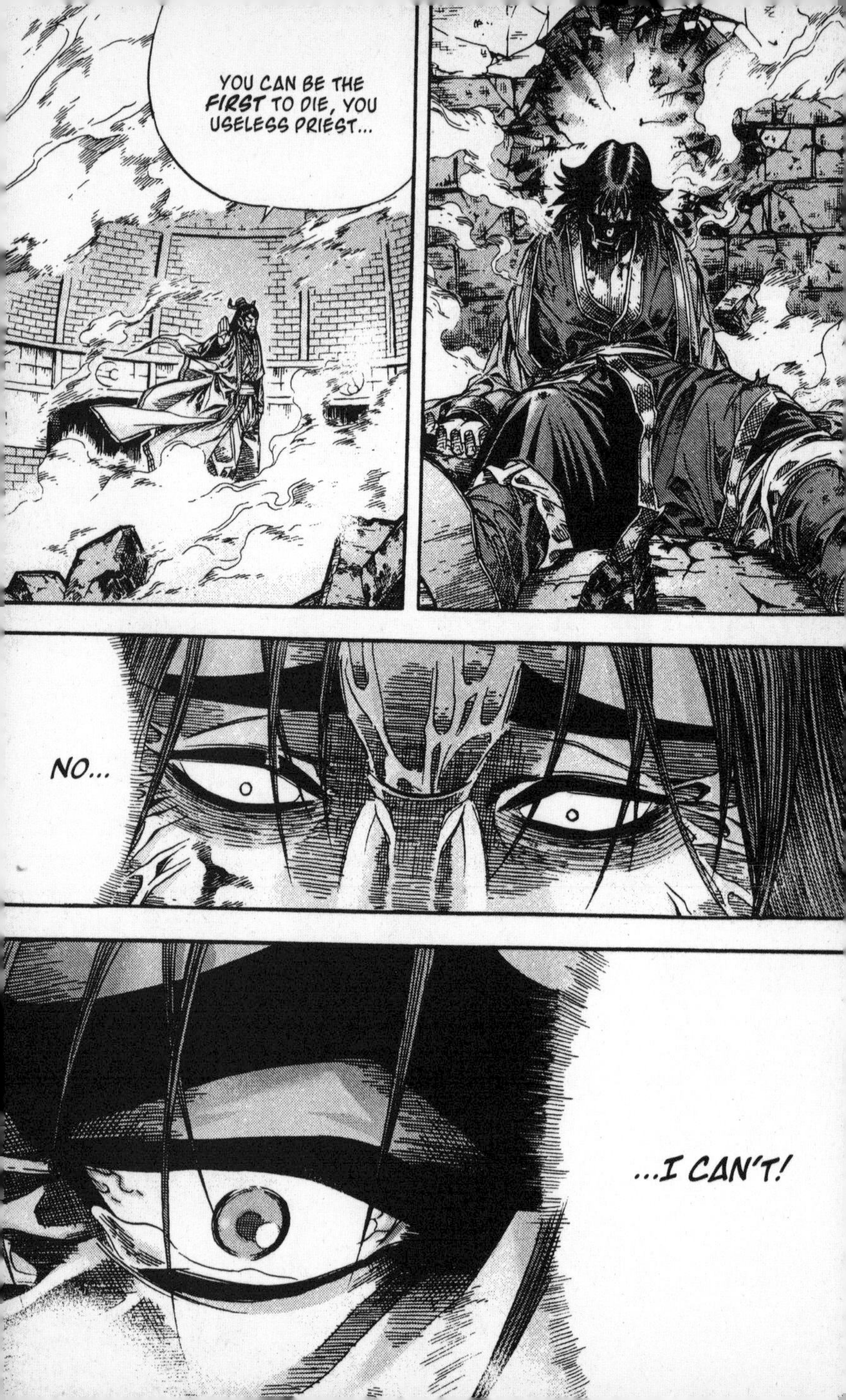
YOU CAN BE THE FIRST TO DIE, YOU USELESS PRIEST...
NO...
...I CAN'T!

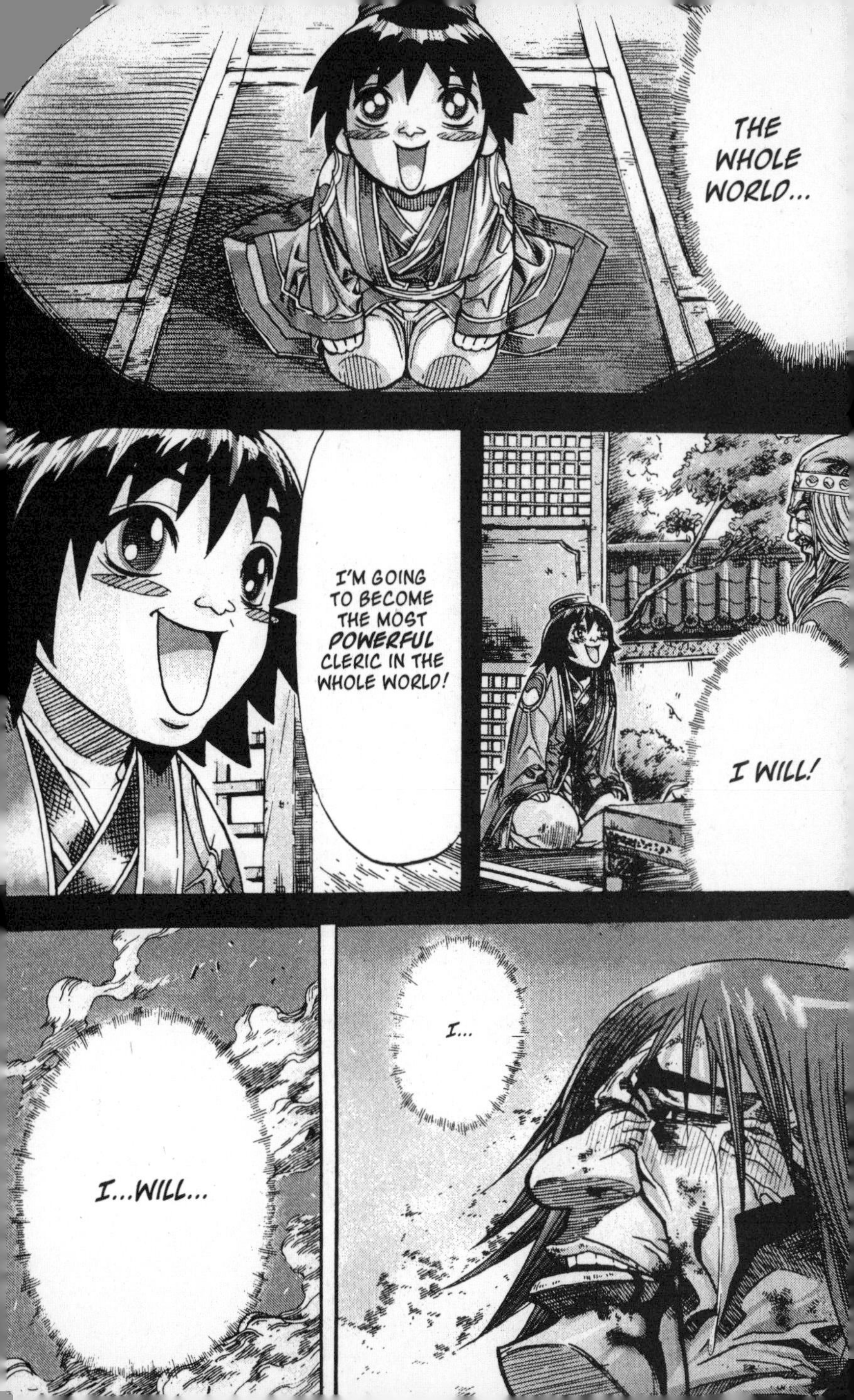
THE WHOLE WORLD...
I WILL!
I'M GOING TO BECOME THE MOST POWERFUL CLERIC IN THE WHOLE WORLD!
I...
I...WILL...

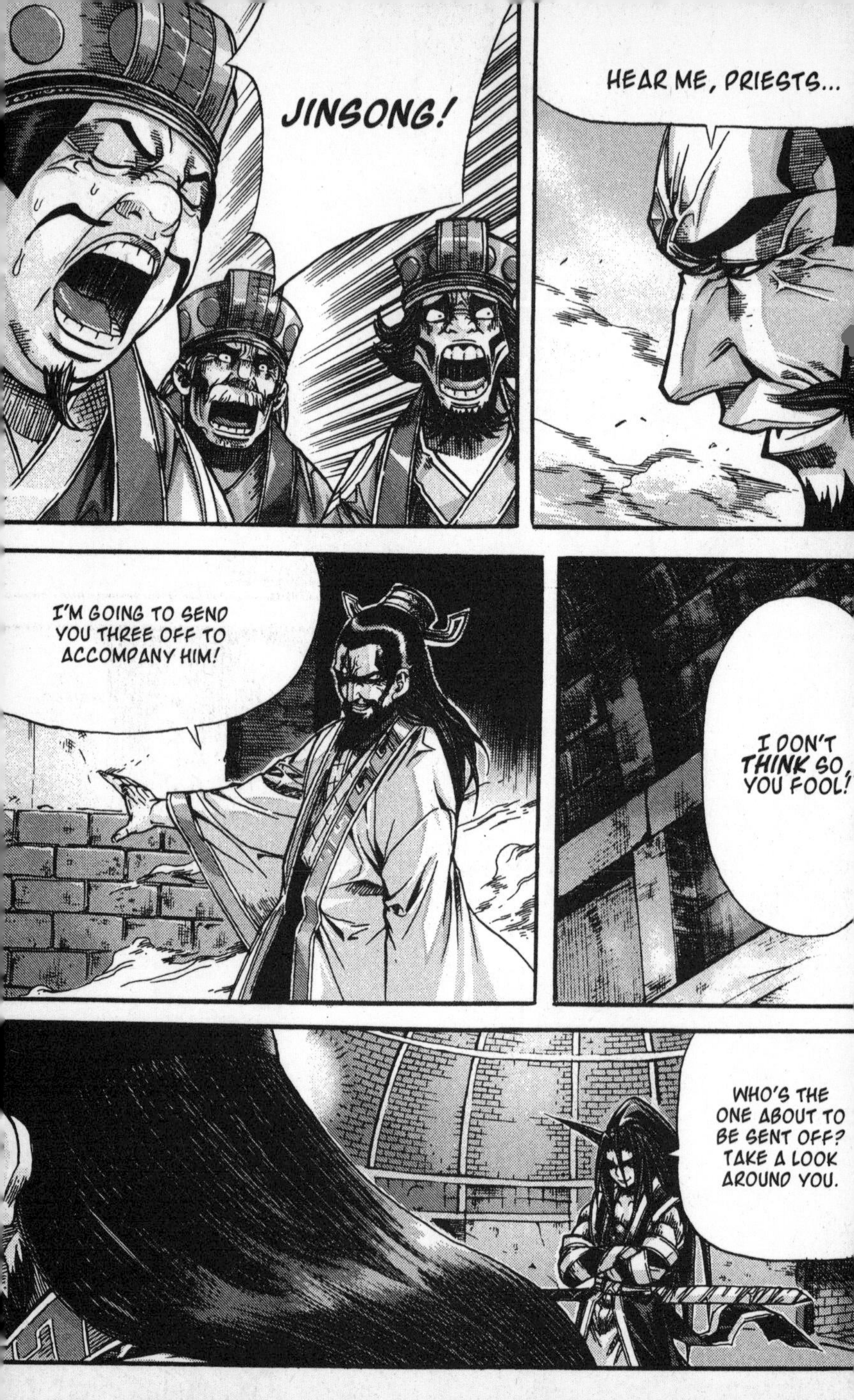
JINSONG!
HEAR ME, PRIESTS...
I'M GOING TO SEND YOU THREE OFF TO ACCOMPANY HIM!
I DON'T THINK SO, YOU FOOL!
WHO'S THE ONE ABOUT TO BE SENT OFF? TAKE A LOOK AROUND YOU.

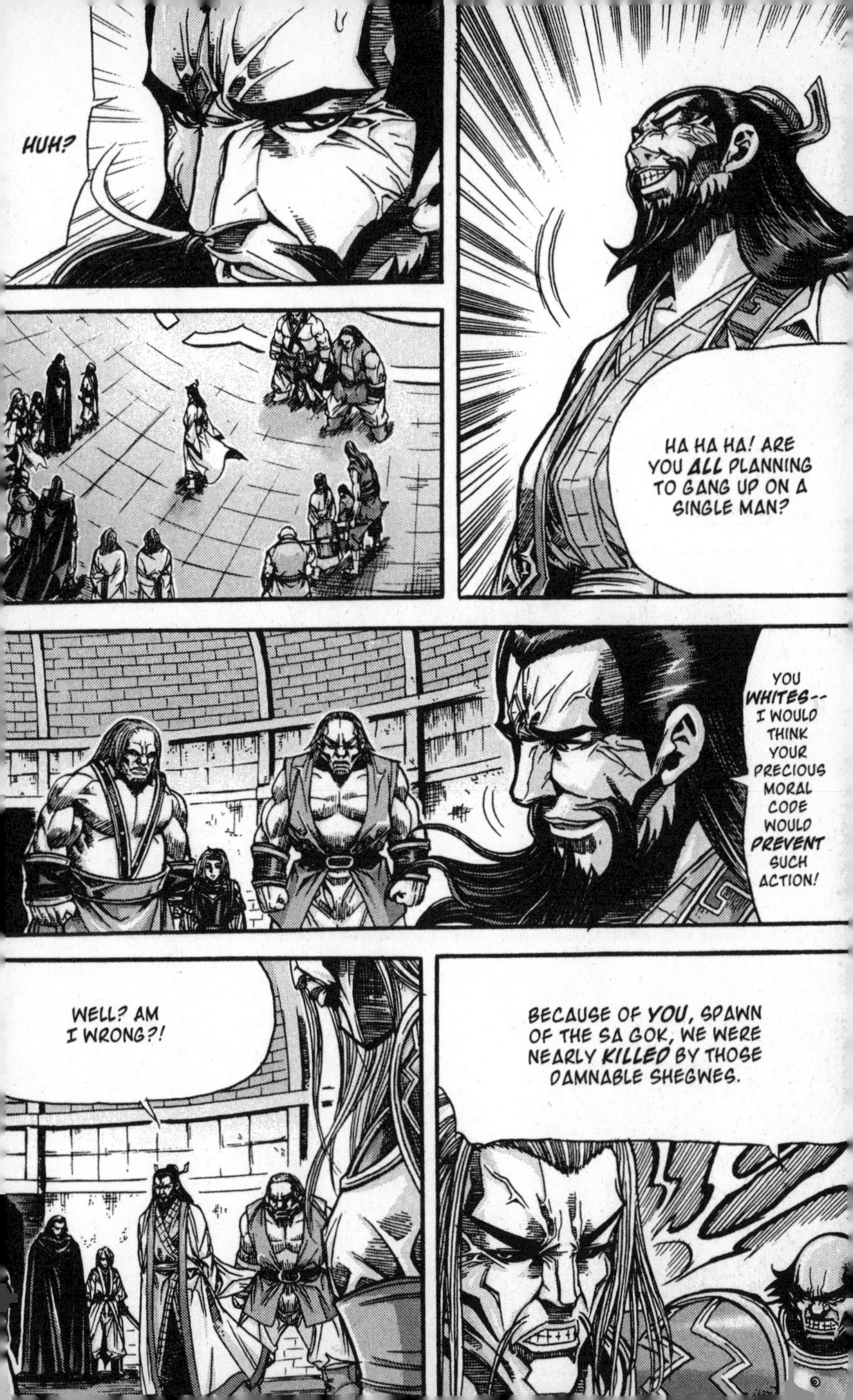
HUH?
HA HA HA! ARE YOU ALL PLANNING TO GANG UP ON A SINGLE MAN?
YOU WHITES-- I WOULD THINK YOUR PRECIOUS MORAL CODE WOULD PREVENT SUCH ACTION!
WELL? AM I WRONG?!
BECAUSE OF YOU, SPAWN OF THE SA GOK, WE WERE NEARLY KILLED BY THOSE DAMNABLE SHEGWES.

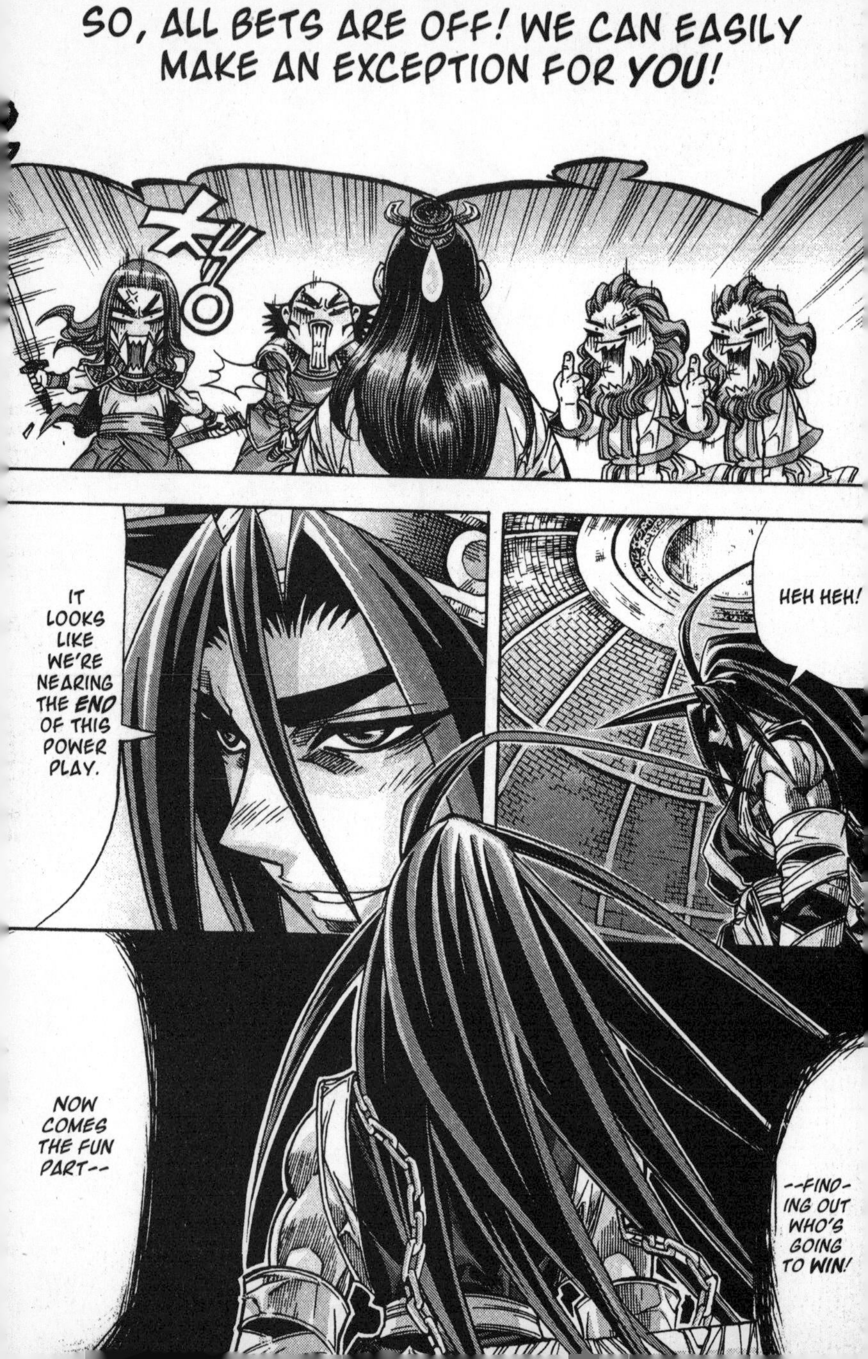
SO, ALL BETS ARE OFF! WE CAN EASILY MAKE AN EXCEPTION FOR YOU!
IT LOOKS LIKE WE'RE NEARING THE END OF THIS POWER PLAY.
HEH HEH!
NOW COMES THE FUN PART--
--FINDING OUT WHO'S GOING TO WIN!

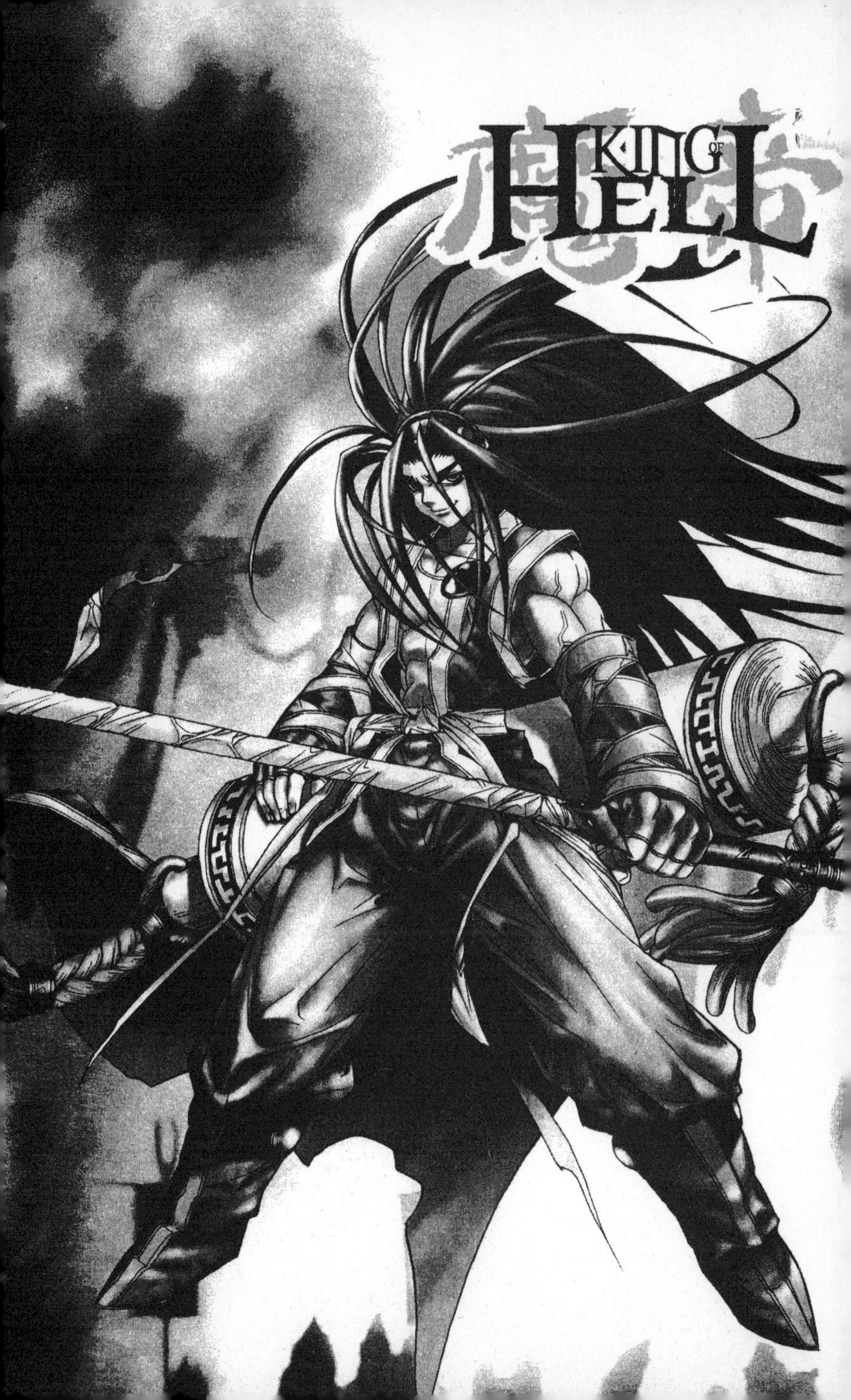
KING OF HELL

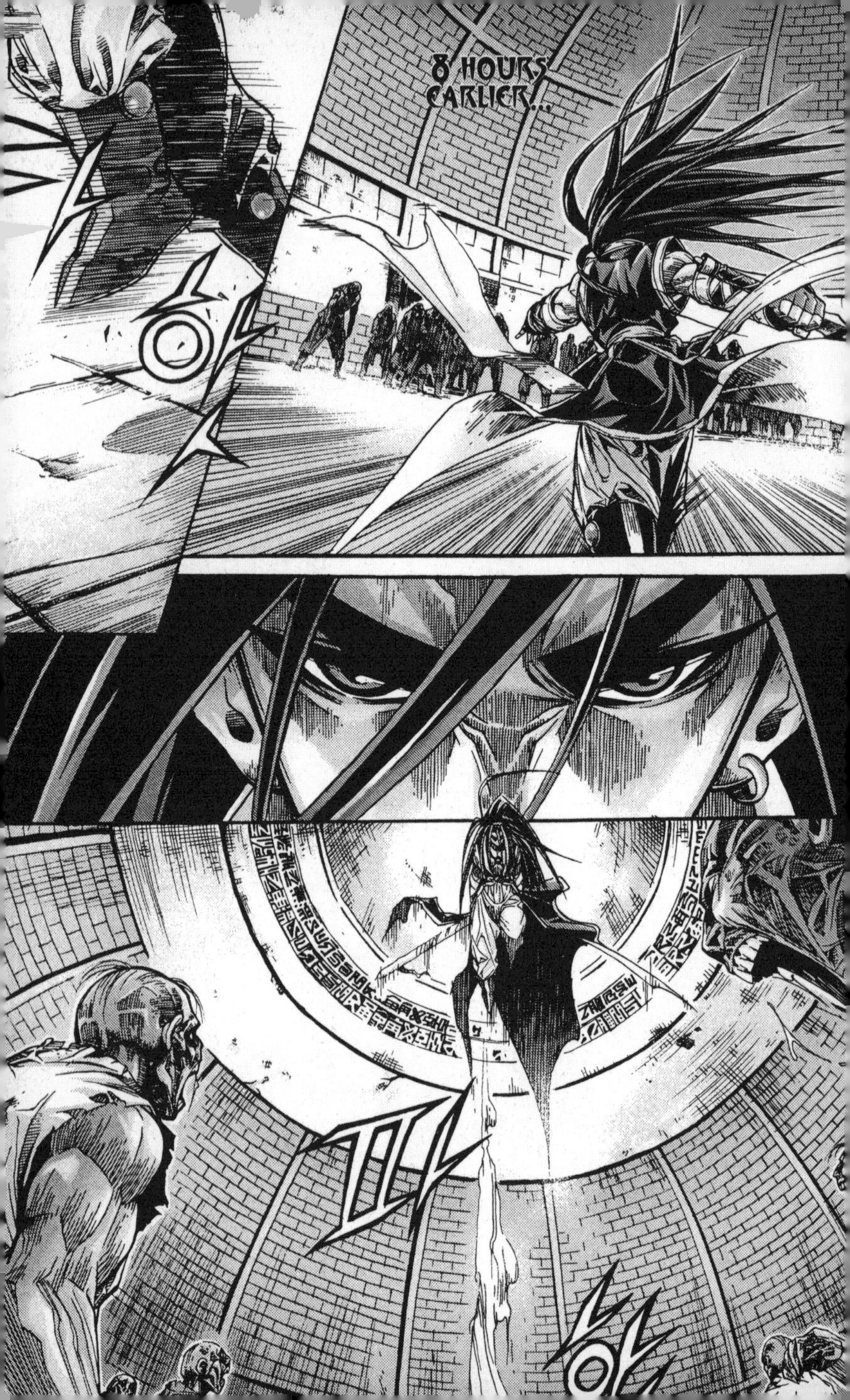
8 HOURS EARLIER...

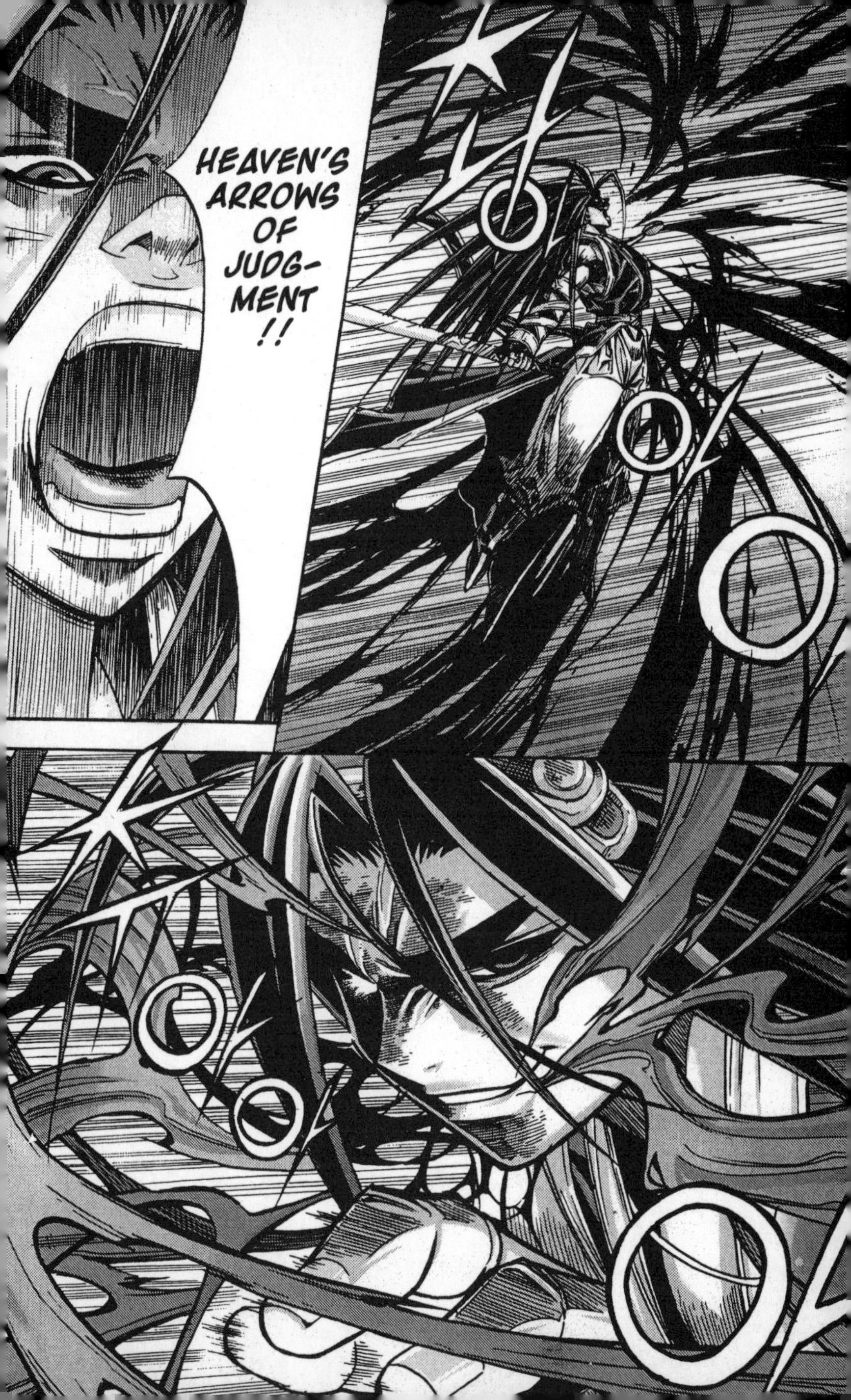
HEAVEN'S ARROWS OF JUDGMENT!!

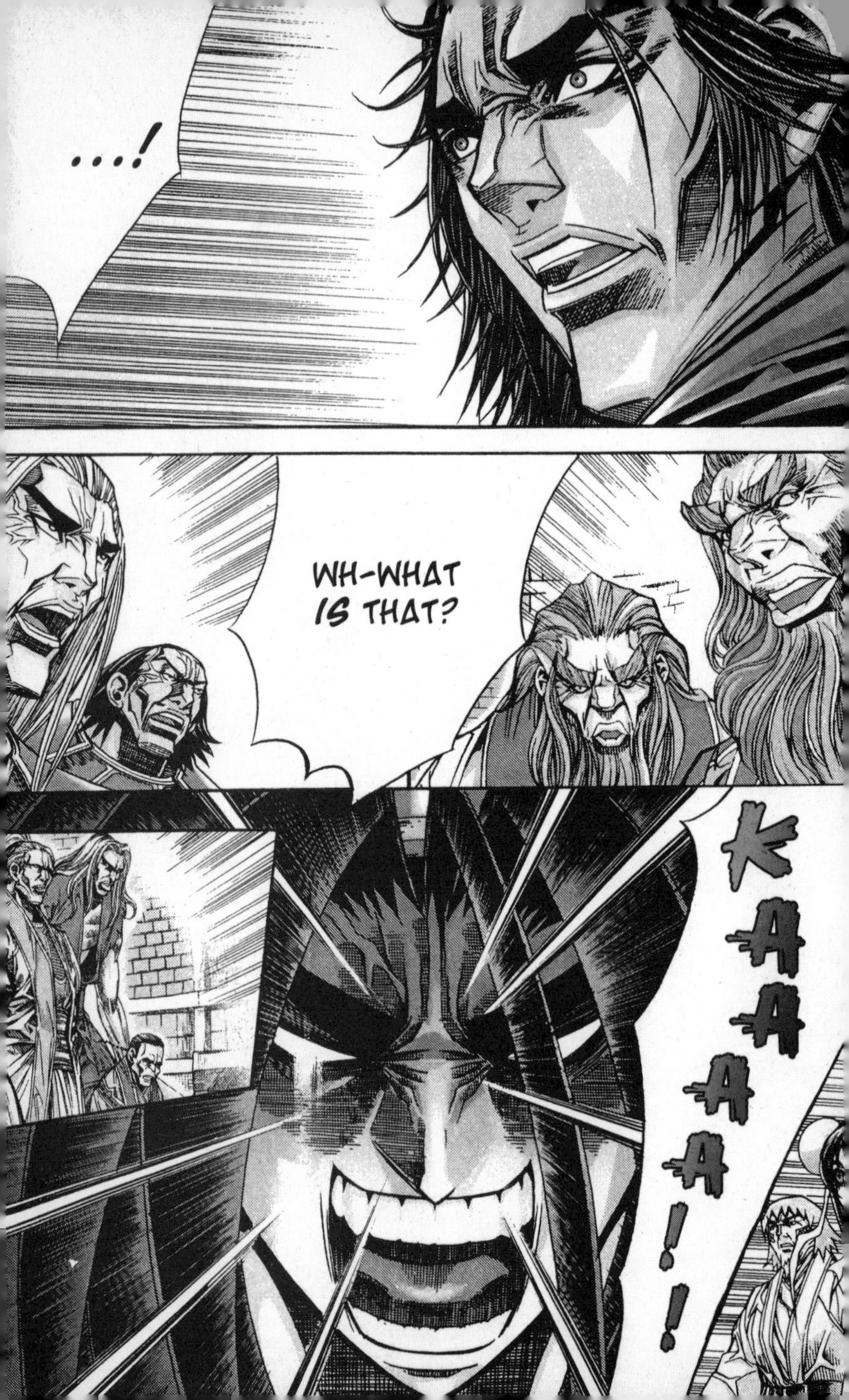
...!
WH-WHAT IS THAT?
KAAAA!!!

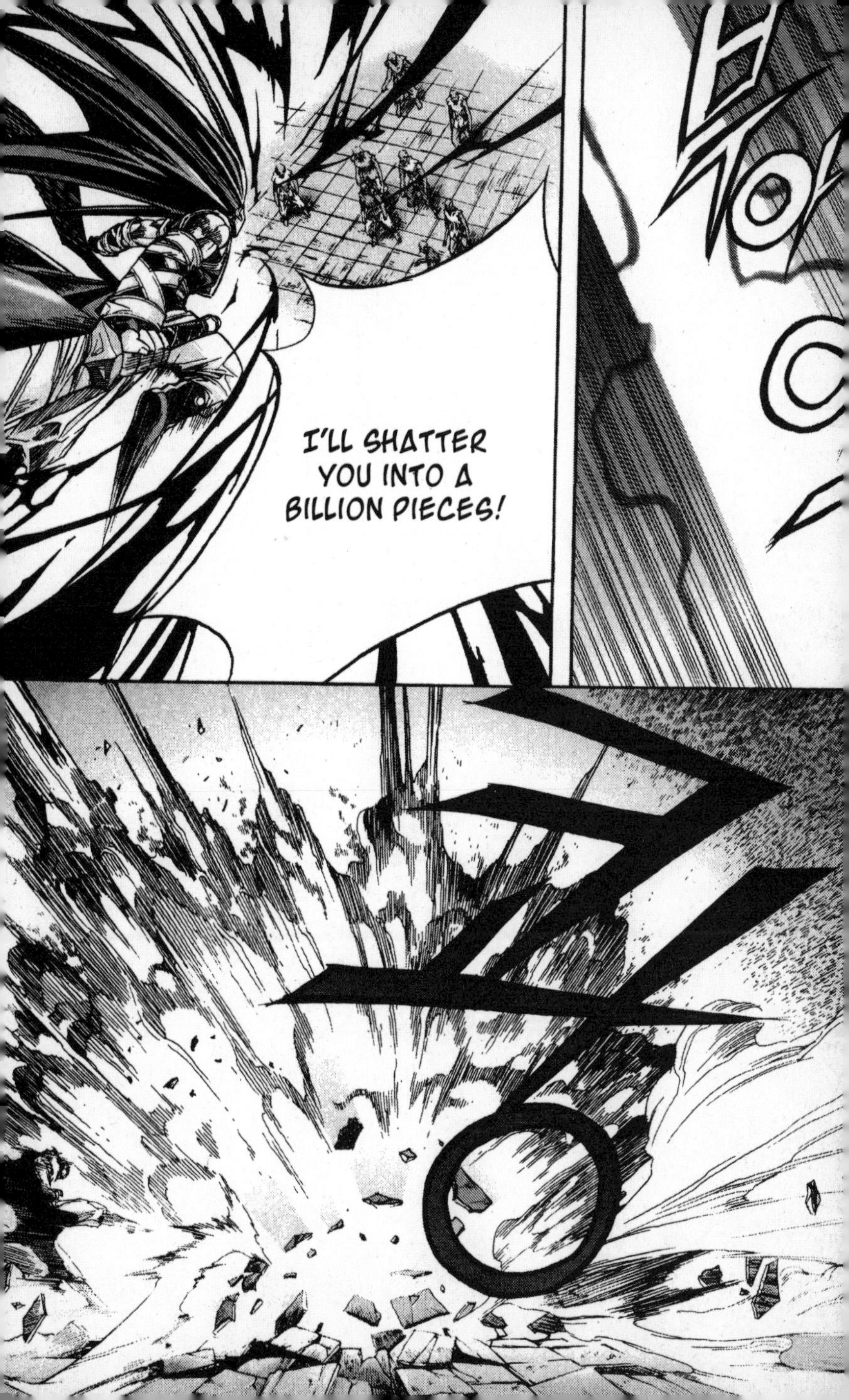
I'LL SHATTER YOU INTO A BILLION PIECES!

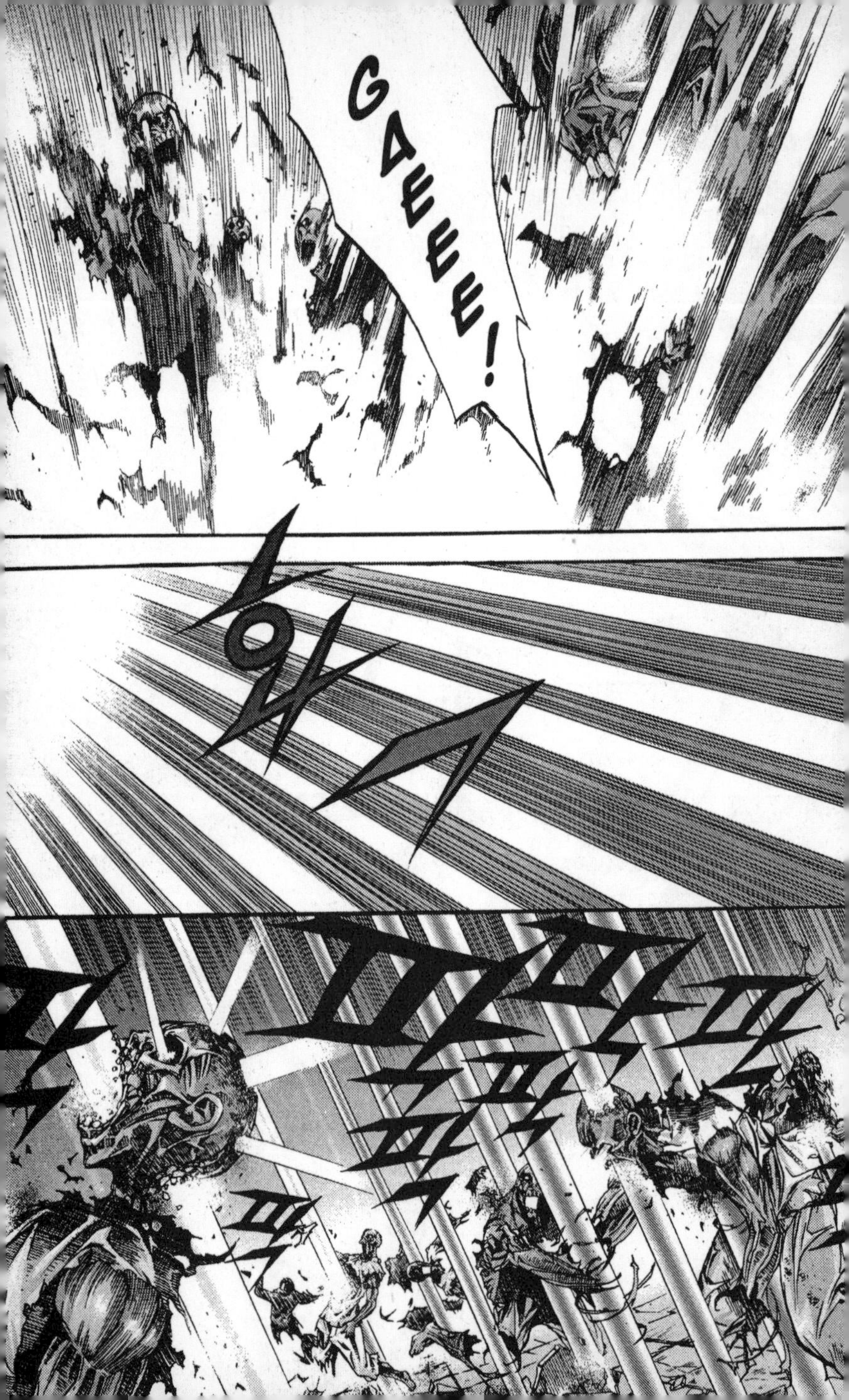
GAEEE!

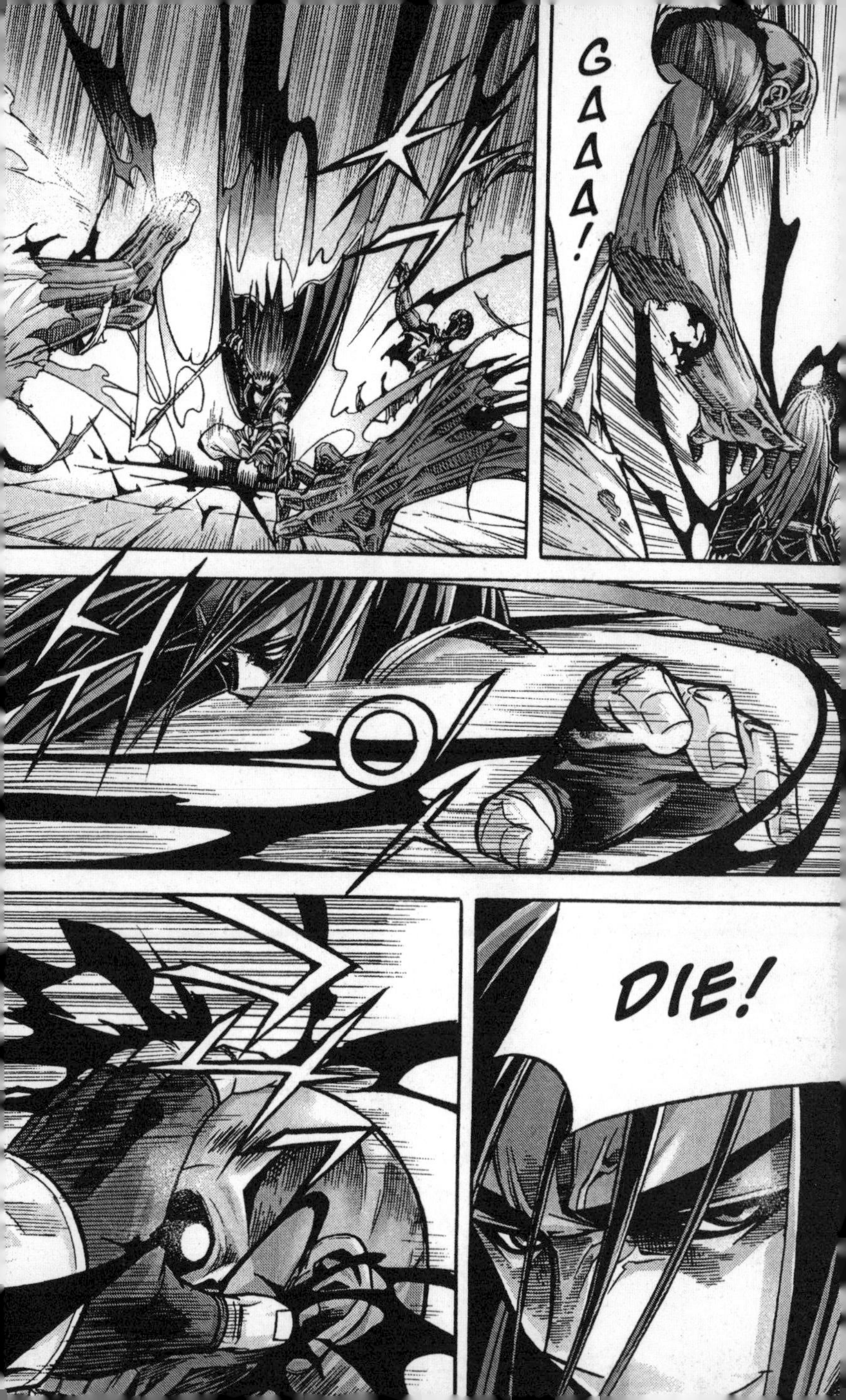

GAAAA!
DIE!

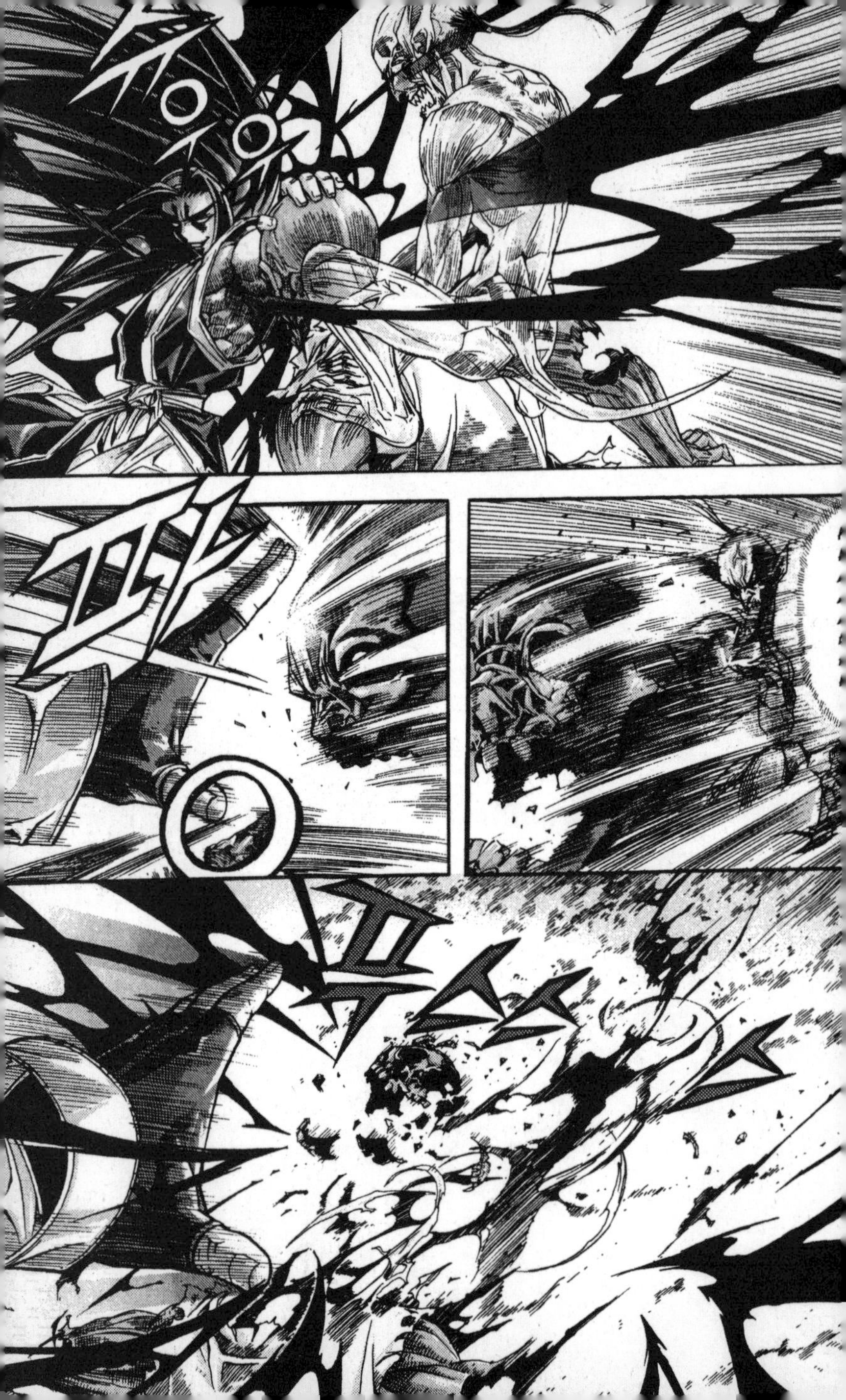

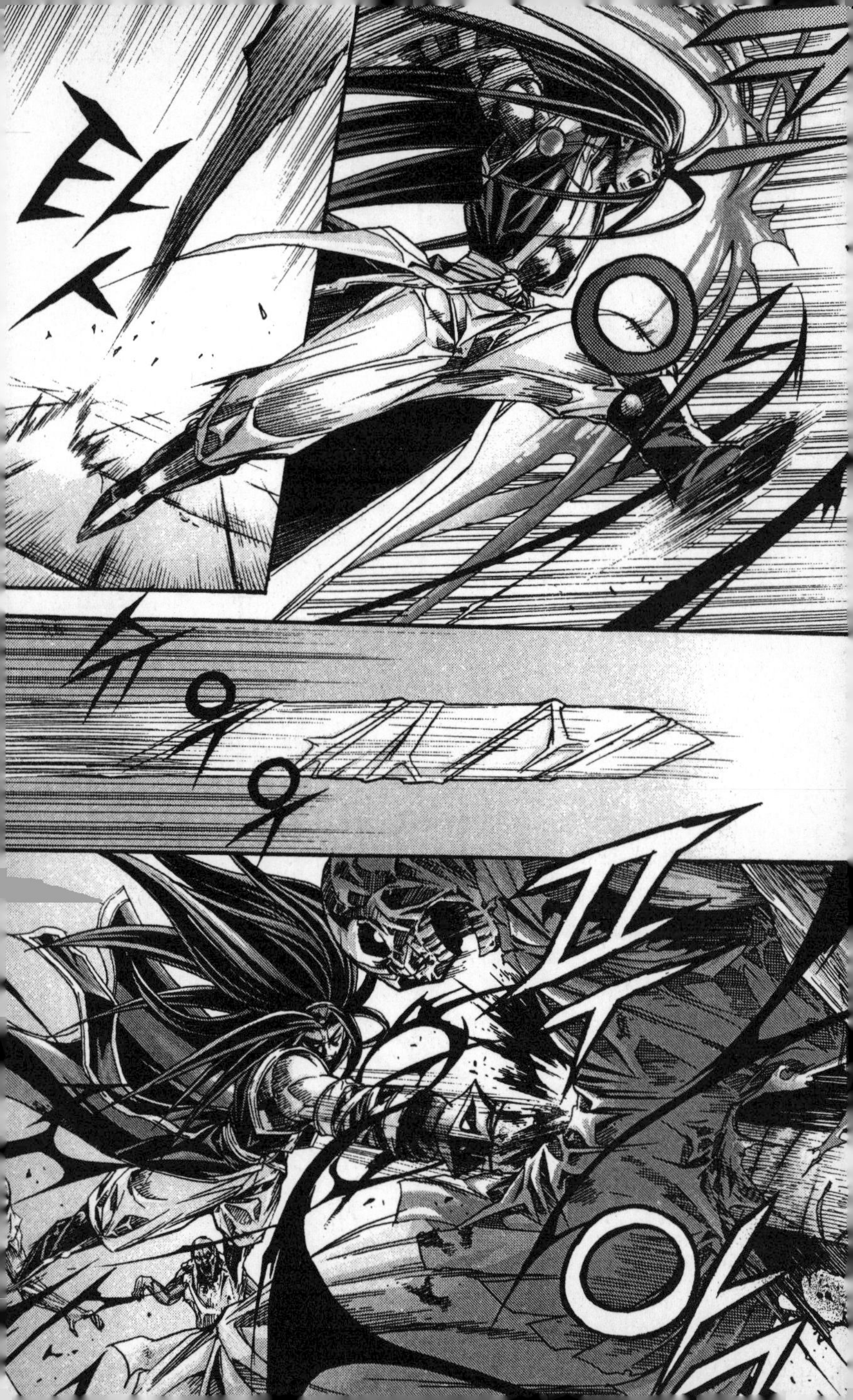

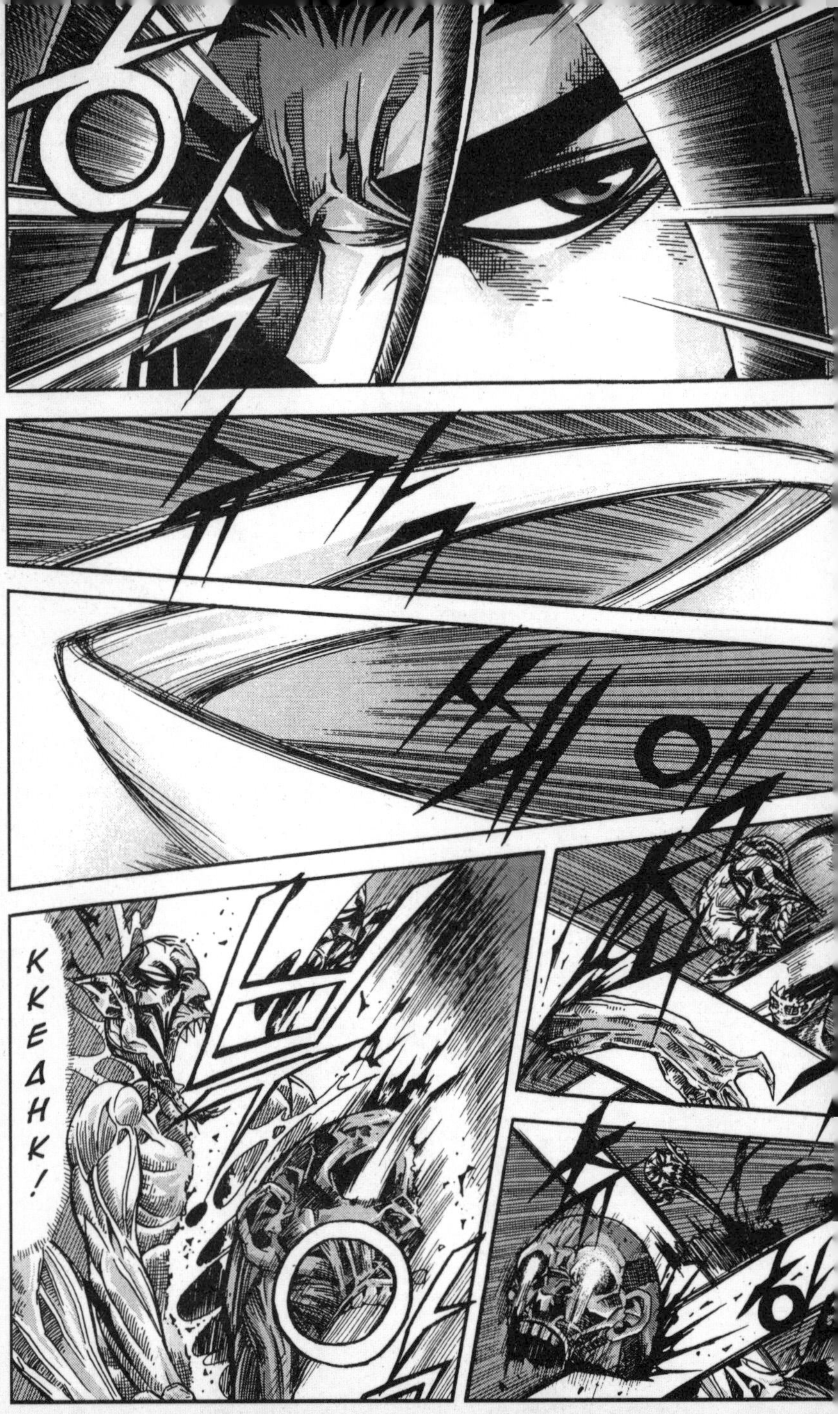
KKEAHK!

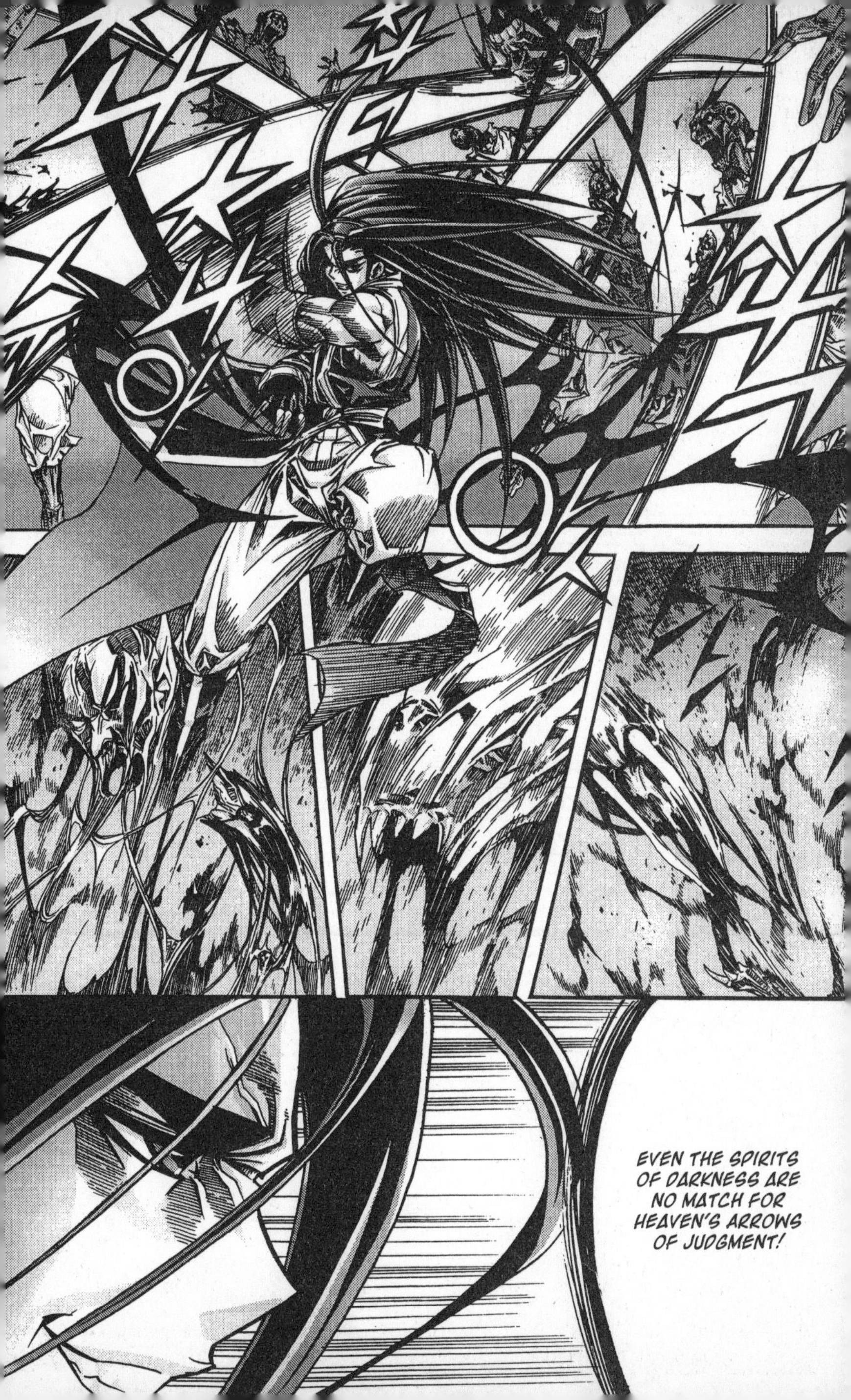
EVEN THE SPIRITS OF DARKNESS ARE NO MATCH FOR HEAVEN'S ARROWS OF JUDGMENT!

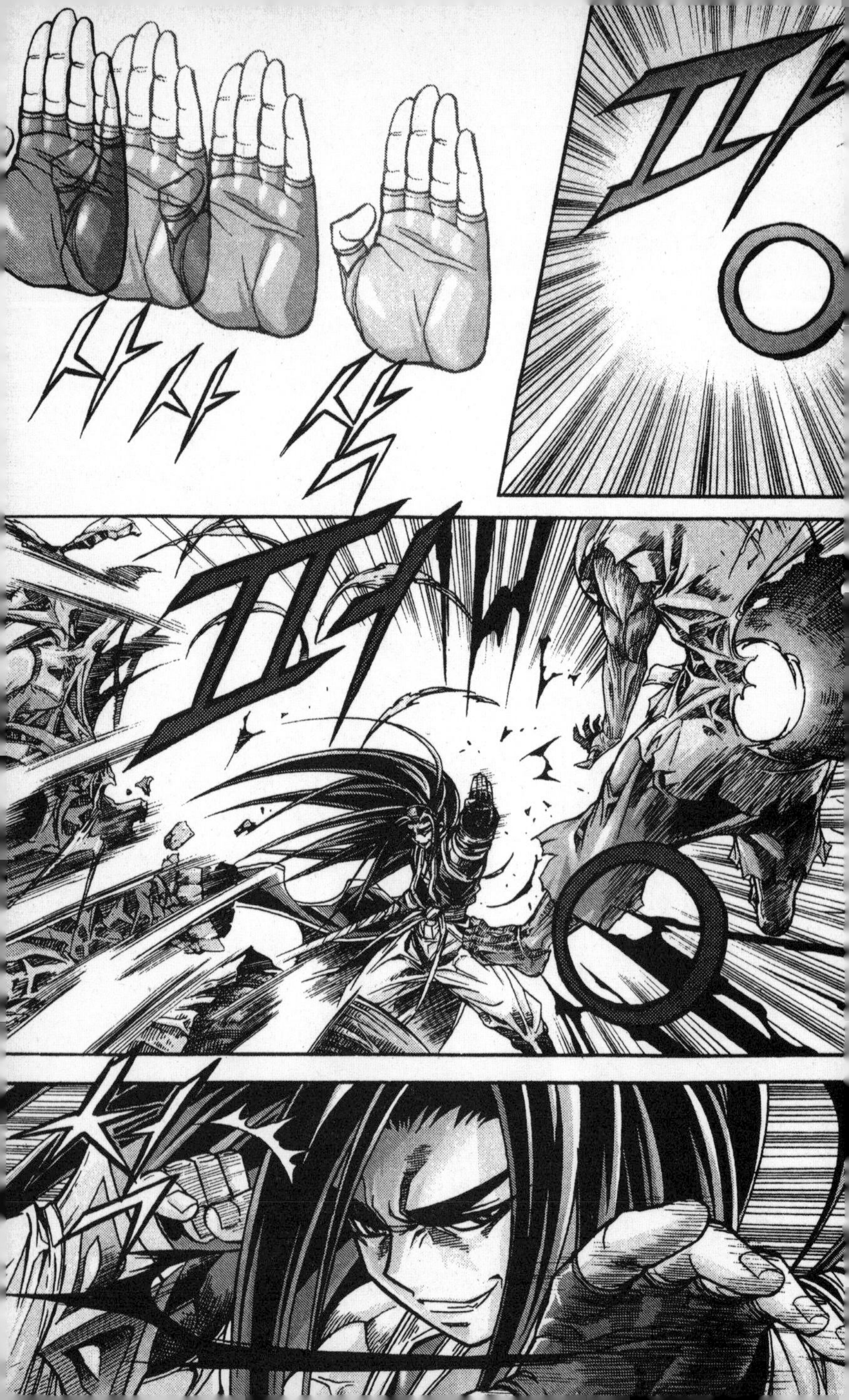

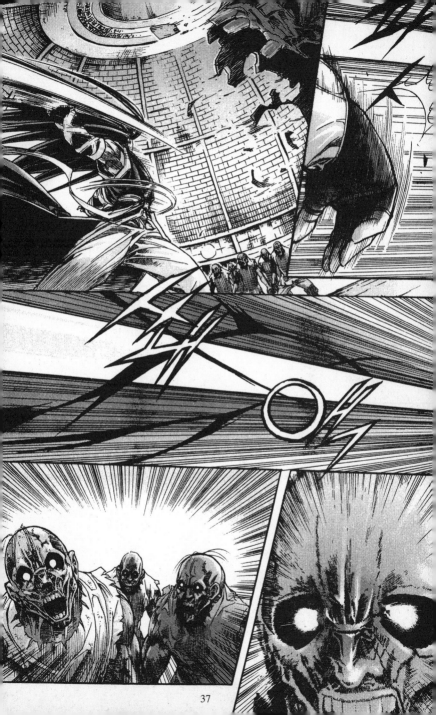

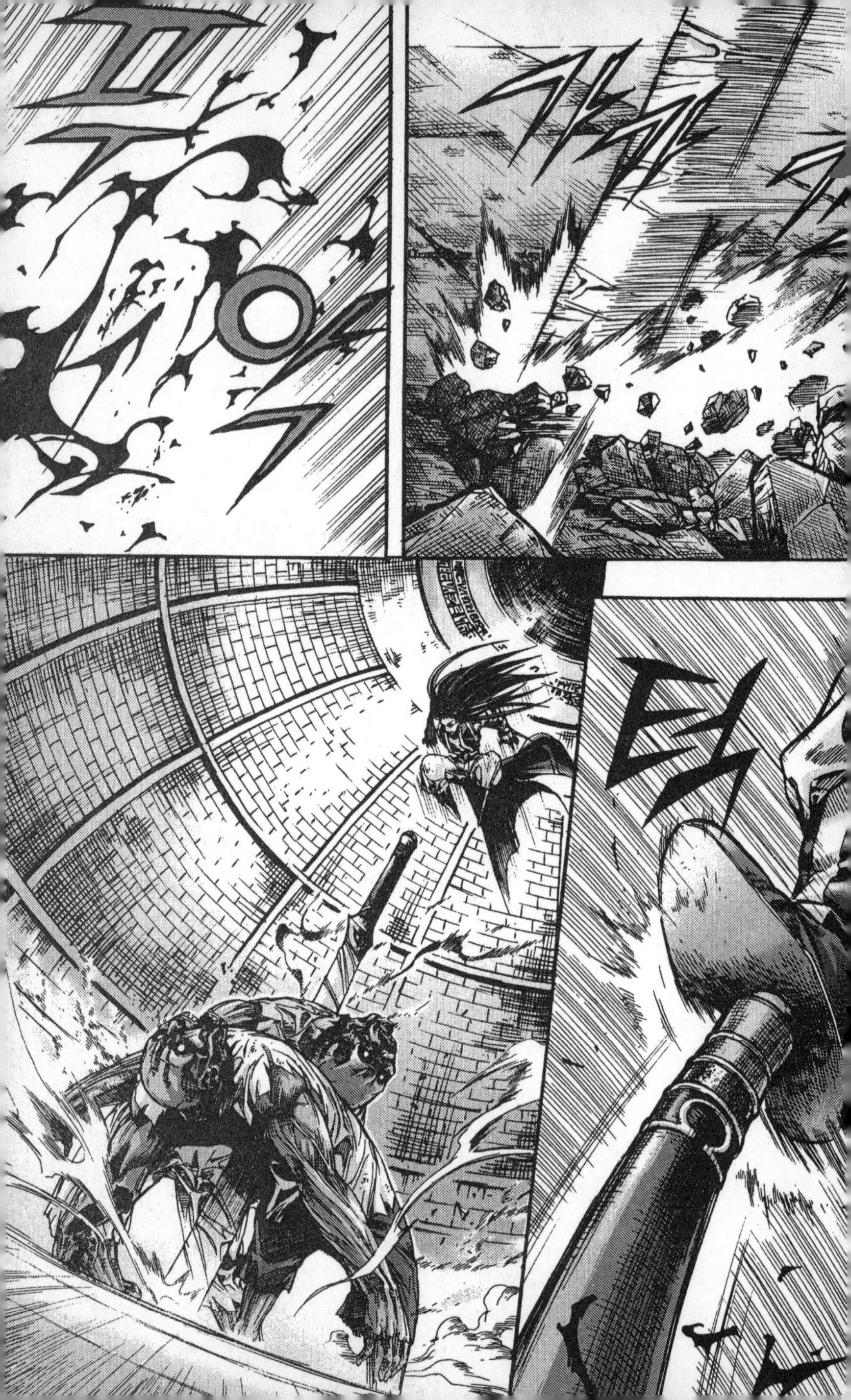
턱

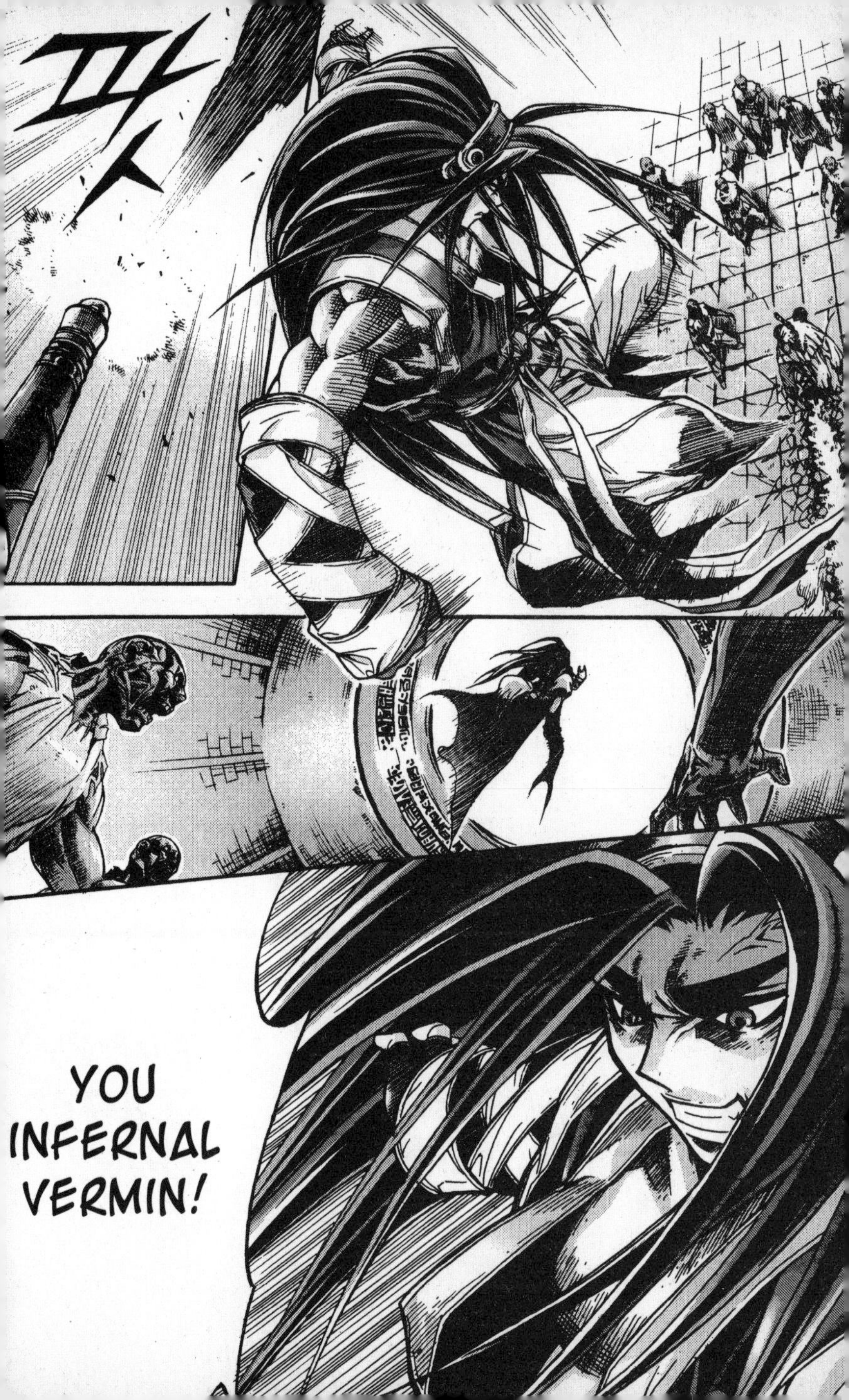
YOU INFERNAL VERMIN!

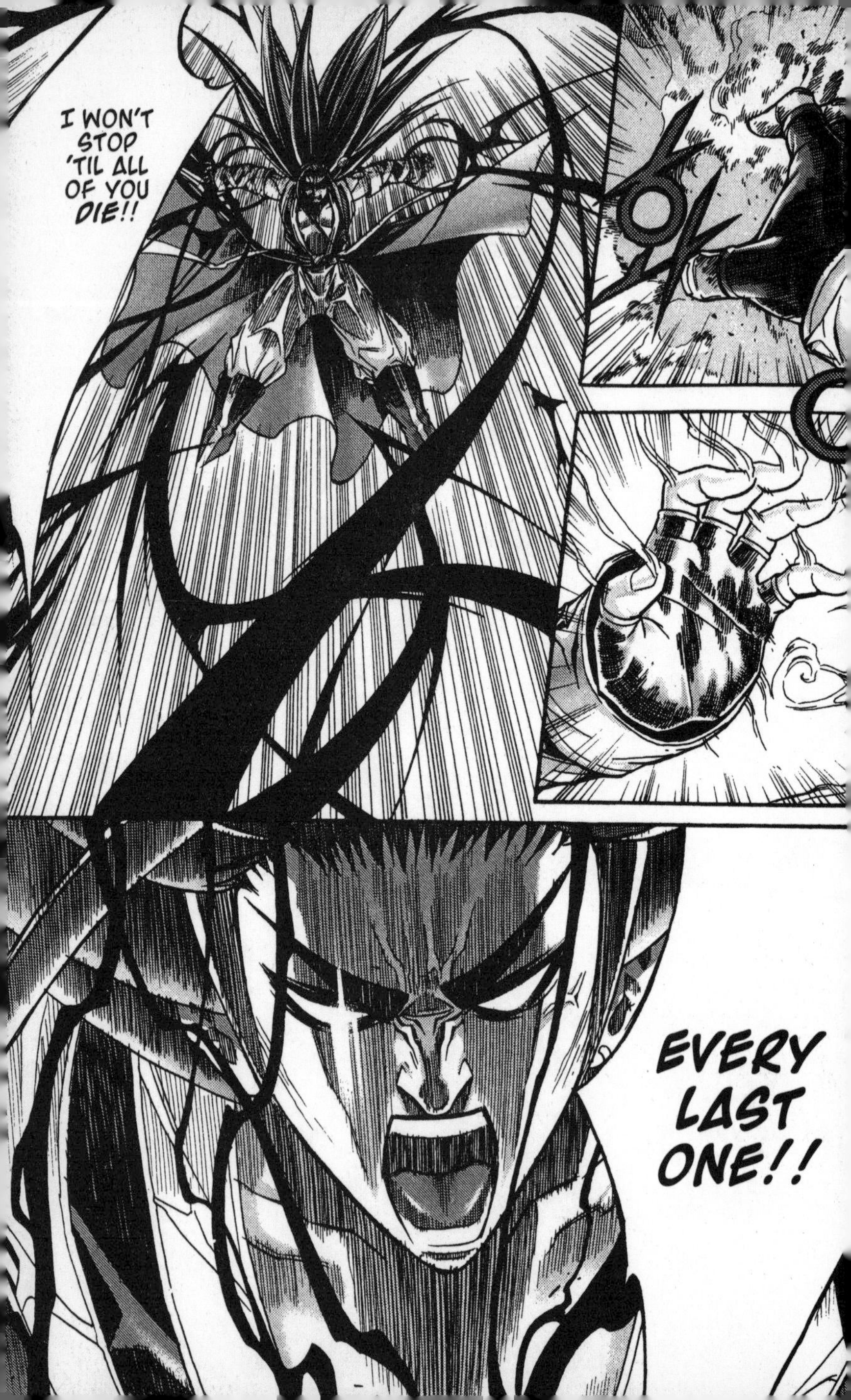
I WON'T STOP 'TIL ALL OF YOU DIE!!
EVERY LAST ONE!!

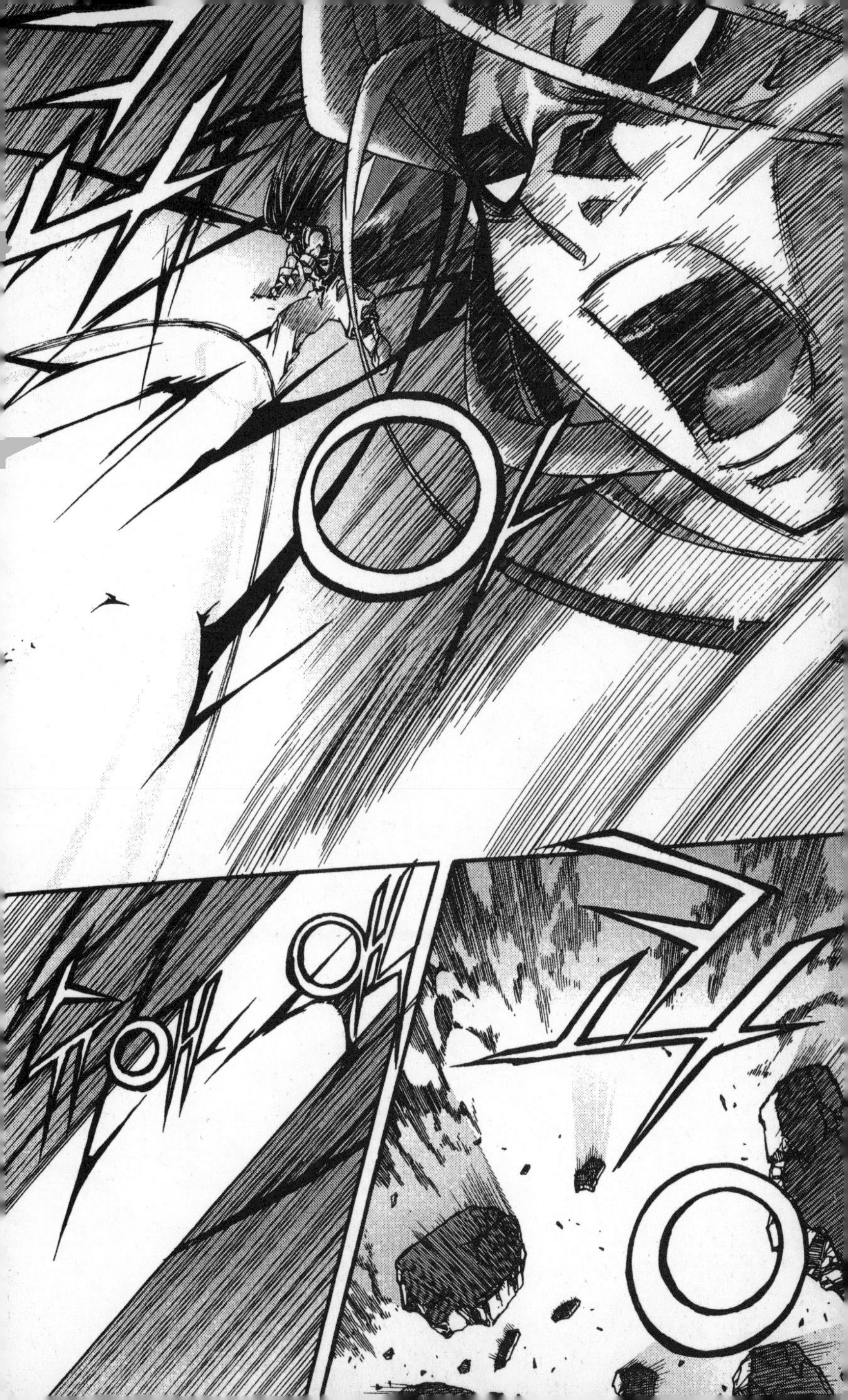

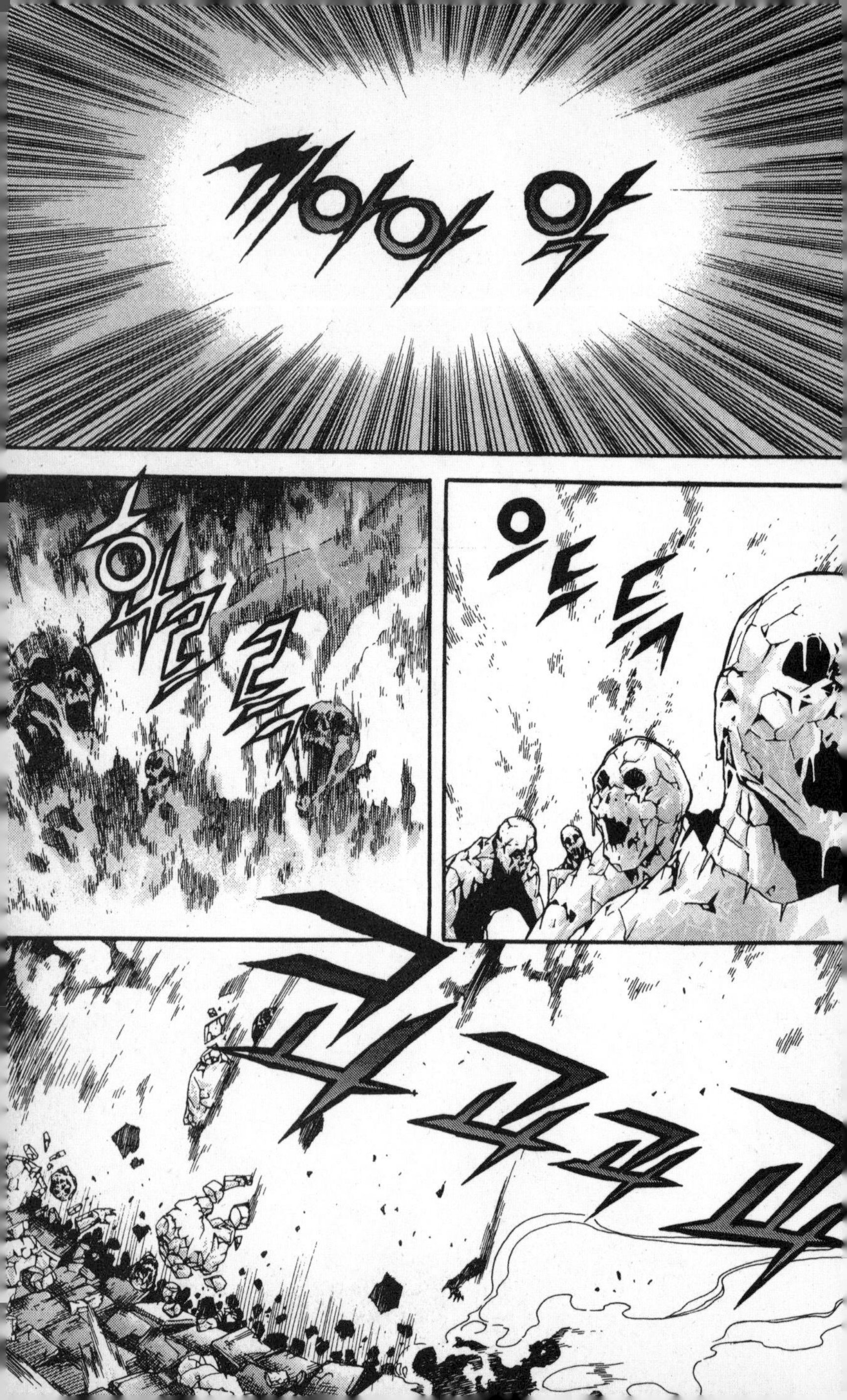
까아아아 앙
화르륵
우드득
쿠구구구

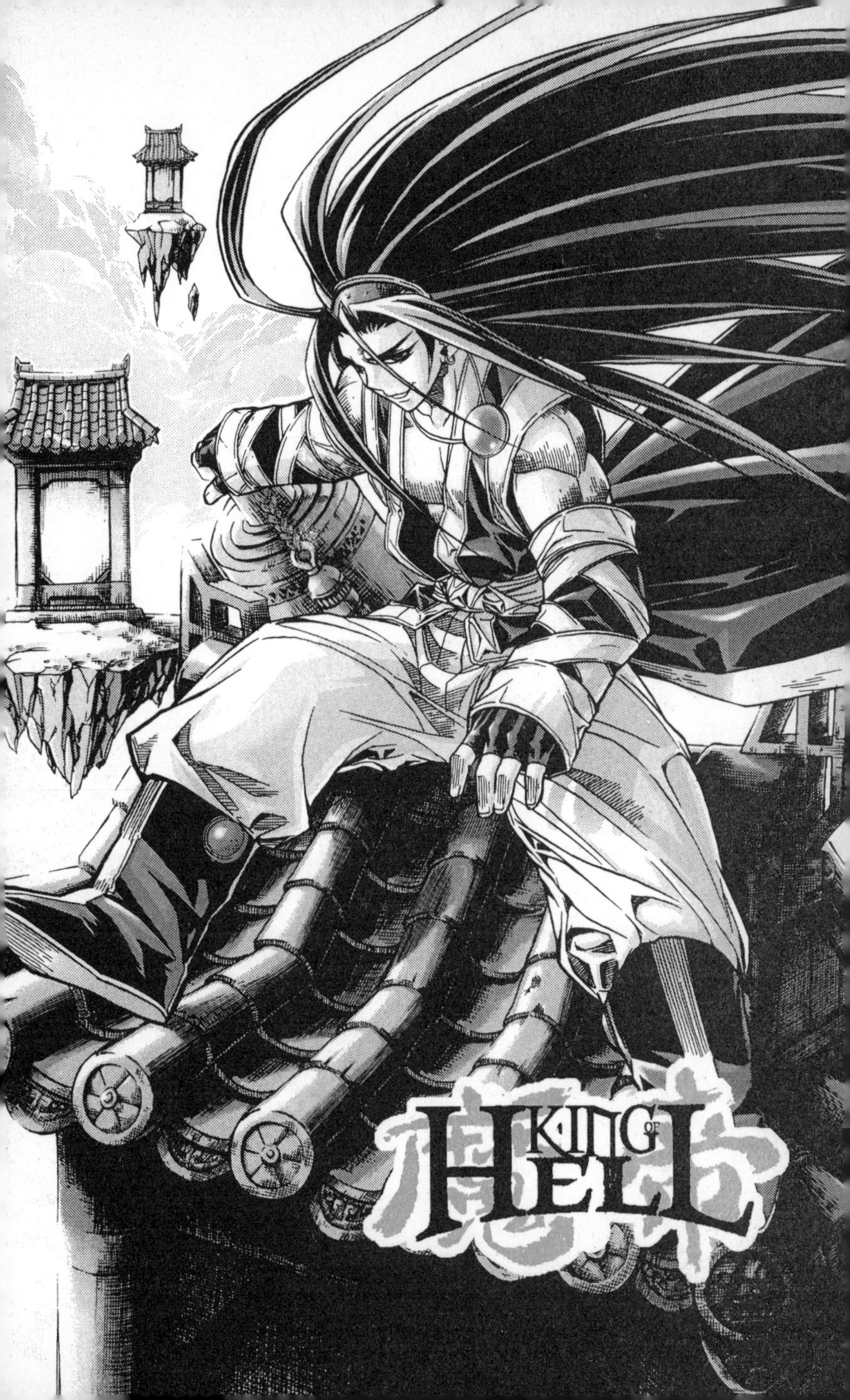
KING OF HELL

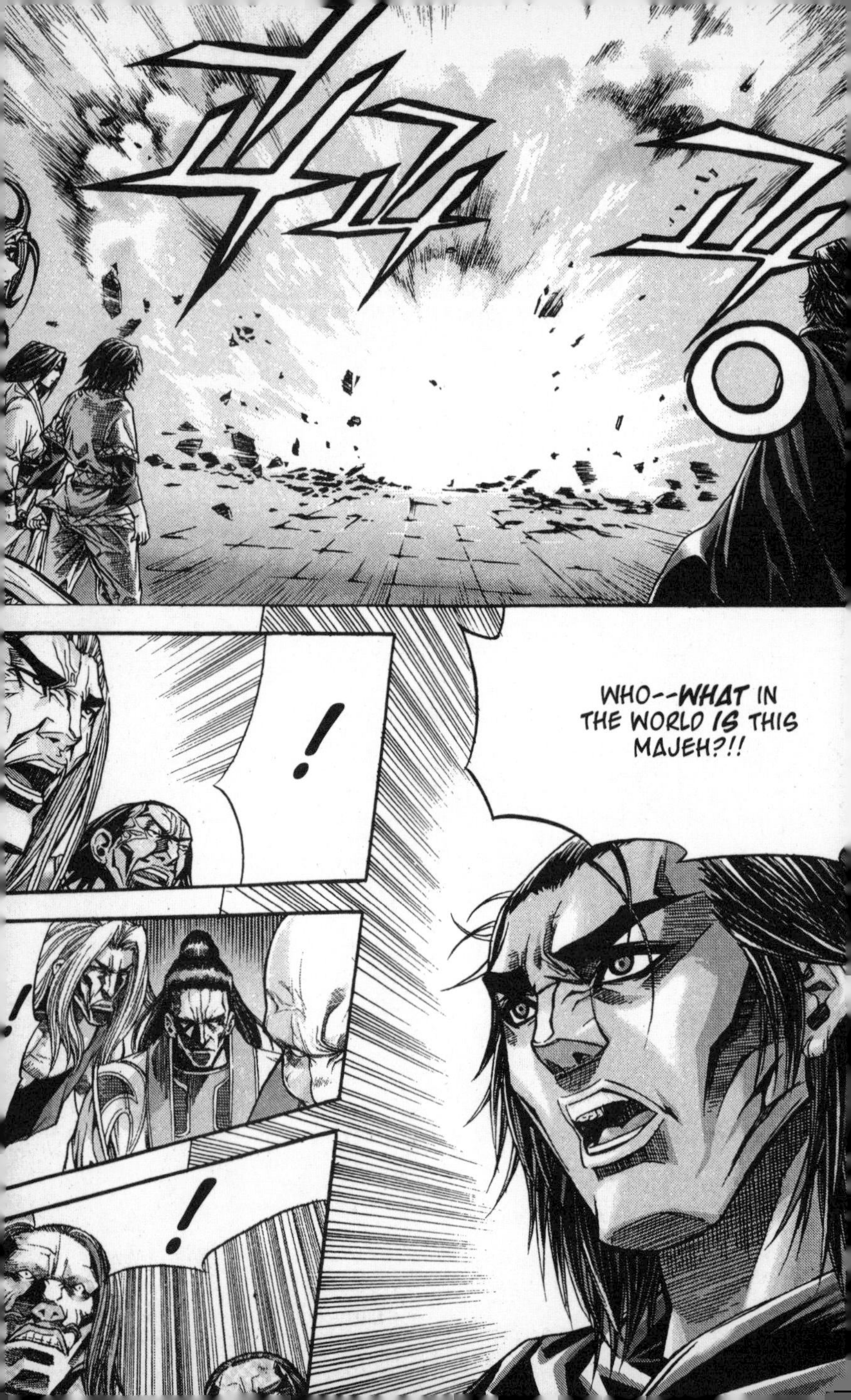
!
!
!
WHO--WHAT IN THE WORLD IS THIS MAJEH?!!

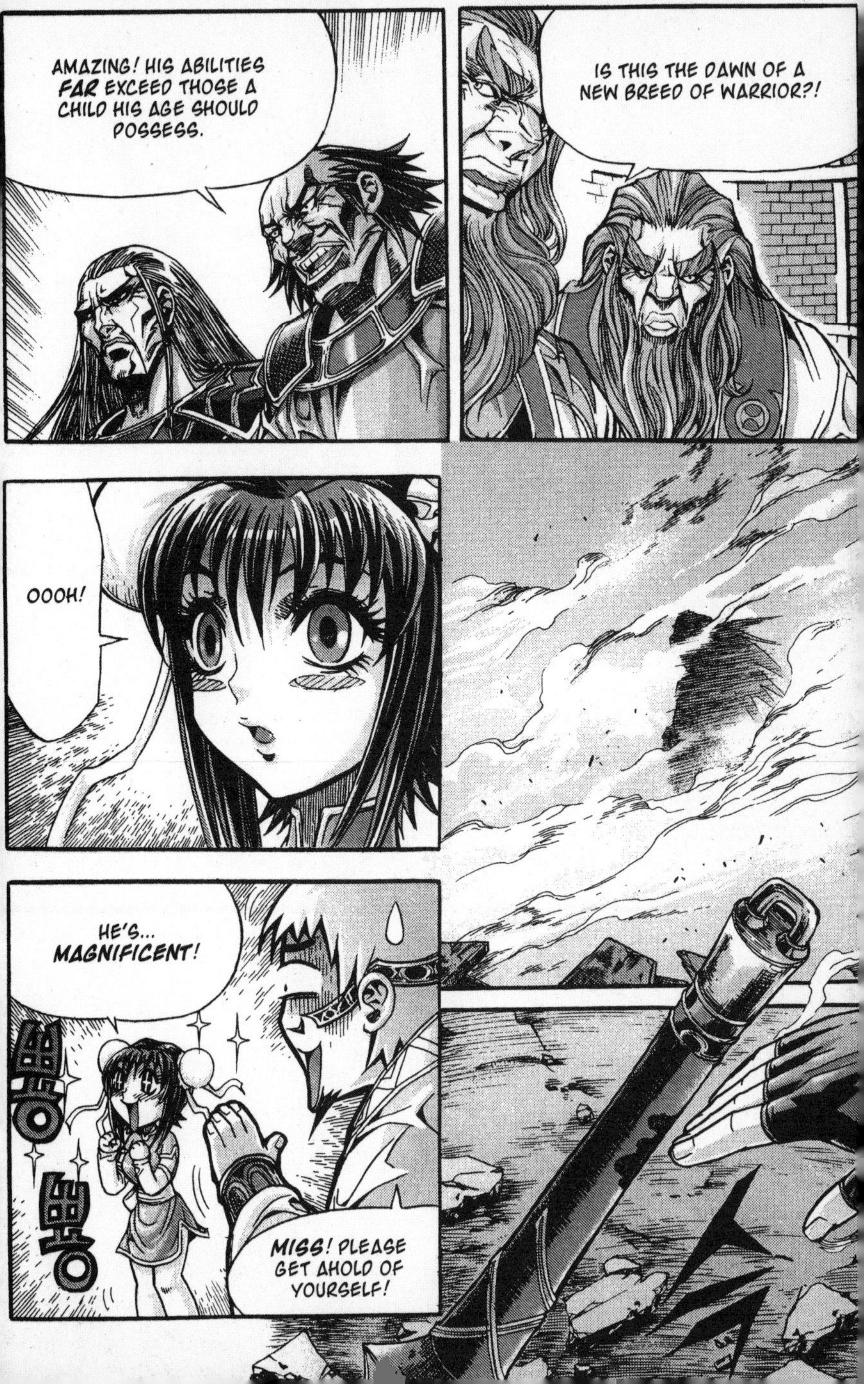
AMAZING! HIS ABILITIES FAR EXCEED THOSE A CHILD HIS AGE SHOULD POSSESS.
IS THIS THE DAWN OF A NEW BREED OF WARRIOR?!
OOOH!
HE'S... MAGNIFICENT!
뿅
뿅
MISS! PLEASE GET AHOLD OF YOURSELF!

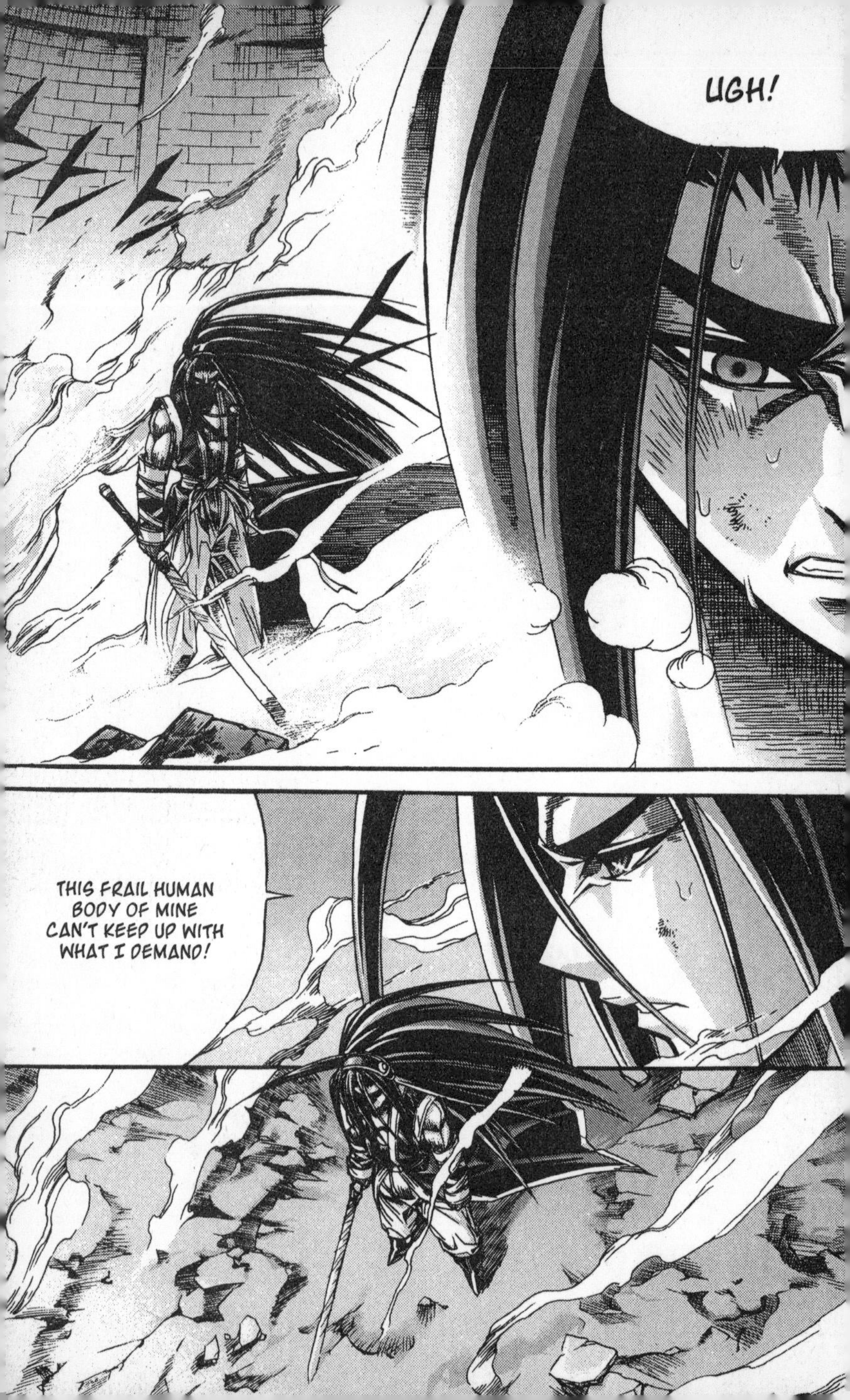
UGH!
THIS FRAIL HUMAN BODY OF MINE CAN'T KEEP UP WITH WHAT I DEMAND!

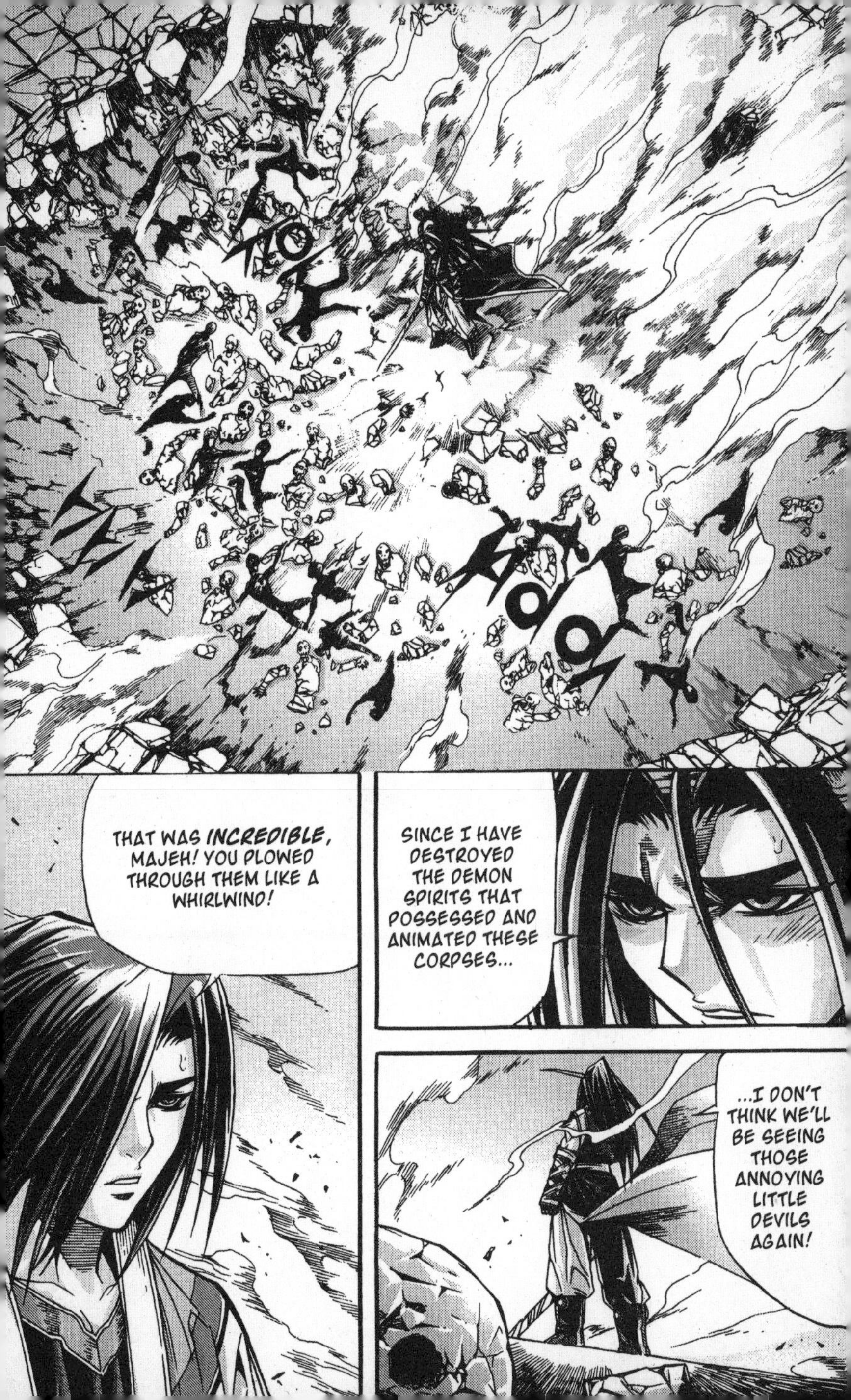

THAT WAS INCREDIBLE, MAJEH! YOU PLOWED THROUGH THEM LIKE A WHIRLWIND!
SINCE I HAVE DESTROYED THE DEMON SPIRITS THAT POSSESSED AND ANIMATED THESE CORPSES...
...I DON'T THINK WE'LL BE SEEING THOSE ANNOYING LITTLE DEVILS AGAIN!

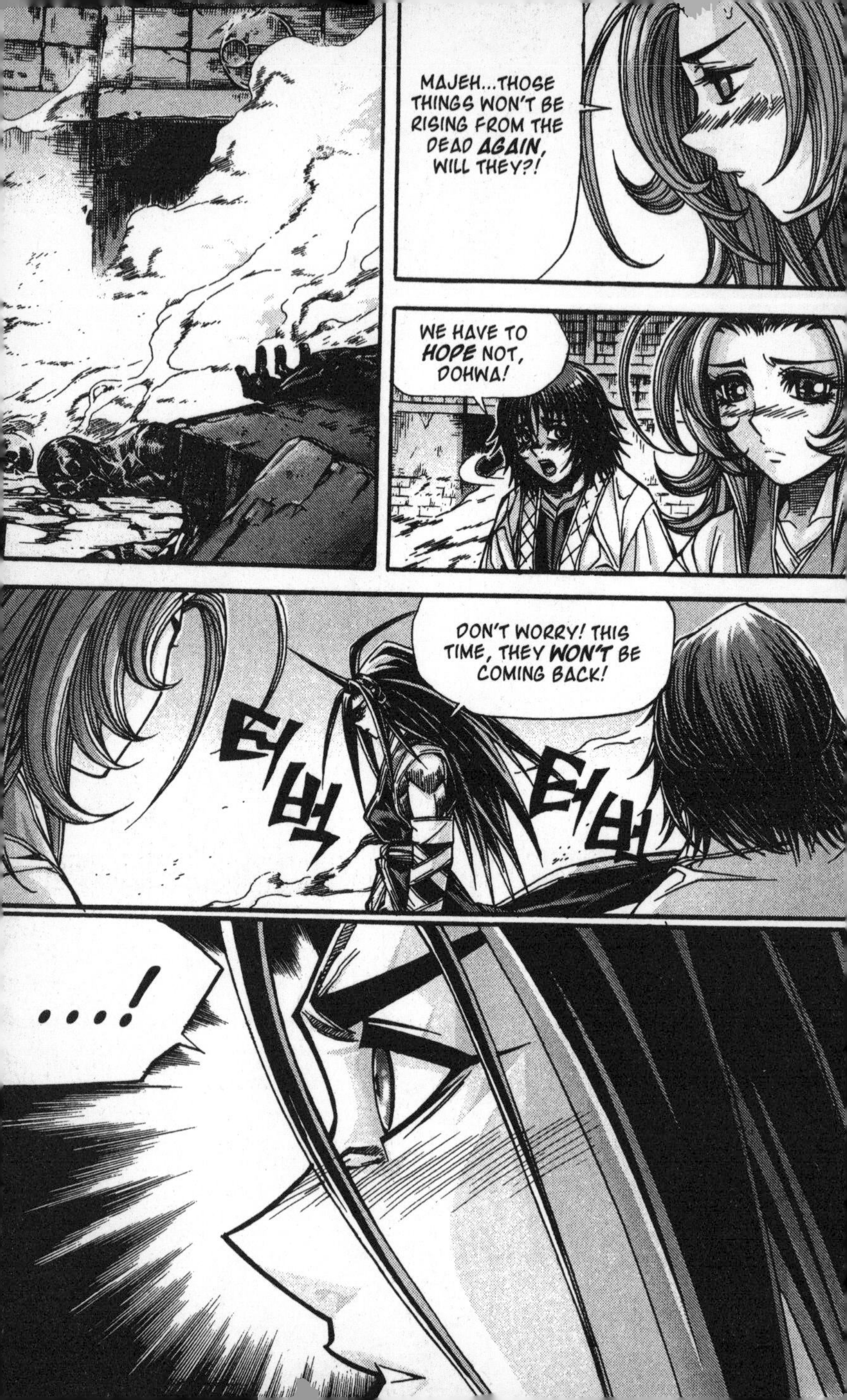
MAJEH...THOSE THINGS WON'T BE RISING FROM THE DEAD AGAIN, WILL THEY?!
WE HAVE TO HOPE NOT, DOHWA!
DON'T WORRY! THIS TIME, THEY WON'T BE COMING BACK!
터벅
터벅
...!

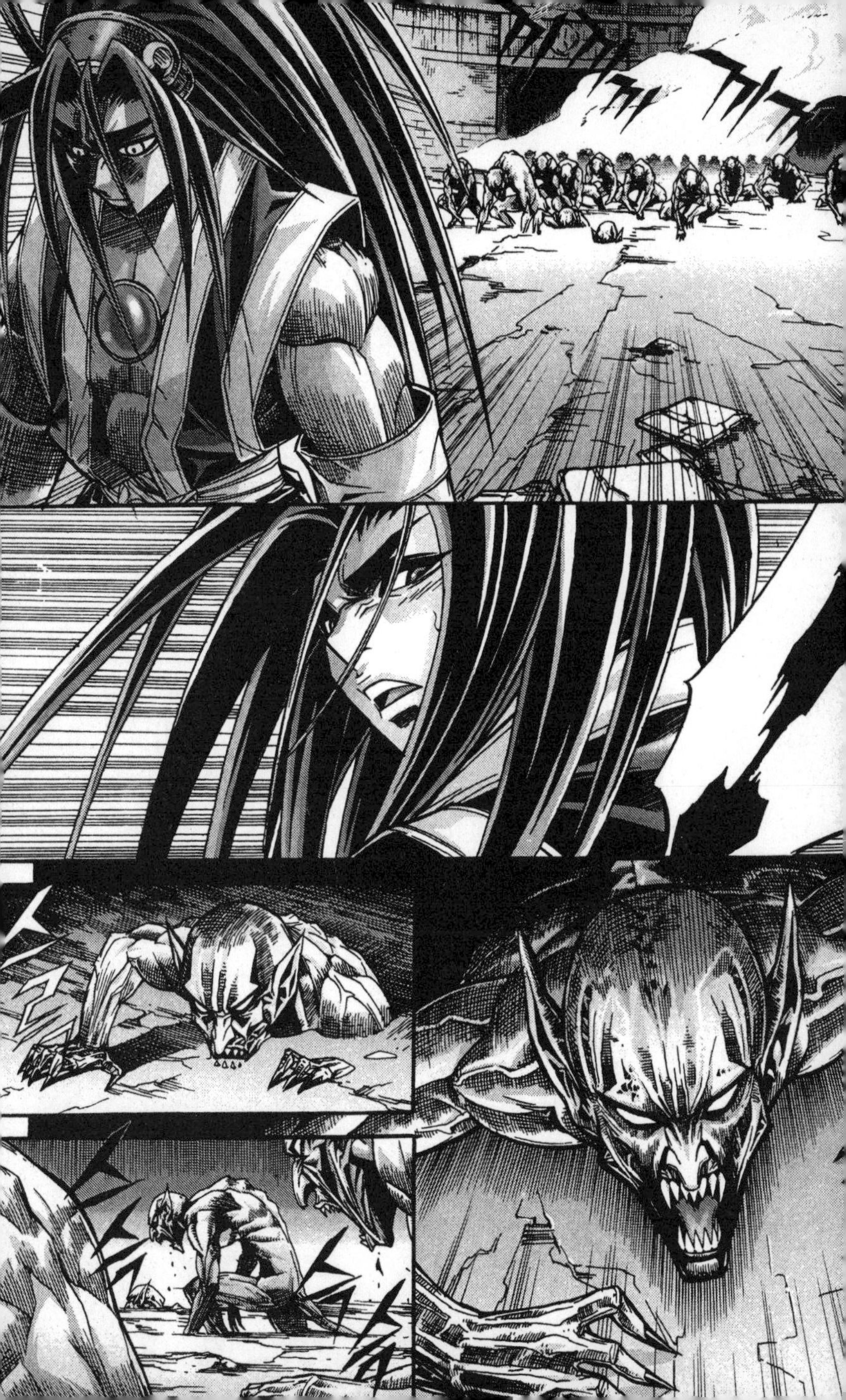

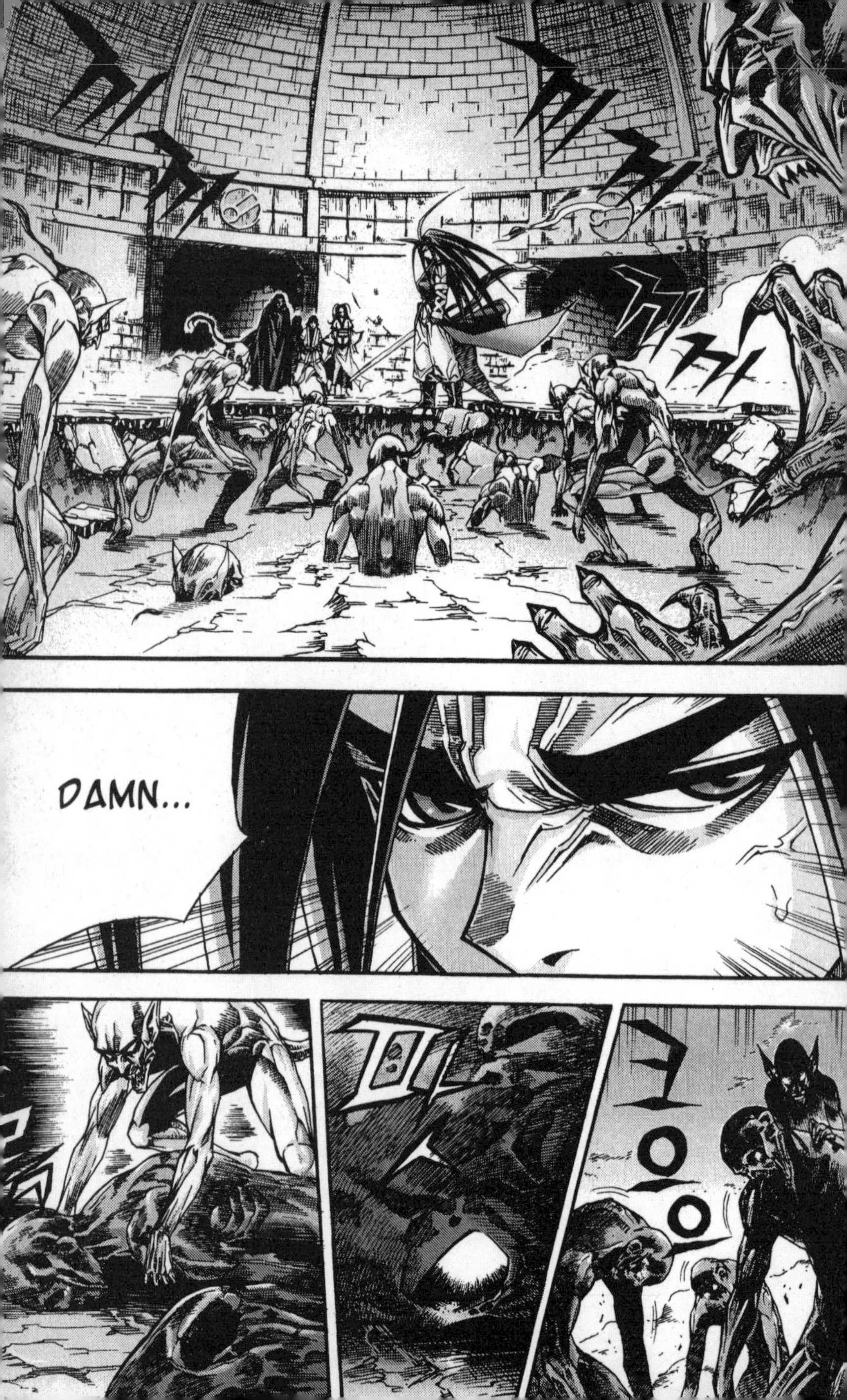
DAMN...

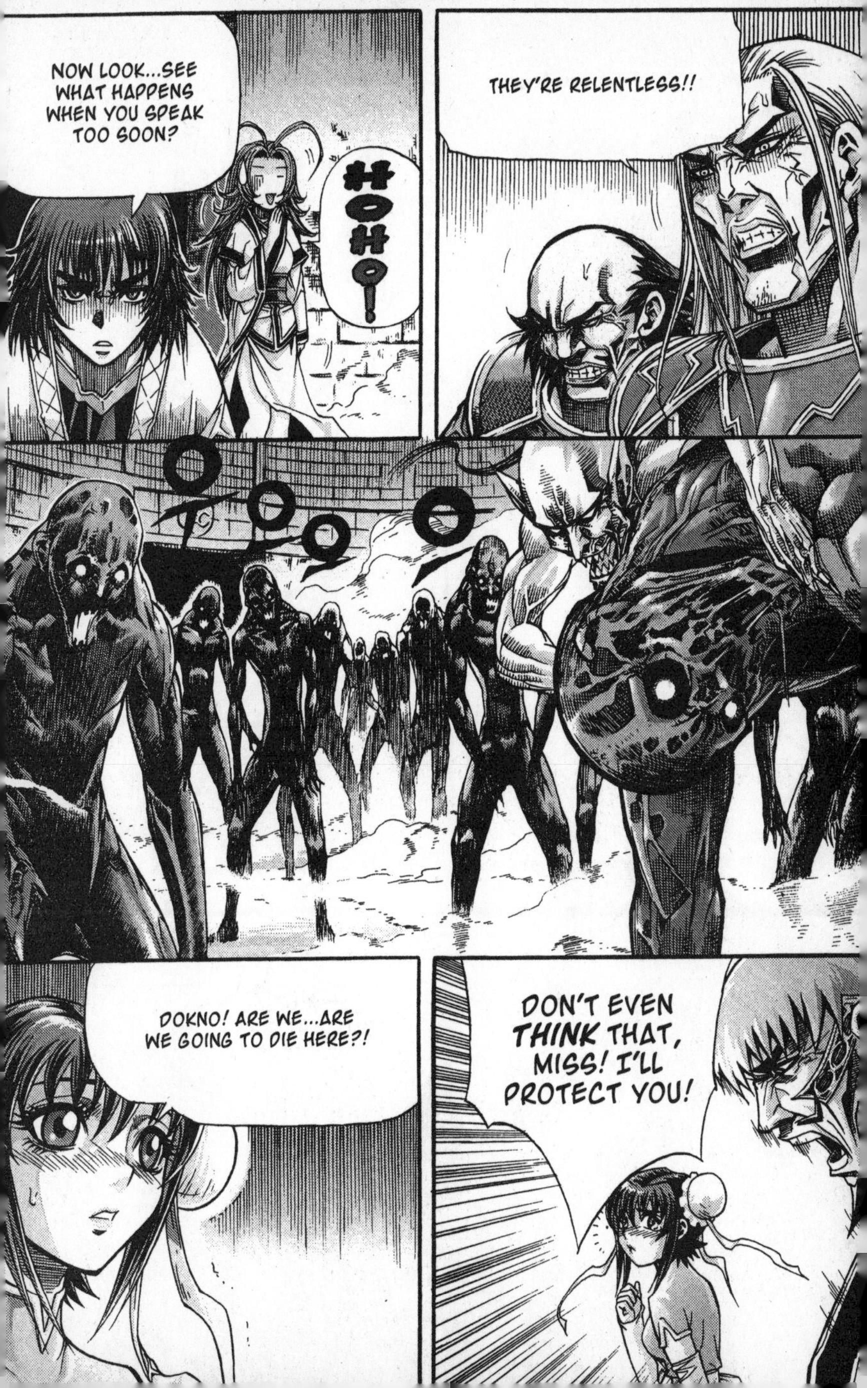
NOW LOOK...SEE WHAT HAPPENS WHEN YOU SPEAK TOO SOON?
HOHOHO!
THEY'RE RELENTLESS!!
DOKNO! ARE WE...ARE WE GOING TO DIE HERE?!
DON'T EVEN THINK THAT, MISS! I'LL PROTECT YOU!

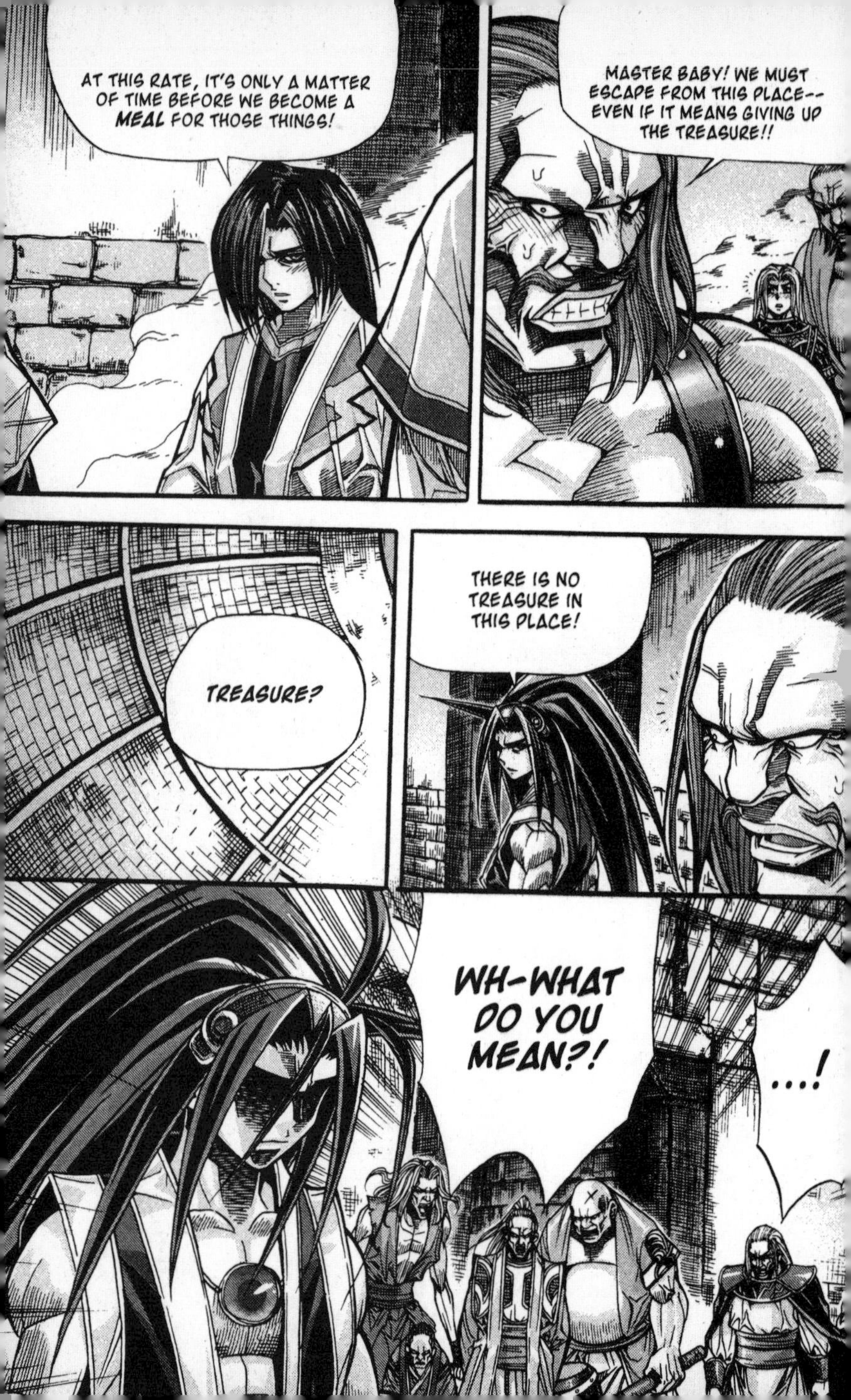
AT THIS RATE, IT'S ONLY A MATTER OF TIME BEFORE WE BECOME A *MEAL* FOR THOSE THINGS!
MASTER BABY! WE MUST ESCAPE FROM THIS PLACE-- EVEN IF IT MEANS GIVING UP THE TREASURE!!
TREASURE?
THERE IS NO TREASURE IN THIS PLACE!
WH-WHAT DO YOU MEAN?!
...!

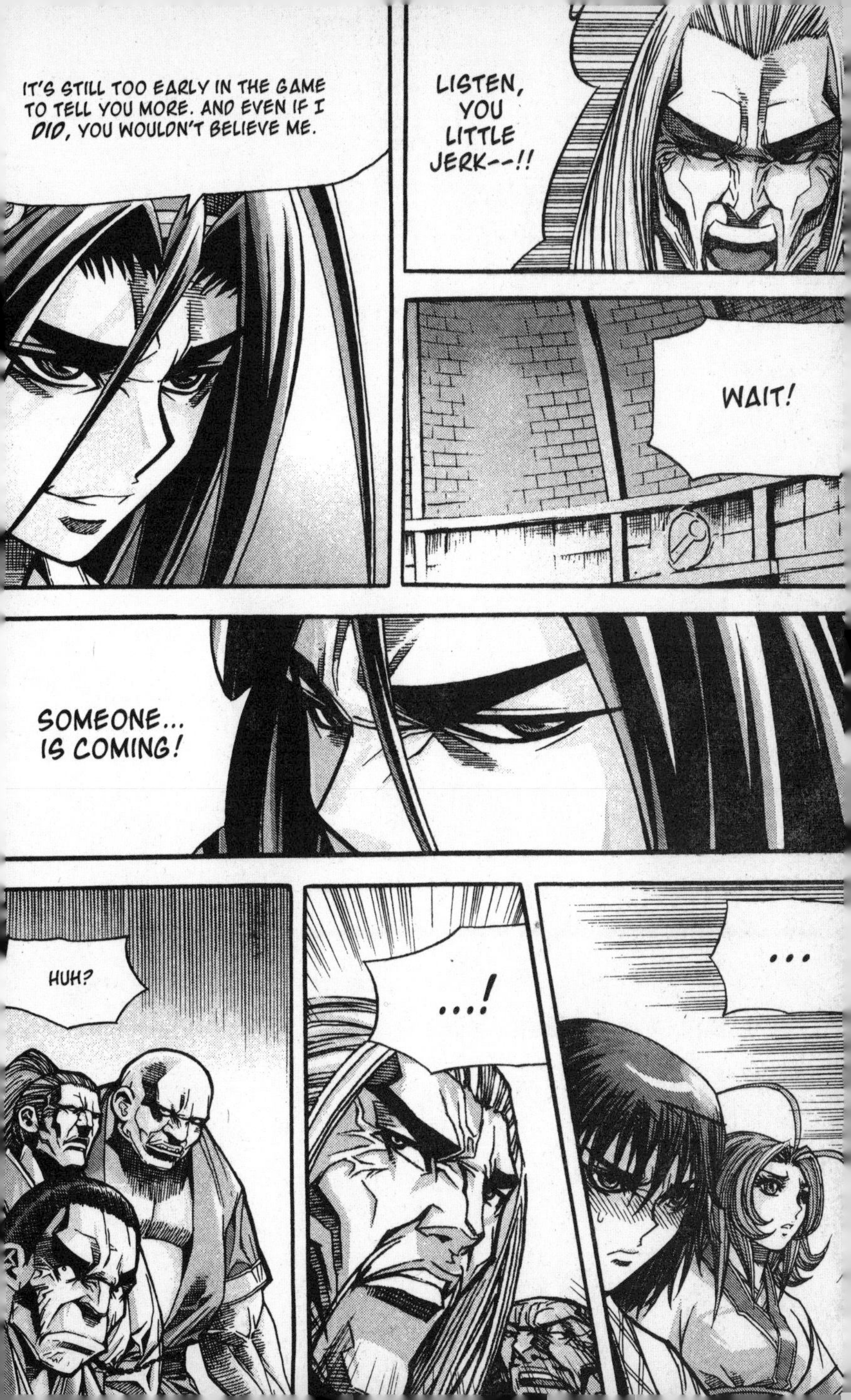
IT'S STILL TOO EARLY IN THE GAME TO TELL YOU MORE. AND EVEN IF I *DID*, YOU WOULDN'T BELIEVE ME.
LISTEN, YOU LITTLE JERK--!!
WAIT!
SOMEONE... IS COMING!
HUH?
...!
...

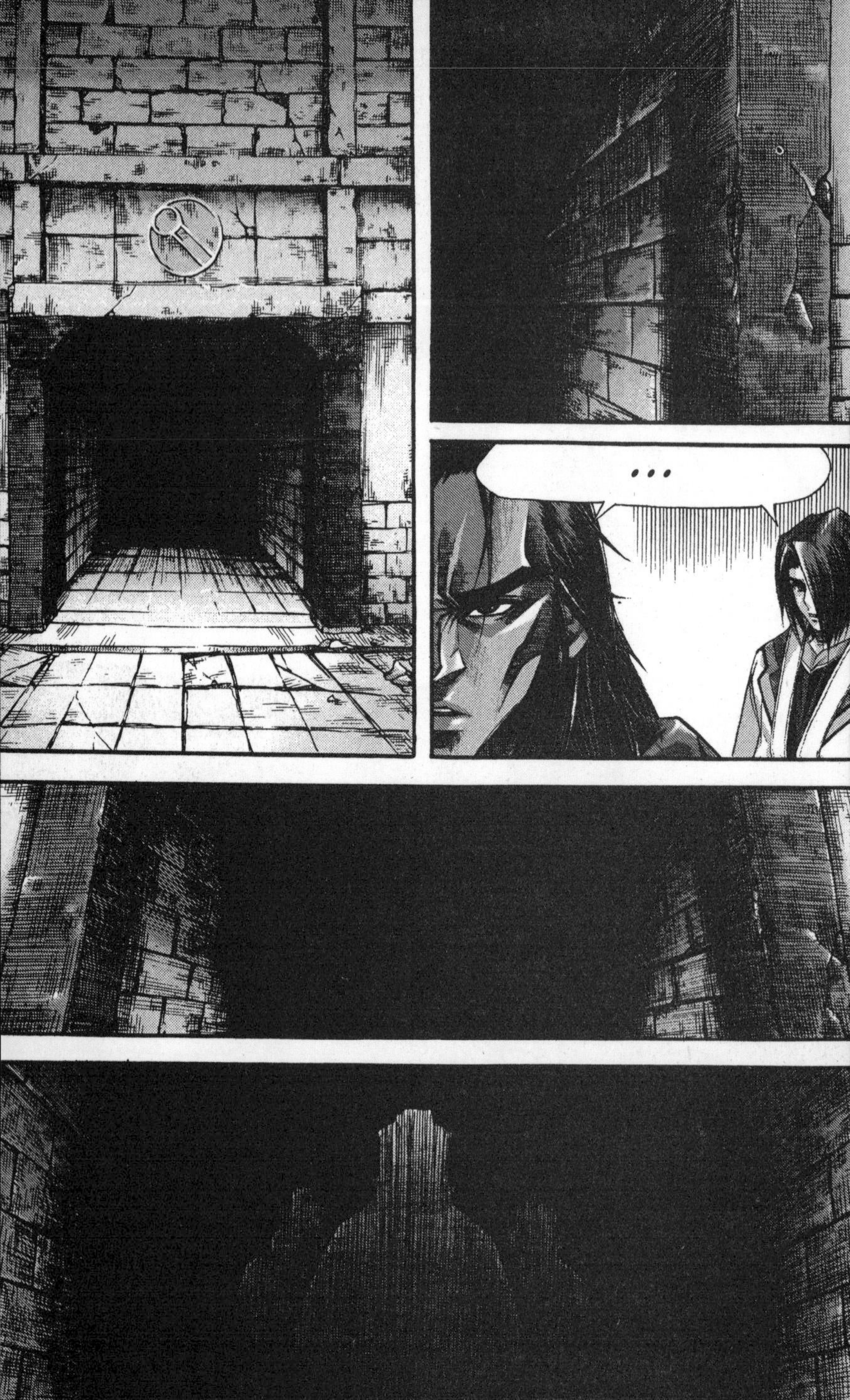
...

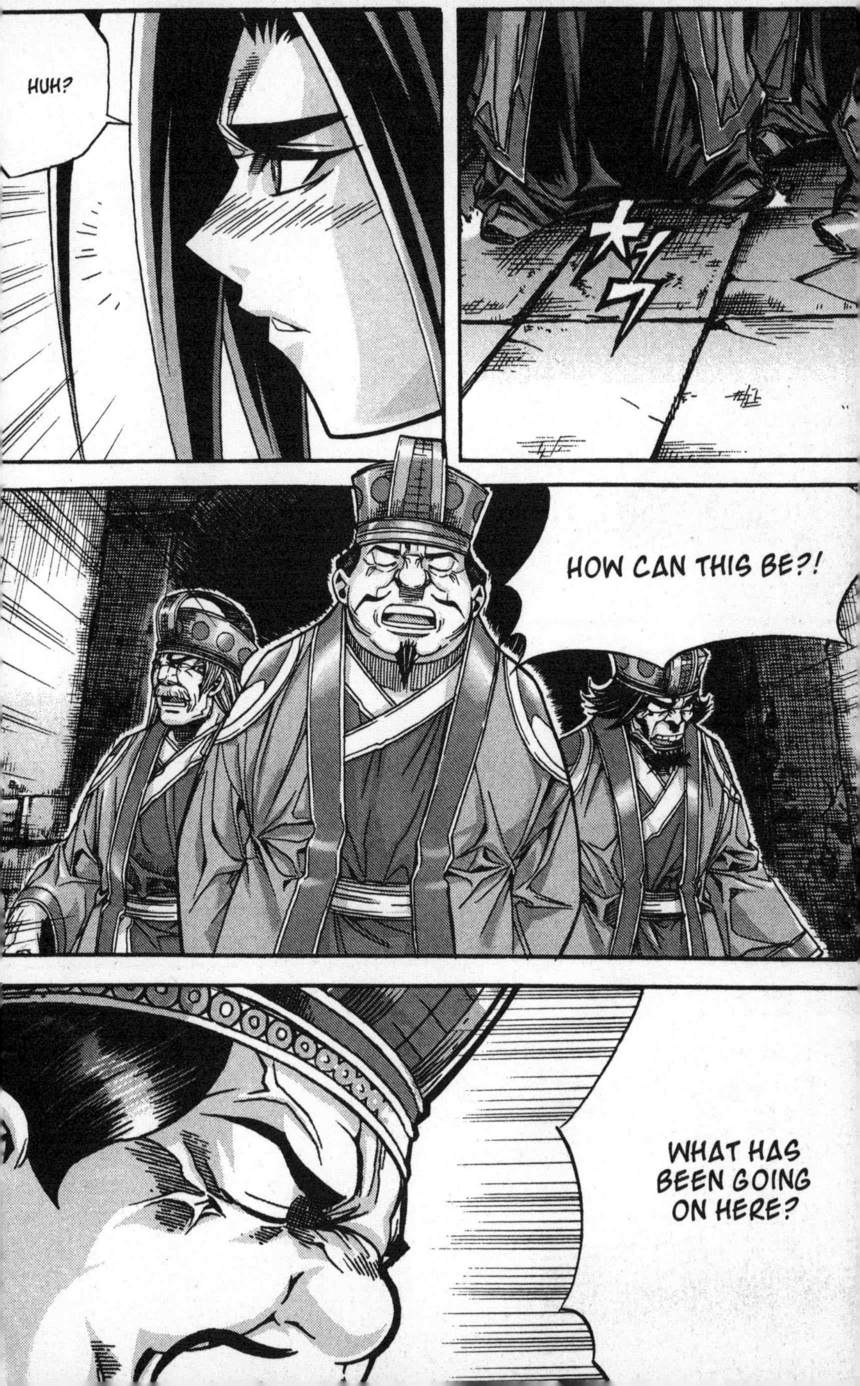
HUH?
HOW CAN THIS BE?!
WHAT HAS BEEN GOING ON HERE?

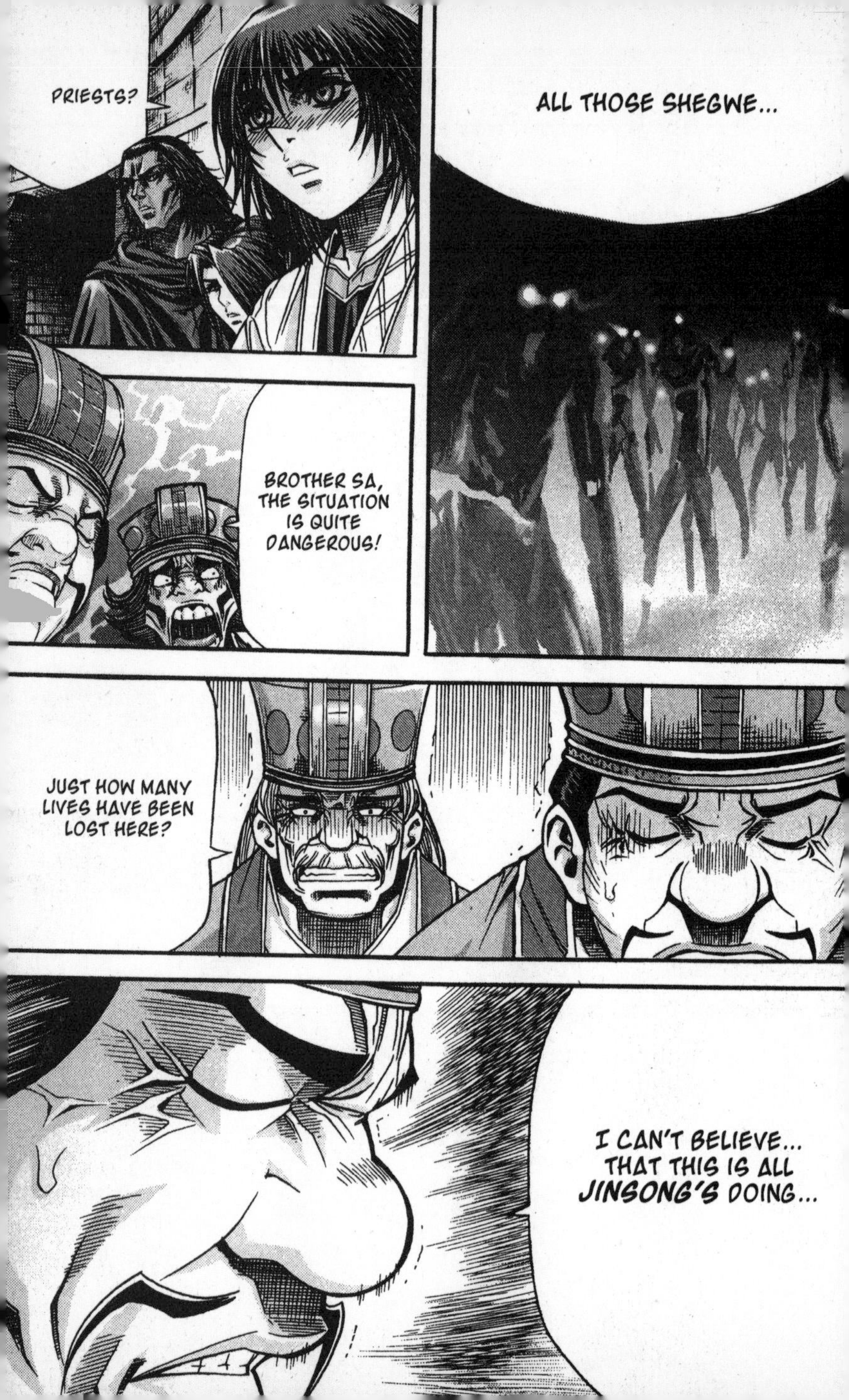
ALL THOSE SHEGWE...
PRIESTS?
BROTHER SA, THE SITUATION IS QUITE DANGEROUS!
JUST HOW MANY LIVES HAVE BEEN LOST HERE?
I CAN'T BELIEVE... THAT THIS IS ALL JINSONG'S DOING...

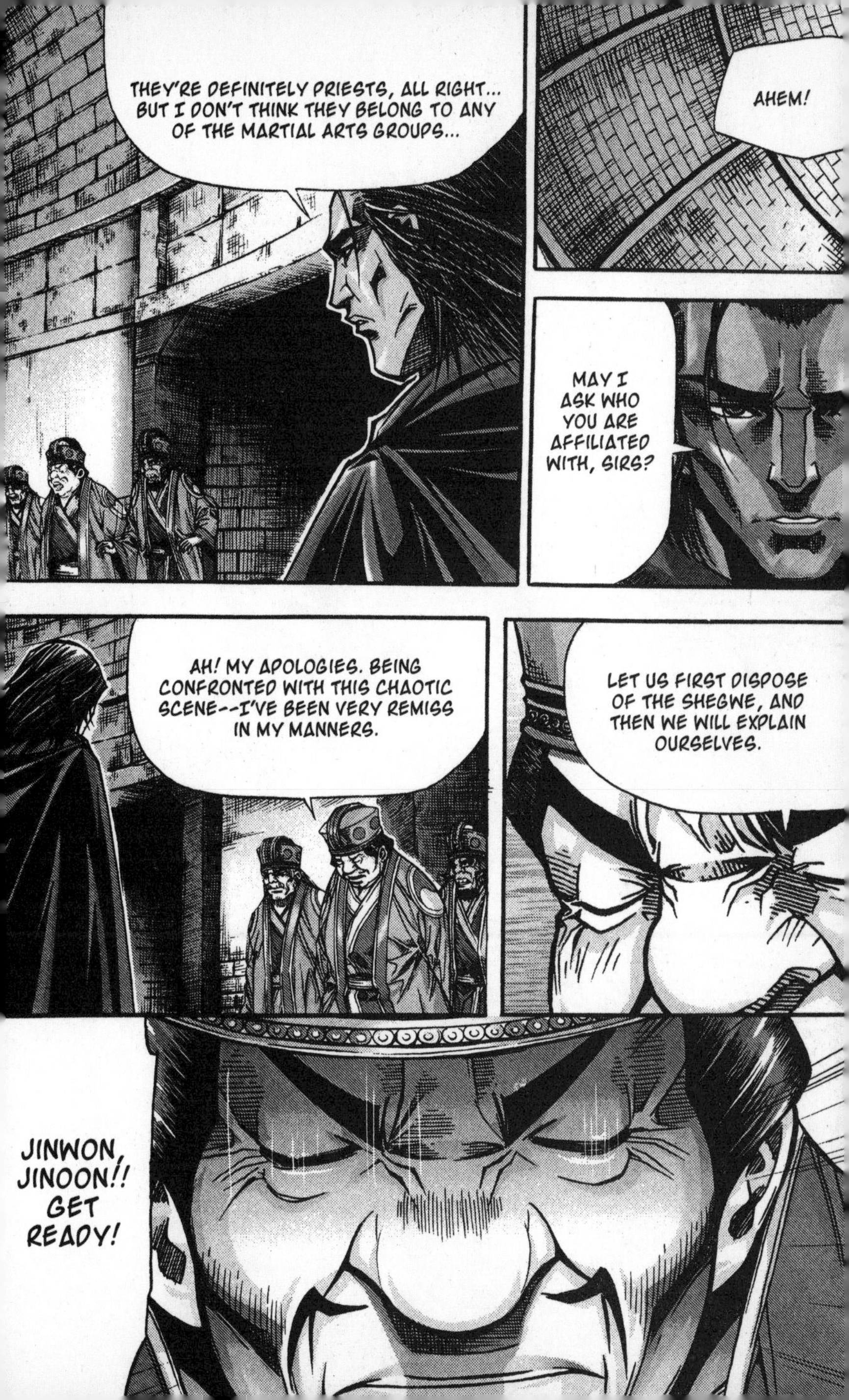
THEY'RE DEFINITELY PRIESTS, ALL RIGHT... BUT I DON'T THINK THEY BELONG TO ANY OF THE MARTIAL ARTS GROUPS...
AHEM!
MAY I ASK WHO YOU ARE AFFILIATED WITH, SIRS?
AH! MY APOLOGIES. BEING CONFRONTED WITH THIS CHAOTIC SCENE--I'VE BEEN VERY REMISS IN MY MANNERS.
LET US FIRST DISPOSE OF THE SHEGWE, AND THEN WE WILL EXPLAIN OURSELVES.
JINWON, JINOON!! GET READY!

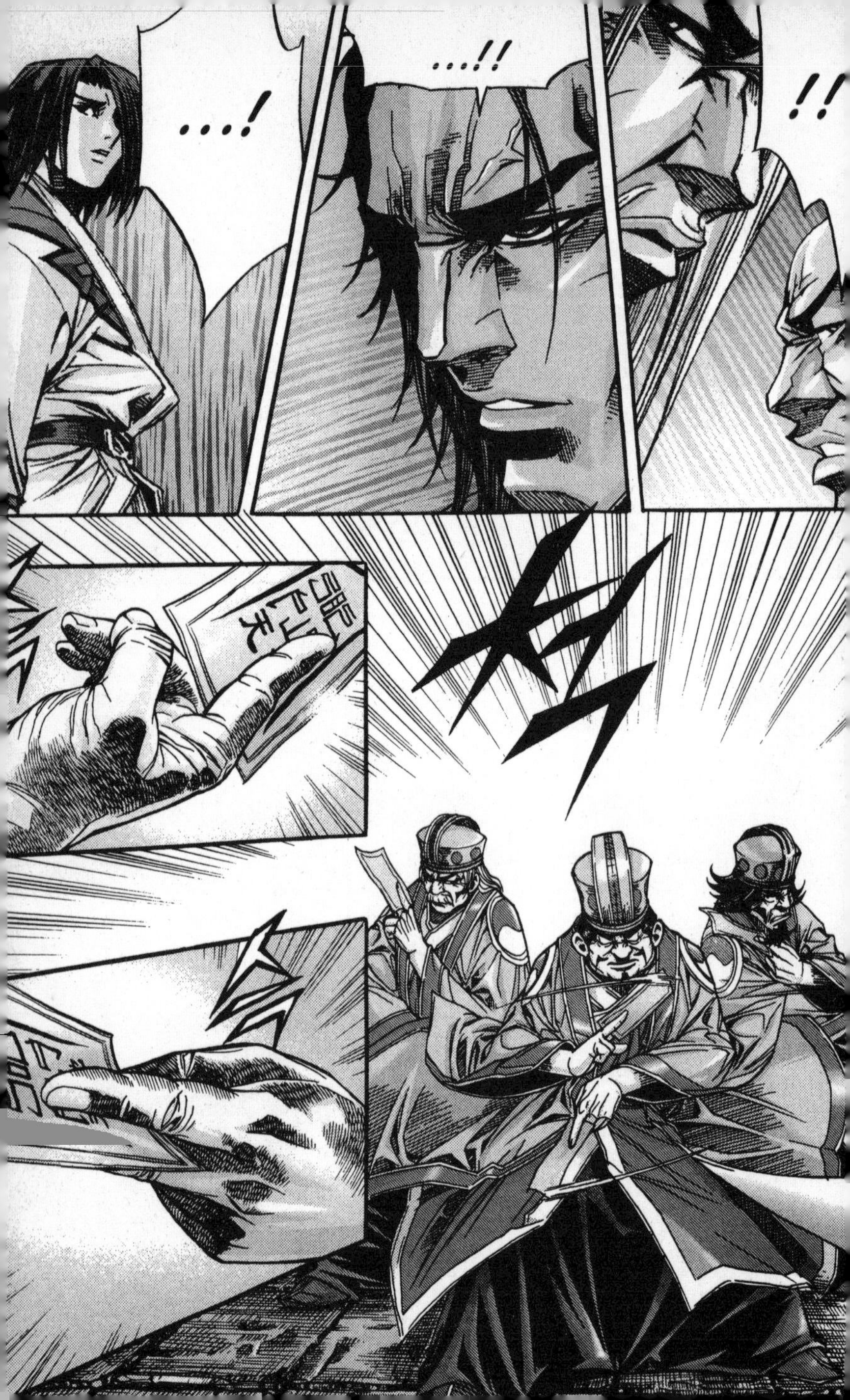
...!
...!!
!!

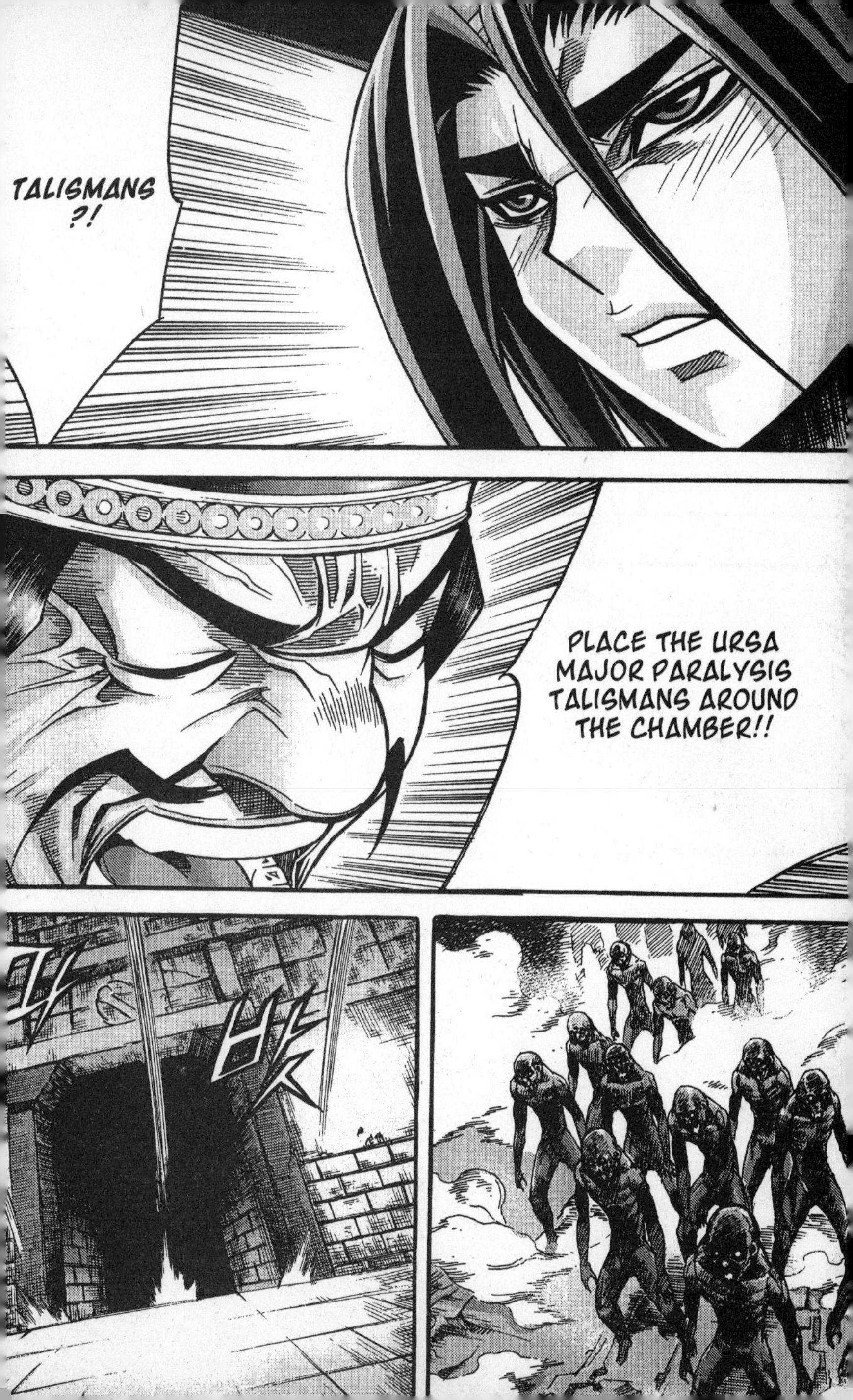
TALISMANS ?!
PLACE THE URSA MAJOR PARALYSIS TALISMANS AROUND THE CHAMBER!!

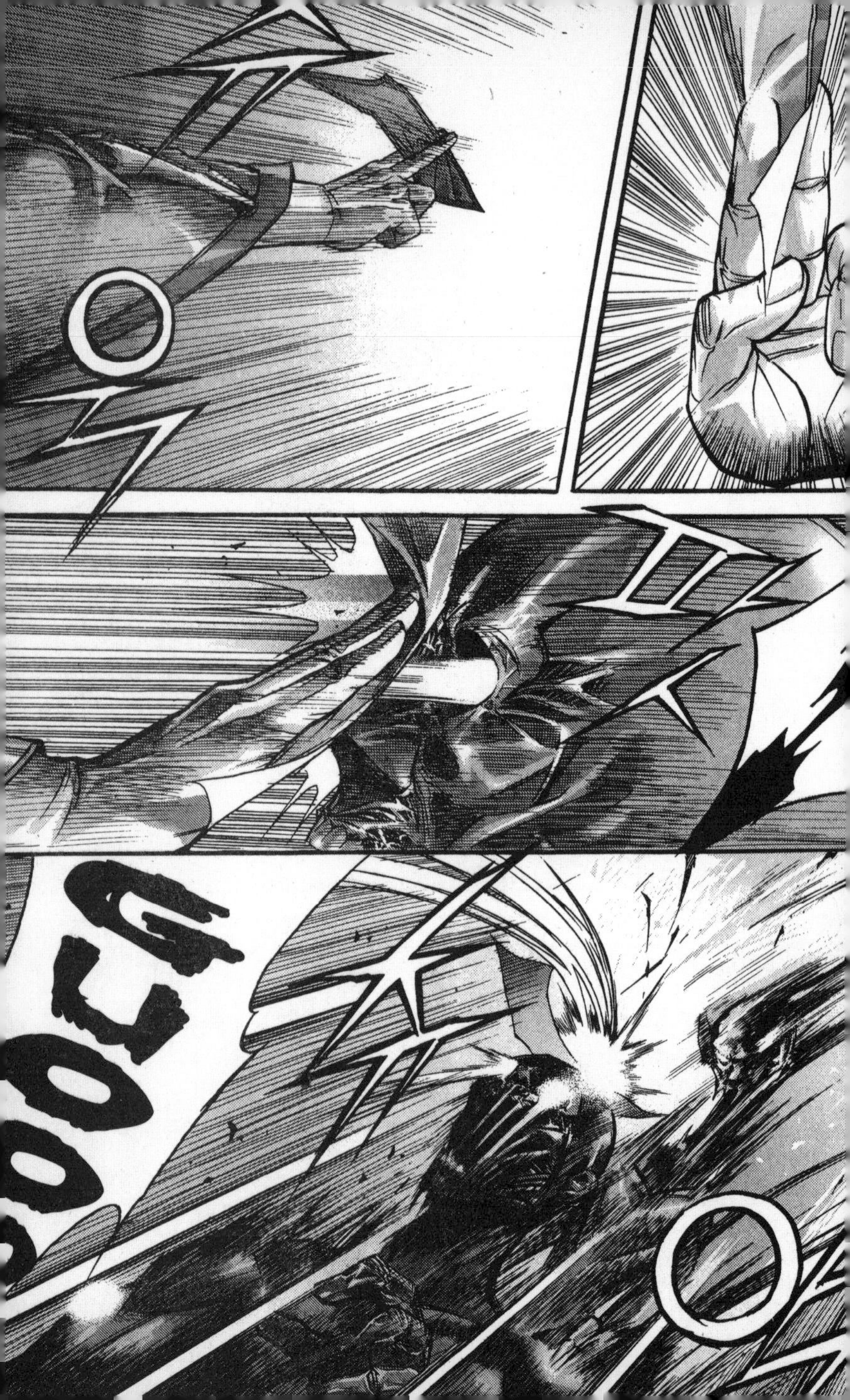

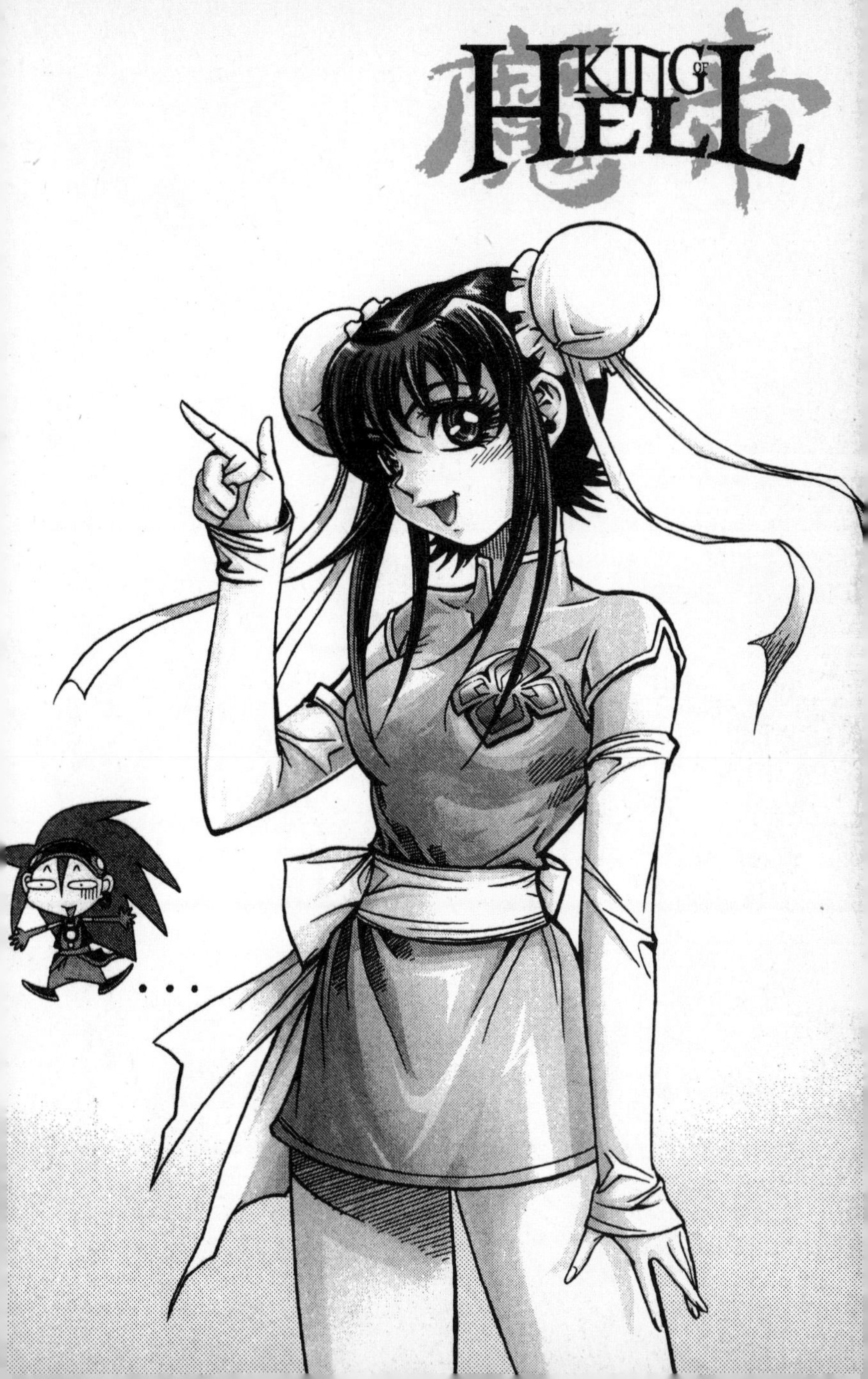
KING OF HELL
...

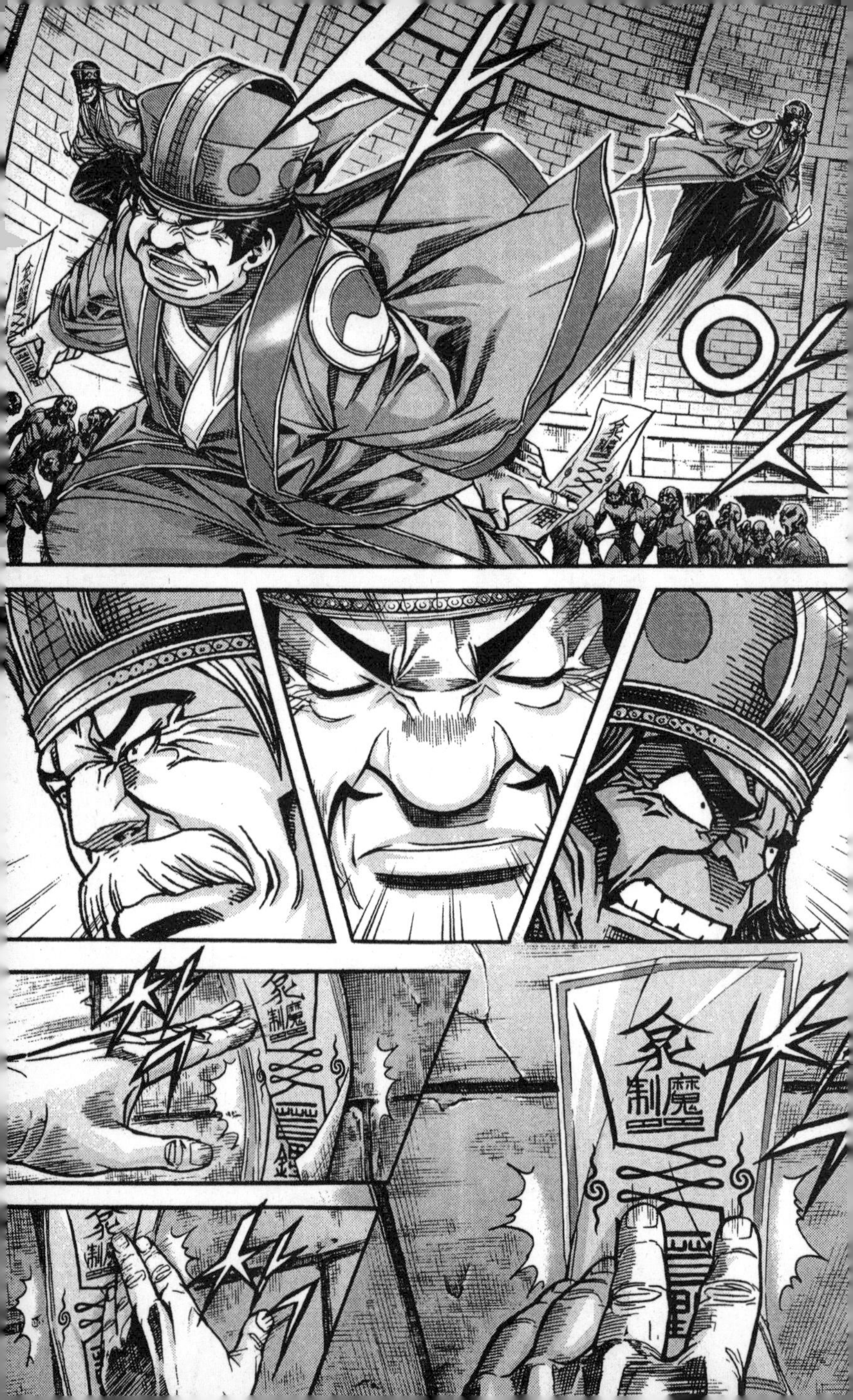
制魔

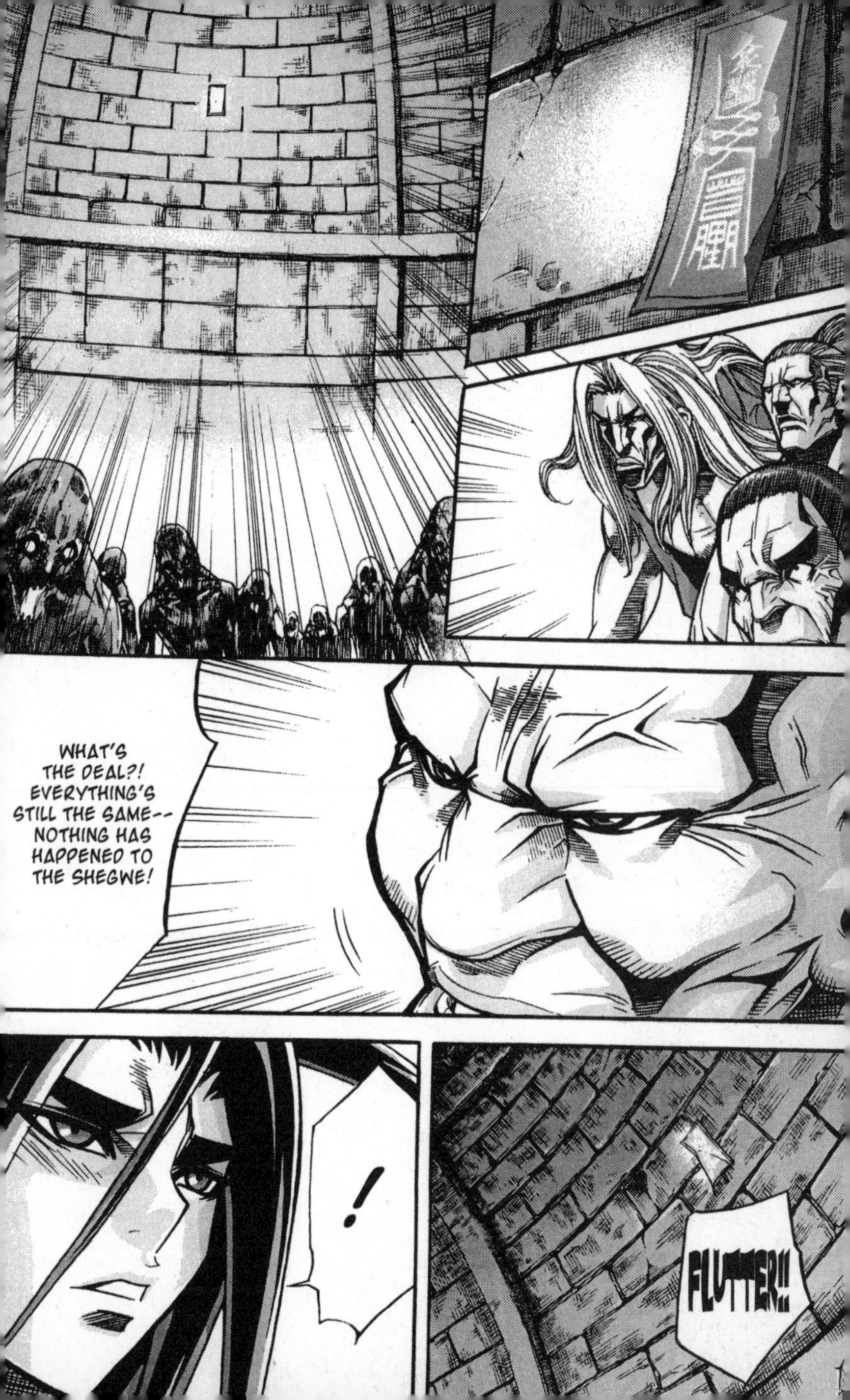
WHAT'S THE DEAL?! EVERYTHING'S STILL THE SAME-- NOTHING HAS HAPPENED TO THE SHEGWE!
!
FLUTTER!!

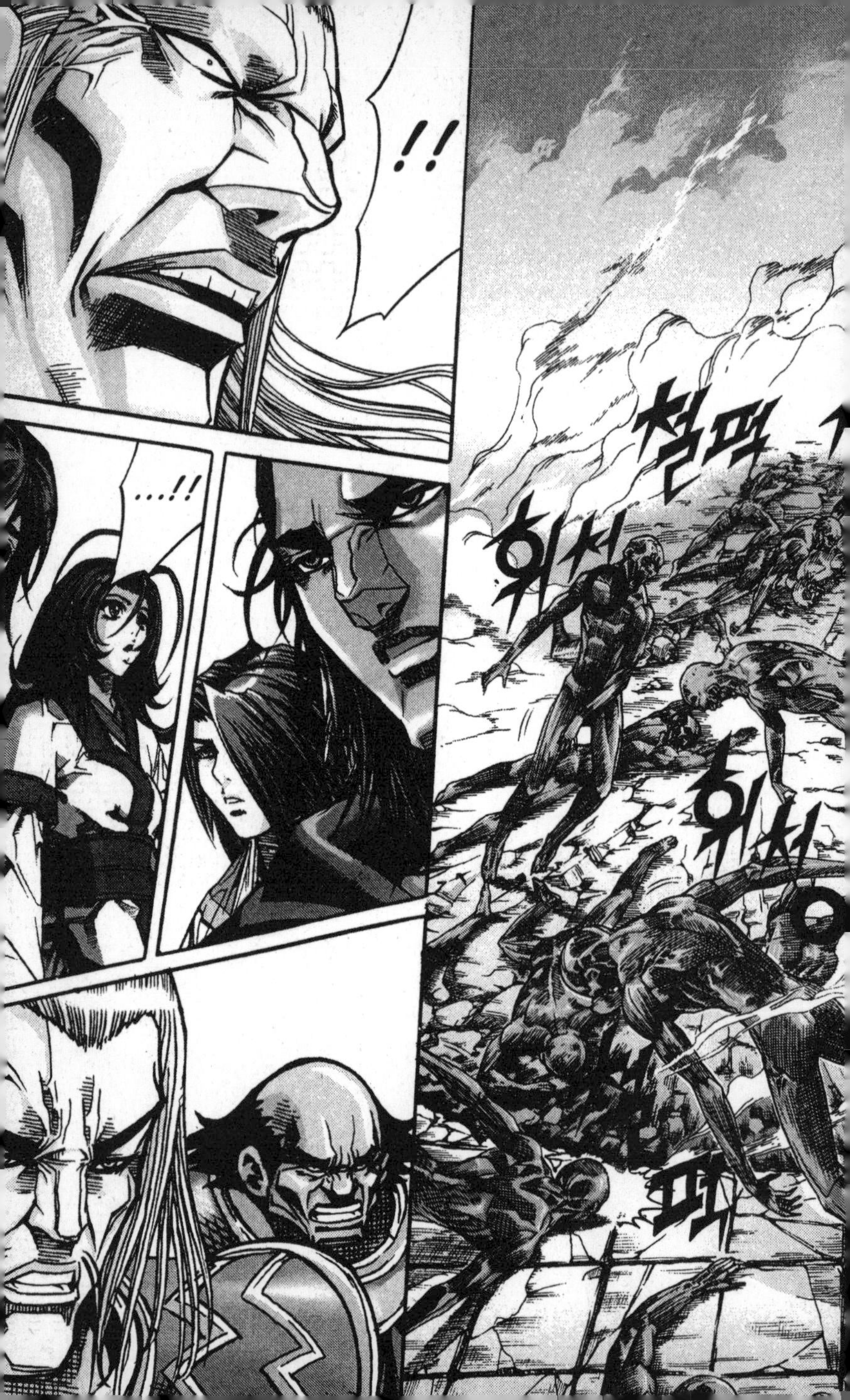
!!
...!!
철퍽

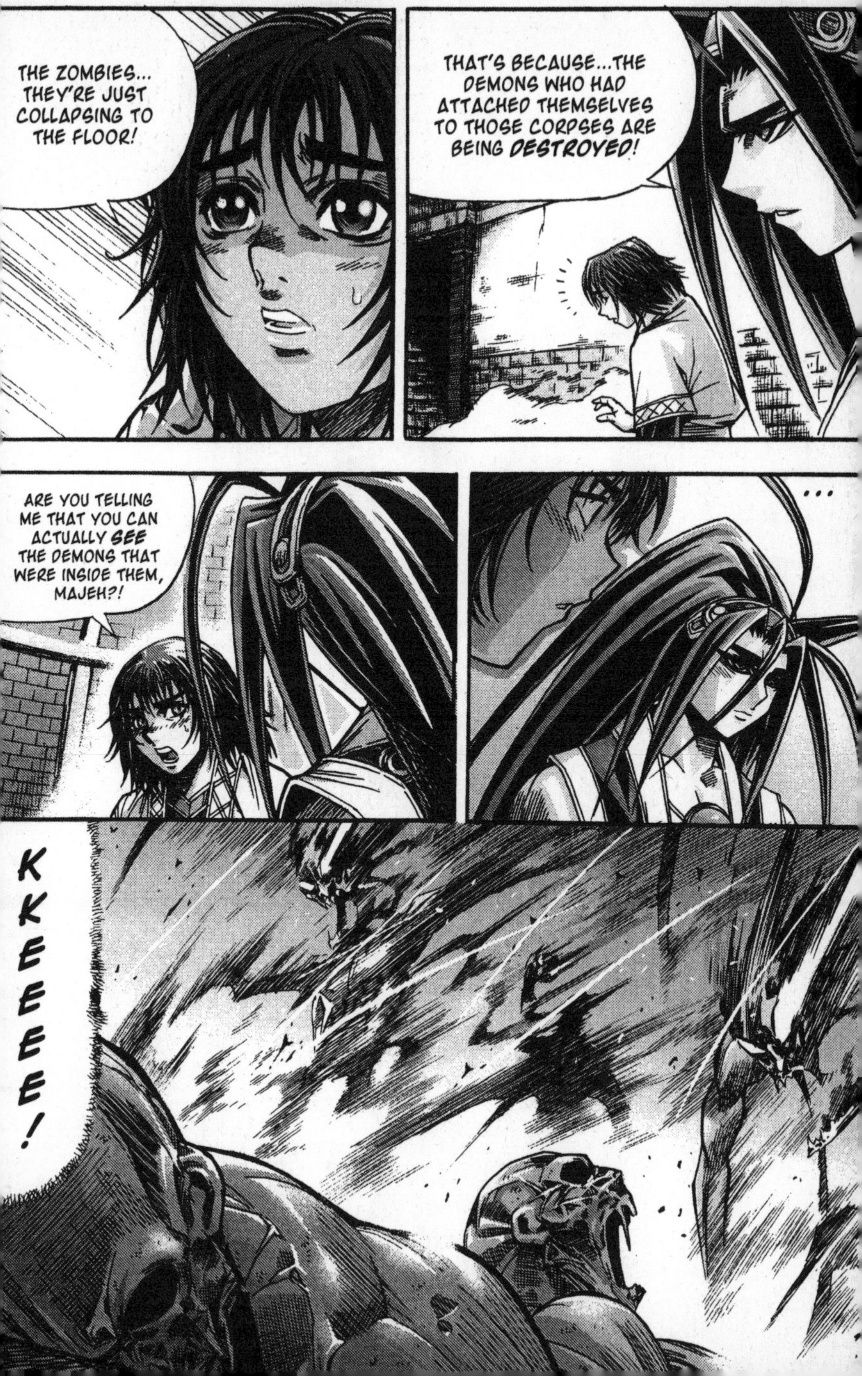
THE ZOMBIES... THEY'RE JUST COLLAPSING TO THE FLOOR!
THAT'S BECAUSE...THE DEMONS WHO HAD ATTACHED THEMSELVES TO THOSE CORPSES ARE BEING DESTROYED!
ARE YOU TELLING ME THAT YOU CAN ACTUALLY SEE THE DEMONS THAT WERE INSIDE THEM, MAJEH?!
...
KKEEEEE!

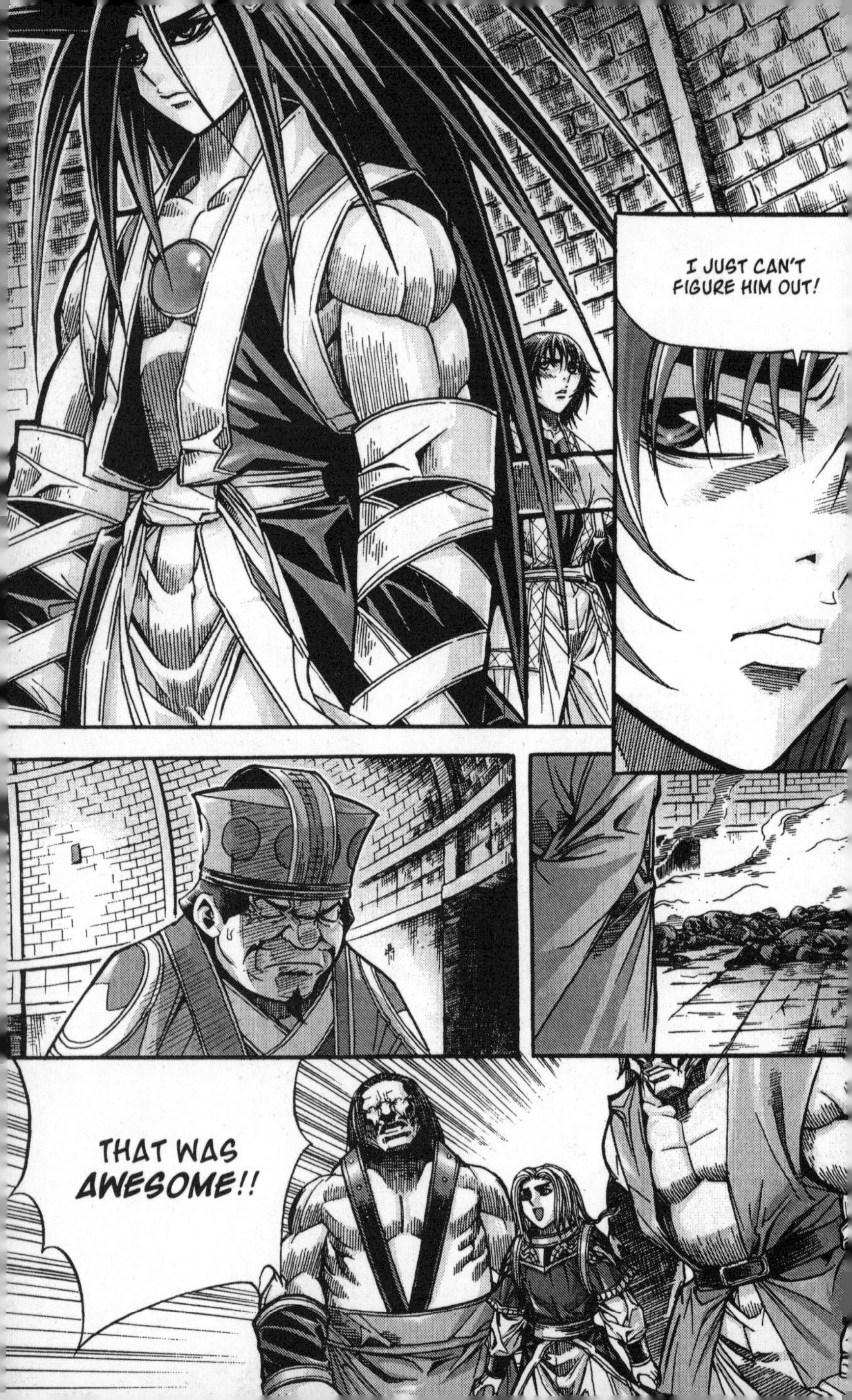
I JUST CAN'T FIGURE HIM OUT!
THAT WAS AWESOME!!

AMAZING! YOU DESTROYED THOSE VICIOUS CREATURES-- WITH ONLY A FEW PIECES OF PAPER!

IT WAS NOT AN EXCEPTIONAL FEAT...

THOSE TALISMANS ARE CALLED THE URSA MAJOR PARALYSIS TALISMANS--AND THEY CAN CONTROL DEMONS!

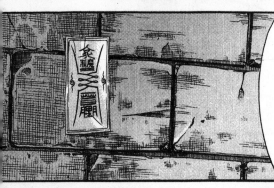

AND THOSE POOR CREATURES...

...ARE MERELY SHEGWE--CORPSES MANIPULATED BY DEMONS.

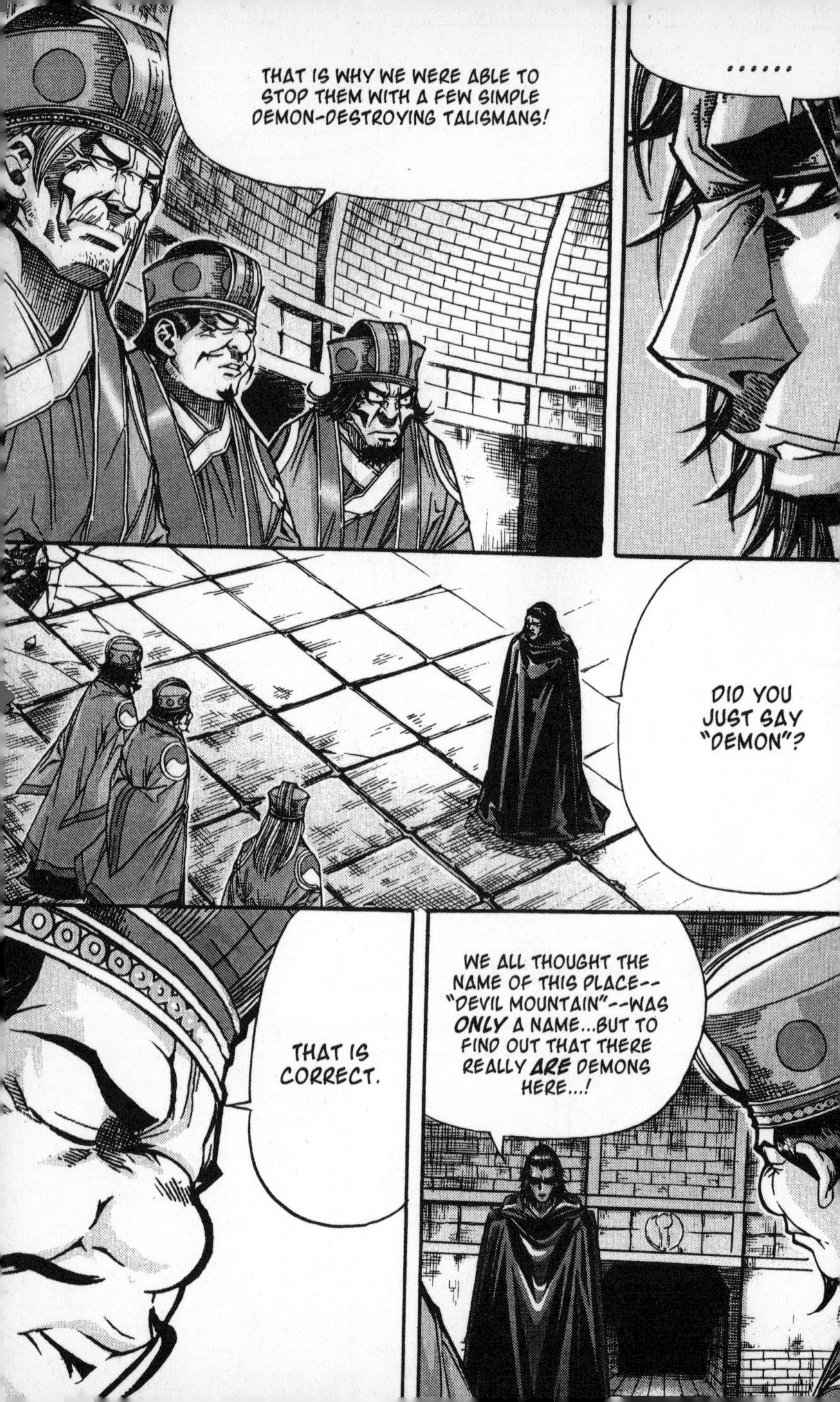
THAT IS WHY WE WERE ABLE TO STOP THEM WITH A FEW SIMPLE DEMON-DESTROYING TALISMANS!
......
DID YOU JUST SAY "DEMON"?
THAT IS CORRECT.
WE ALL THOUGHT THE NAME OF THIS PLACE--"DEVIL MOUNTAIN"--WAS *ONLY* A NAME...BUT TO FIND OUT THAT THERE REALLY *ARE* DEMONS HERE...!

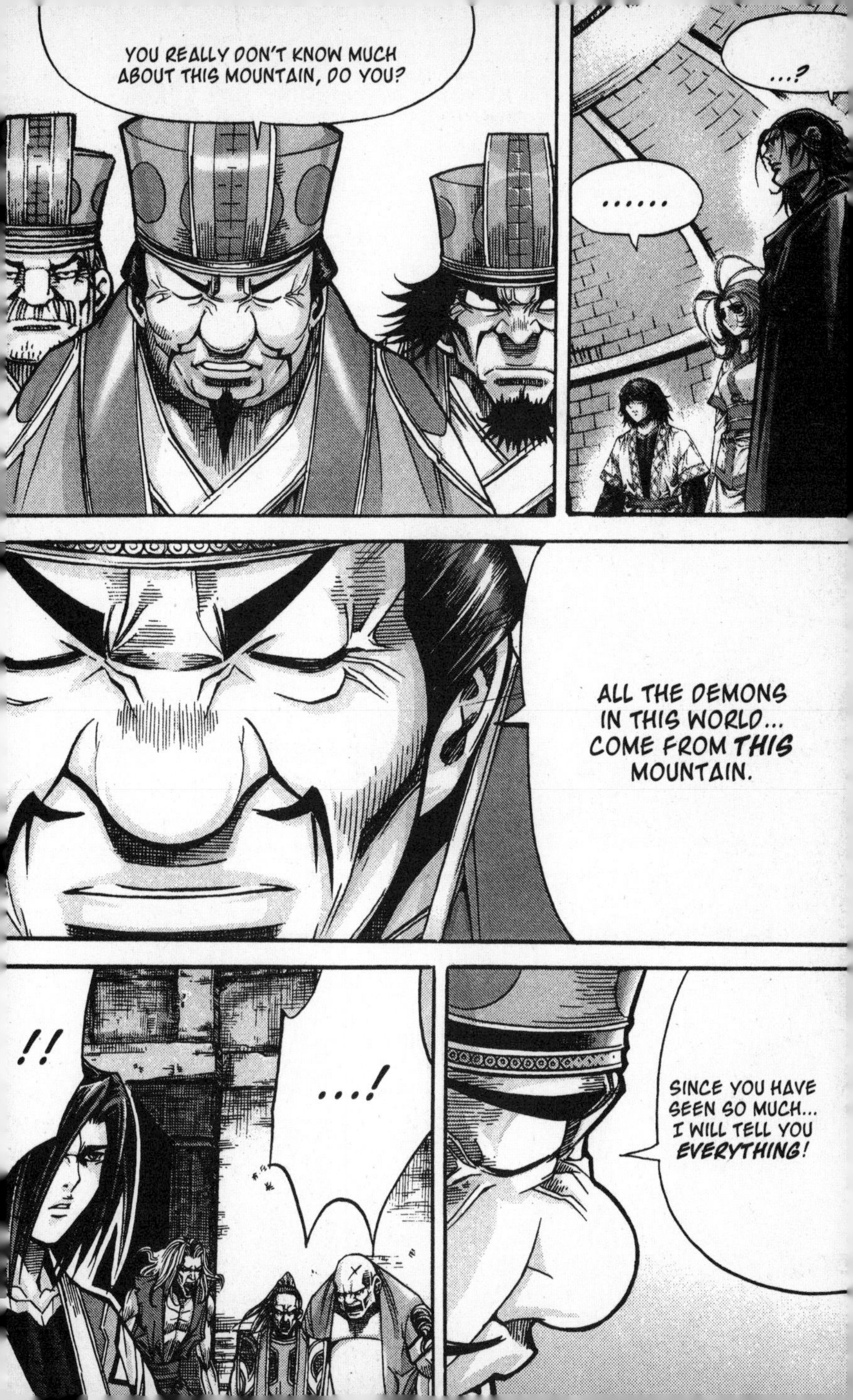
YOU REALLY DON'T KNOW MUCH ABOUT THIS MOUNTAIN, DO YOU?
...?
......
ALL THE DEMONS IN THIS WORLD... COME FROM THIS MOUNTAIN.
!!
...!
SINCE YOU HAVE SEEN SO MUCH... I WILL TELL YOU EVERYTHING!

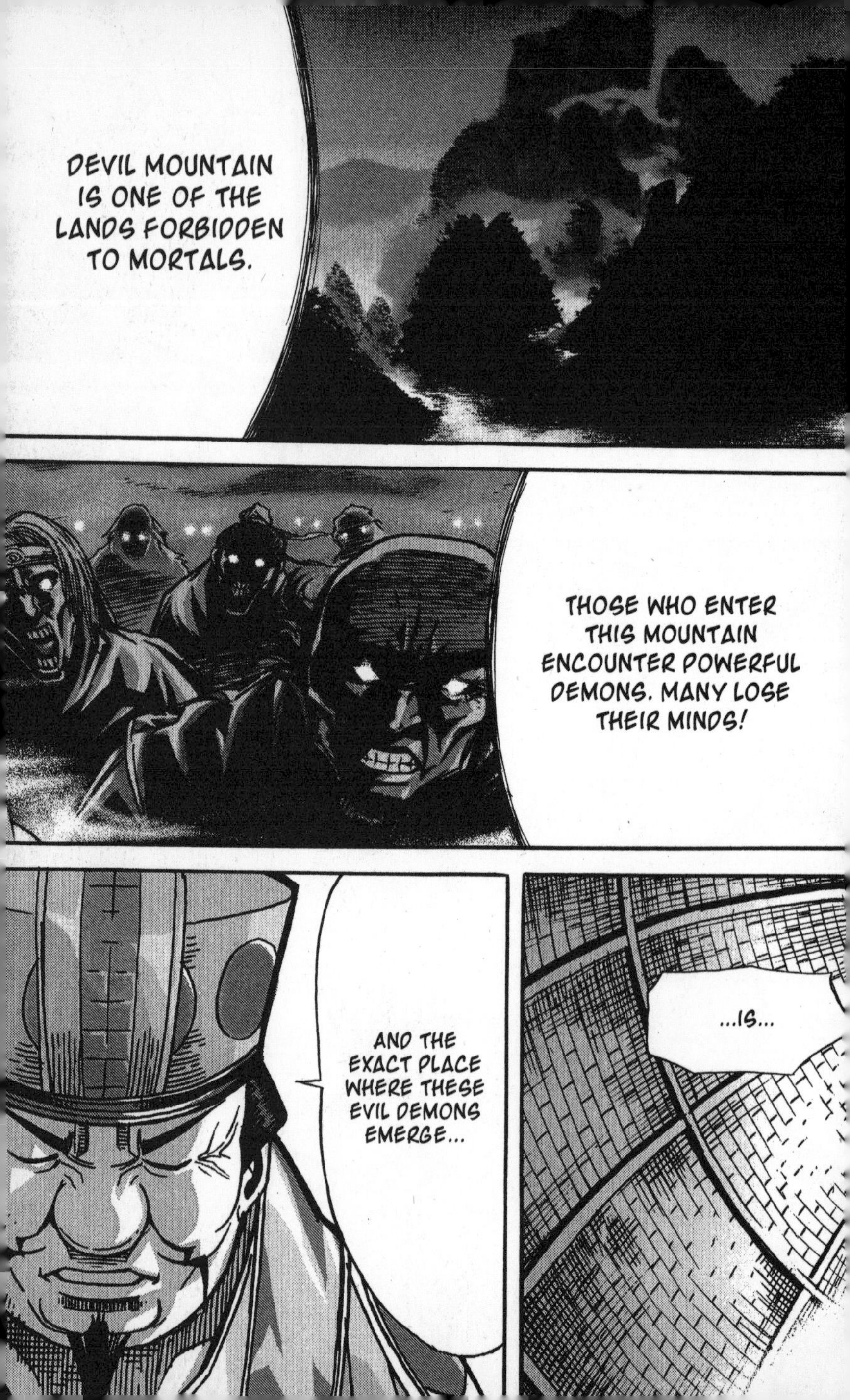
DEVIL MOUNTAIN IS ONE OF THE LANDS FORBIDDEN TO MORTALS.
THOSE WHO ENTER THIS MOUNTAIN ENCOUNTER POWERFUL DEMONS. MANY LOSE THEIR MINDS!
AND THE EXACT PLACE WHERE THESE EVIL DEMONS EMERGE...
...IS...

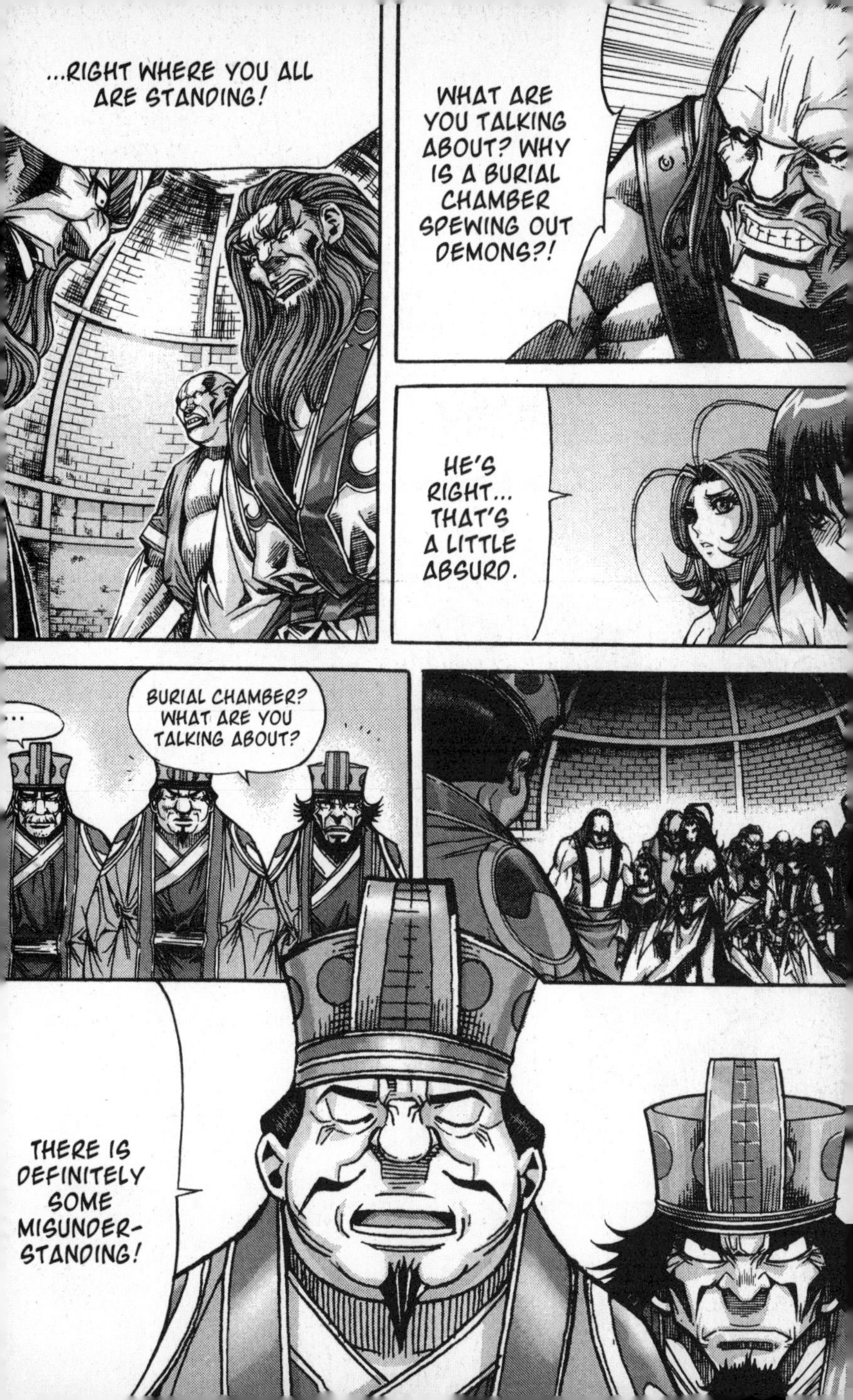
...RIGHT WHERE YOU ALL ARE STANDING!
WHAT ARE YOU TALKING ABOUT? WHY IS A BURIAL CHAMBER SPEWING OUT DEMONS?!
HE'S RIGHT... THAT'S A LITTLE ABSURD.
...
BURIAL CHAMBER? WHAT ARE YOU TALKING ABOUT?
THERE IS DEFINITELY SOME MISUNDER-STANDING!

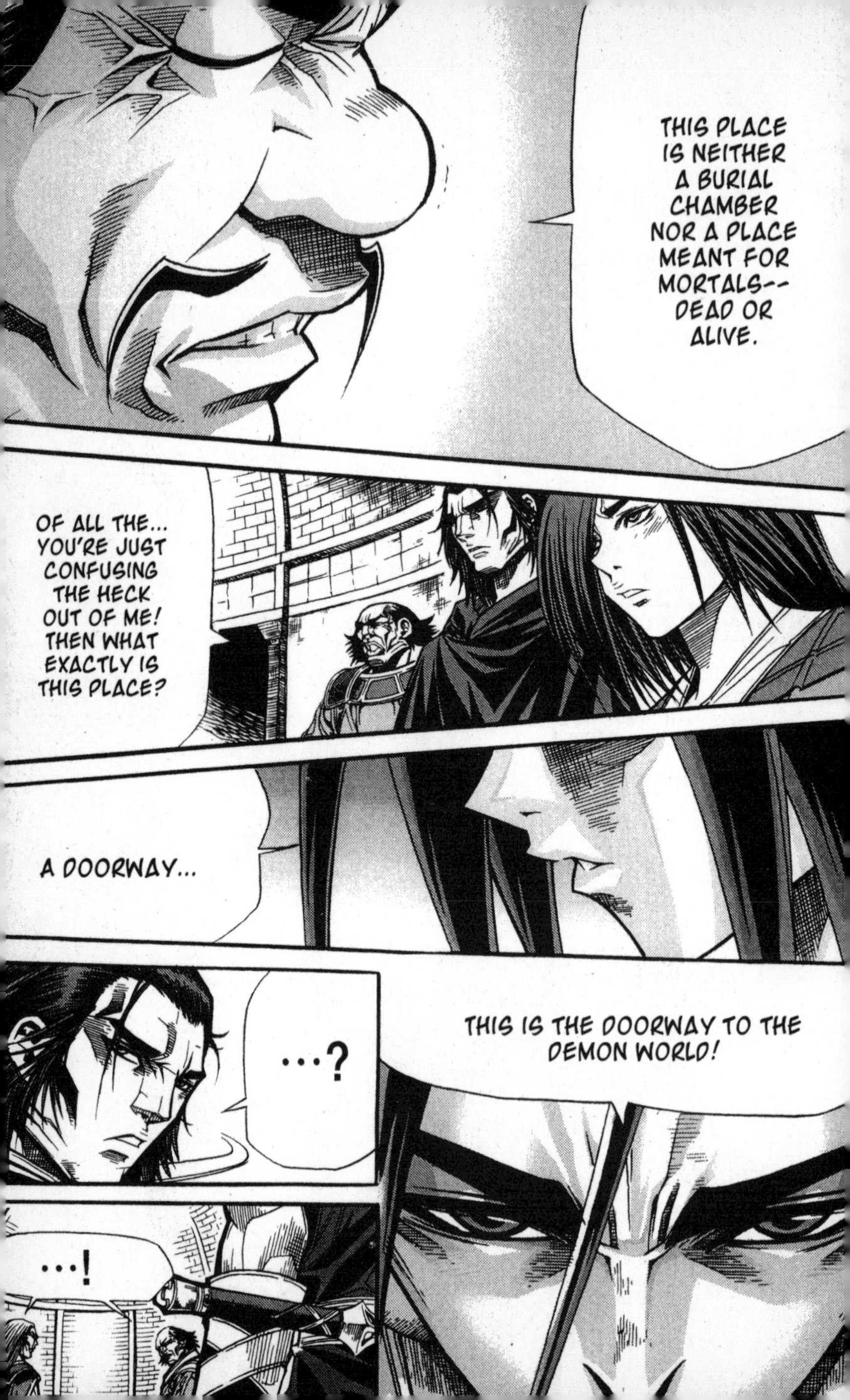
THIS PLACE IS NEITHER A BURIAL CHAMBER NOR A PLACE MEANT FOR MORTALS-- DEAD OR ALIVE.
OF ALL THE... YOU'RE JUST CONFUSING THE HECK OUT OF ME! THEN WHAT EXACTLY IS THIS PLACE?
A DOORWAY...
THIS IS THE DOORWAY TO THE DEMON WORLD!
...?
...!

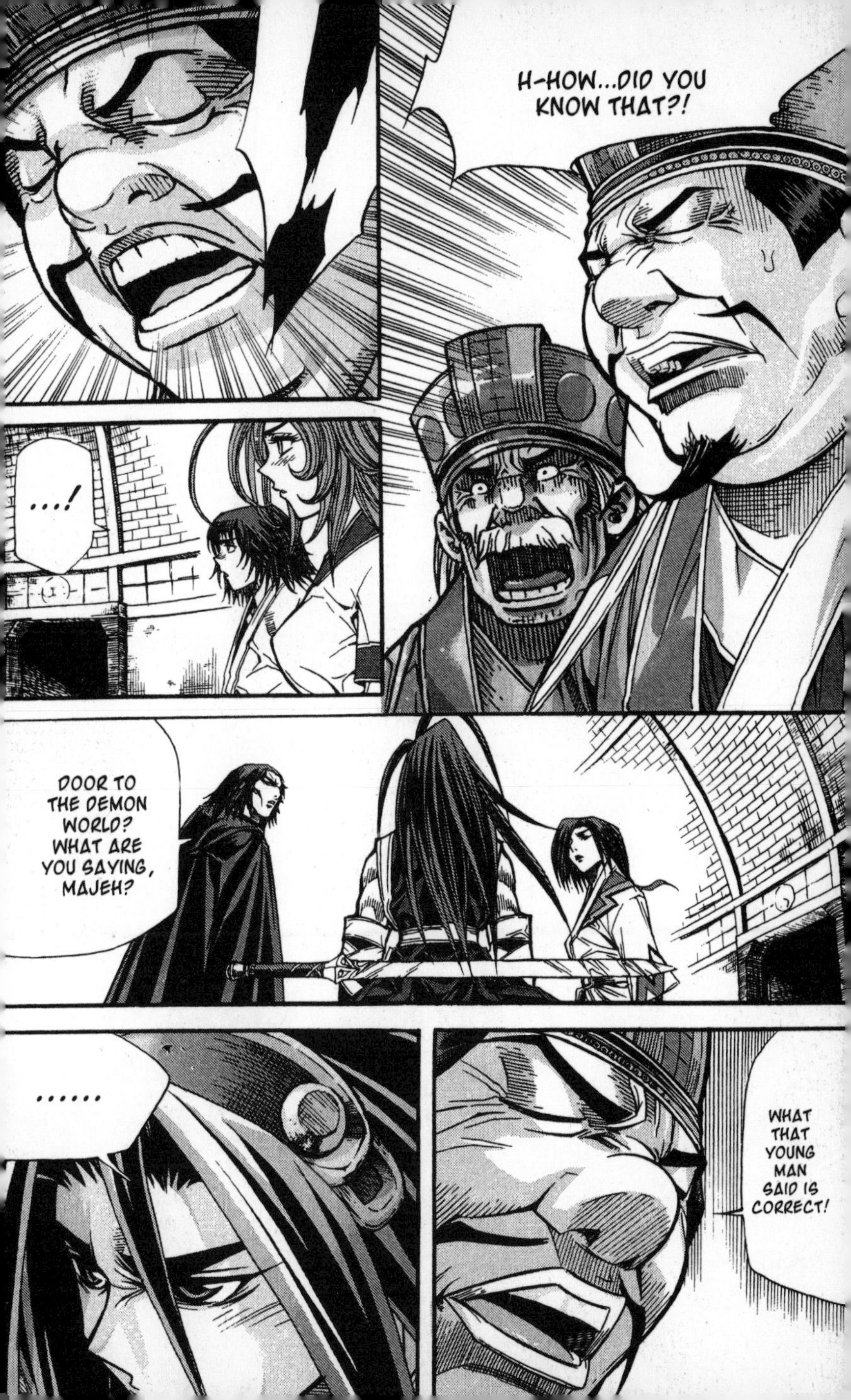

H-HOW...DID YOU KNOW THAT?!
...!
DOOR TO THE DEMON WORLD? WHAT ARE YOU SAYING, MAJEH?
......
WHAT THAT YOUNG MAN SAID IS CORRECT!

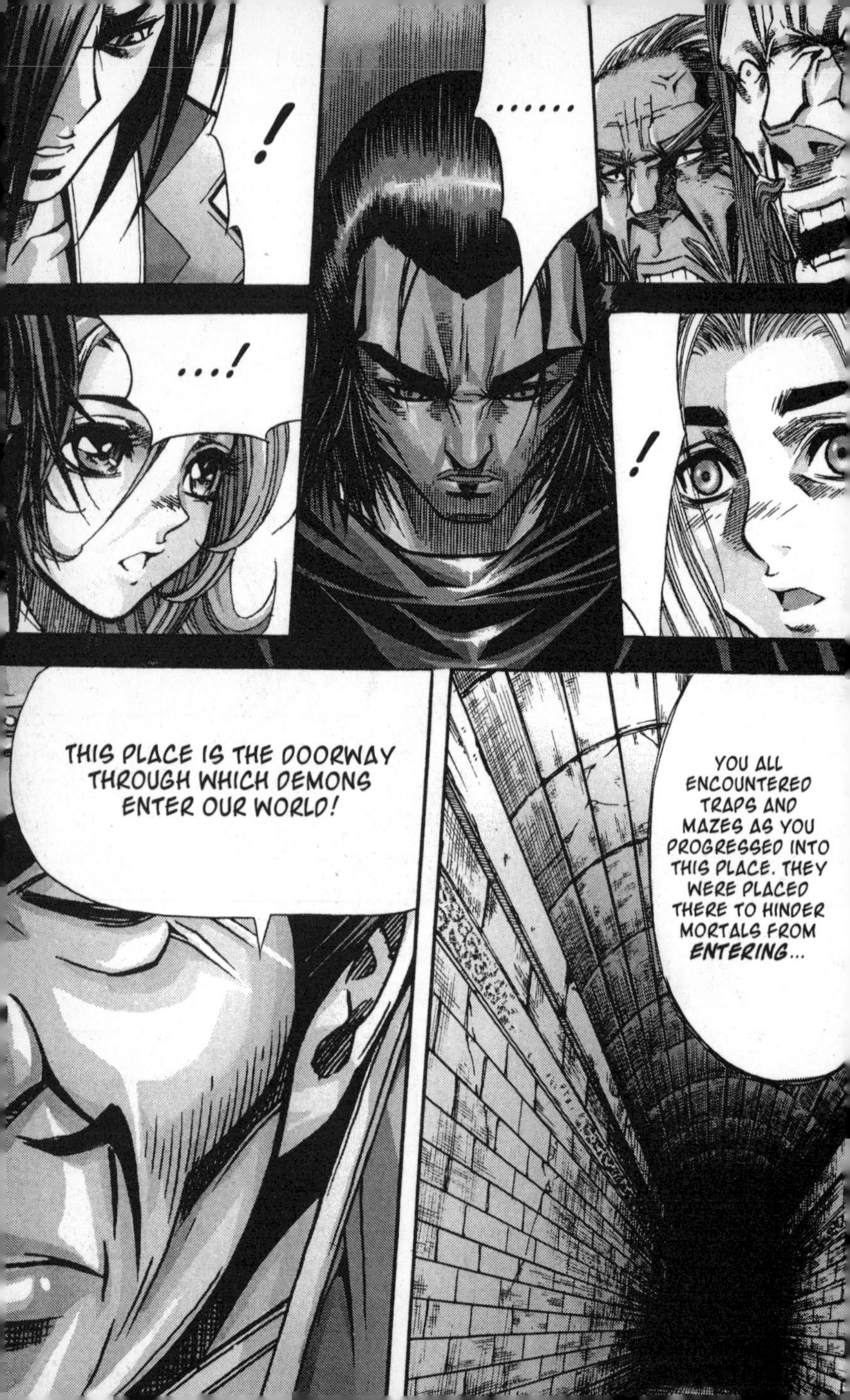
......
!
...!
!
THIS PLACE IS THE DOORWAY THROUGH WHICH DEMONS ENTER OUR WORLD!
YOU ALL ENCOUNTERED TRAPS AND MAZES AS YOU PROGRESSED INTO THIS PLACE. THEY WERE PLACED THERE TO HINDER MORTALS FROM ENTERING...

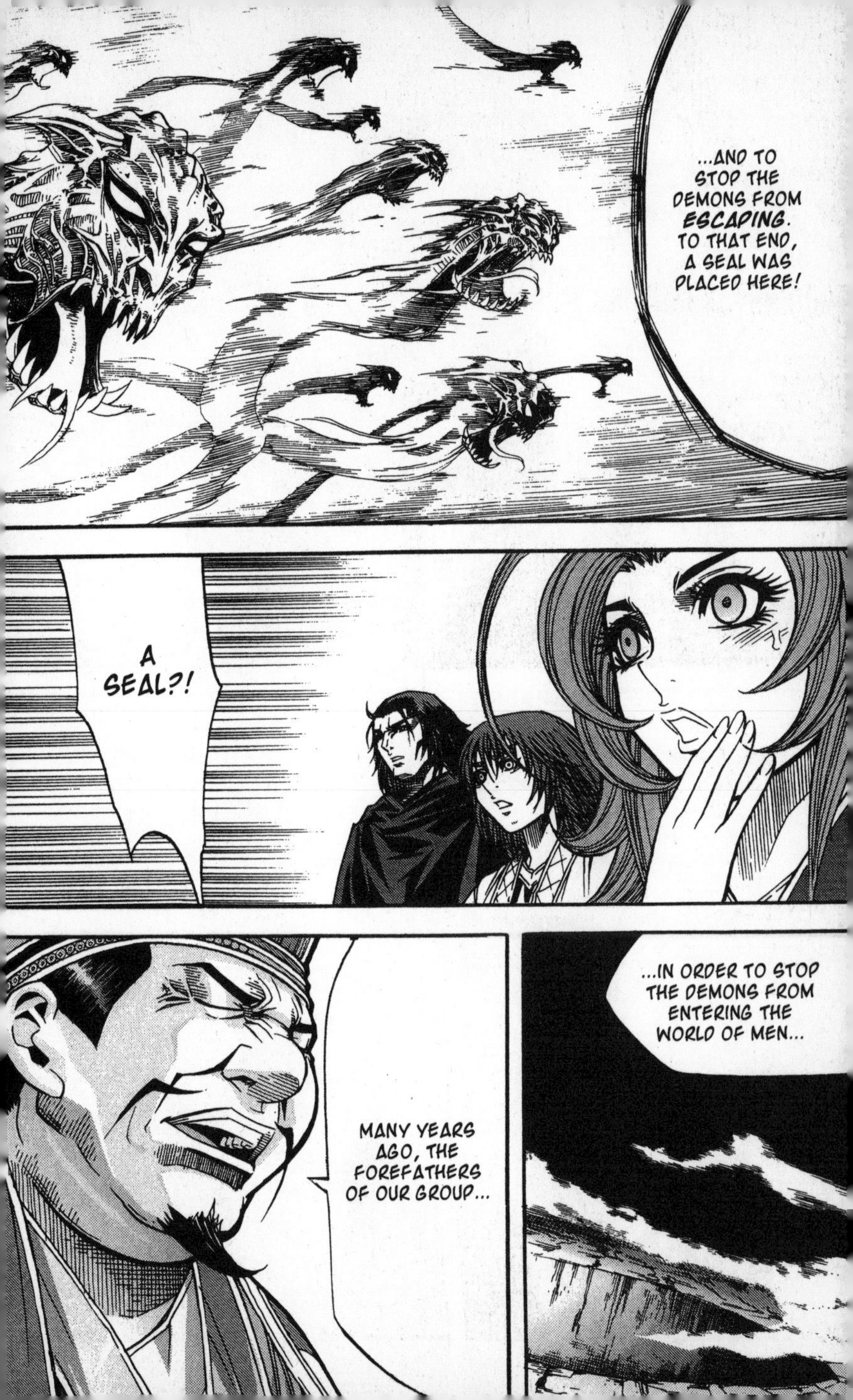
...AND TO STOP THE DEMONS FROM ESCAPING. TO THAT END, A SEAL WAS PLACED HERE!
A SEAL?!
...IN ORDER TO STOP THE DEMONS FROM ENTERING THE WORLD OF MEN...
MANY YEARS AGO, THE FOREFATHERS OF OUR GROUP...

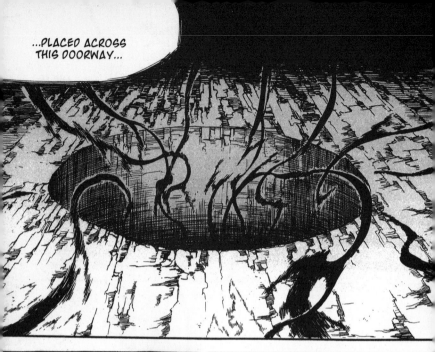

...PLACED ACROSS THIS DOORWAY...

...A MYSTIC SEAL!

TELL US, PRIESTS-- ARE YOU ALSO THE ONES WHO CREATED THOSE UNDEAD MONSTERS WHO ATTACKED US?!

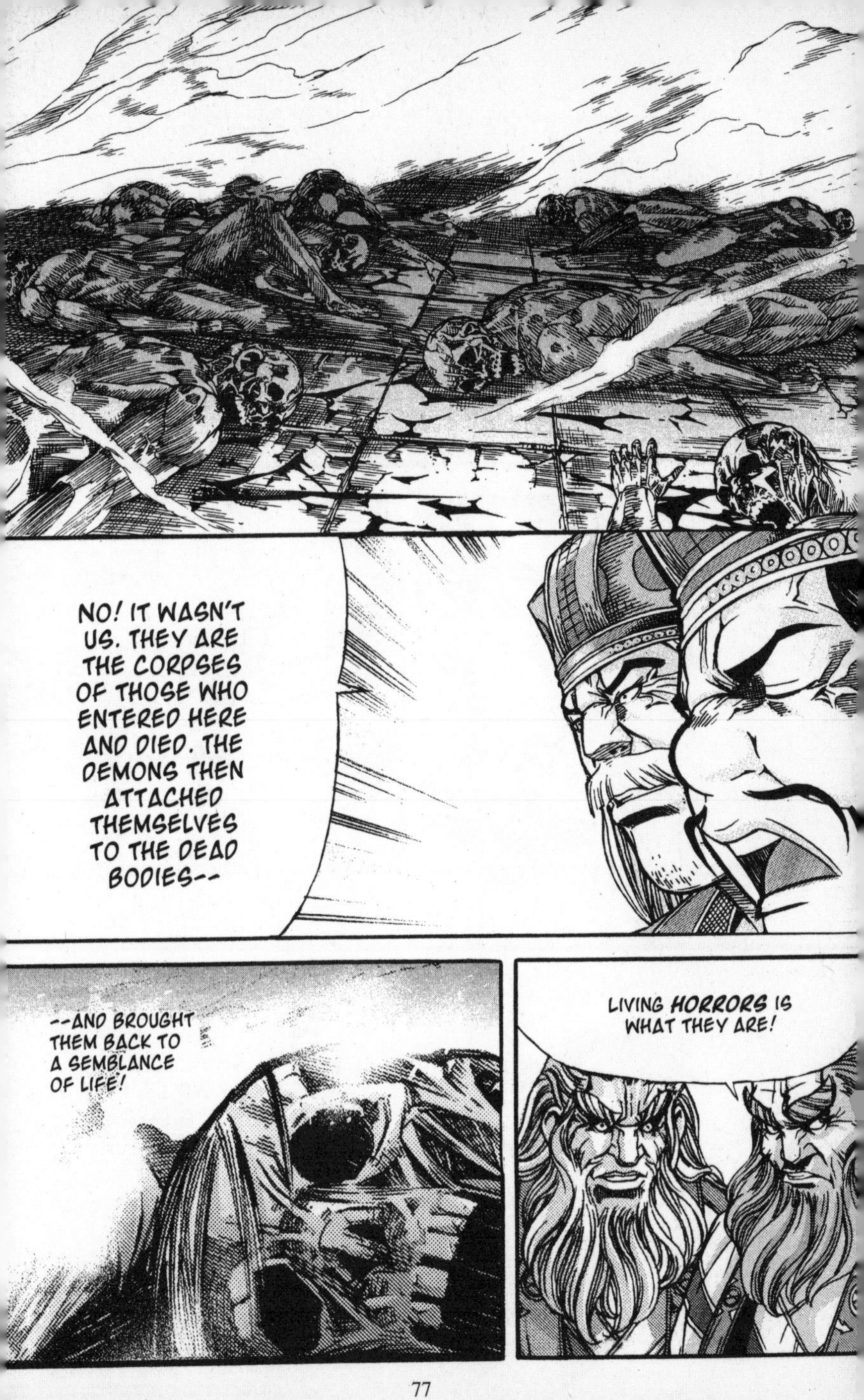
NO! IT WASN'T US. THEY ARE THE CORPSES OF THOSE WHO ENTERED HERE AND DIED. THE DEMONS THEN ATTACHED THEMSELVES TO THE DEAD BODIES--
--AND BROUGHT THEM BACK TO A SEMBLANCE OF LIFE!
LIVING HORRORS IS WHAT THEY ARE!

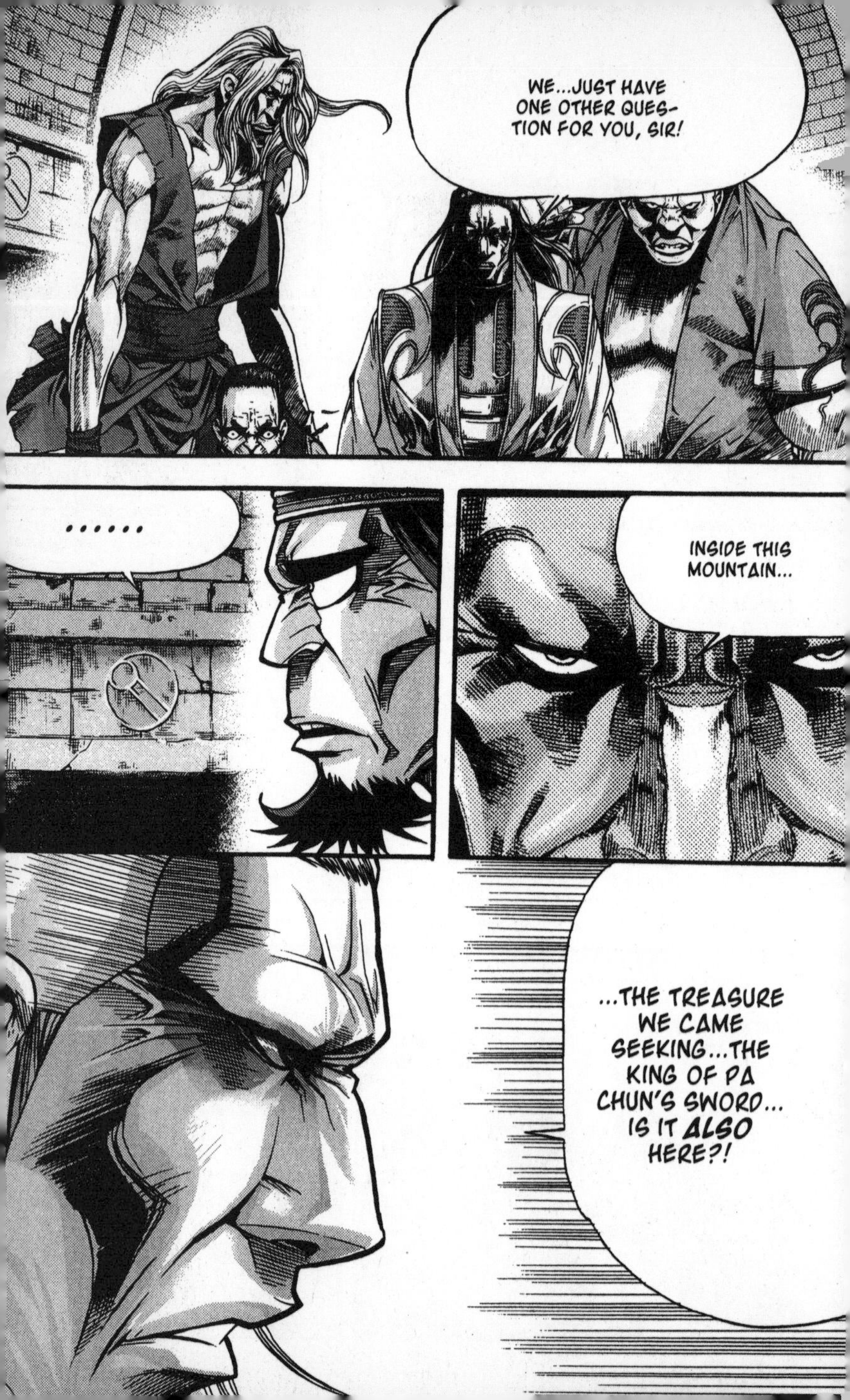

WE...JUST HAVE ONE OTHER QUES- TION FOR YOU, SIR!
......
INSIDE THIS MOUNTAIN...
...THE TREASURE WE CAME SEEKING...THE KING OF PA CHUN'S SWORD... IS IT ALSO HERE?!

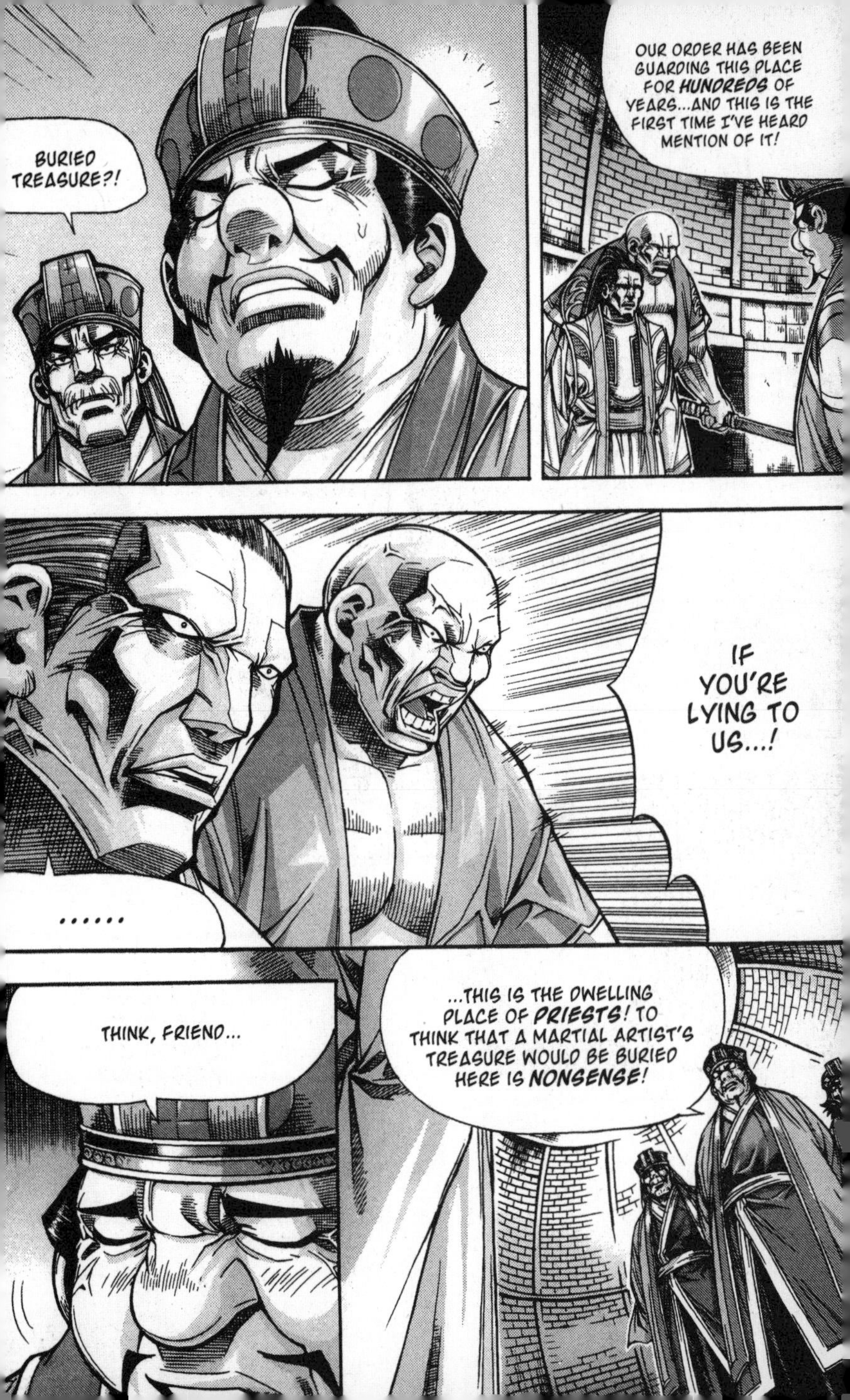
BURIED TREASURE?!
OUR ORDER HAS BEEN GUARDING THIS PLACE FOR HUNDREDS OF YEARS...AND THIS IS THE FIRST TIME I'VE HEARD MENTION OF IT!
IF YOU'RE LYING TO US...!
......
THINK, FRIEND...
...THIS IS THE DWELLING PLACE OF PRIESTS! TO THINK THAT A MARTIAL ARTIST'S TREASURE WOULD BE BURIED HERE IS NONSENSE!

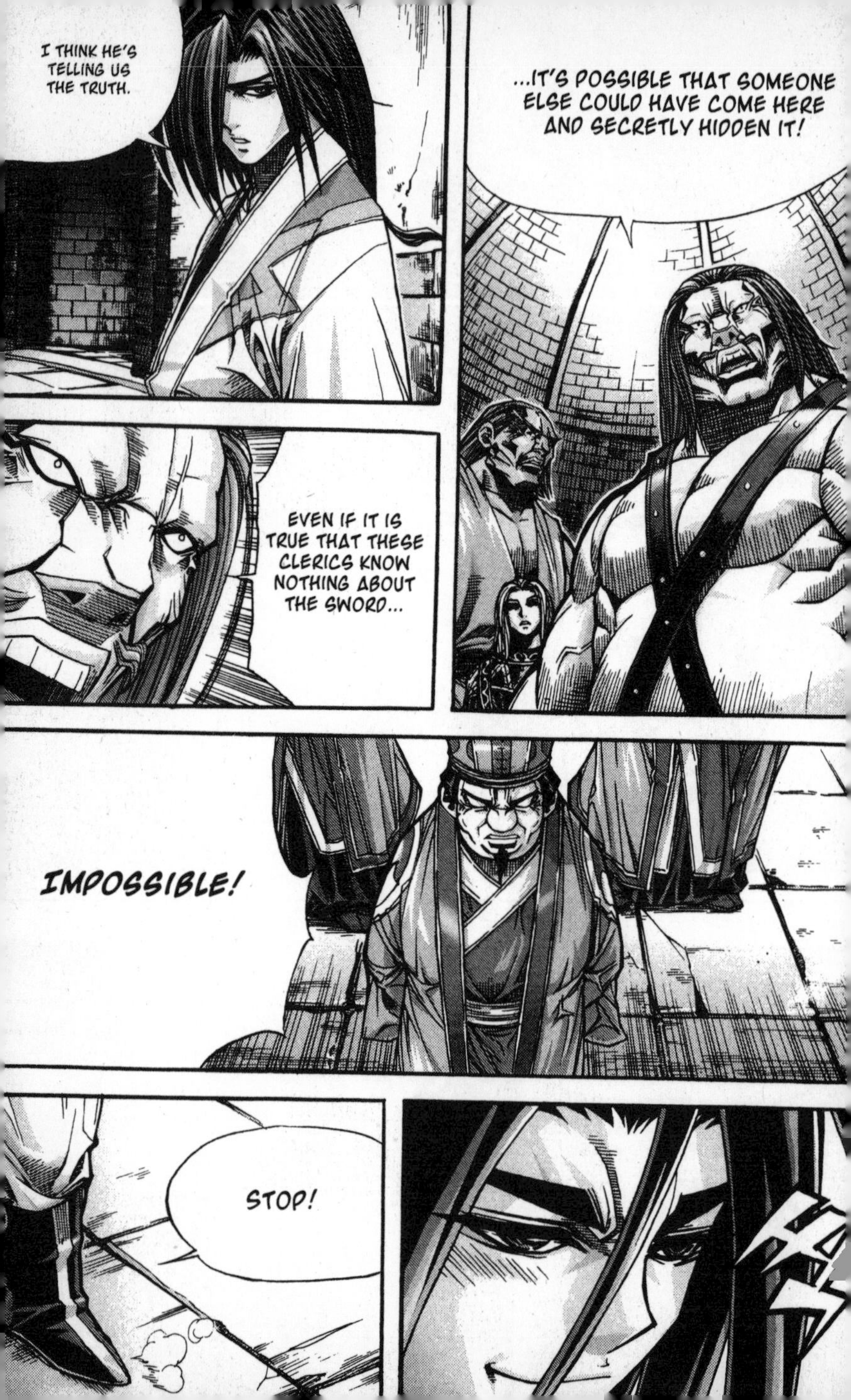
I THINK HE'S TELLING US THE TRUTH.
...IT'S POSSIBLE THAT SOMEONE ELSE COULD HAVE COME HERE AND SECRETLY HIDDEN IT!
EVEN IF IT IS TRUE THAT THESE CLERICS KNOW NOTHING ABOUT THE SWORD...
IMPOSSIBLE!
STOP!

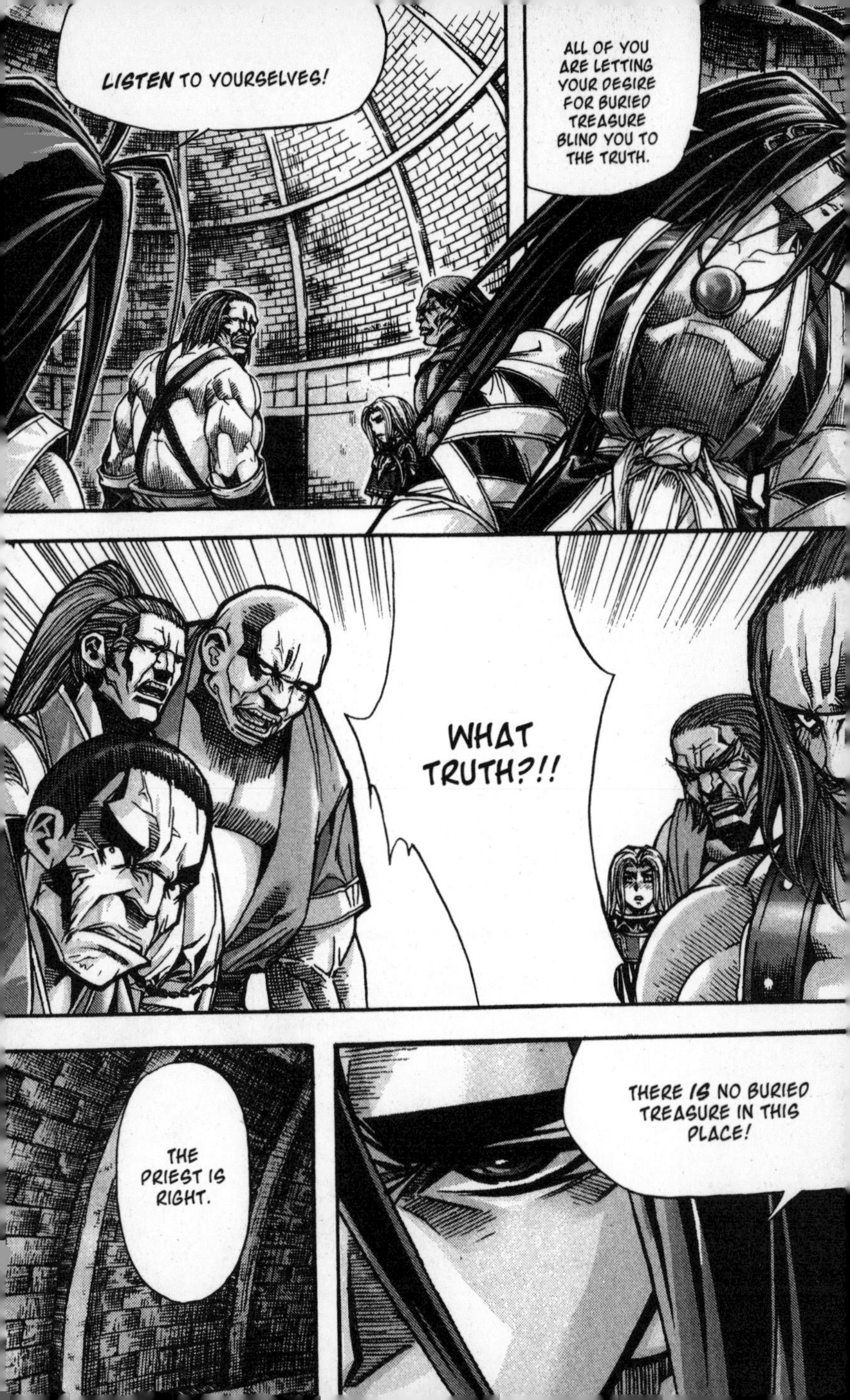
LISTEN TO YOURSELVES!
ALL OF YOU ARE LETTING YOUR DESIRE FOR BURIED TREASURE BLIND YOU TO THE TRUTH.
WHAT TRUTH?!!
THERE IS NO BURIED TREASURE IN THIS PLACE!
THE PRIEST IS RIGHT.

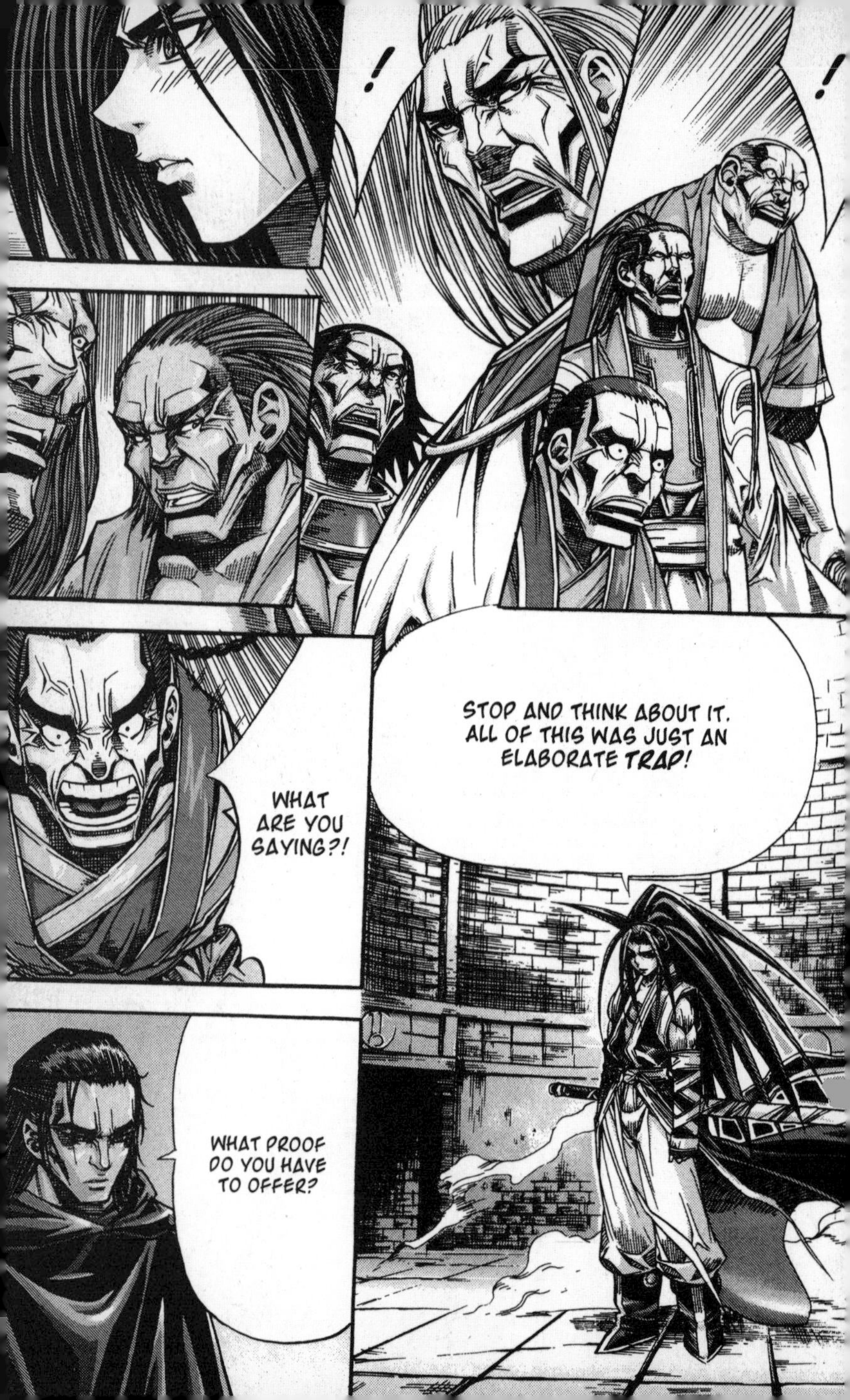
!
!
STOP AND THINK ABOUT IT. ALL OF THIS WAS JUST AN ELABORATE TRAP!
WHAT ARE YOU SAYING?!
WHAT PROOF DO YOU HAVE TO OFFER?

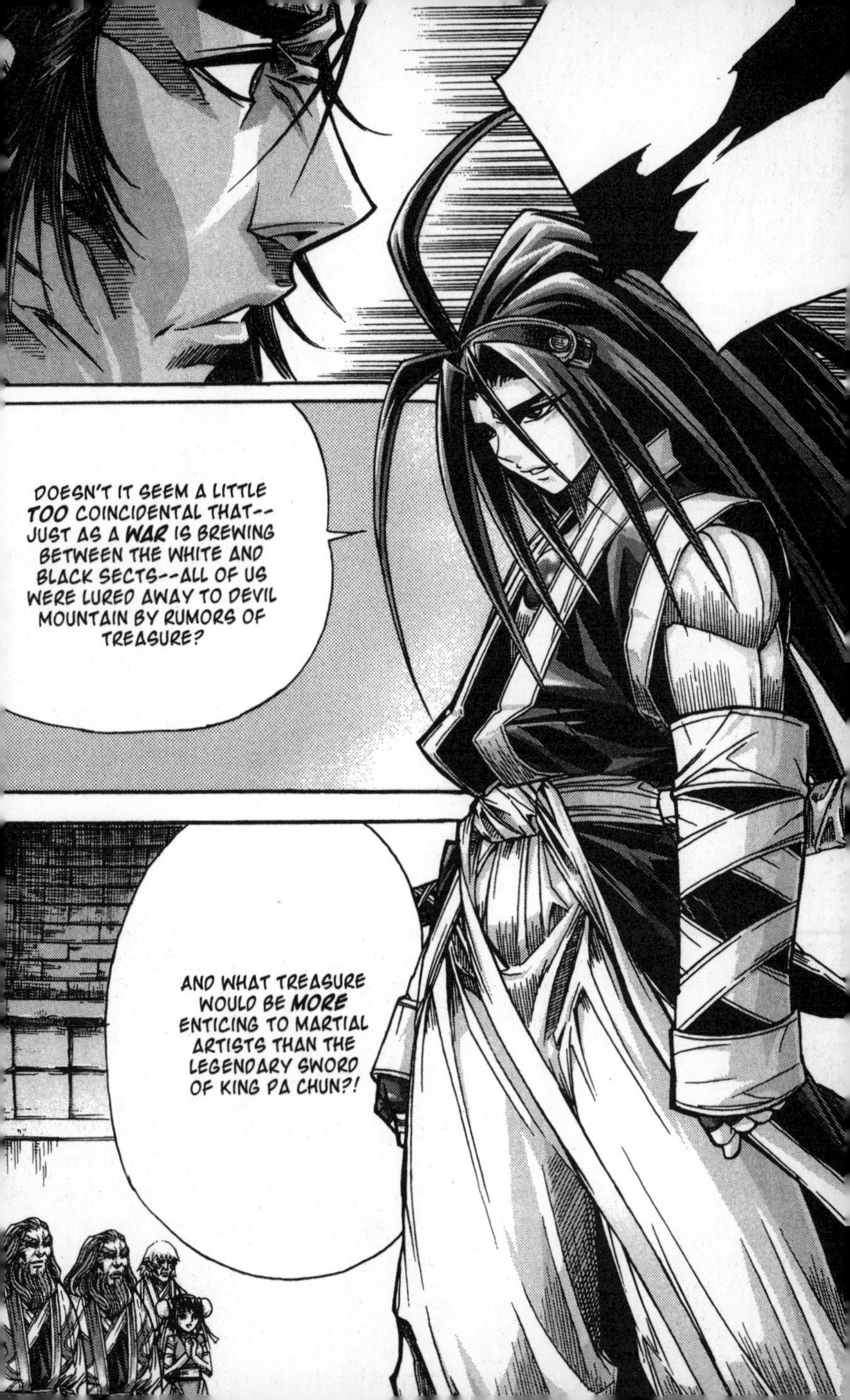
DOESN'T IT SEEM A LITTLE TOO COINCIDENTAL THAT--JUST AS A WAR IS BREWING BETWEEN THE WHITE AND BLACK SECTS--ALL OF US WERE LURED AWAY TO DEVIL MOUNTAIN BY RUMORS OF TREASURE?
AND WHAT TREASURE WOULD BE MORE ENTICING TO MARTIAL ARTISTS THAN THE LEGENDARY SWORD OF KING PA CHUN?!

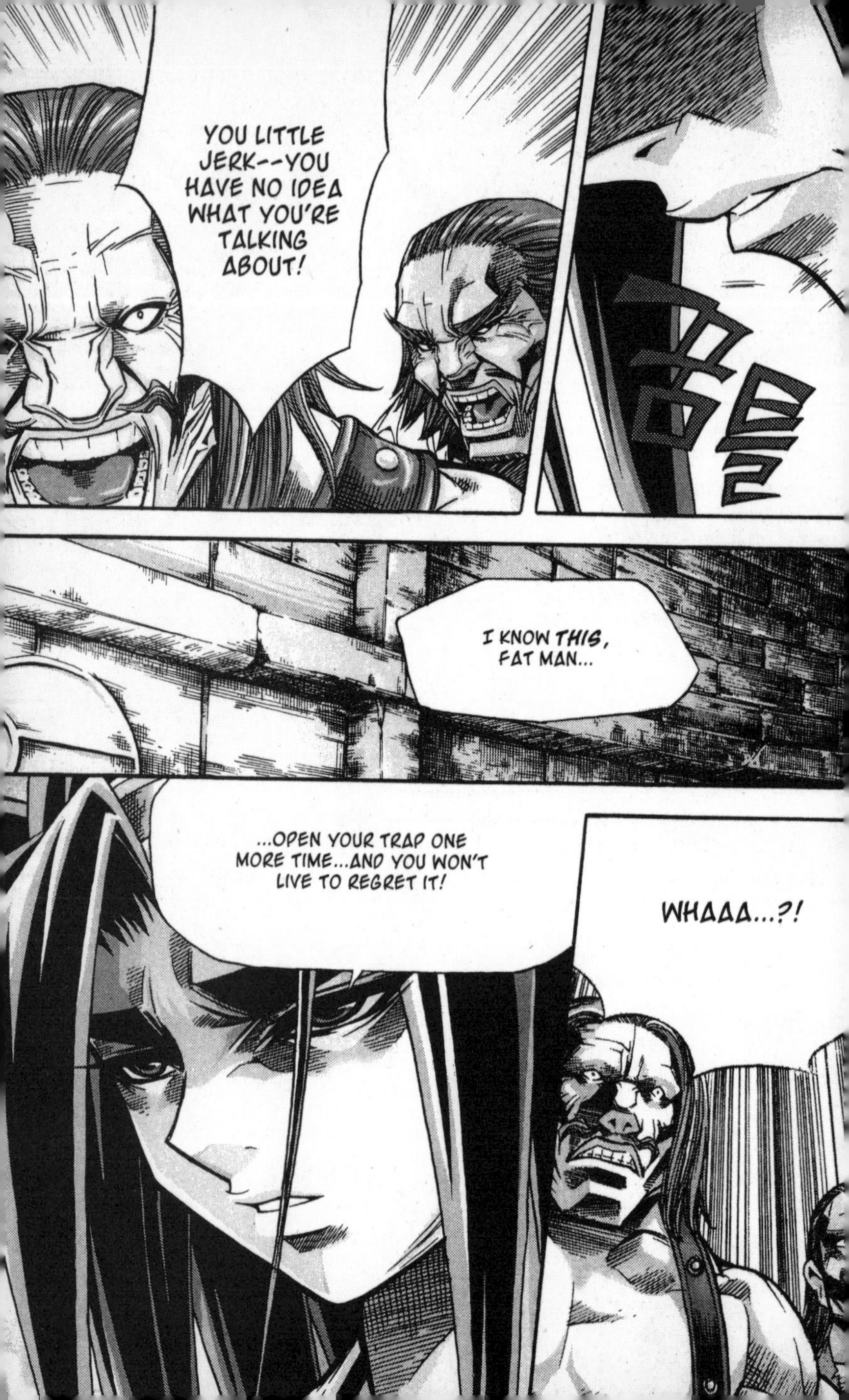
YOU LITTLE JERK--YOU HAVE NO IDEA WHAT YOU'RE TALKING ABOUT!
I KNOW THIS, FAT MAN...
...OPEN YOUR TRAP ONE MORE TIME...AND YOU WON'T LIVE TO REGRET IT!
WHAAA...?!

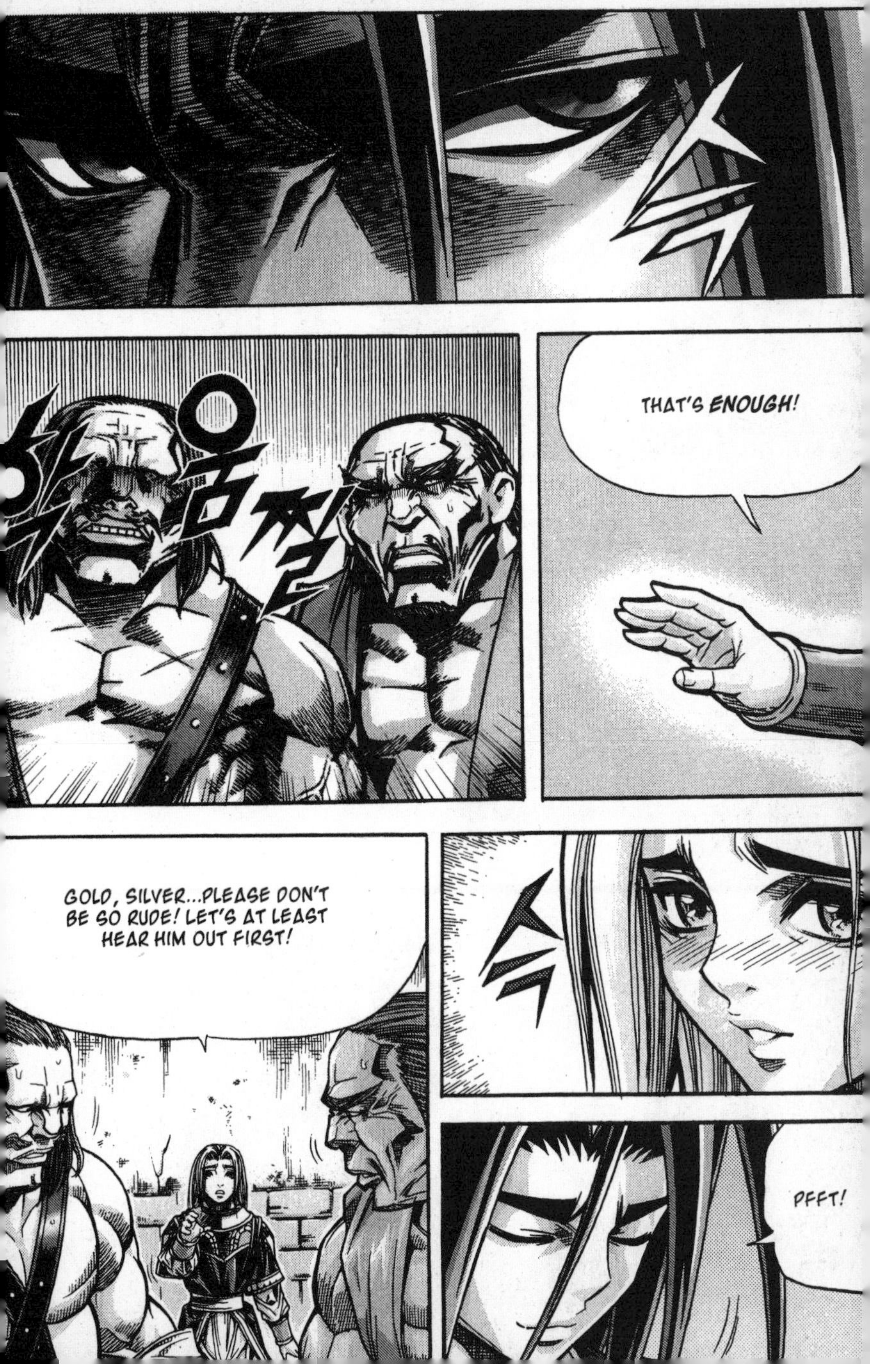
THAT'S ENOUGH!
GOLD, SILVER...PLEASE DON'T BE SO RUDE! LET'S AT LEAST HEAR HIM OUT FIRST!
PFFT!

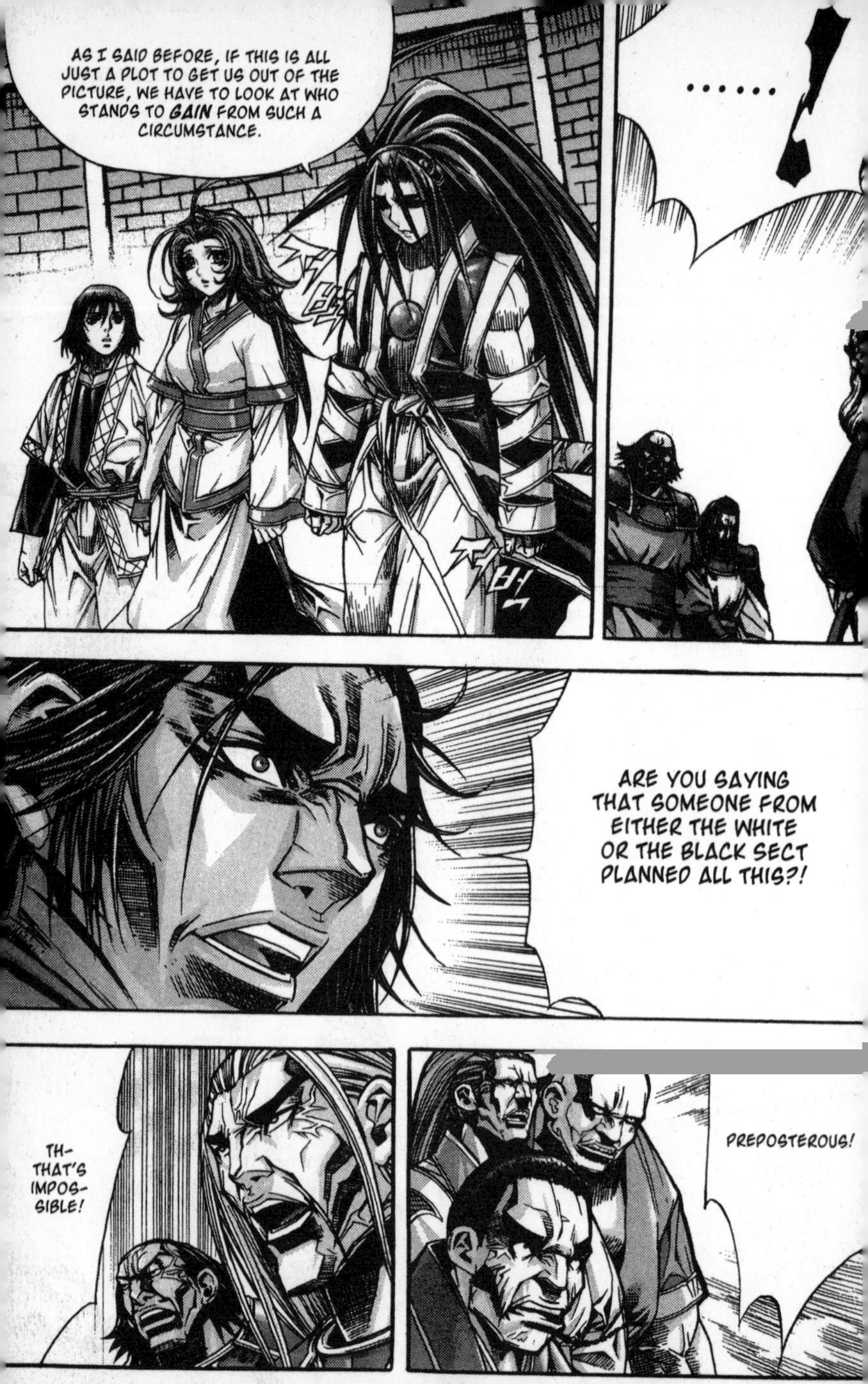
AS I SAID BEFORE, IF THIS IS ALL JUST A PLOT TO GET US OUT OF THE PICTURE, WE HAVE TO LOOK AT WHO STANDS TO GAIN FROM SUCH A CIRCUMSTANCE.
......!
ARE YOU SAYING THAT SOMEONE FROM EITHER THE WHITE OR THE BLACK SECT PLANNED ALL THIS?!
TH-THAT'S IMPOSSIBLE!
PREPOSTEROUS!

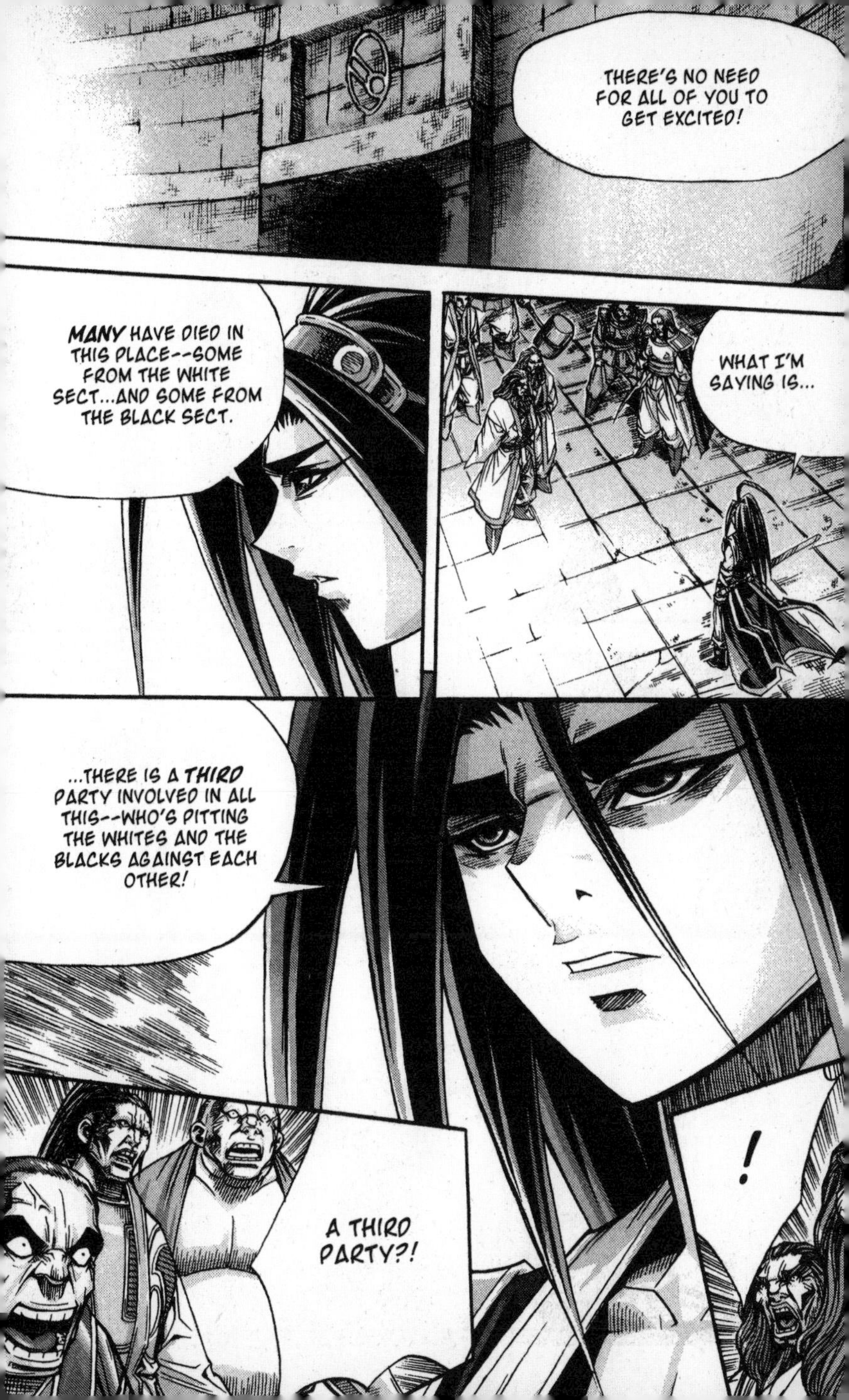
THERE'S NO NEED FOR ALL OF YOU TO GET EXCITED!
MANY HAVE DIED IN THIS PLACE--SOME FROM THE WHITE SECT...AND SOME FROM THE BLACK SECT.
WHAT I'M SAYING IS...
...THERE IS A THIRD PARTY INVOLVED IN ALL THIS--WHO'S PITTING THE WHITES AND THE BLACKS AGAINST EACH OTHER!
!
A THIRD PARTY?!

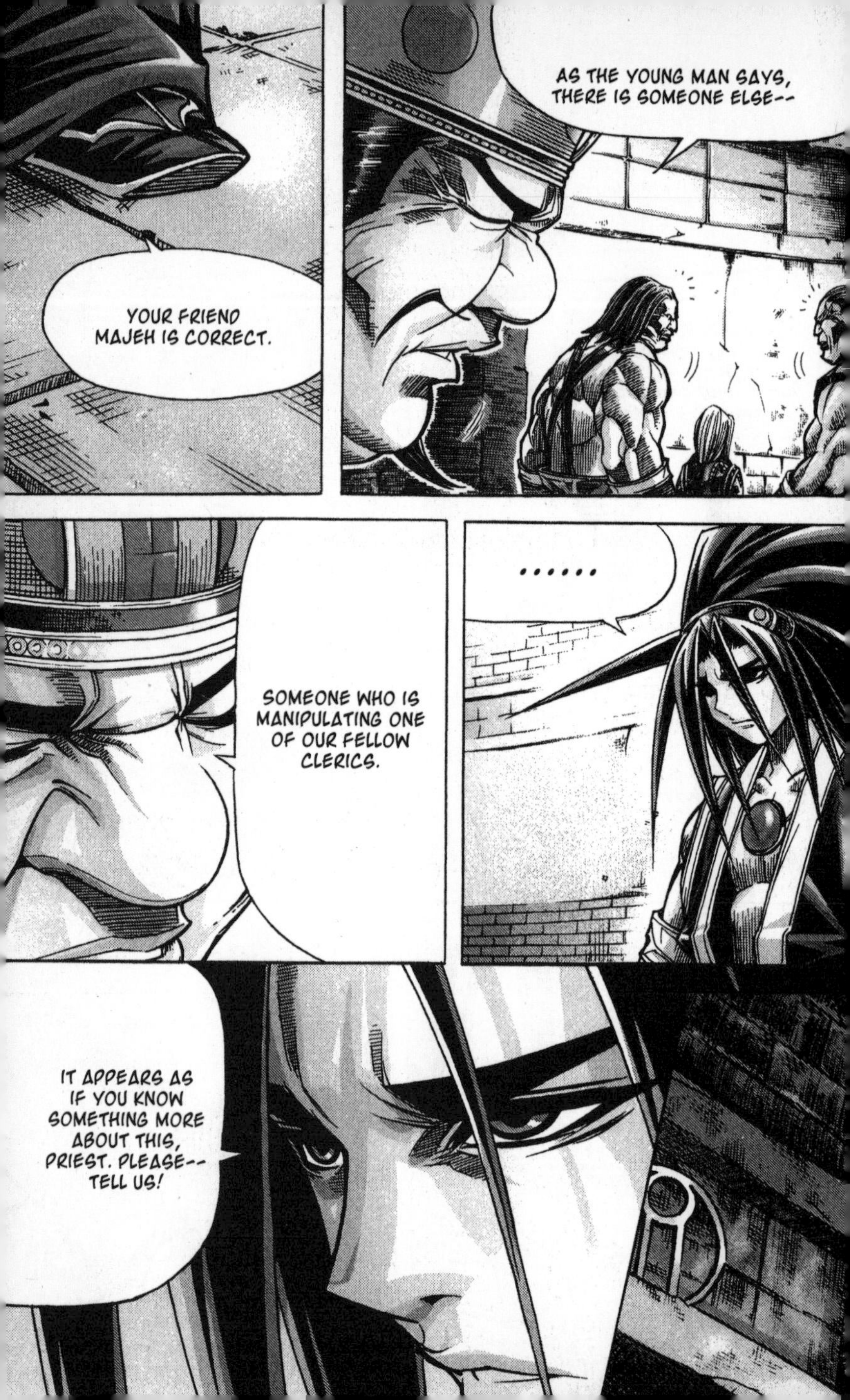
YOUR FRIEND MAJEH IS CORRECT.
AS THE YOUNG MAN SAYS, THERE IS SOMEONE ELSE--
SOMEONE WHO IS MANIPULATING ONE OF OUR FELLOW CLERICS.
......
IT APPEARS AS IF YOU KNOW SOMETHING MORE ABOUT THIS, PRIEST. PLEASE--TELL US!

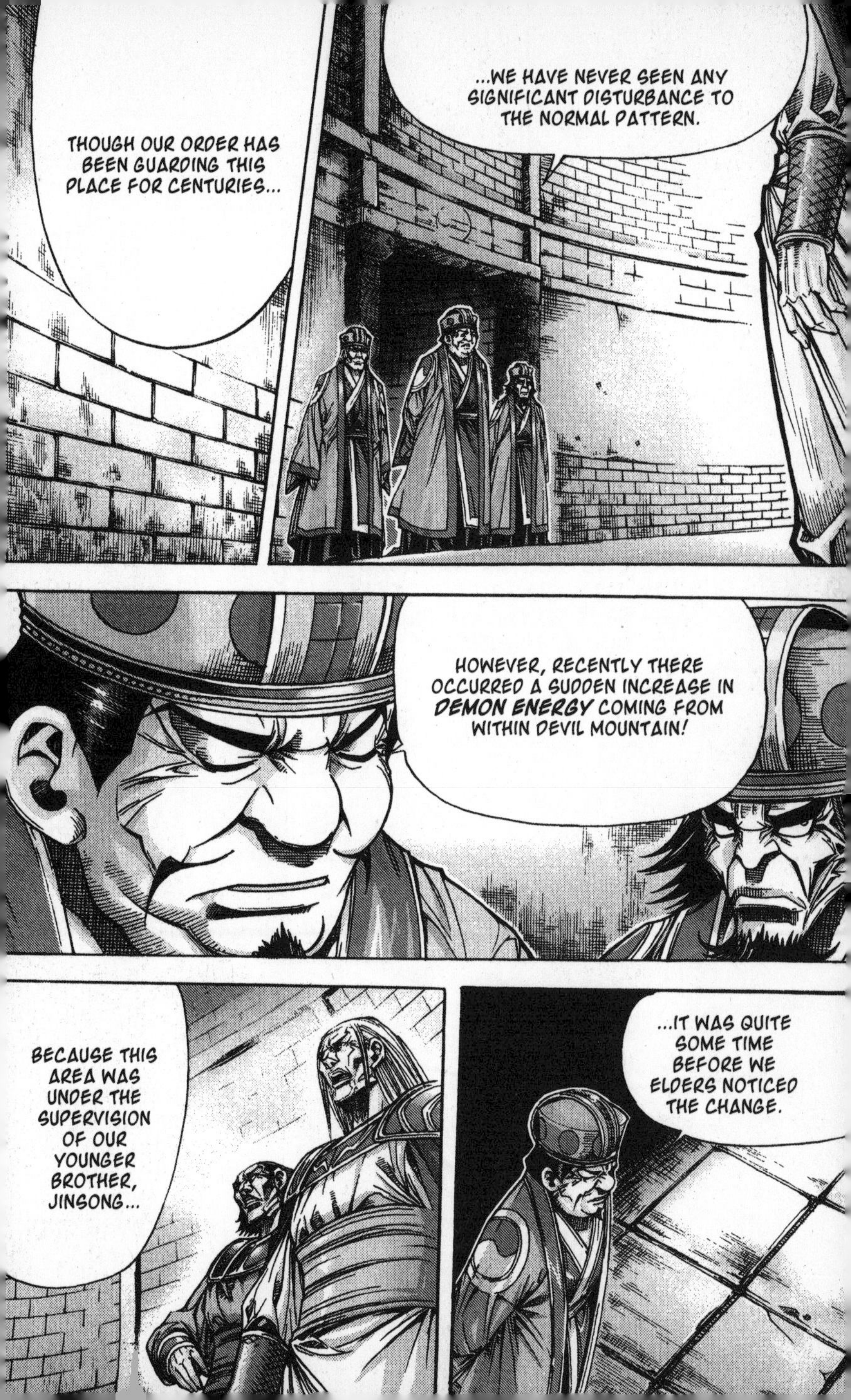
THOUGH OUR ORDER HAS BEEN GUARDING THIS PLACE FOR CENTURIES...
...WE HAVE NEVER SEEN ANY SIGNIFICANT DISTURBANCE TO THE NORMAL PATTERN.
HOWEVER, RECENTLY THERE OCCURRED A SUDDEN INCREASE IN *DEMON ENERGY* COMING FROM WITHIN DEVIL MOUNTAIN!
BECAUSE THIS AREA WAS UNDER THE SUPERVISION OF OUR YOUNGER BROTHER, JINSONG...
...IT WAS QUITE SOME TIME BEFORE WE ELDERS NOTICED THE CHANGE.

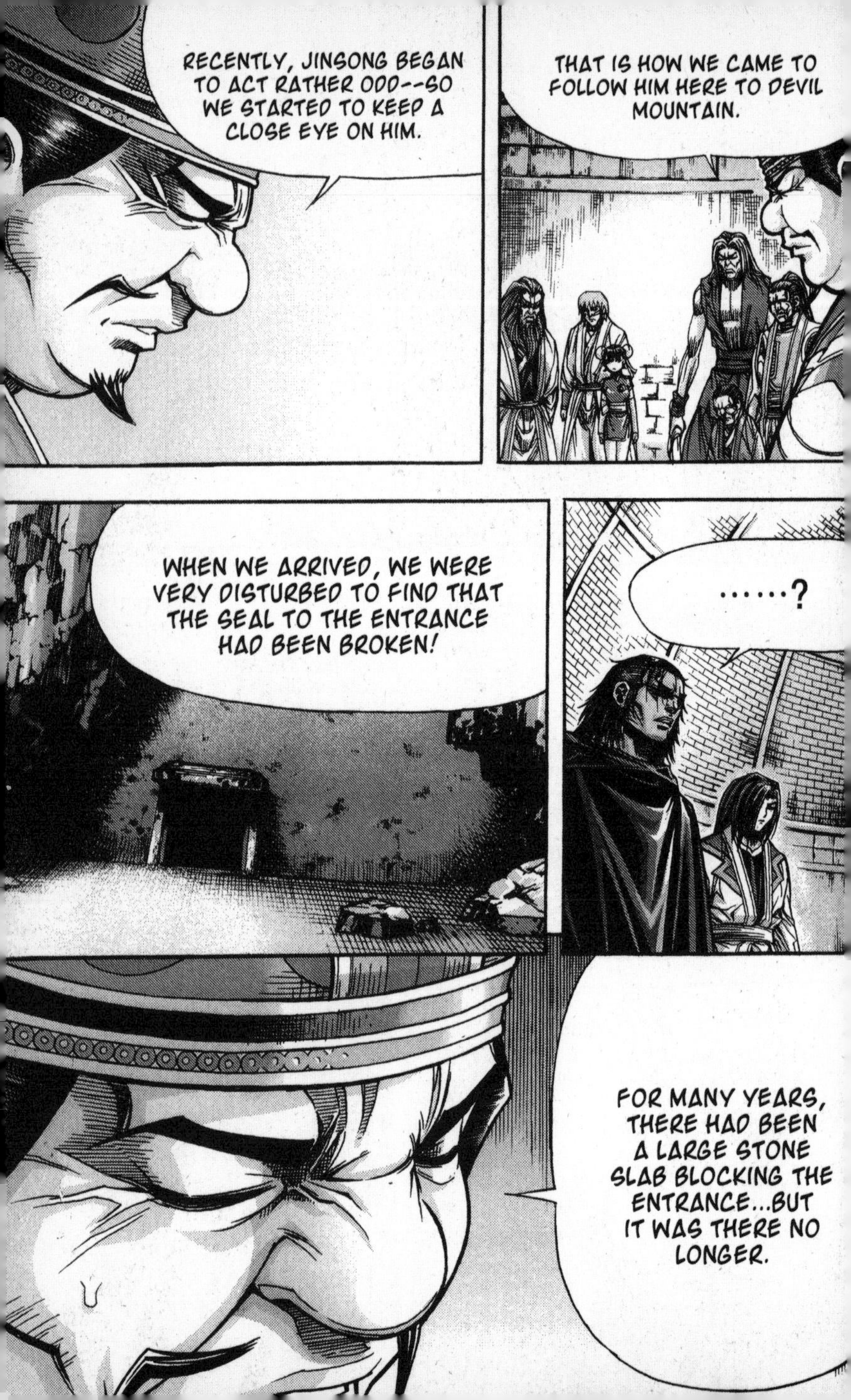
RECENTLY, JINSONG BEGAN TO ACT RATHER ODD--SO WE STARTED TO KEEP A CLOSE EYE ON HIM.
THAT IS HOW WE CAME TO FOLLOW HIM HERE TO DEVIL MOUNTAIN.
WHEN WE ARRIVED, WE WERE VERY DISTURBED TO FIND THAT THE SEAL TO THE ENTRANCE HAD BEEN BROKEN!
......?
FOR MANY YEARS, THERE HAD BEEN A LARGE STONE SLAB BLOCKING THE ENTRANCE...BUT IT WAS THERE NO LONGER.

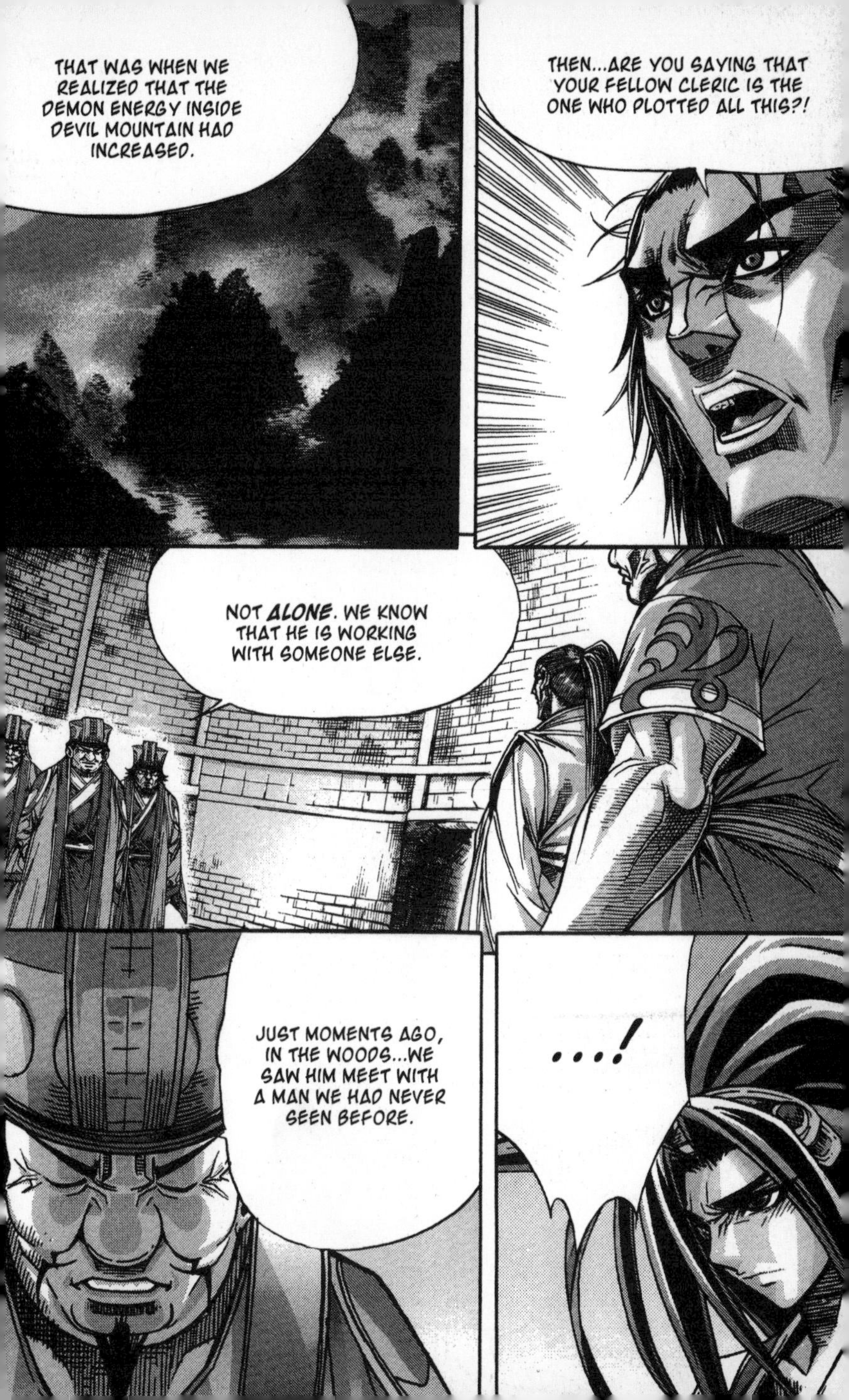
THAT WAS WHEN WE REALIZED THAT THE DEMON ENERGY INSIDE DEVIL MOUNTAIN HAD INCREASED.
THEN...ARE YOU SAYING THAT YOUR FELLOW CLERIC IS THE ONE WHO PLOTTED ALL THIS?!
NOT ALONE. WE KNOW THAT HE IS WORKING WITH SOMEONE ELSE.
JUST MOMENTS AGO, IN THE WOODS...WE SAW HIM MEET WITH A MAN WE HAD NEVER SEEN BEFORE.
...!

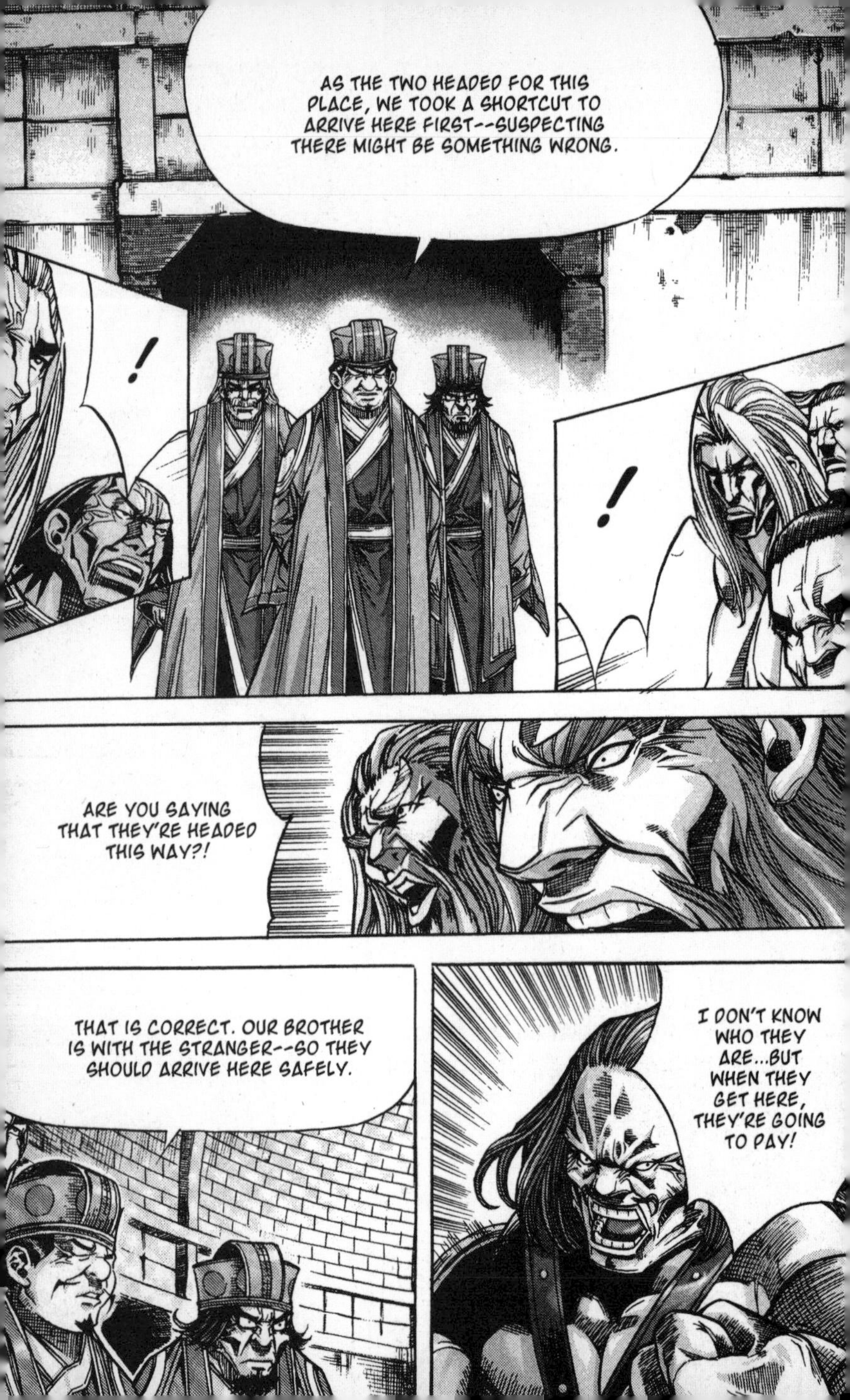
AS THE TWO HEADED FOR THIS PLACE, WE TOOK A SHORTCUT TO ARRIVE HERE FIRST--SUSPECTING THERE MIGHT BE SOMETHING WRONG.
!
!
ARE YOU SAYING THAT THEY'RE HEADED THIS WAY?!
THAT IS CORRECT. OUR BROTHER IS WITH THE STRANGER--SO THEY SHOULD ARRIVE HERE SAFELY.
I DON'T KNOW WHO THEY ARE...BUT WHEN THEY GET HERE, THEY'RE GOING TO PAY!

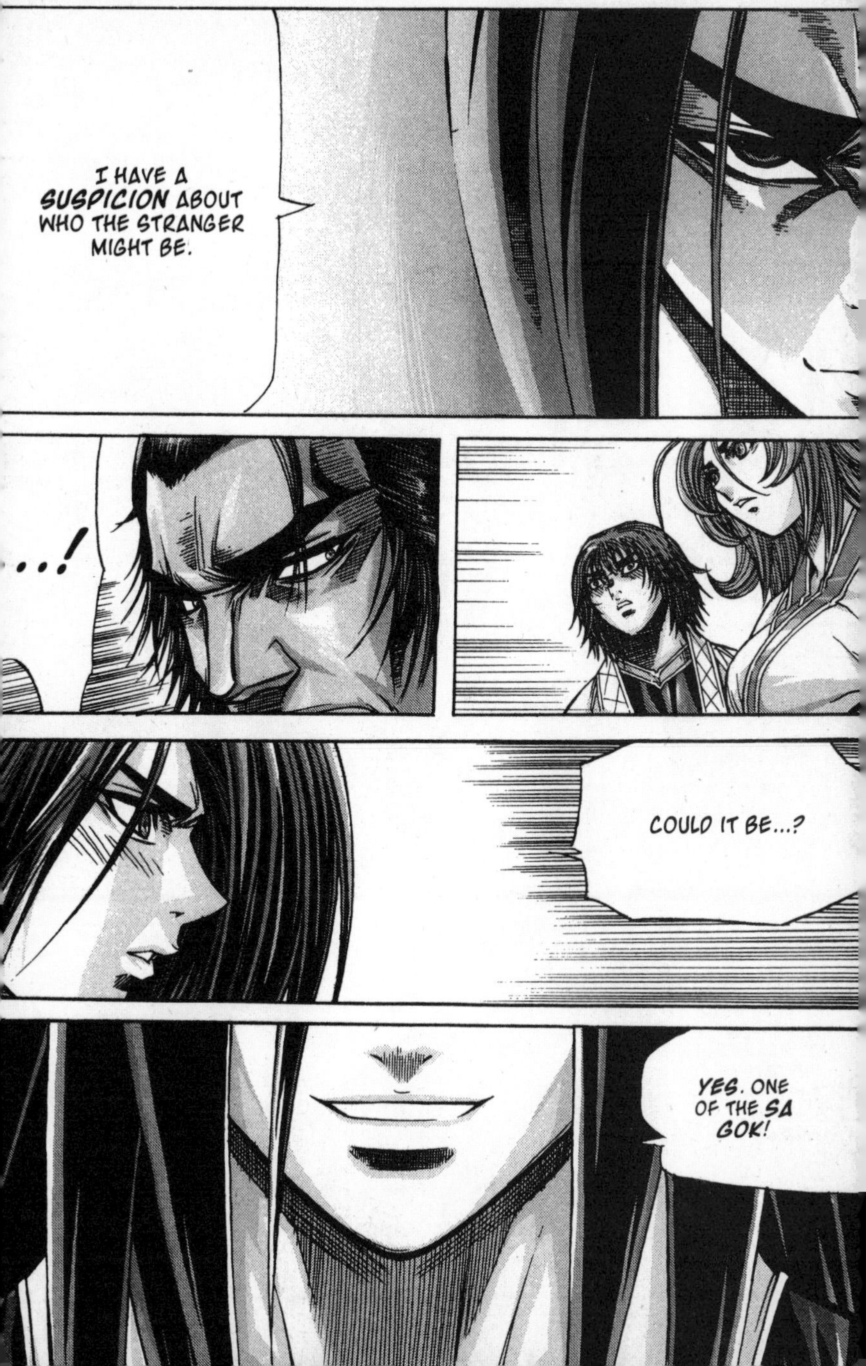
I HAVE A SUSPICION ABOUT WHO THE STRANGER MIGHT BE.
..!
COULD IT BE...?
YES. ONE OF THE SA GOK!

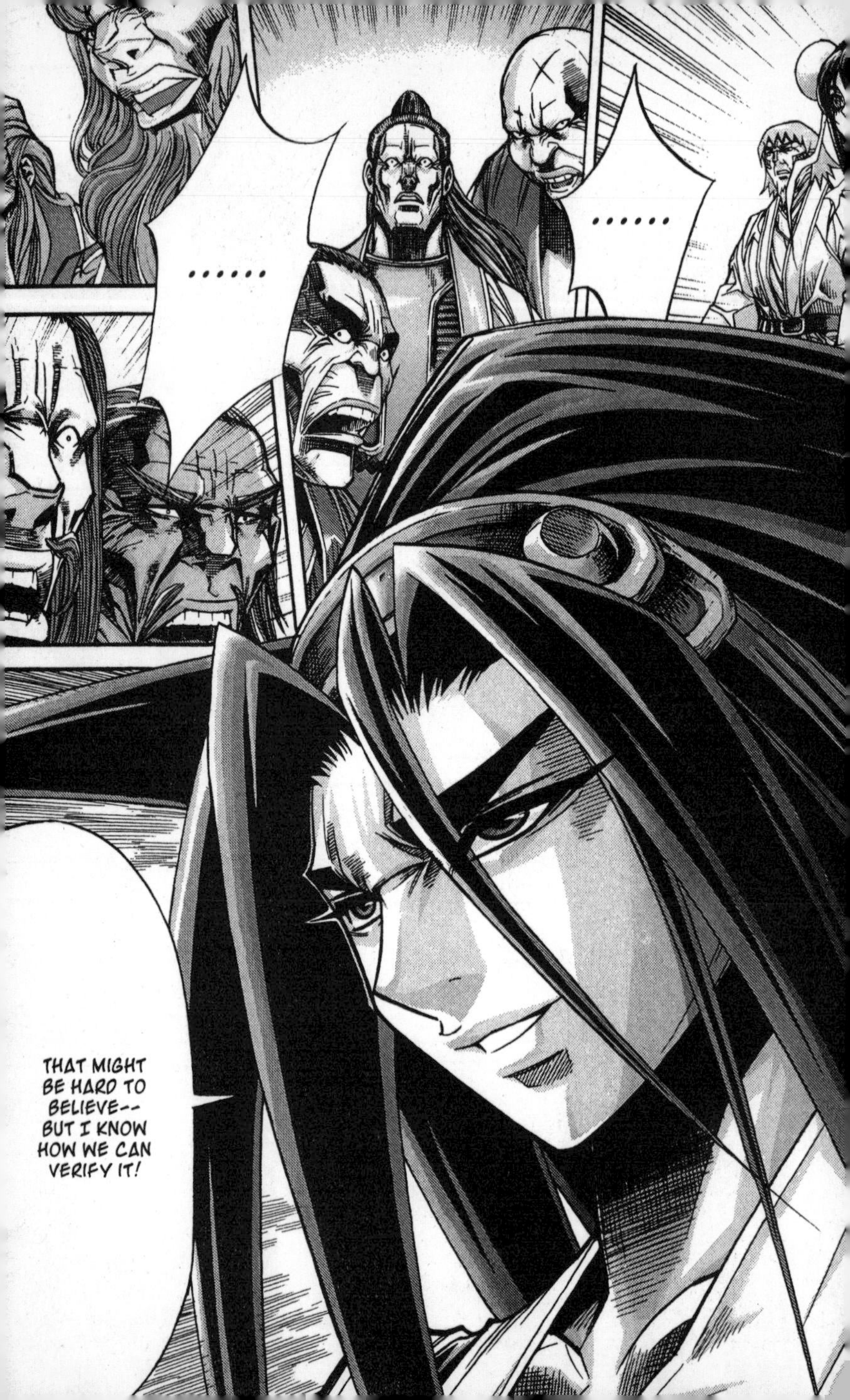
......
......
THAT MIGHT BE HARD TO BELIEVE-- BUT I KNOW HOW WE CAN VERIFY IT!

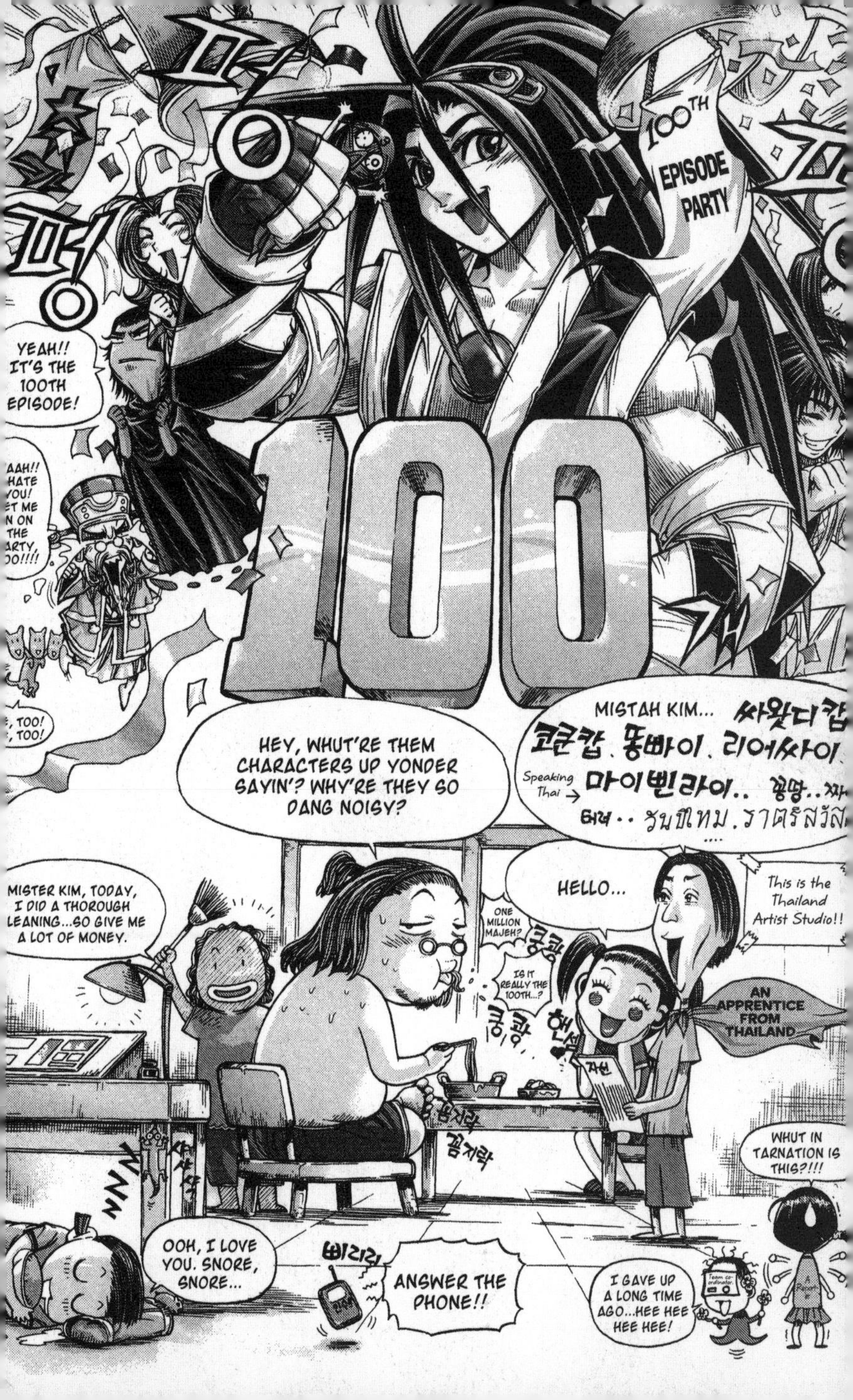
100TH EPISODE PARTY
YEAH!! IT'S THE 100TH EPISODE!
AAH!! HATE YOU! ET ME N ON THE ARTY, OO!!!!
, TOO! , TOO!
100
HEY, WHUT'RE THEM CHARACTERS UP YONDER SAYIN'? WHY'RE THEY SO DANG NOISY?
MISTAH KIM... 싸왓디 캅 코쿤캅. 똥빠이. 리어싸이 마이 뻰라이.. 쨩땅.. 쨔 허녀.. ชนกไทม. ราตรีสวัส ....
Speaking Thai →
MISTER KIM, TODAY, I DID A THOROUGH LEANING...SO GIVE ME A LOT OF MONEY.
HELLO...
This is the Thailand Artist Studio!!
ONE MILLION MAJEH?
IS IT REALLY THE 100TH...?
AN APPRENTICE FROM THAILAND
WHUT IN TARNATION IS THIS?!!!
OOH, I LOVE YOU. SNORE, SNORE...
ANSWER THE PHONE!!
I GAVE UP A LONG TIME AGO...HEE HEE HEE HEE!
Team coordinator

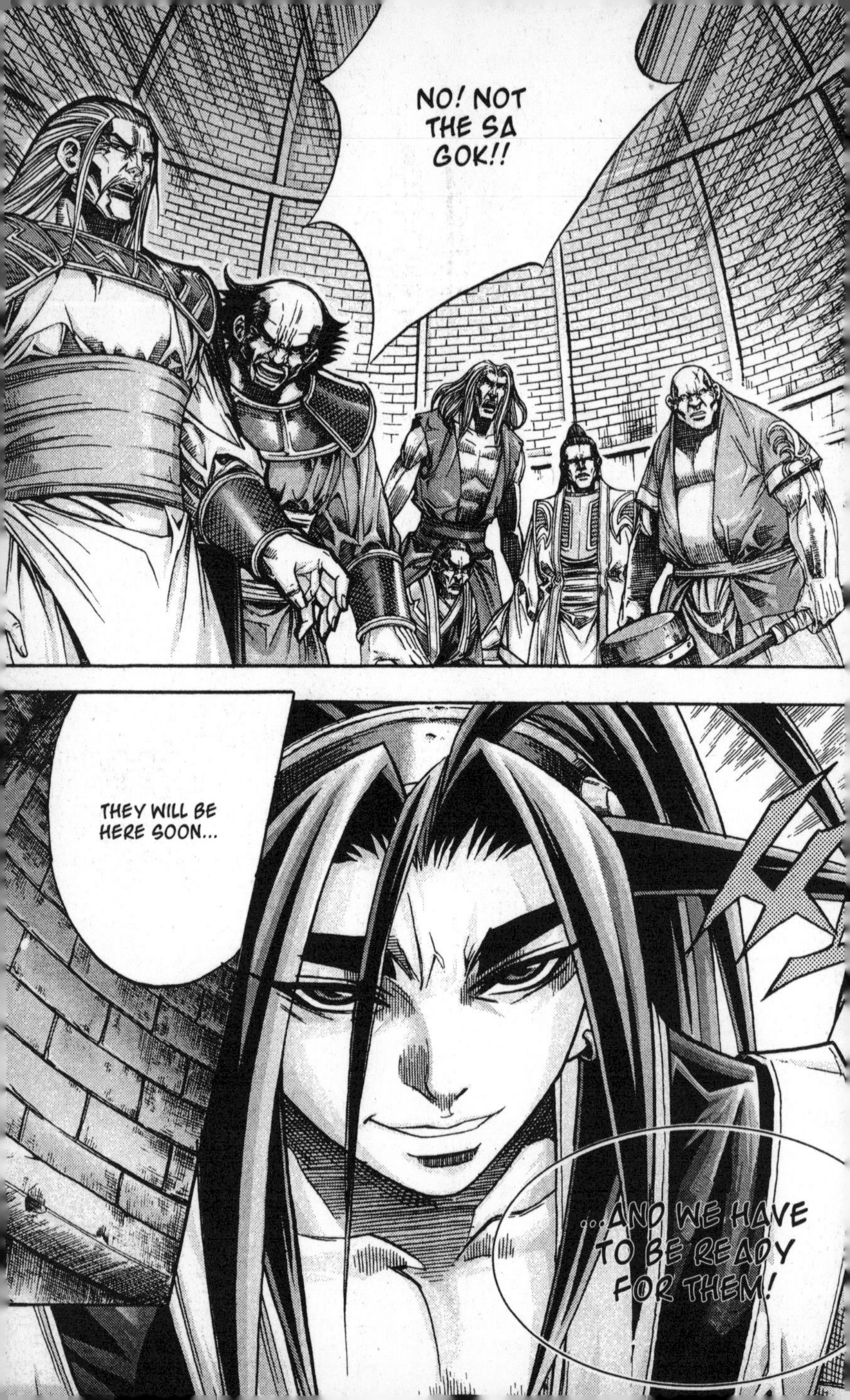
NO! NOT THE SA GOK!!
THEY WILL BE HERE SOON...
...AND WE HAVE TO BE READY FOR THEM!

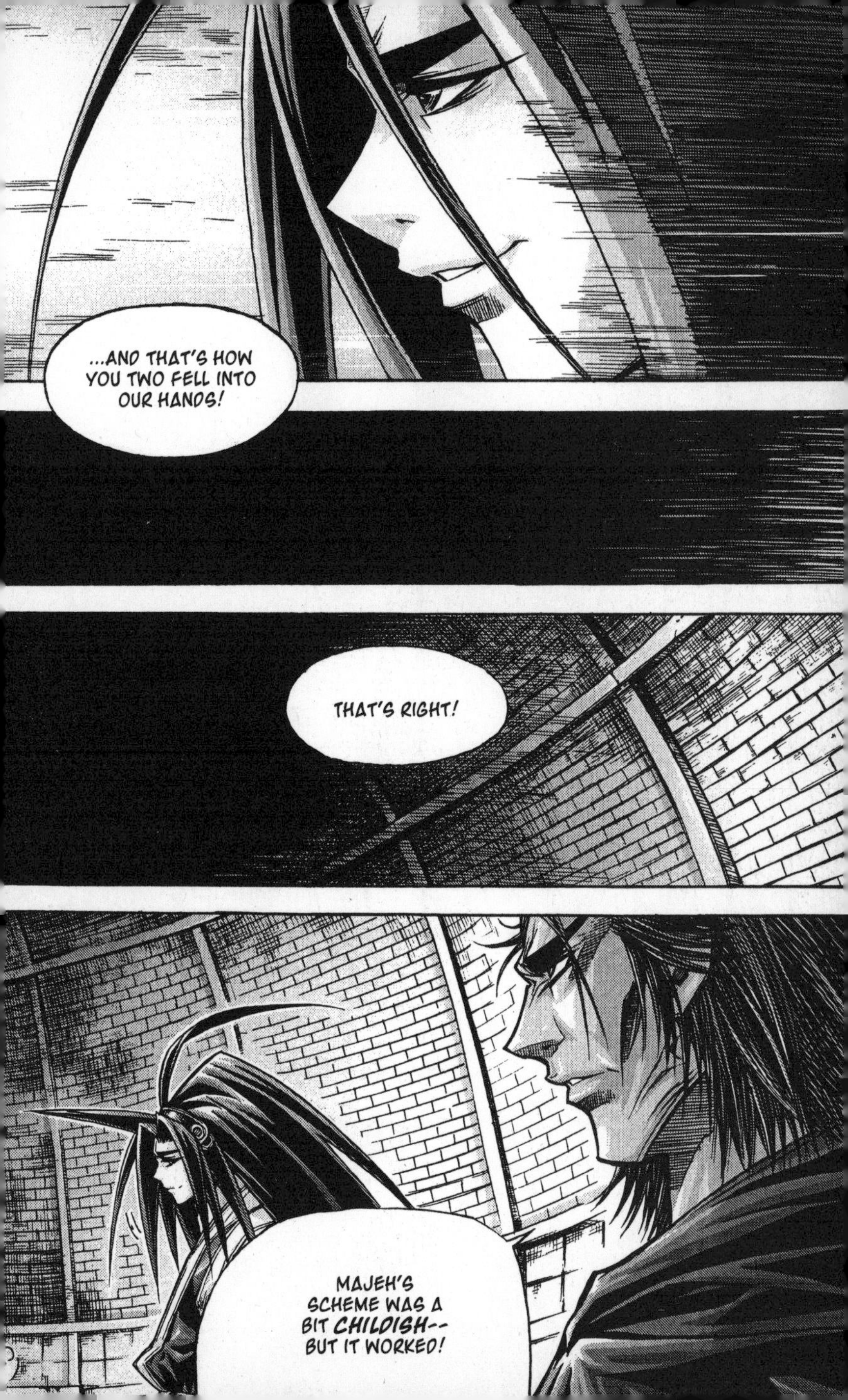
...AND THAT'S HOW YOU TWO FELL INTO OUR HANDS!
THAT'S RIGHT!
MAJEH'S SCHEME WAS A BIT CHILDISH--BUT IT WORKED!

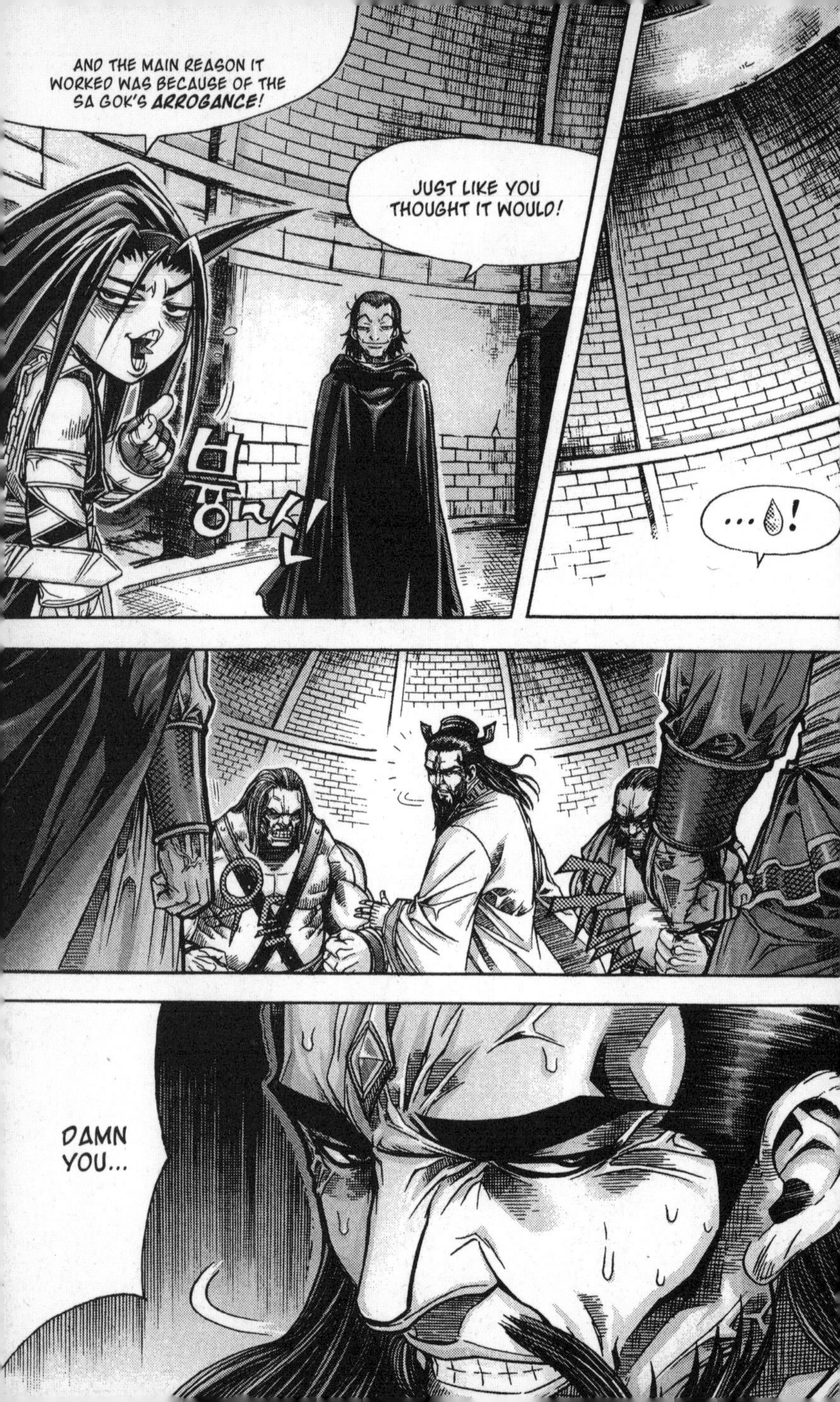
AND THE MAIN REASON IT WORKED WAS BECAUSE OF THE SA GOK'S ARROGANCE!
JUST LIKE YOU THOUGHT IT WOULD!
...!
DAMN YOU...

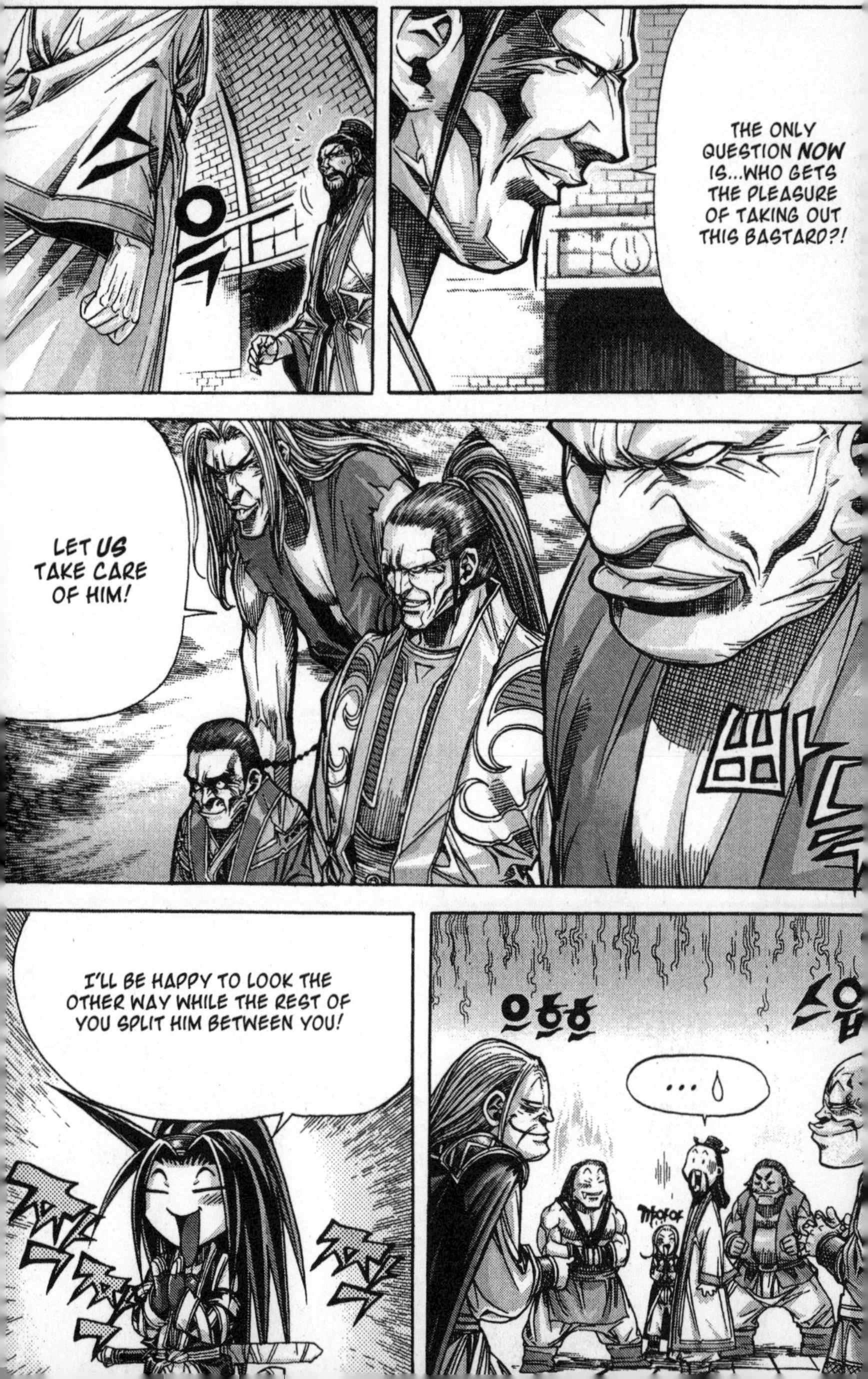
THE ONLY QUESTION NOW IS...WHO GETS THE PLEASURE OF TAKING OUT THIS BASTARD?!
LET US TAKE CARE OF HIM!
I'LL BE HAPPY TO LOOK THE OTHER WAY WHILE THE REST OF YOU SPLIT HIM BETWEEN YOU!
...

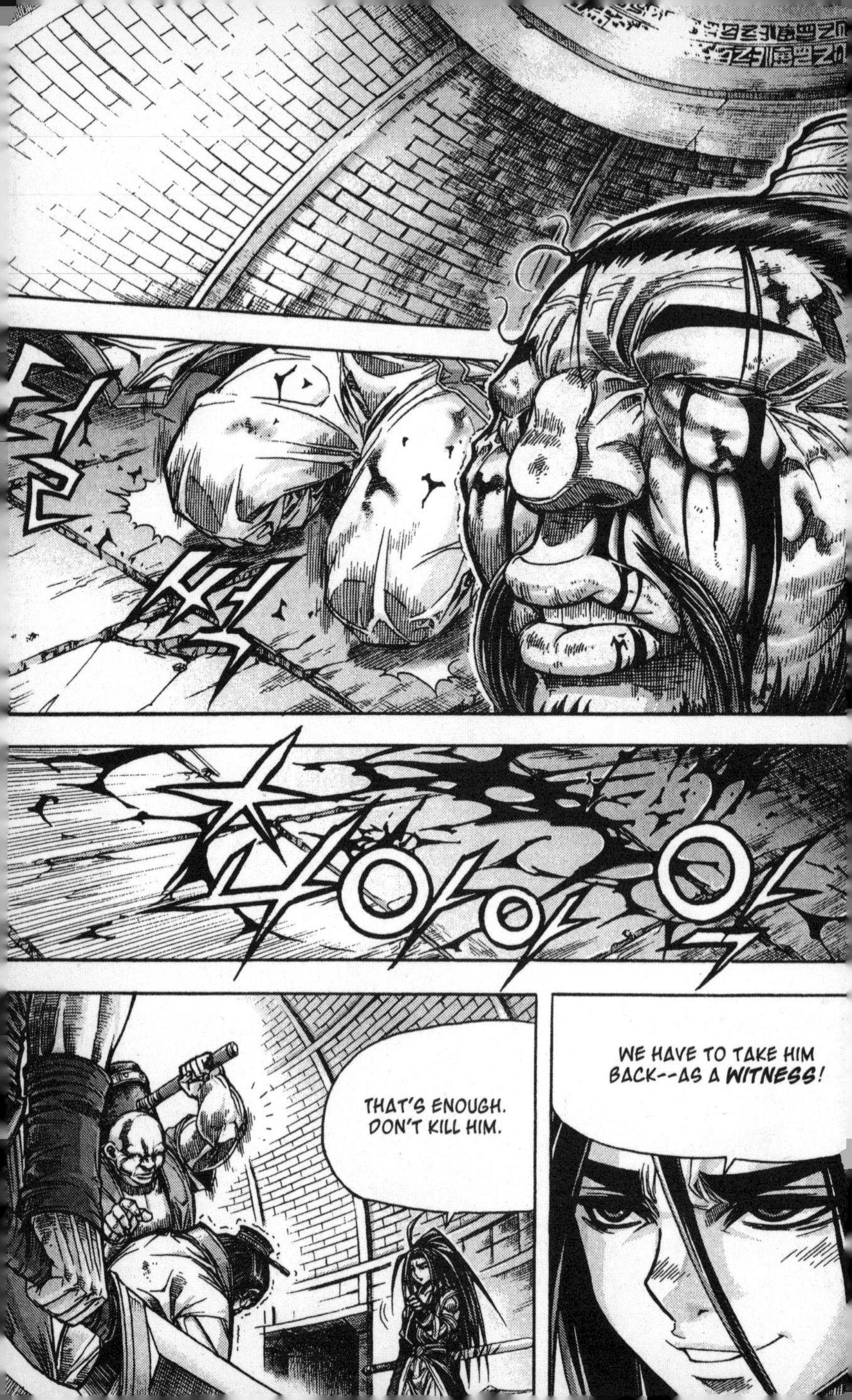
THAT'S ENOUGH. DON'T KILL HIM.
WE HAVE TO TAKE HIM BACK--AS A WITNESS!

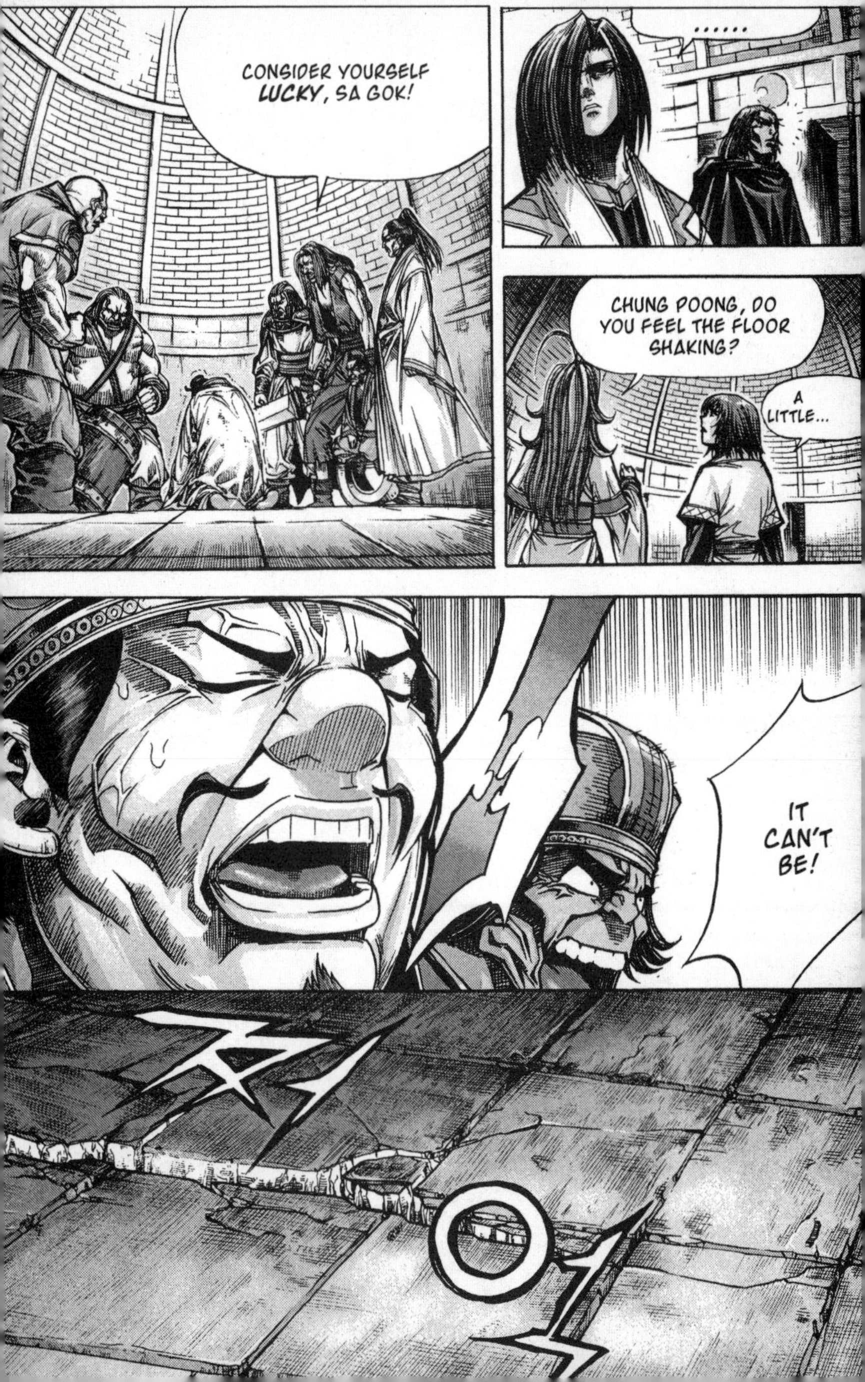
CONSIDER YOURSELF LUCKY, SA GOK!
......
CHUNG POONG, DO YOU FEEL THE FLOOR SHAKING?
A LITTLE...
IT CAN'T BE!

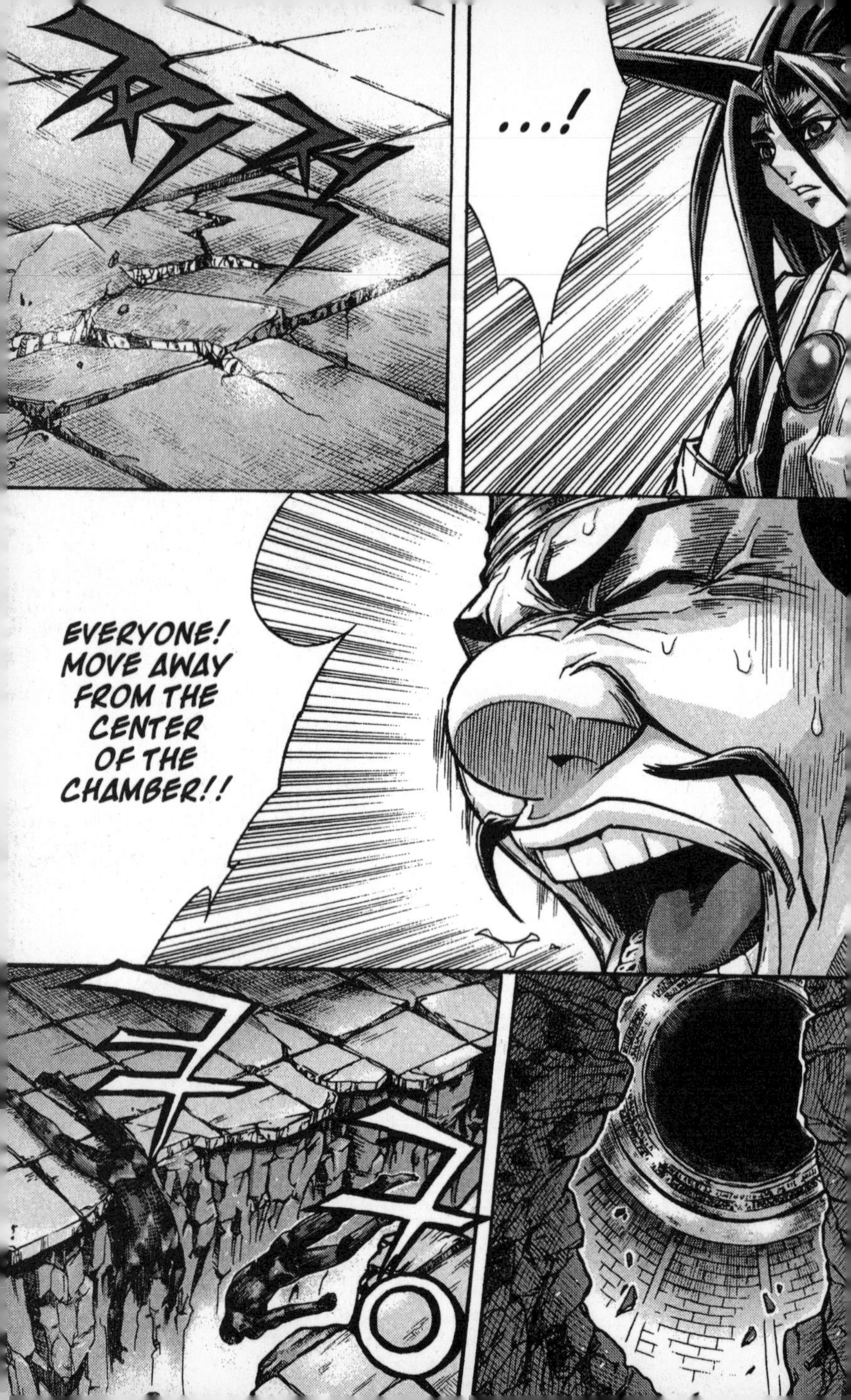
...!
EVERYONE! MOVE AWAY FROM THE CENTER OF THE CHAMBER!!

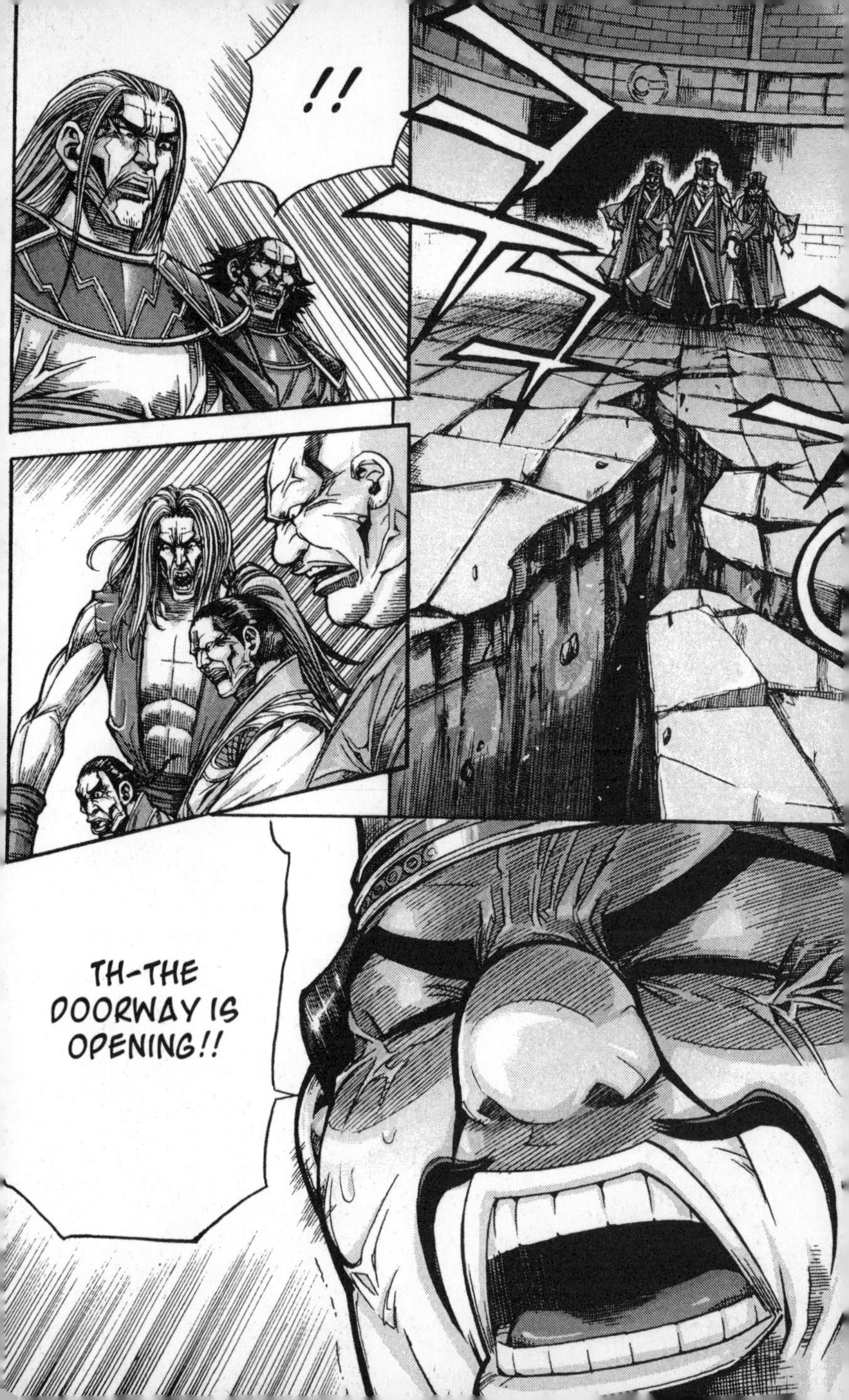
!!
TH-THE DOORWAY IS OPENING!!

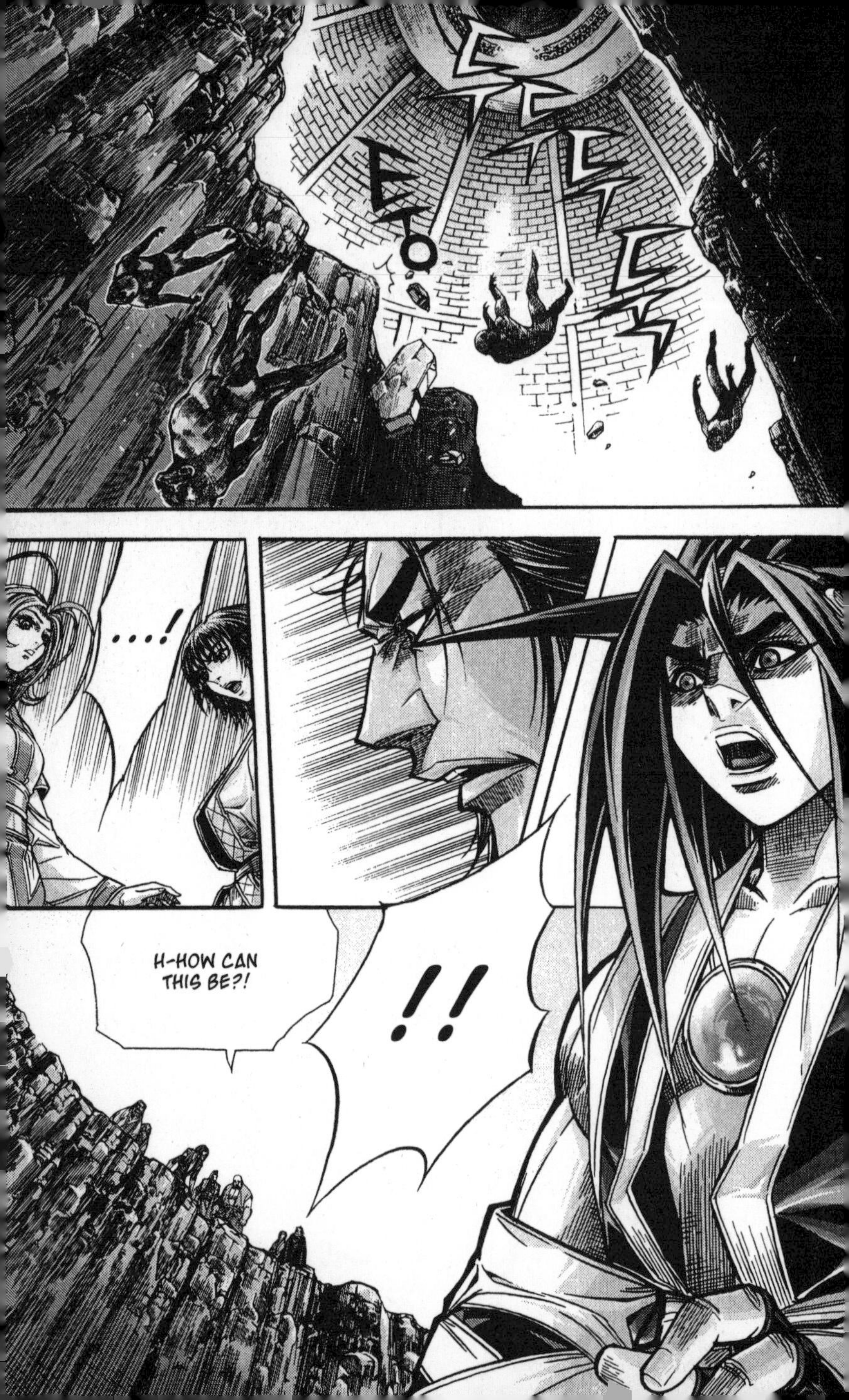
...!
H-HOW CAN THIS BE?!
!!

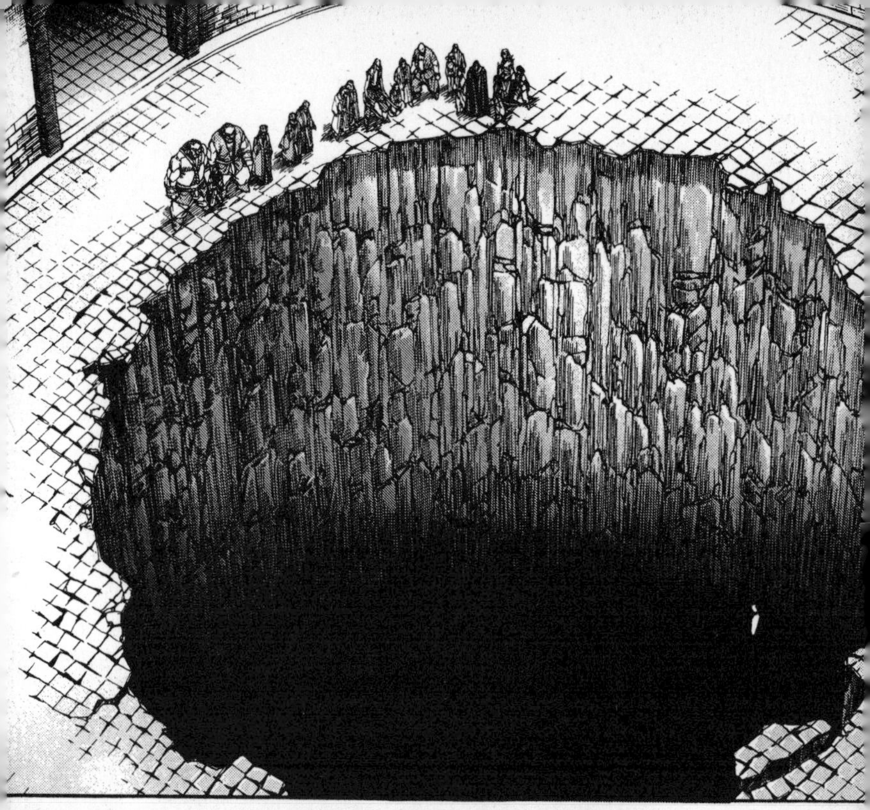

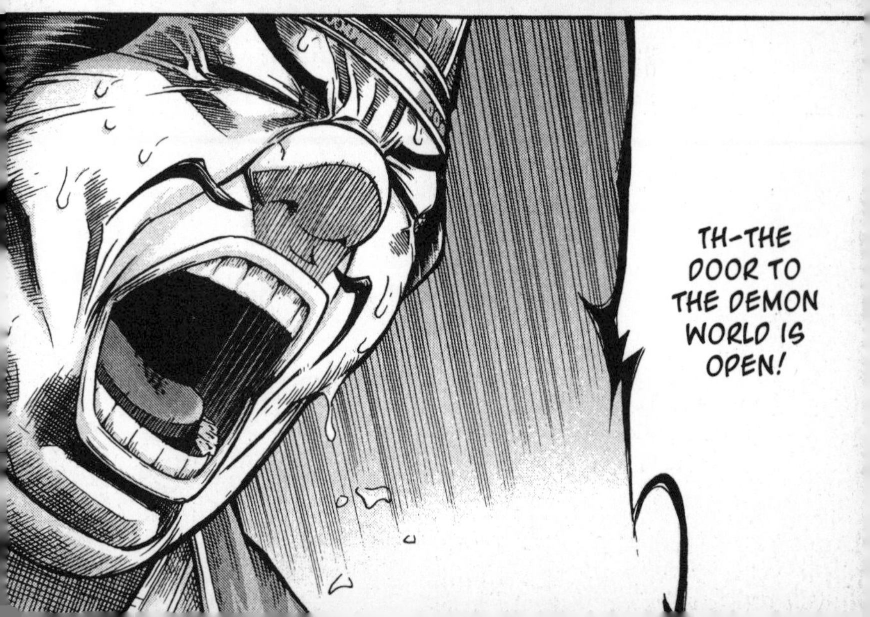
TH-THE DOOR TO THE DEMON WORLD IS OPEN!

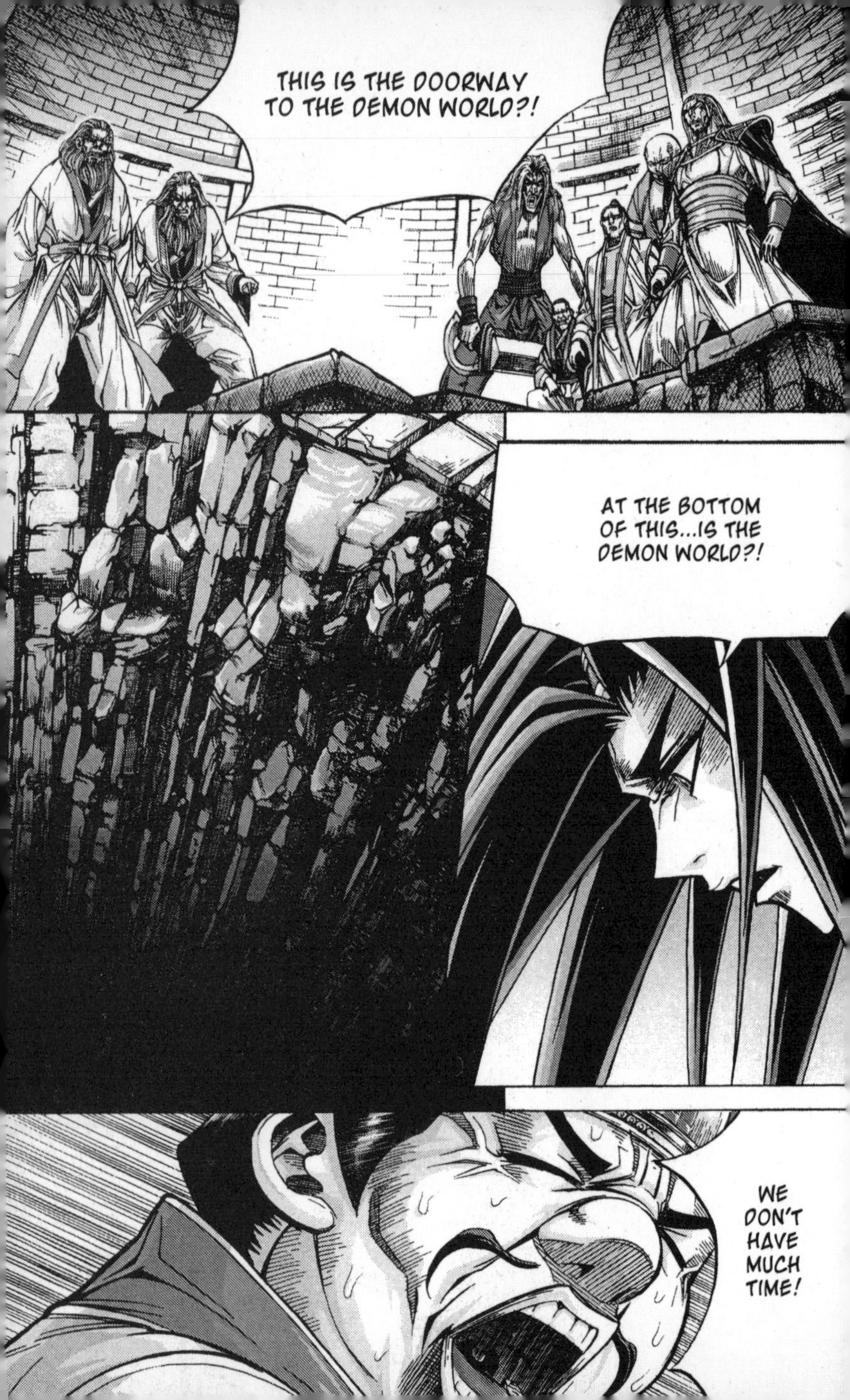
THIS IS THE DOORWAY TO THE DEMON WORLD?!
AT THE BOTTOM OF THIS...IS THE DEMON WORLD?!
WE DON'T HAVE MUCH TIME!

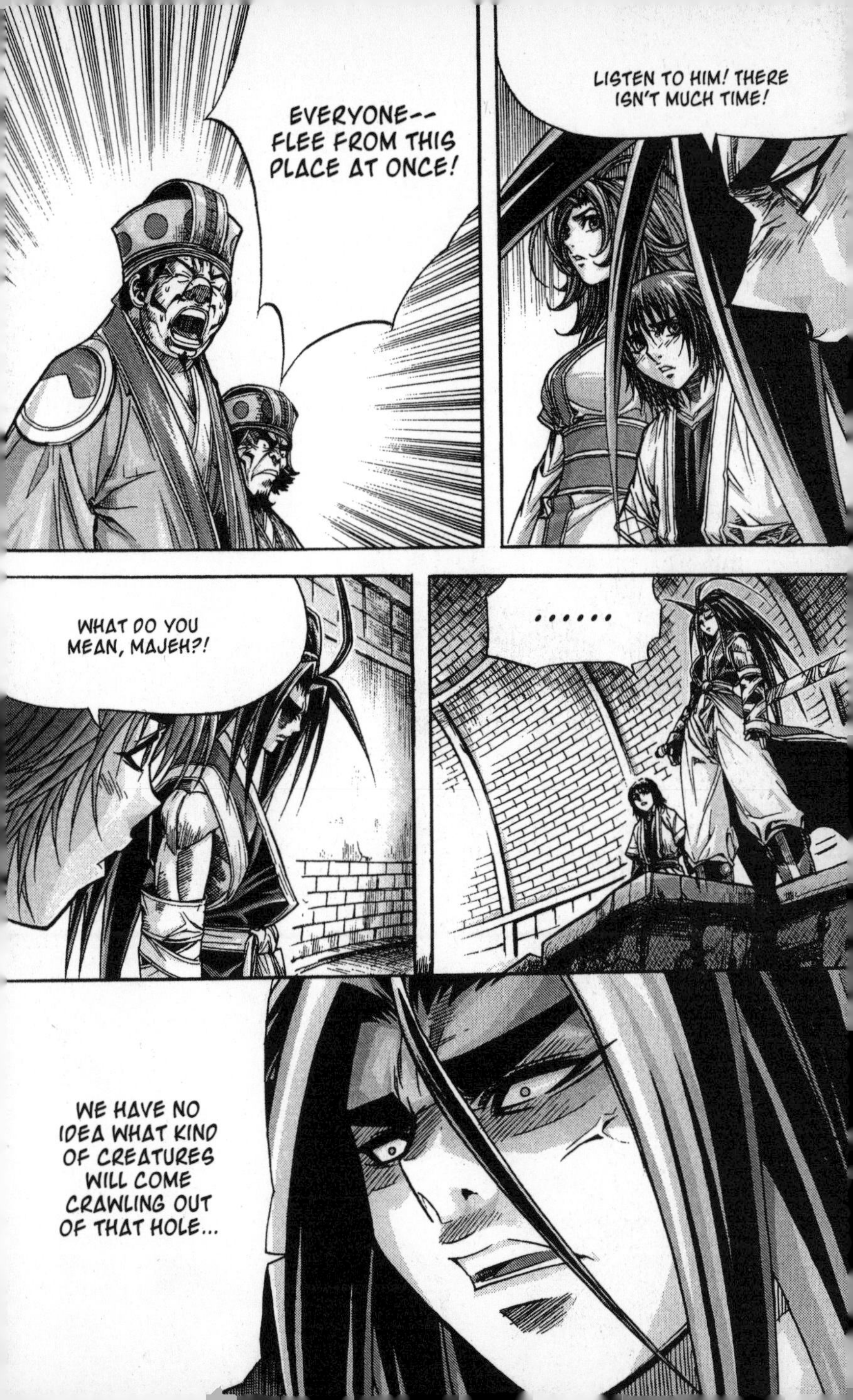
EVERYONE-- FLEE FROM THIS PLACE AT ONCE!
LISTEN TO HIM! THERE ISN'T MUCH TIME!
WHAT DO YOU MEAN, MAJEH?!
......
WE HAVE NO IDEA WHAT KIND OF CREATURES WILL COME CRAWLING OUT OF THAT HOLE...

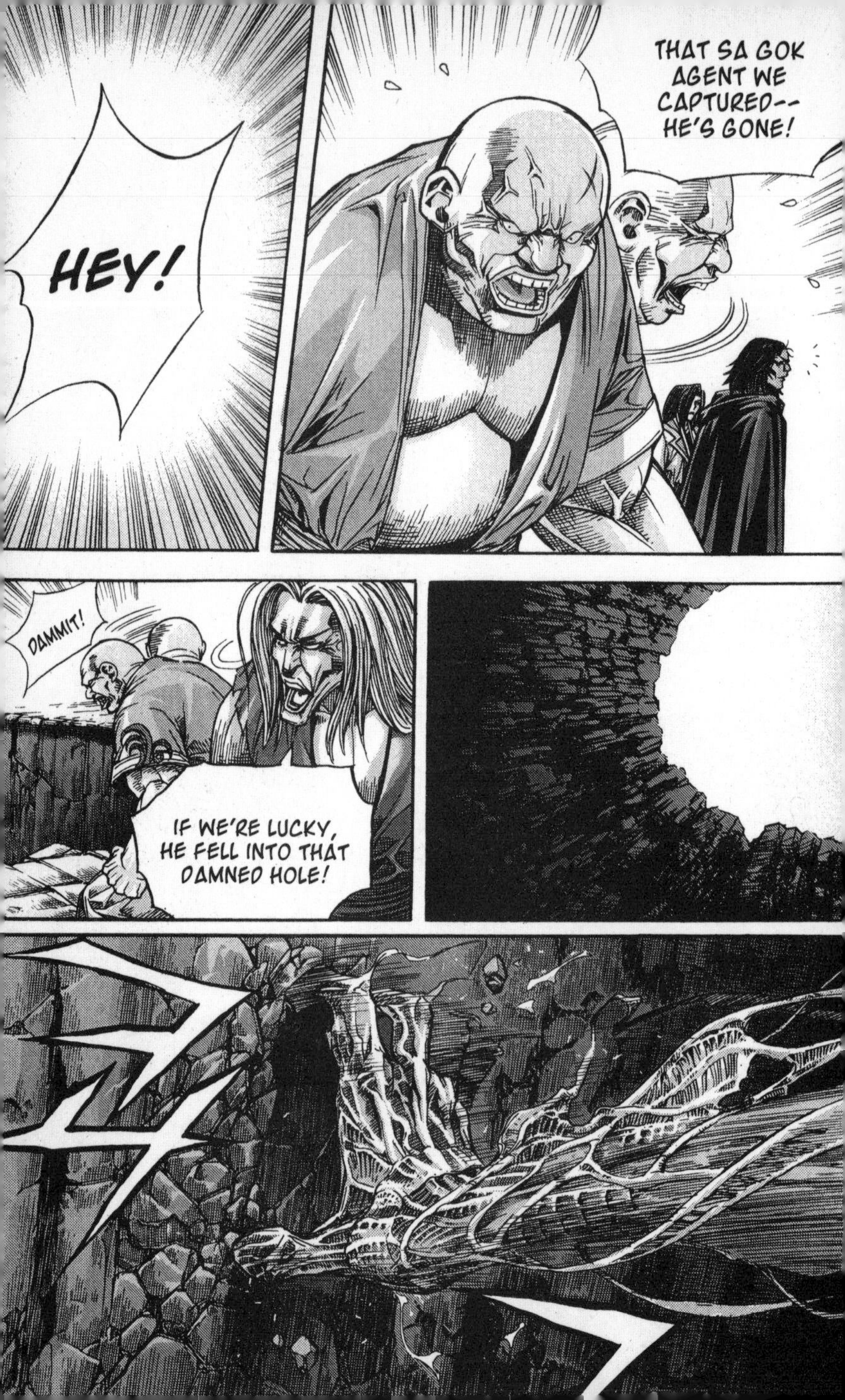
HEY!
THAT SA GOK AGENT WE CAPTURED--HE'S GONE!
DAMMIT!
IF WE'RE LUCKY, HE FELL INTO THAT DAMNED HOLE!

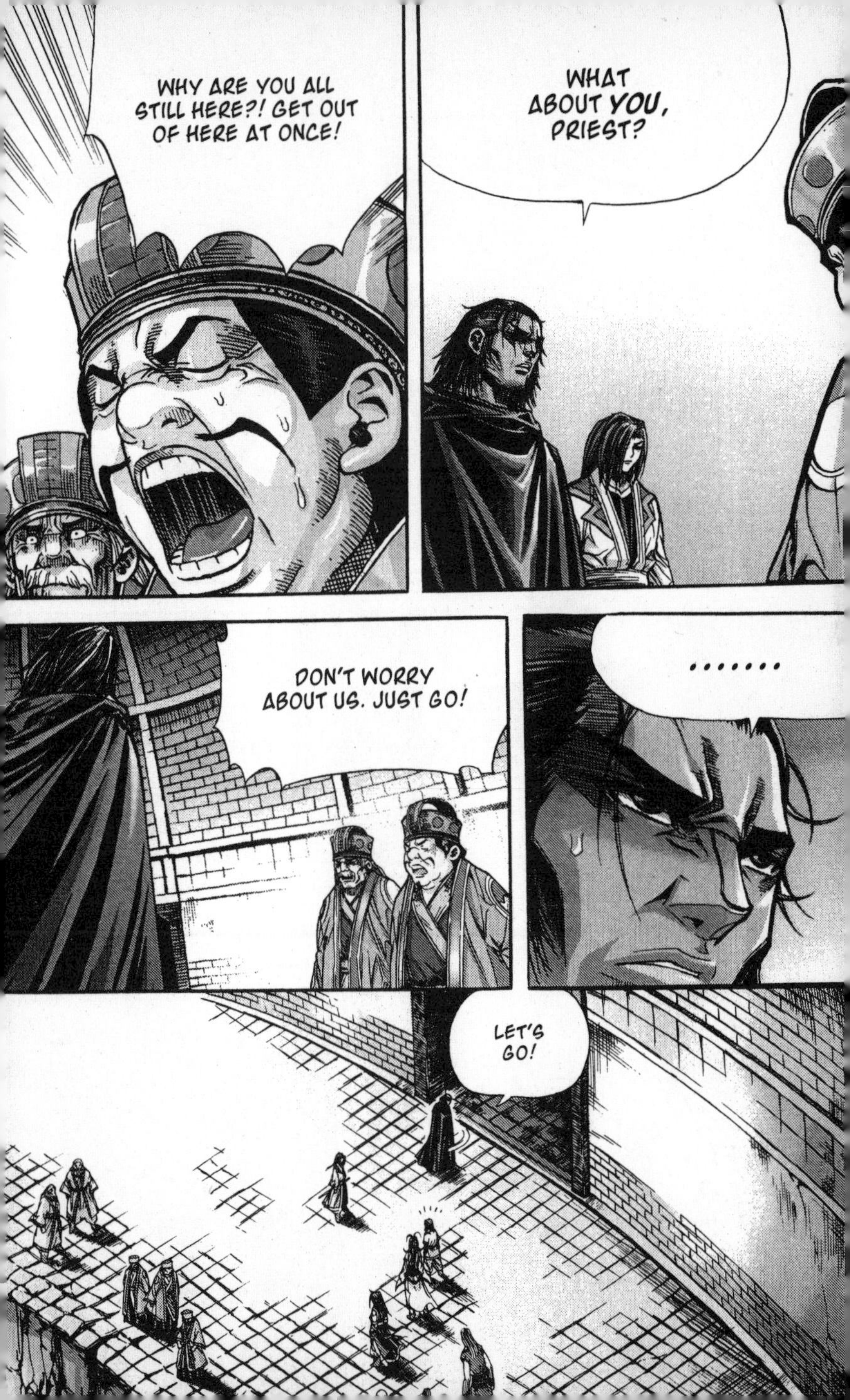
WHY ARE YOU ALL STILL HERE?! GET OUT OF HERE AT ONCE!
WHAT ABOUT YOU, PRIEST?
DON'T WORRY ABOUT US. JUST GO!
....
LET'S GO!

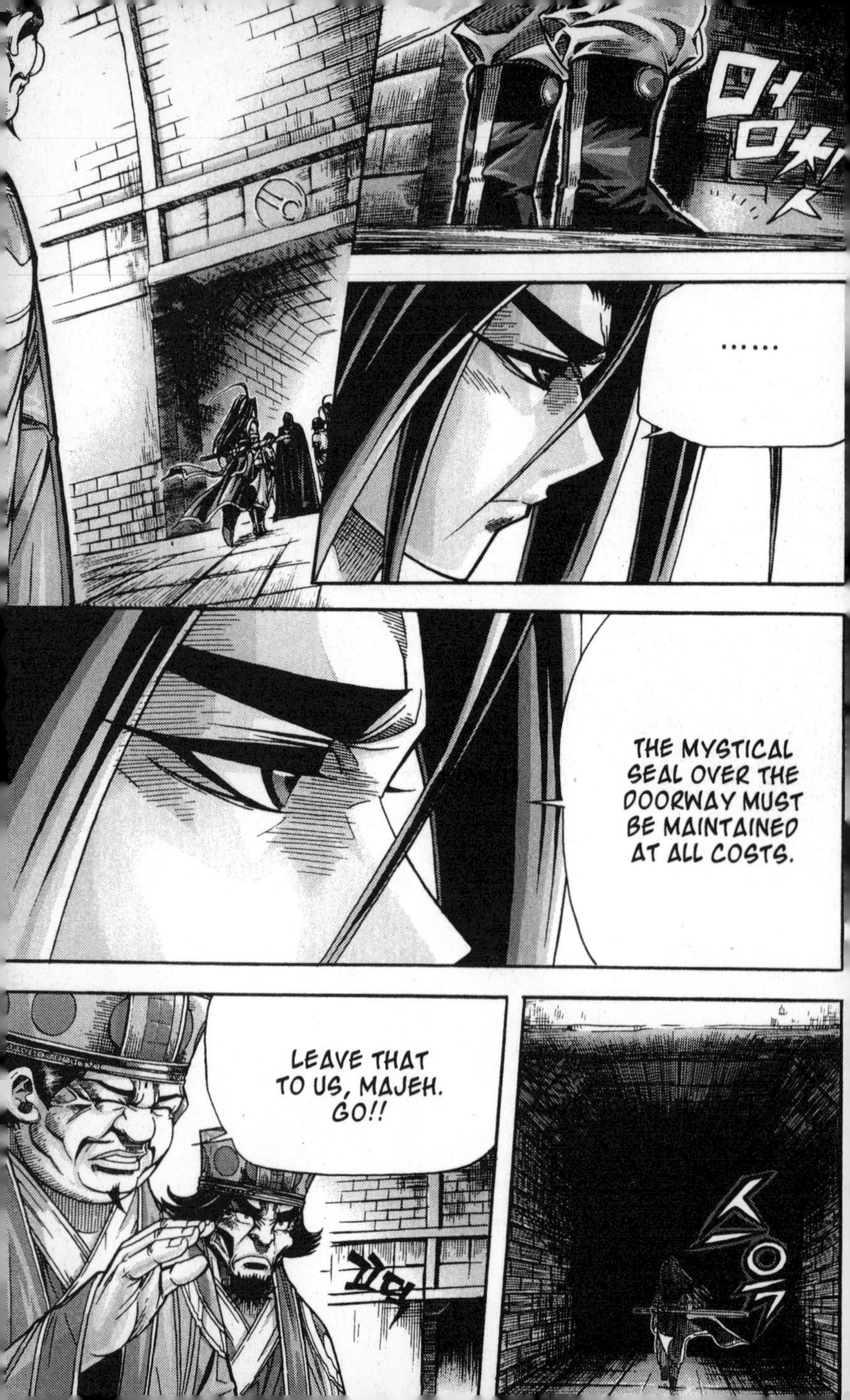
......
THE MYSTICAL SEAL OVER THE DOORWAY MUST BE MAINTAINED AT ALL COSTS.
LEAVE THAT TO US, MAJEH. GO!!

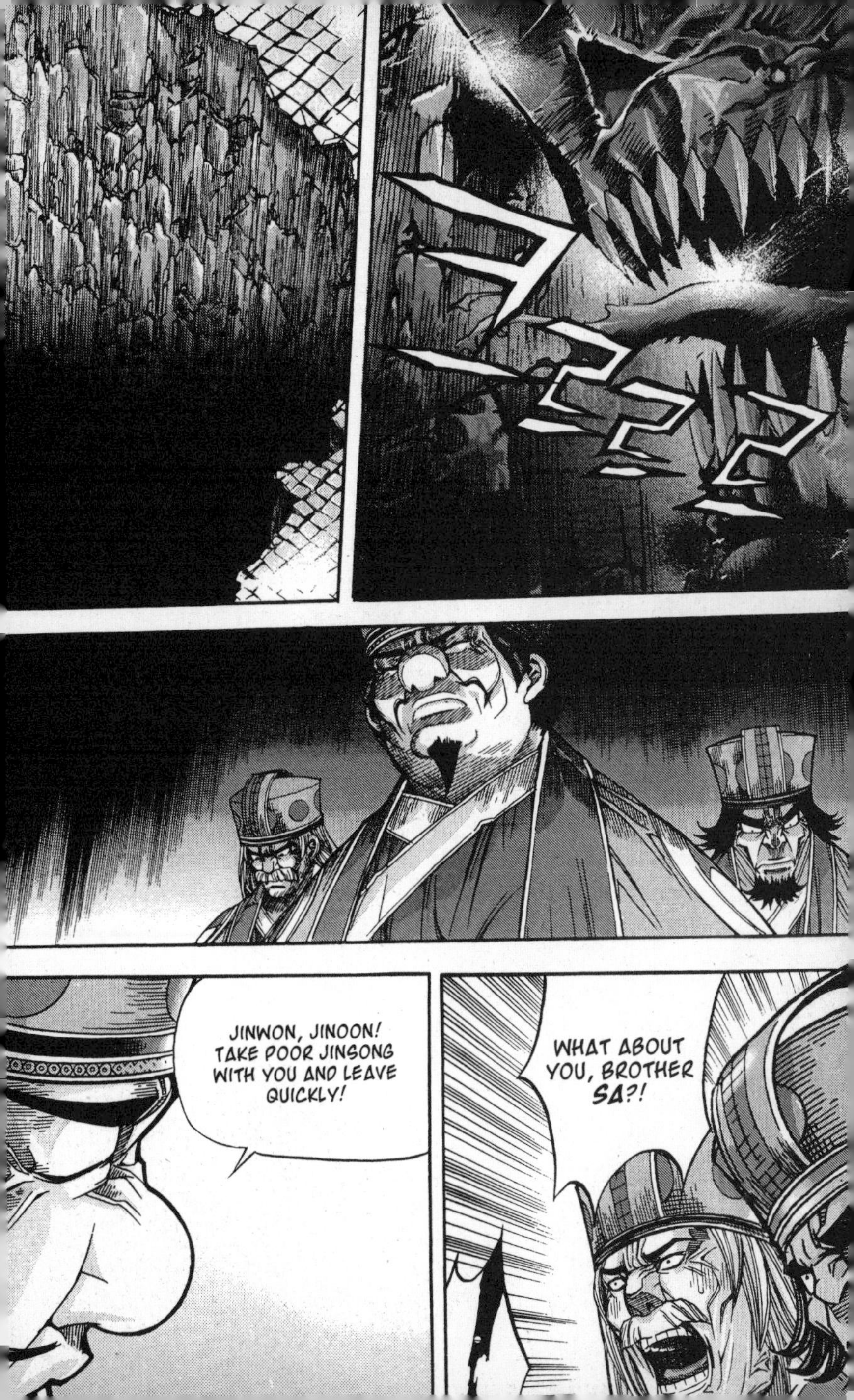
JINWON, JINOON! TAKE POOR JINSONG WITH YOU AND LEAVE QUICKLY!
WHAT ABOUT YOU, BROTHER SA?!

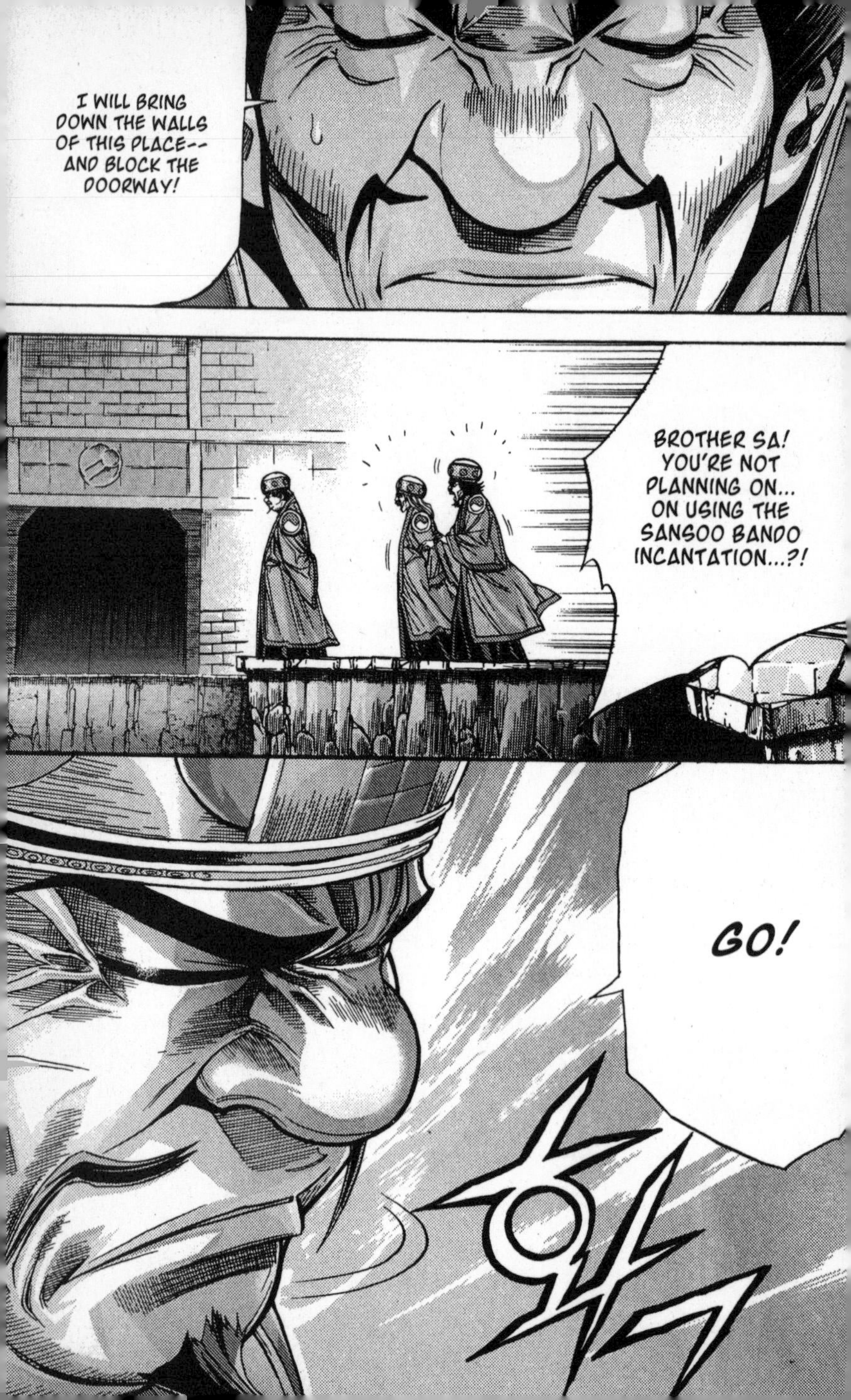
I WILL BRING DOWN THE WALLS OF THIS PLACE-- AND BLOCK THE DOORWAY!
BROTHER SA! YOU'RE NOT PLANNING ON... ON USING THE SANSOO BANDO INCANTATION...?!
GO!

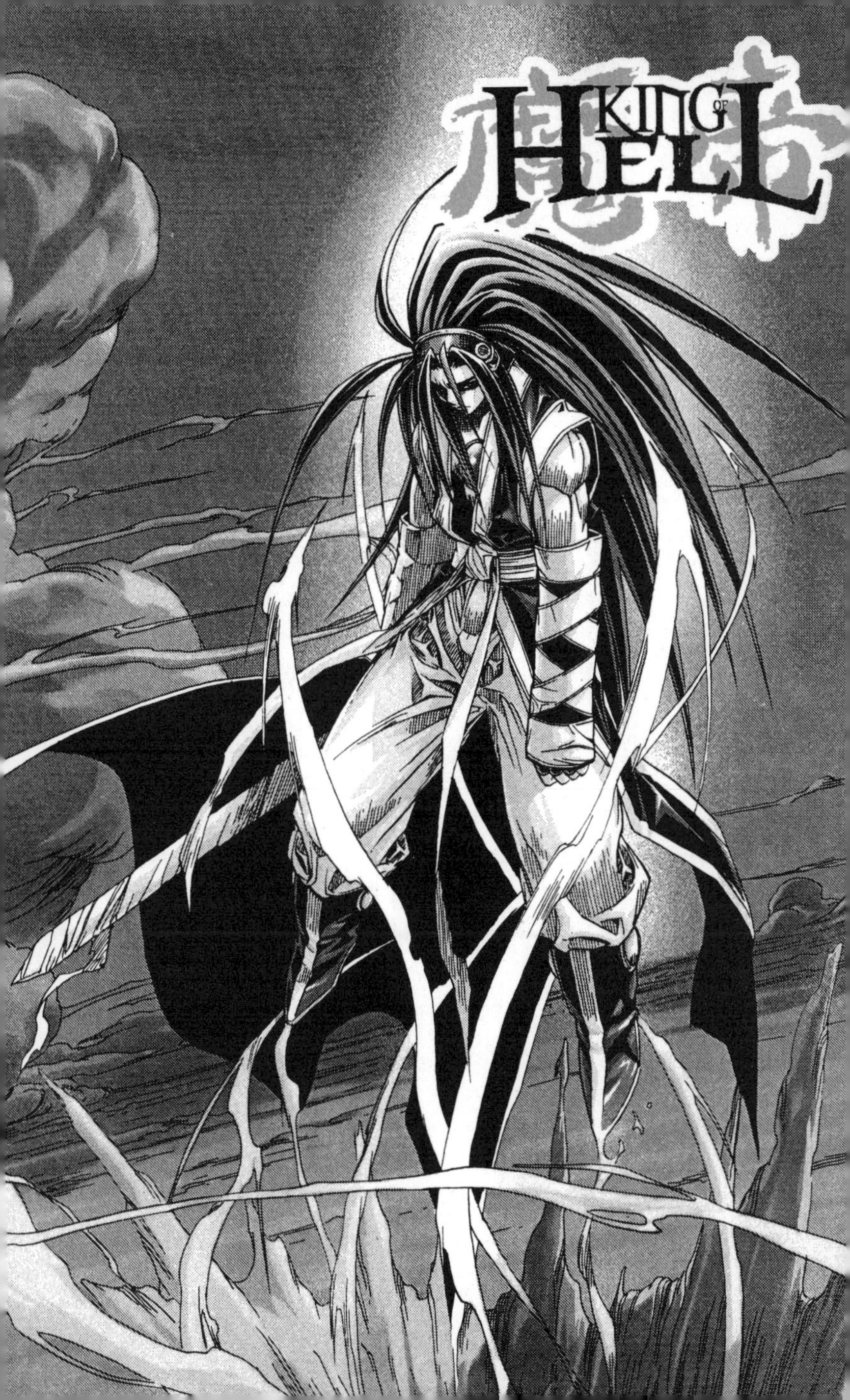
KING OF HELL

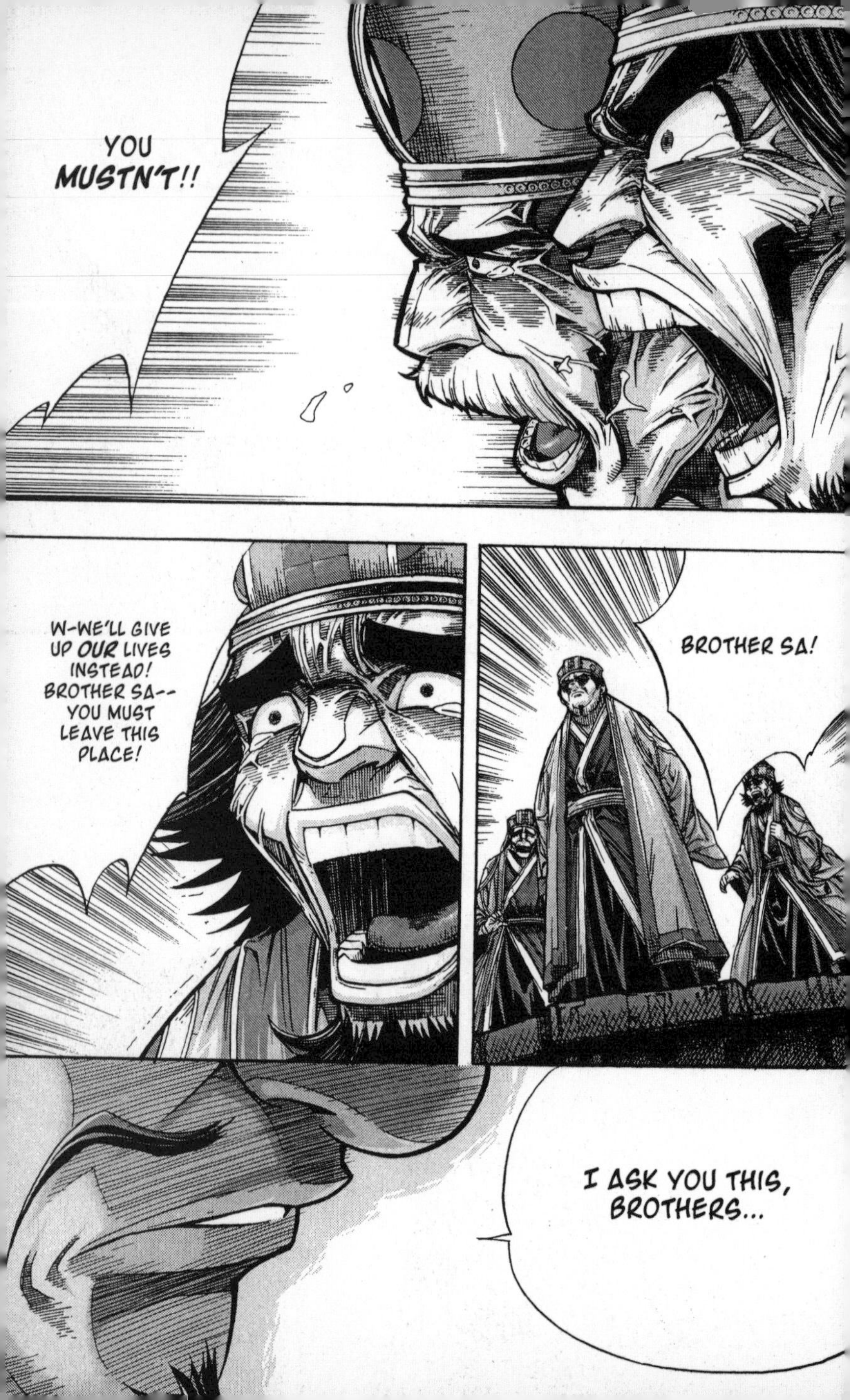
YOU MUSTN'T!!
W-WE'LL GIVE UP OUR LIVES INSTEAD! BROTHER SA-- YOU MUST LEAVE THIS PLACE!
BROTHER SA!
I ASK YOU THIS, BROTHERS...

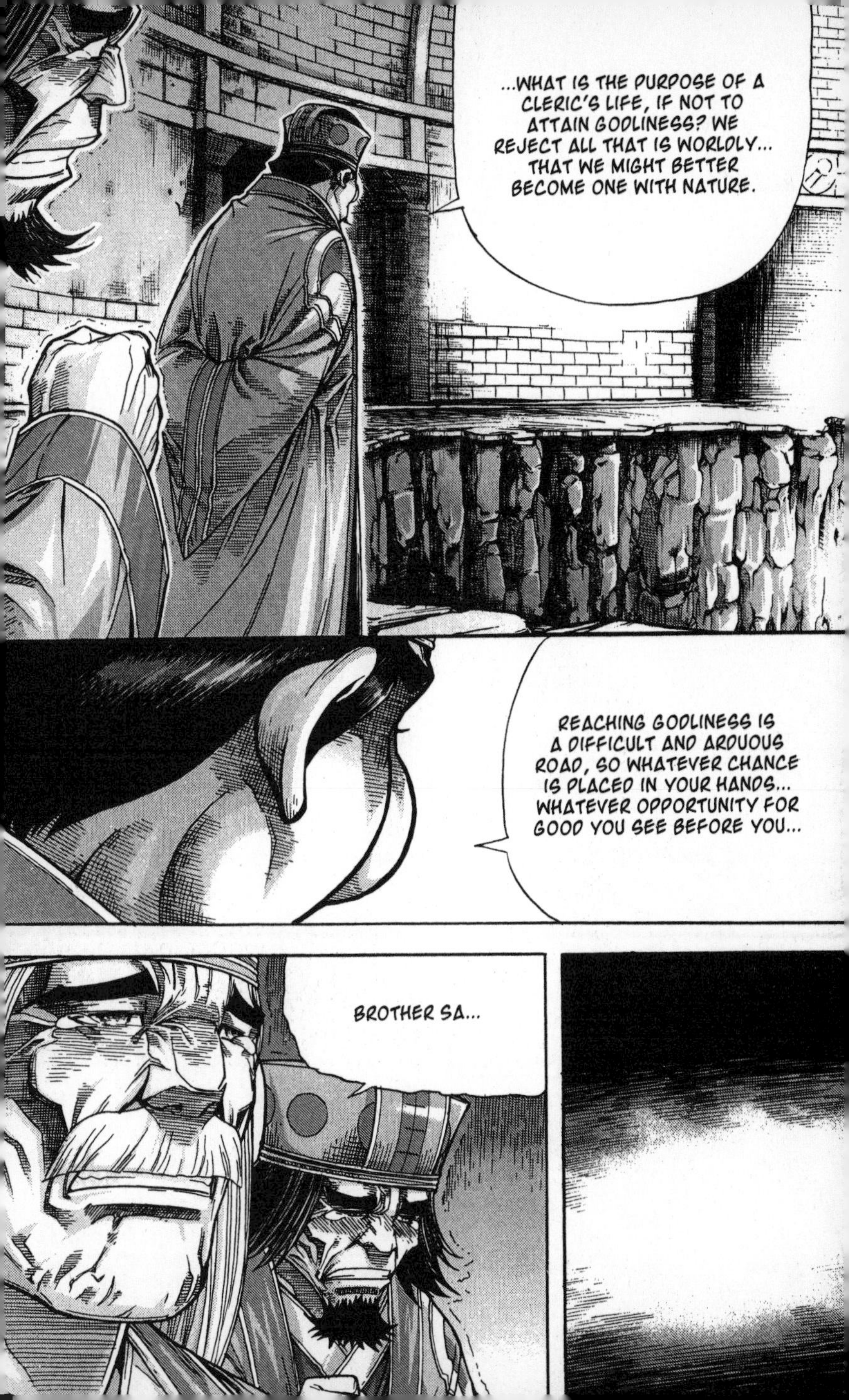
...WHAT IS THE PURPOSE OF A CLERIC'S LIFE, IF NOT TO ATTAIN GODLINESS? WE REJECT ALL THAT IS WORLDLY... THAT WE MIGHT BETTER BECOME ONE WITH NATURE.
REACHING GODLINESS IS A DIFFICULT AND ARDUOUS ROAD, SO WHATEVER CHANCE IS PLACED IN YOUR HANDS... WHATEVER OPPORTUNITY FOR GOOD YOU SEE BEFORE YOU...
BROTHER SA...

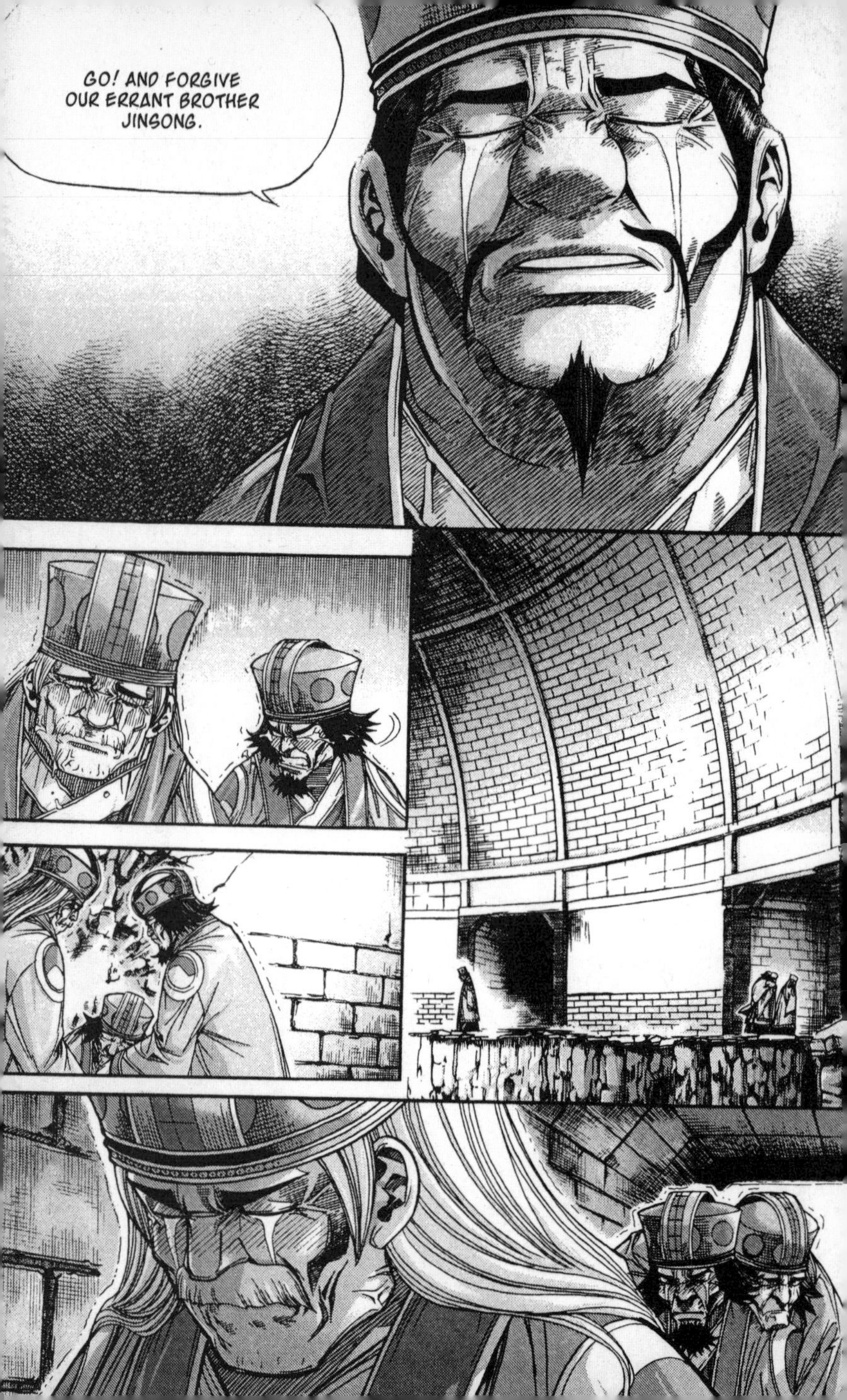
GO! AND FORGIVE OUR ERRANT BROTHER JINSONG.

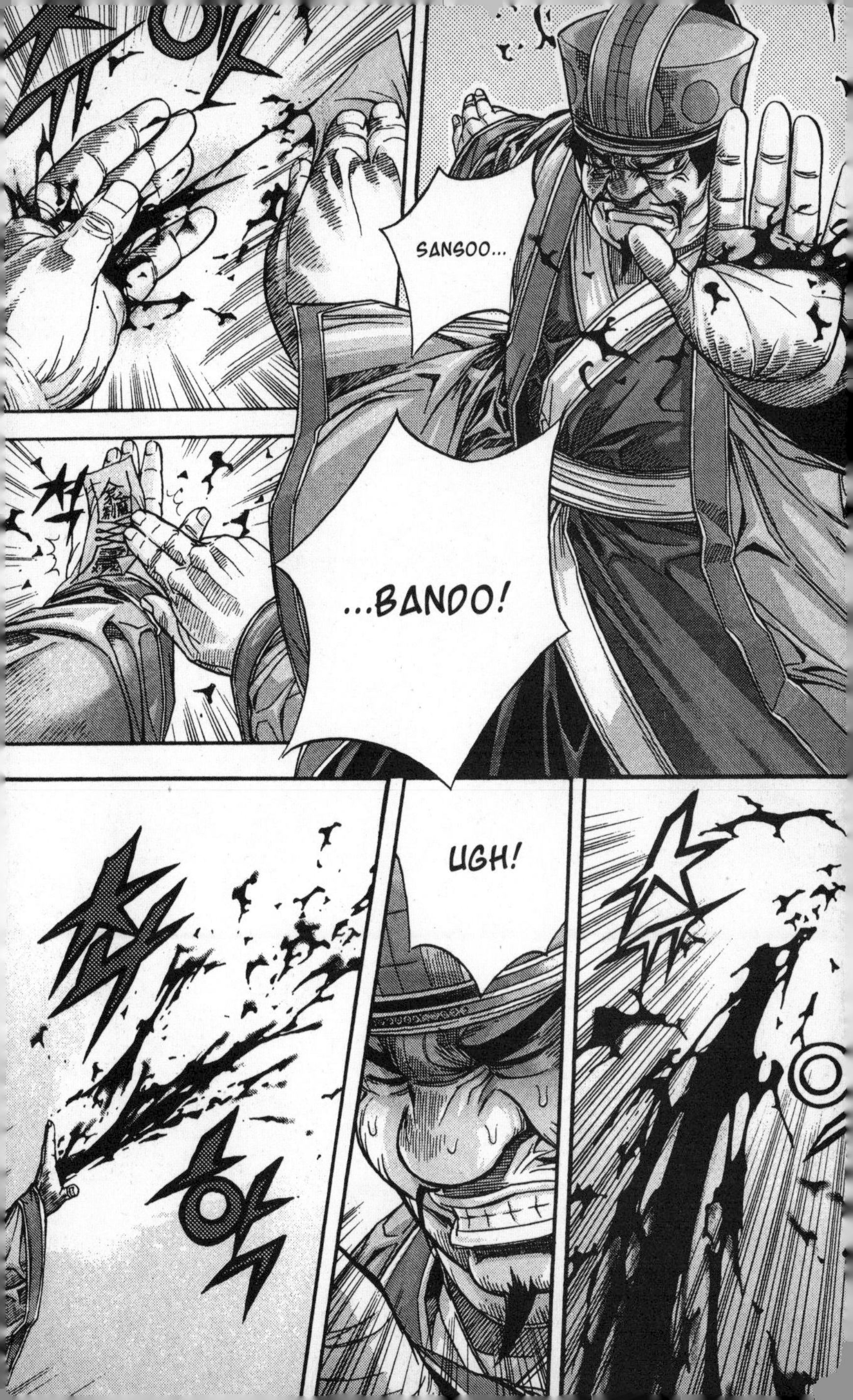
SANSOO...
...BANDO!
UGH!

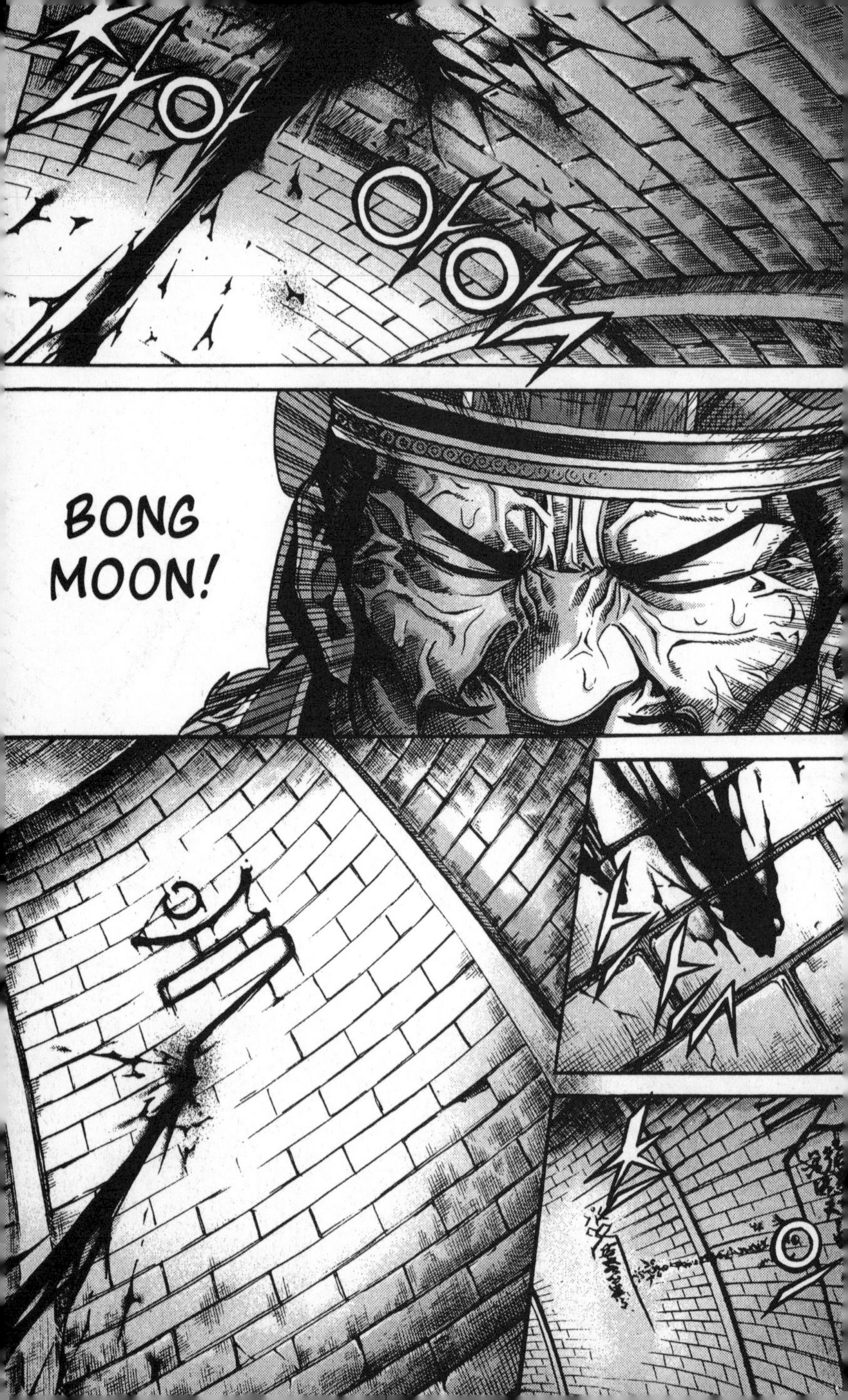
BONG
MOON!

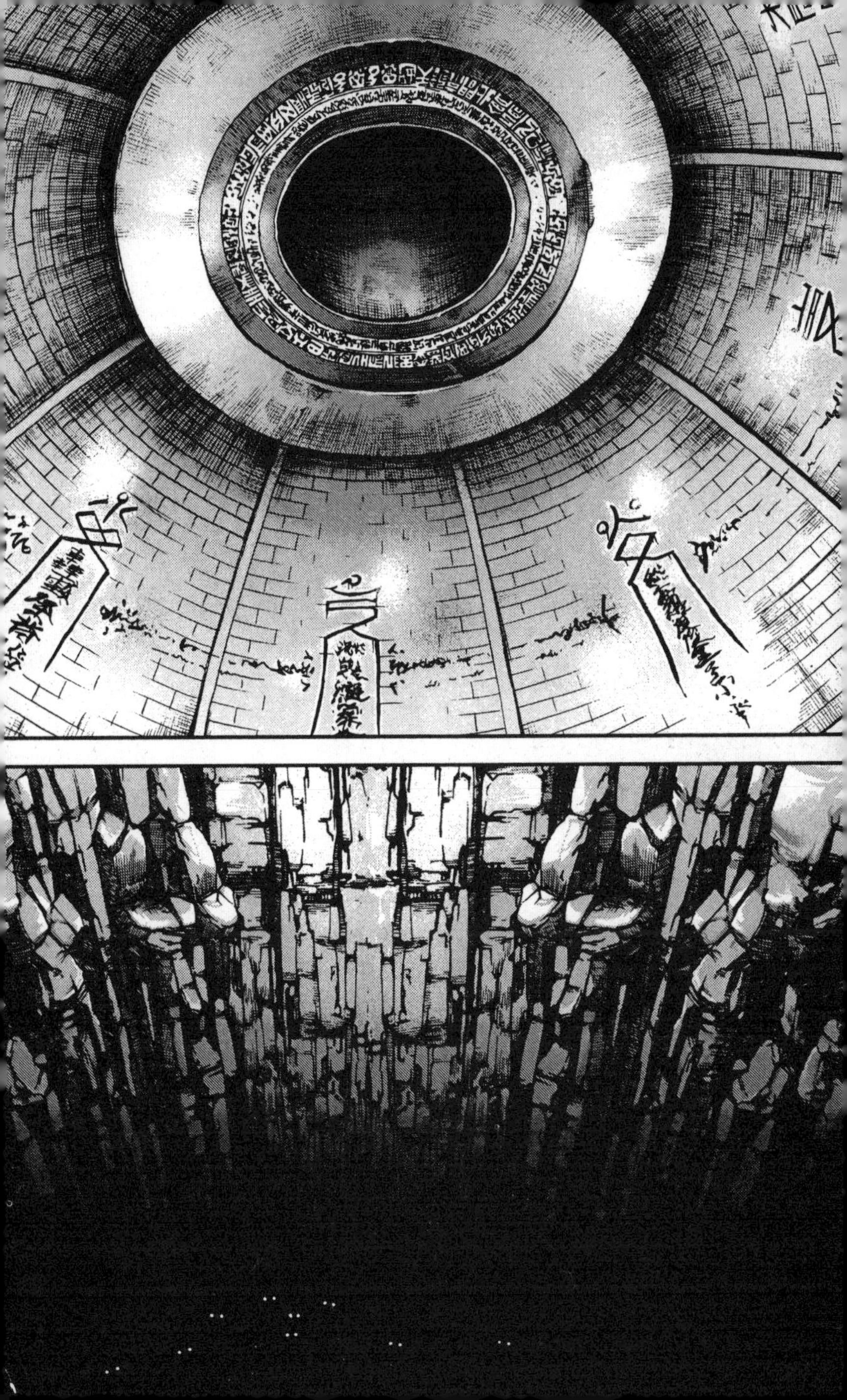

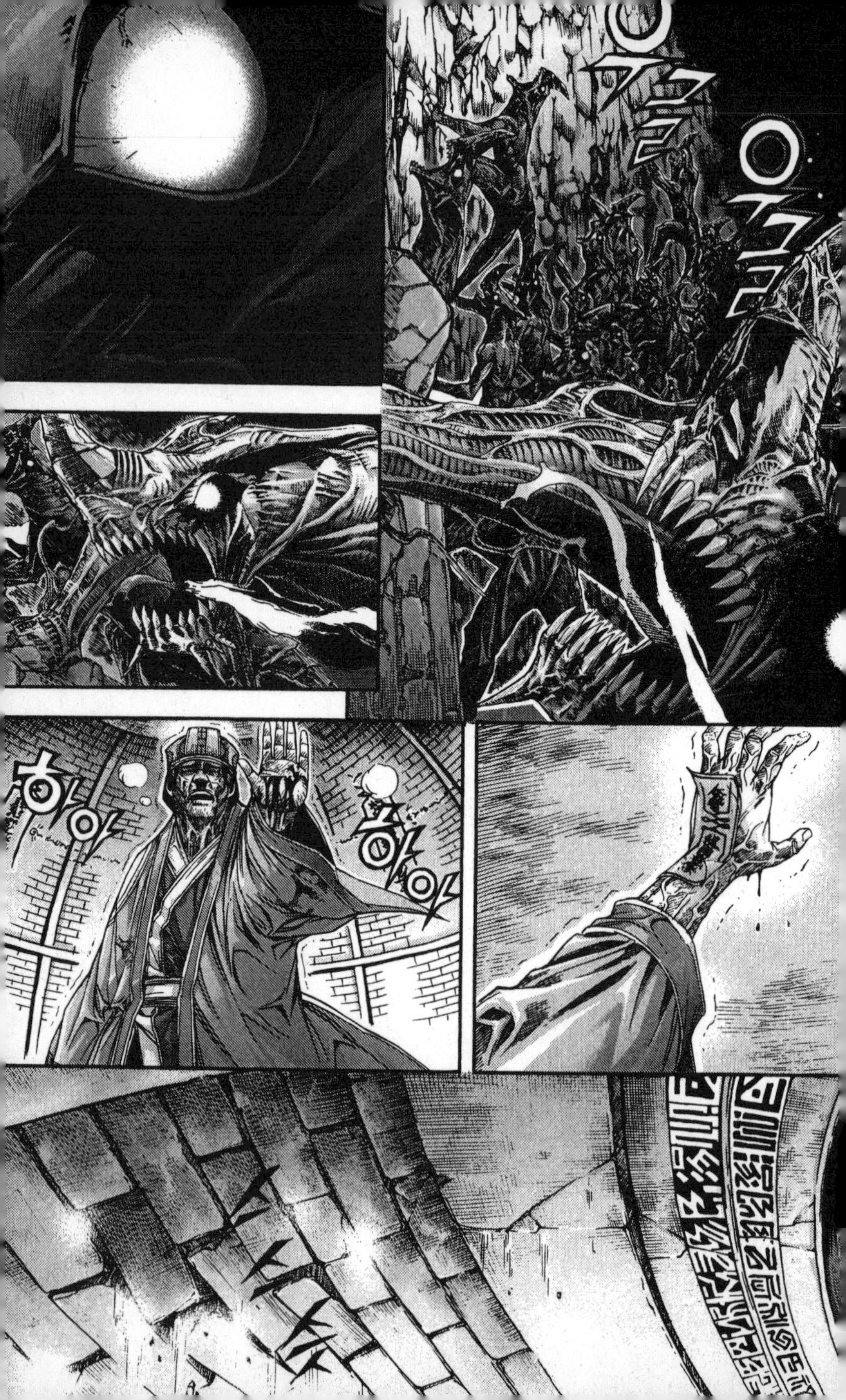

하아

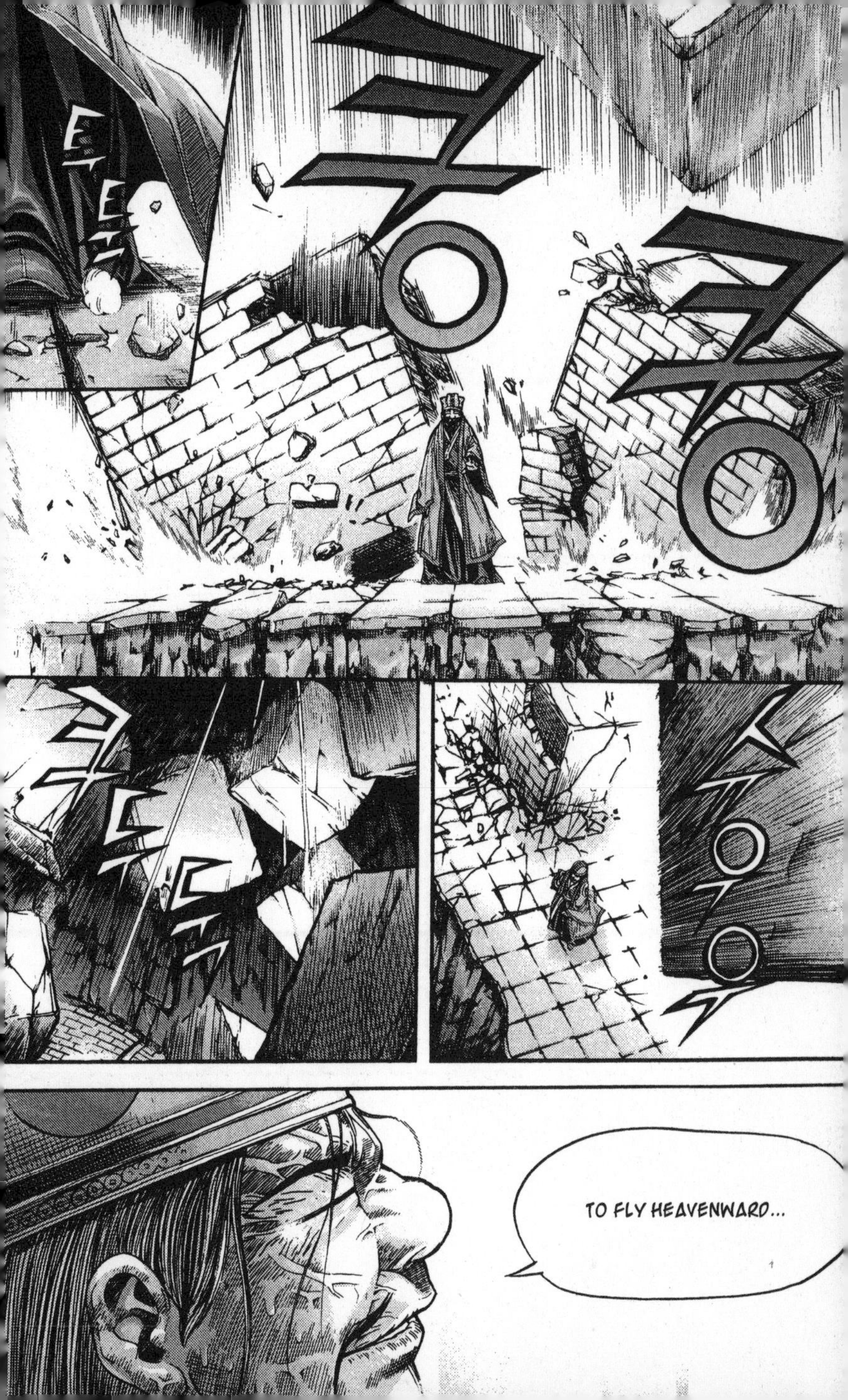
TO FLY HEAVENWARD...

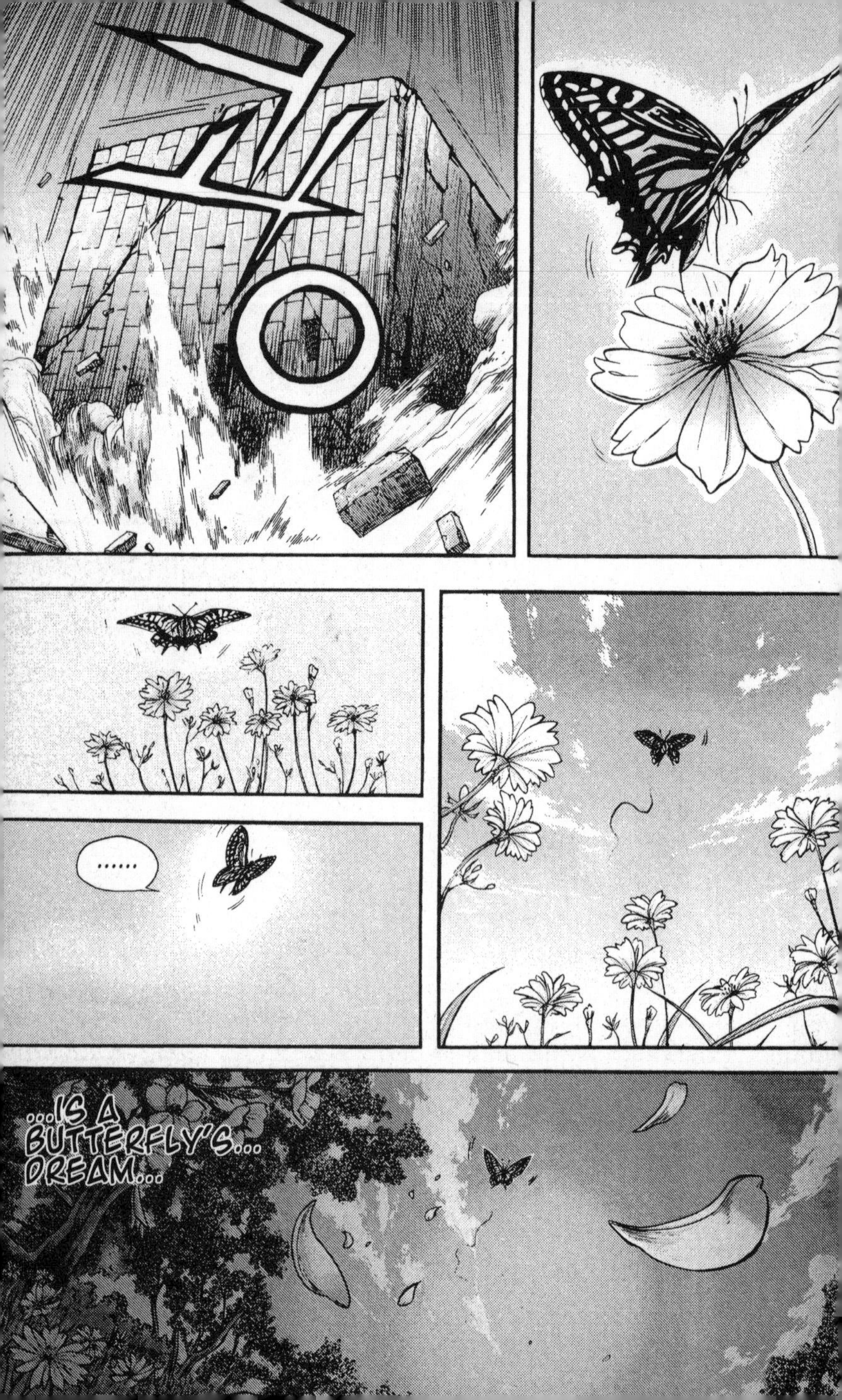

......
...IS A BUTTERFLY'S... DREAM...

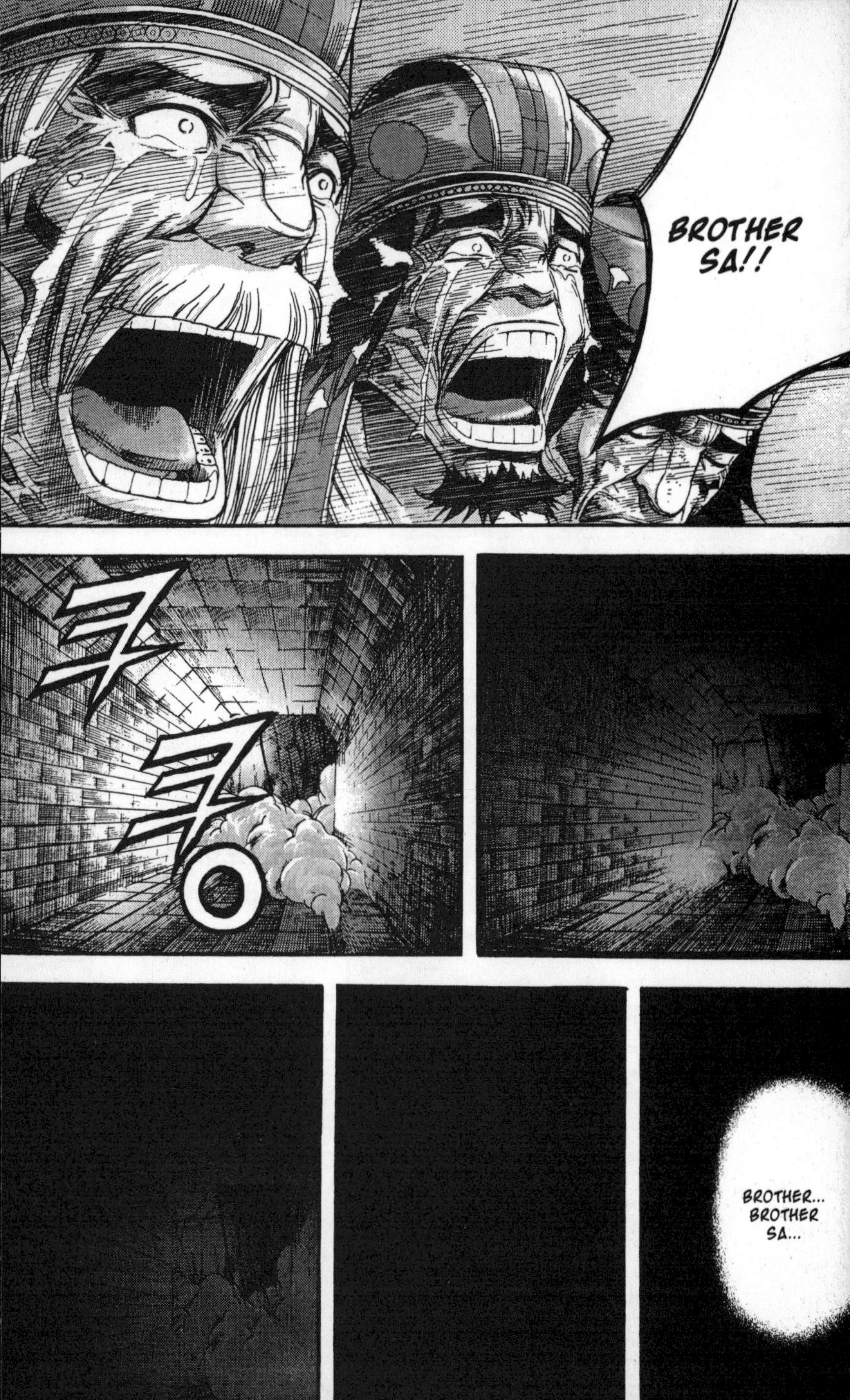
BROTHER SA!!
BROTHER... BROTHER SA...

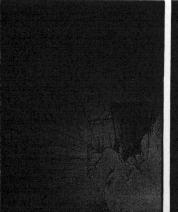

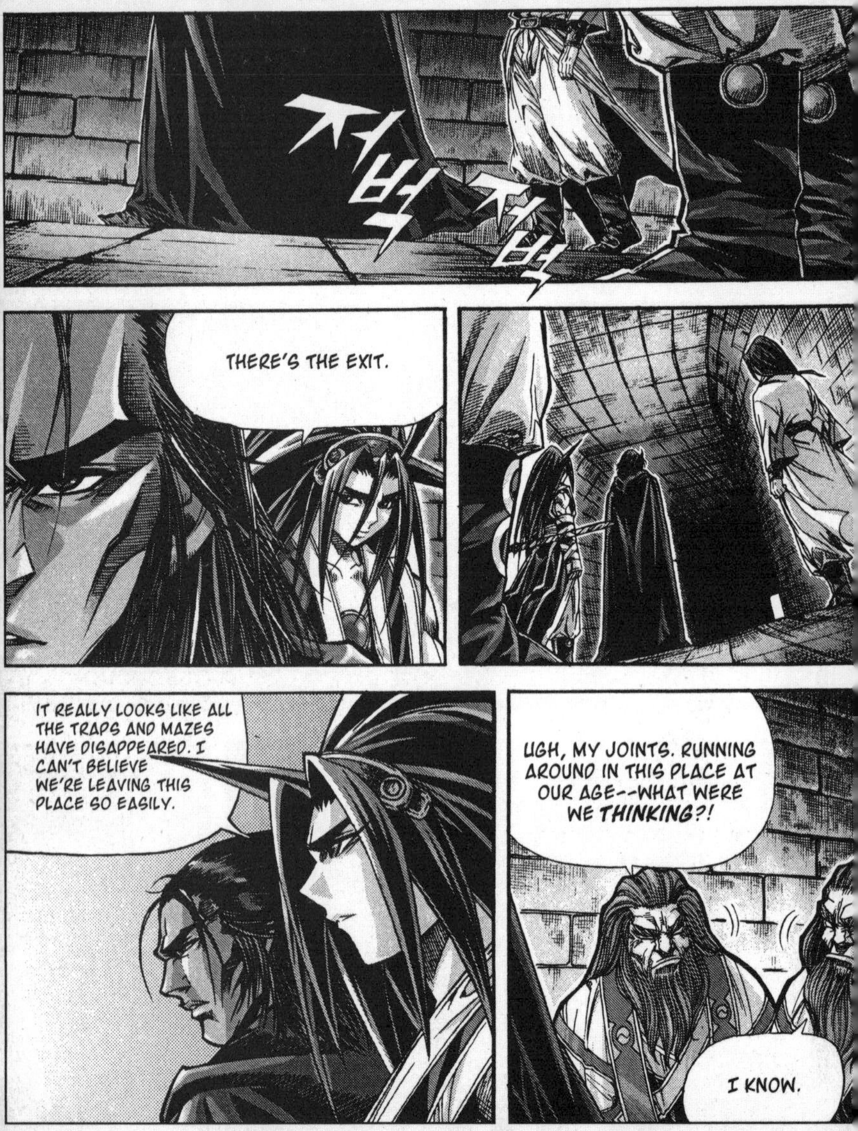
저벅 저벅
THERE'S THE EXIT.
IT REALLY LOOKS LIKE ALL THE TRAPS AND MAZES HAVE DISAPPEARED. I CAN'T BELIEVE WE'RE LEAVING THIS PLACE SO EASILY.
UGH, MY JOINTS. RUNNING AROUND IN THIS PLACE AT OUR AGE--WHAT WERE WE *THINKING*?!
I KNOW.

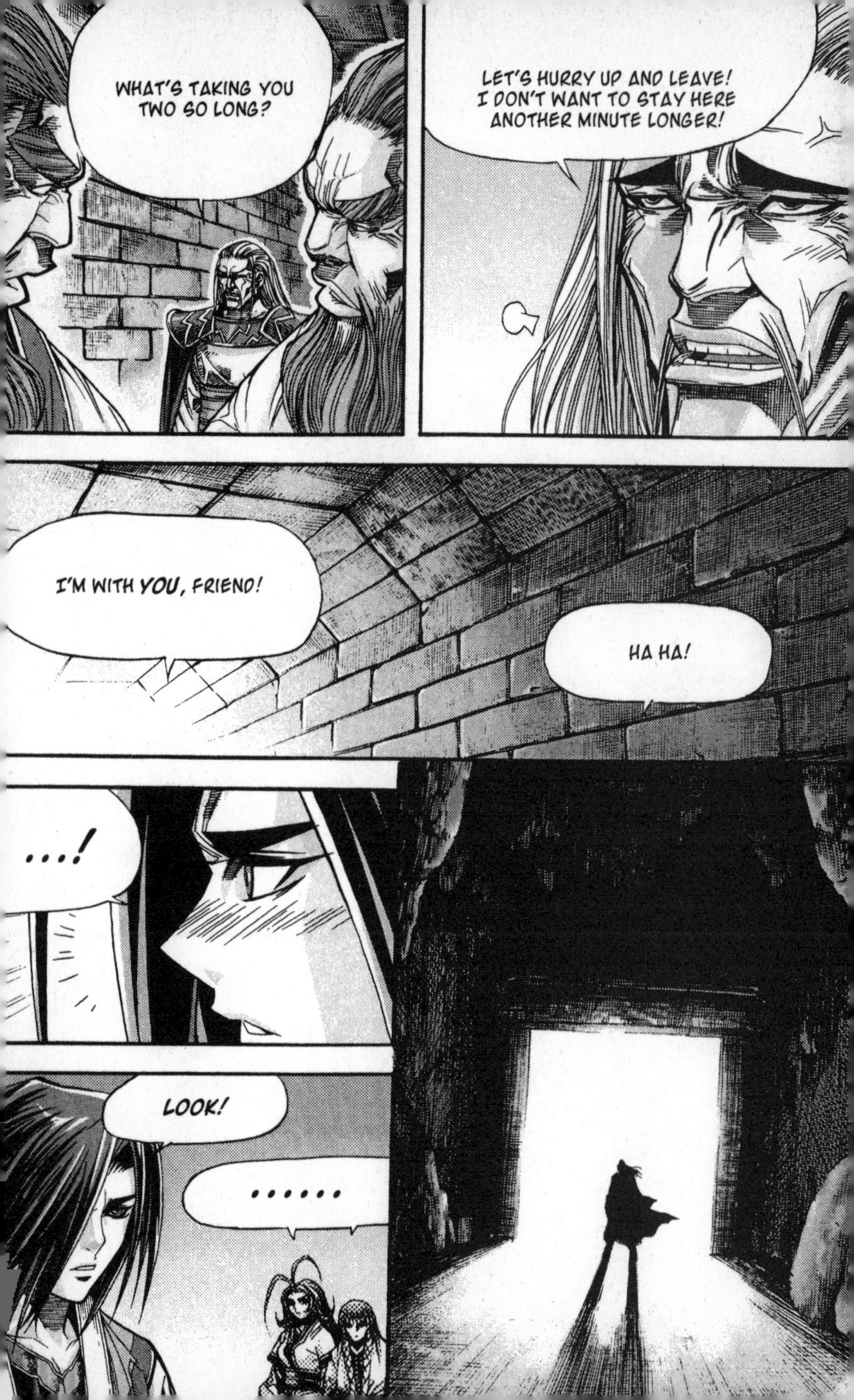
WHAT'S TAKING YOU TWO SO LONG?
LET'S HURRY UP AND LEAVE! I DON'T WANT TO STAY HERE ANOTHER MINUTE LONGER!
I'M WITH YOU, FRIEND!
HA HA!
...!
LOOK!
......

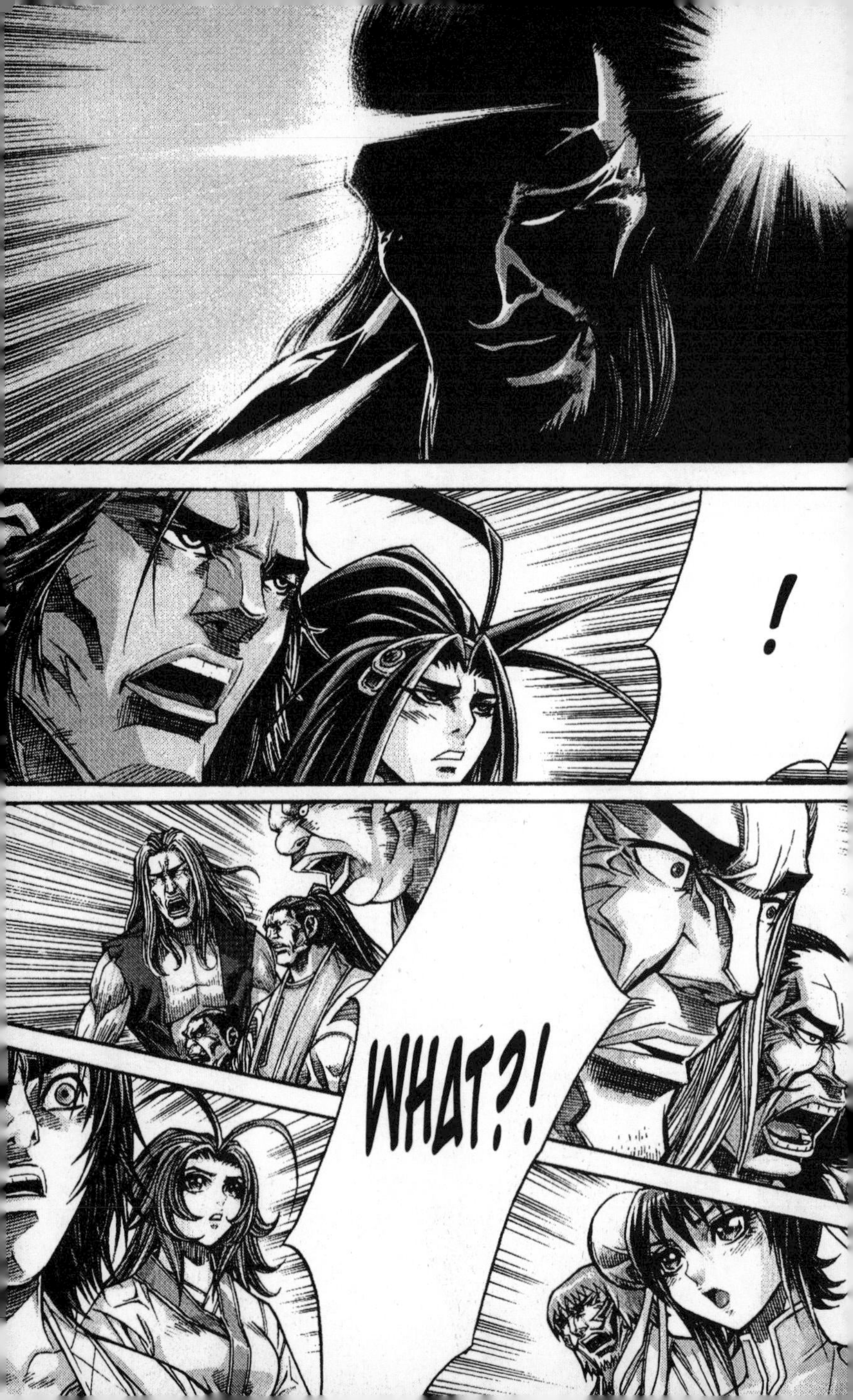
!
WHAT?!

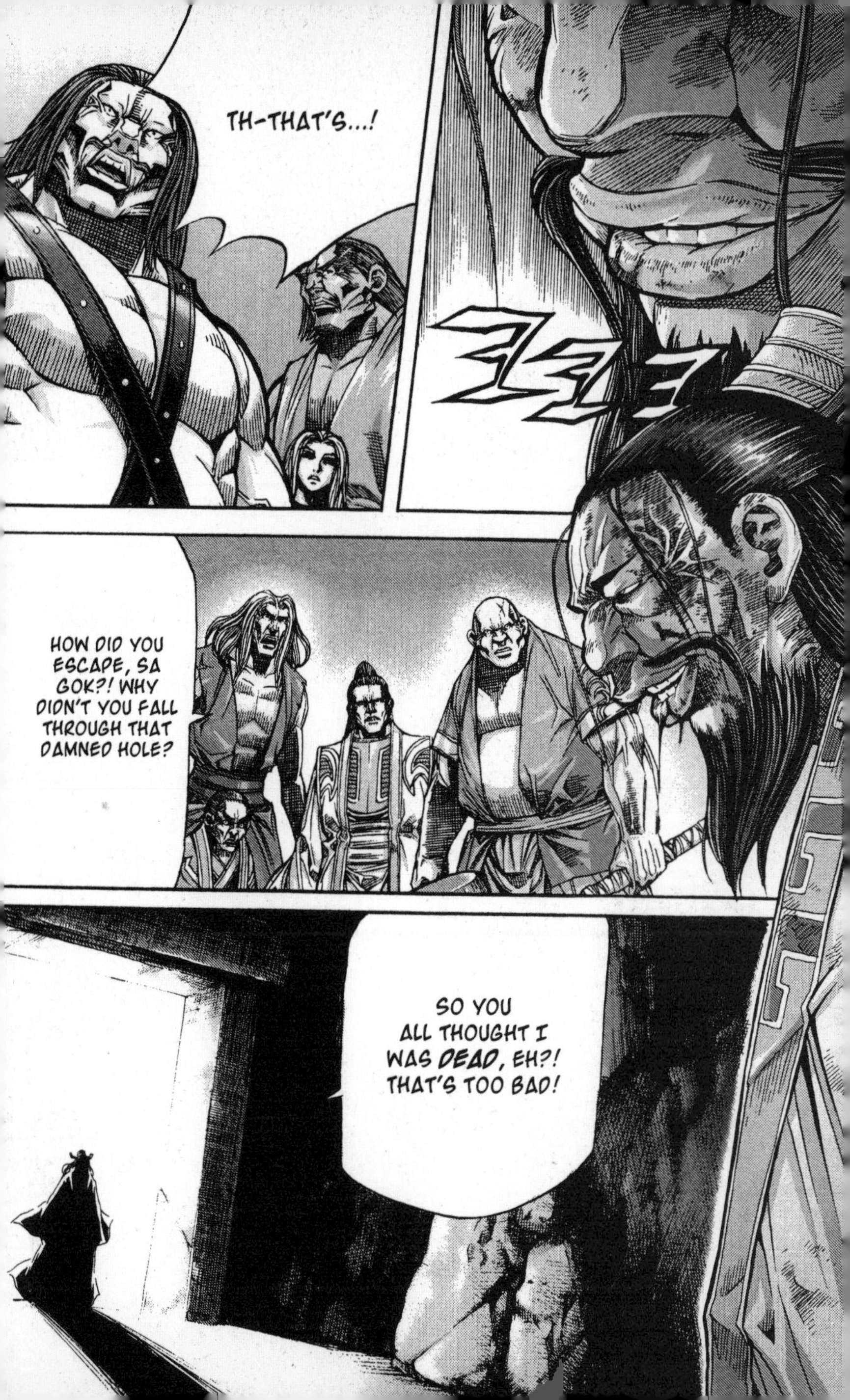
TH-THAT'S...!
HOW DID YOU ESCAPE, SA GOK?! WHY DIDN'T YOU FALL THROUGH THAT DAMNED HOLE?
SO YOU ALL THOUGHT I WAS DEAD, EH?! THAT'S TOO BAD!

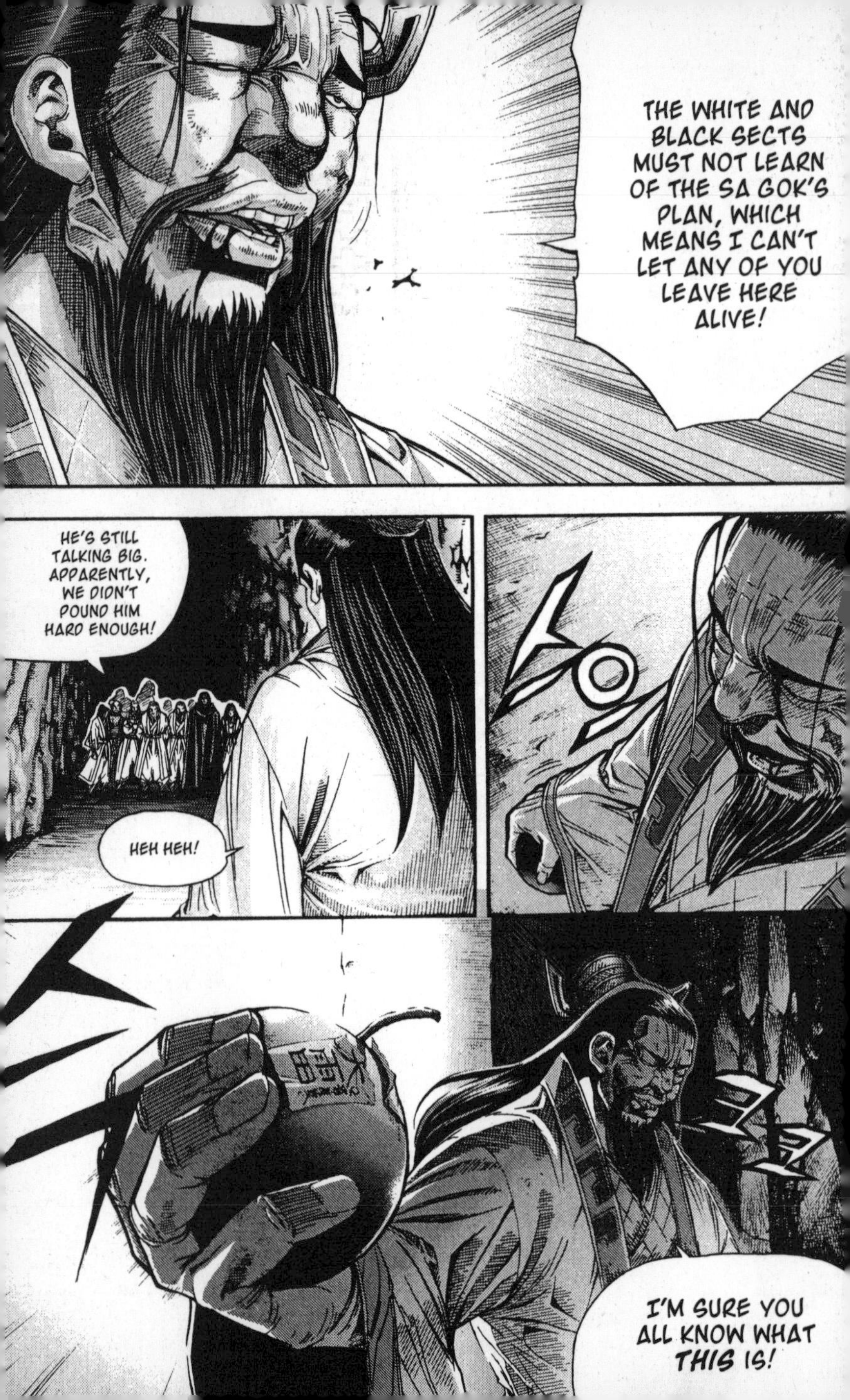
THE WHITE AND BLACK SECTS MUST NOT LEARN OF THE SA GOK'S PLAN, WHICH MEANS I CAN'T LET ANY OF YOU LEAVE HERE ALIVE!
HE'S STILL TALKING BIG. APPARENTLY, WE DIDN'T POUND HIM HARD ENOUGH!
HEH HEH!
I'M SURE YOU ALL KNOW WHAT THIS IS!

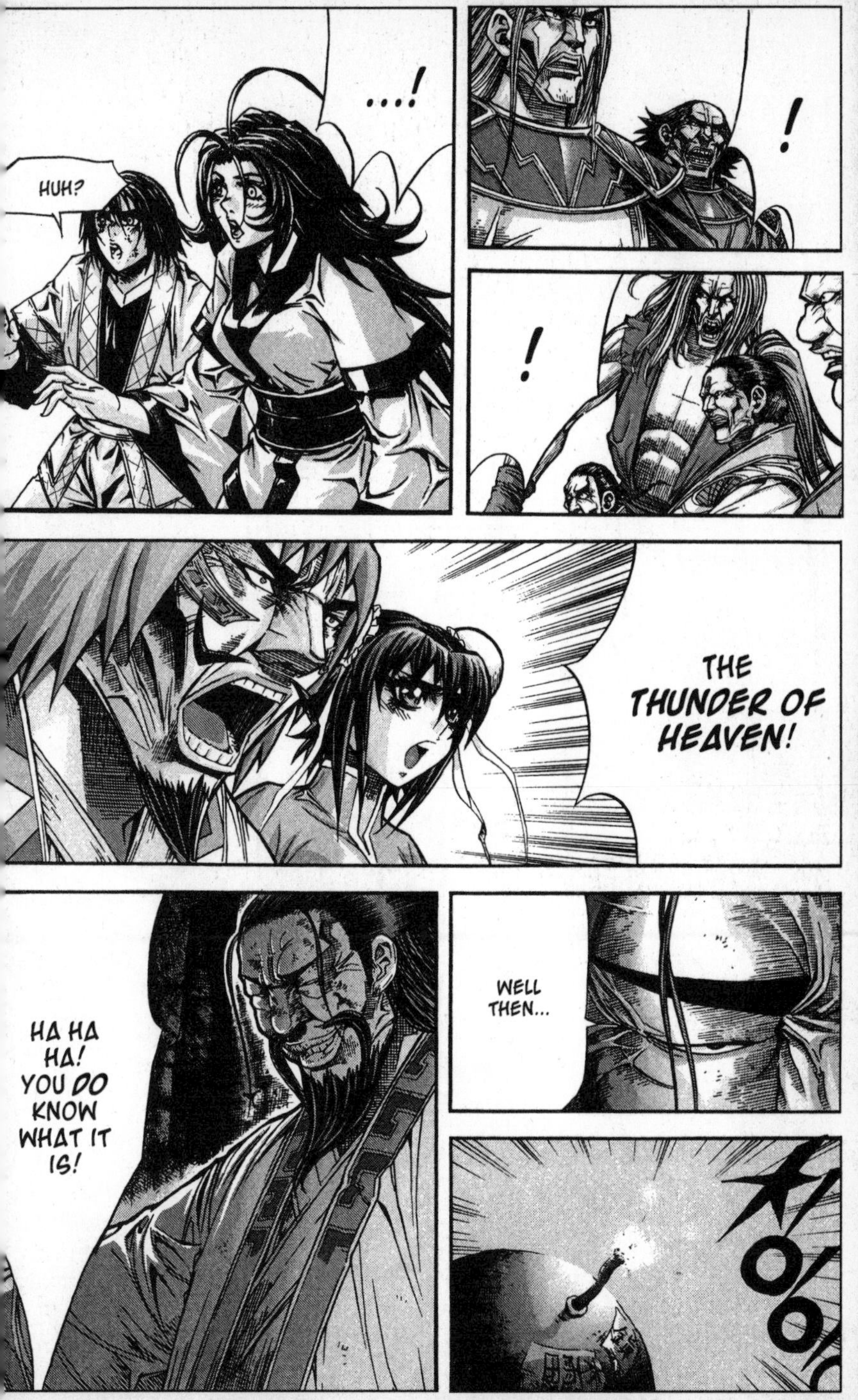
HUH?
...!
!
!
THE THUNDER OF HEAVEN!
HA HA HA! YOU DO KNOW WHAT IT IS!
WELL THEN...

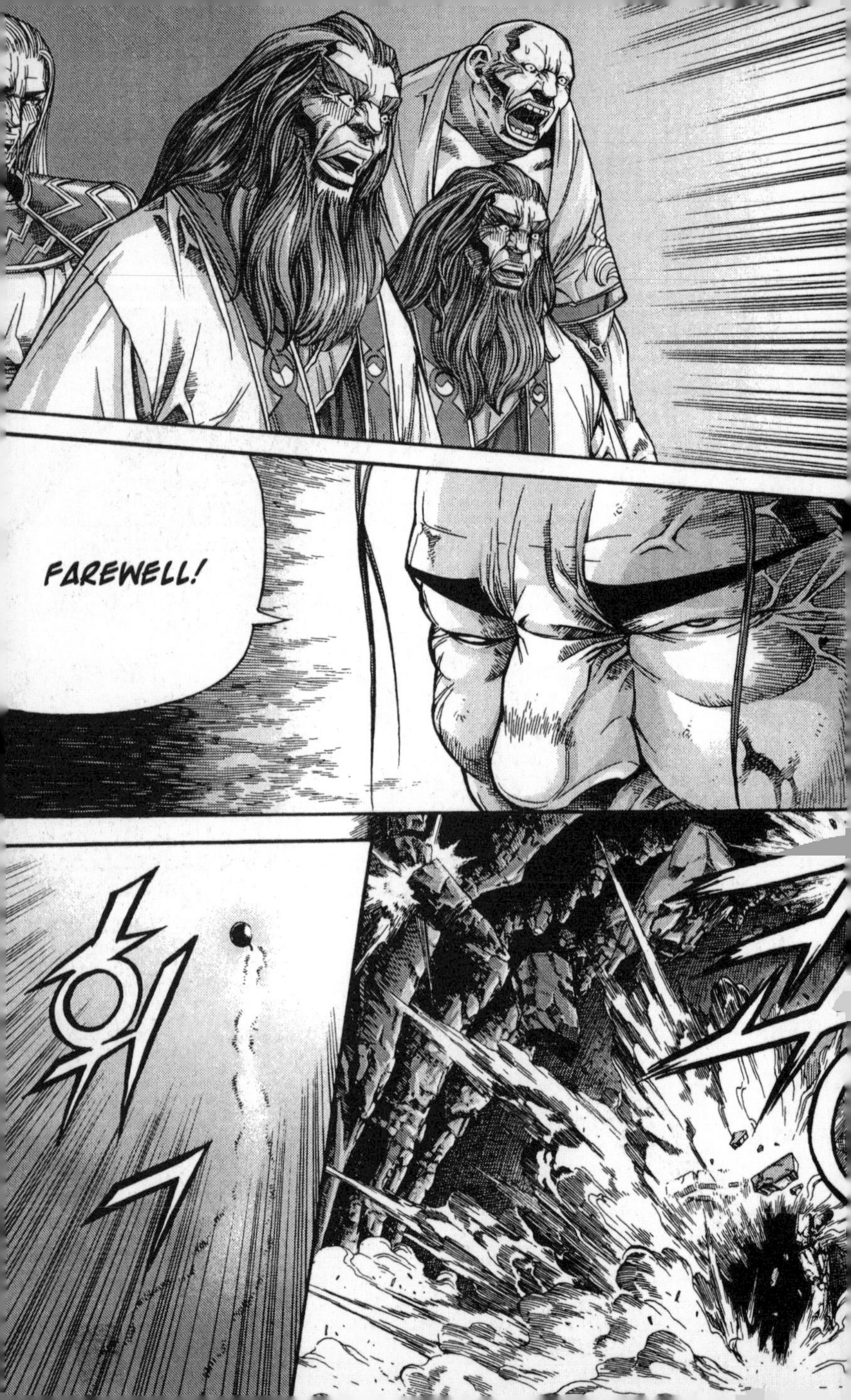
FAREWELL!

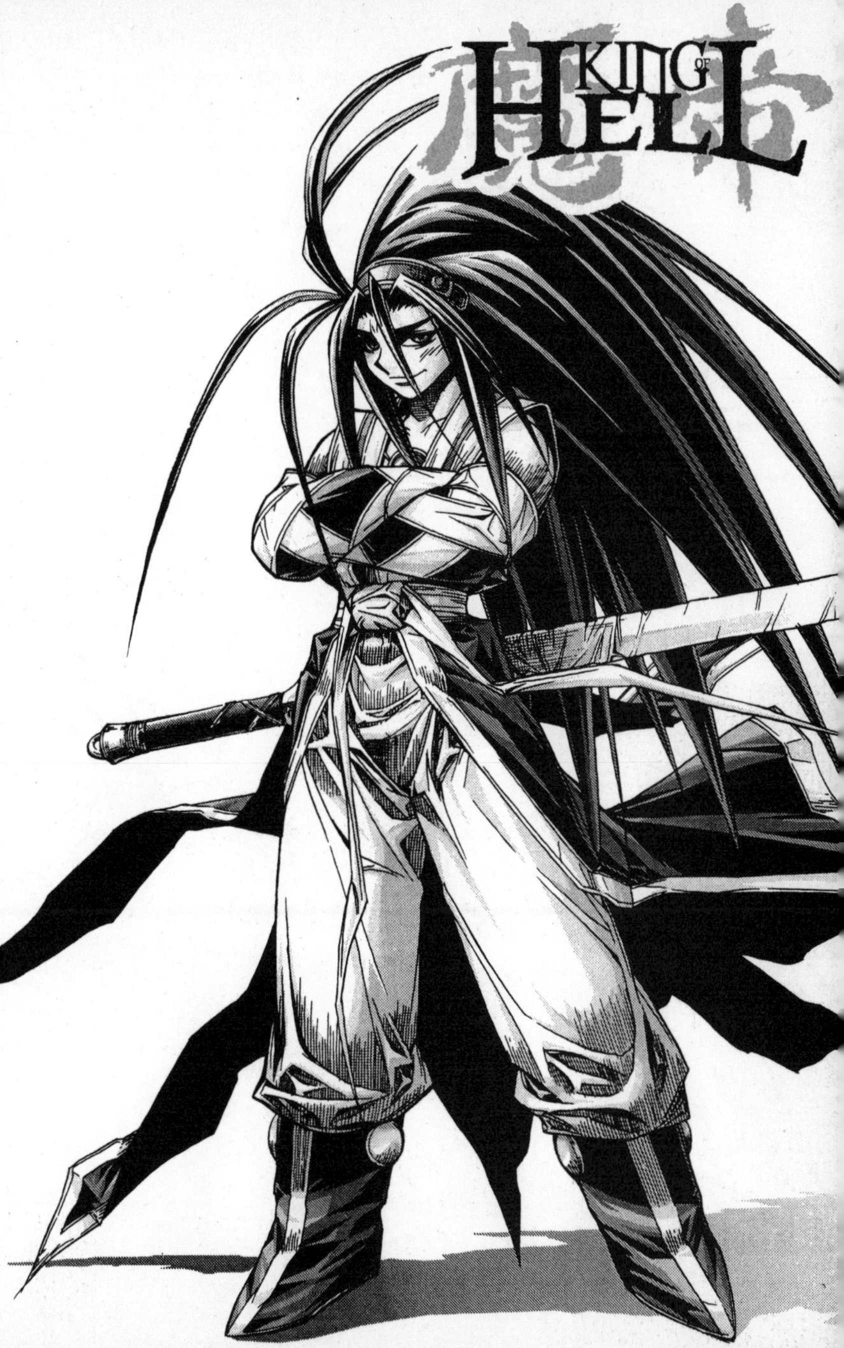

KING OF HELL

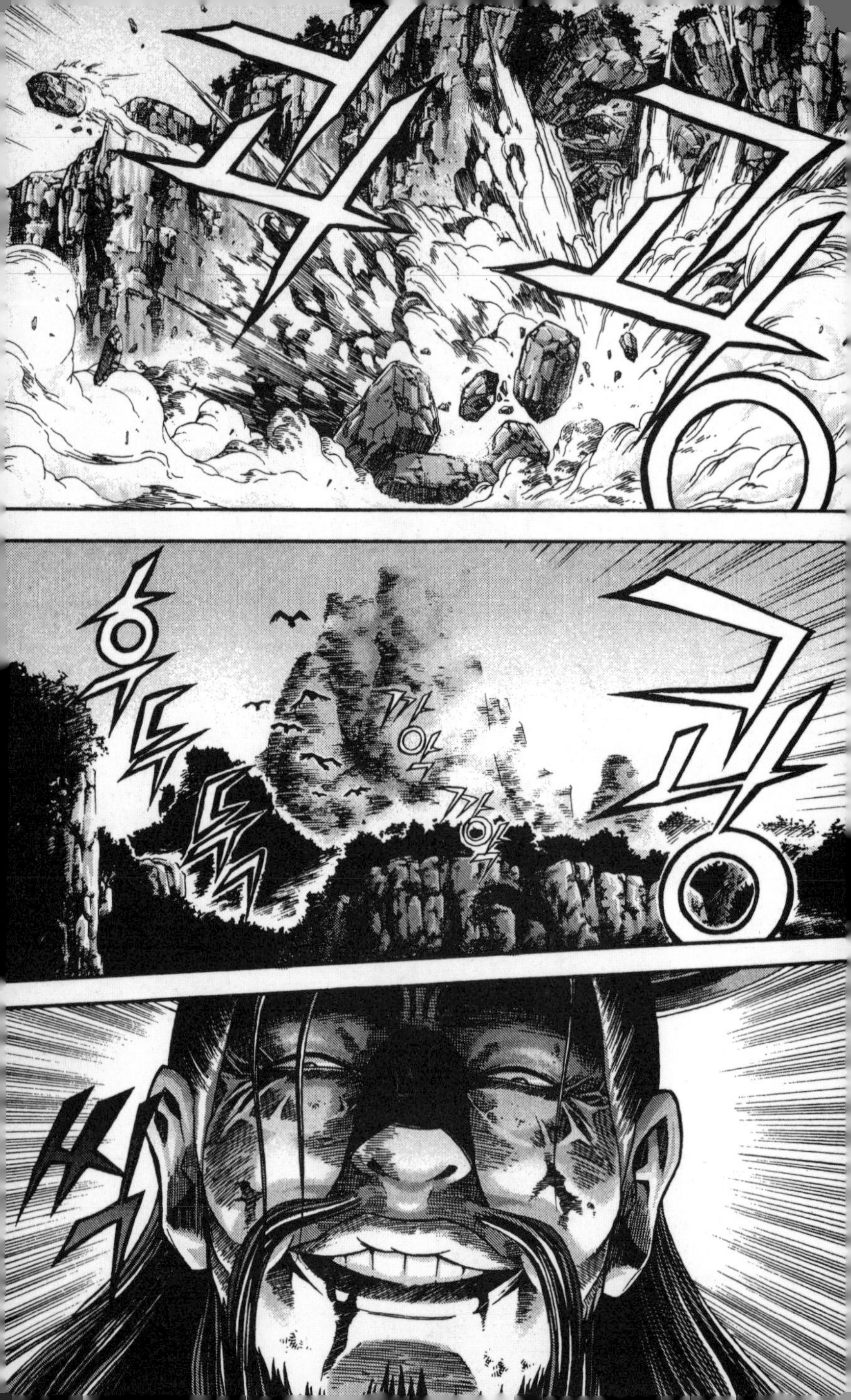
까악
까악

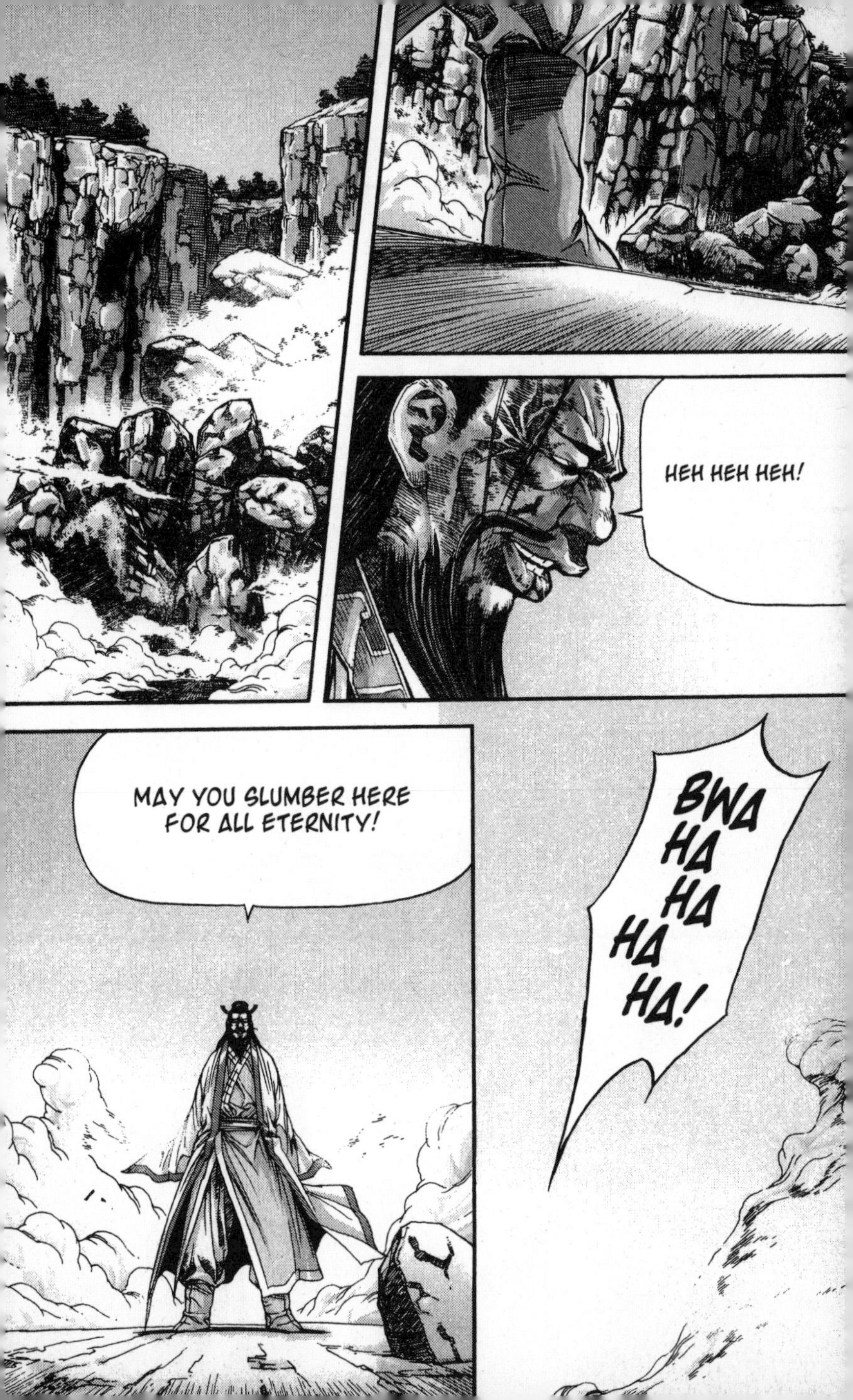
HEH HEH HEH!
MAY YOU SLUMBER HERE FOR ALL ETERNITY!
BWA HA HA HA HA!

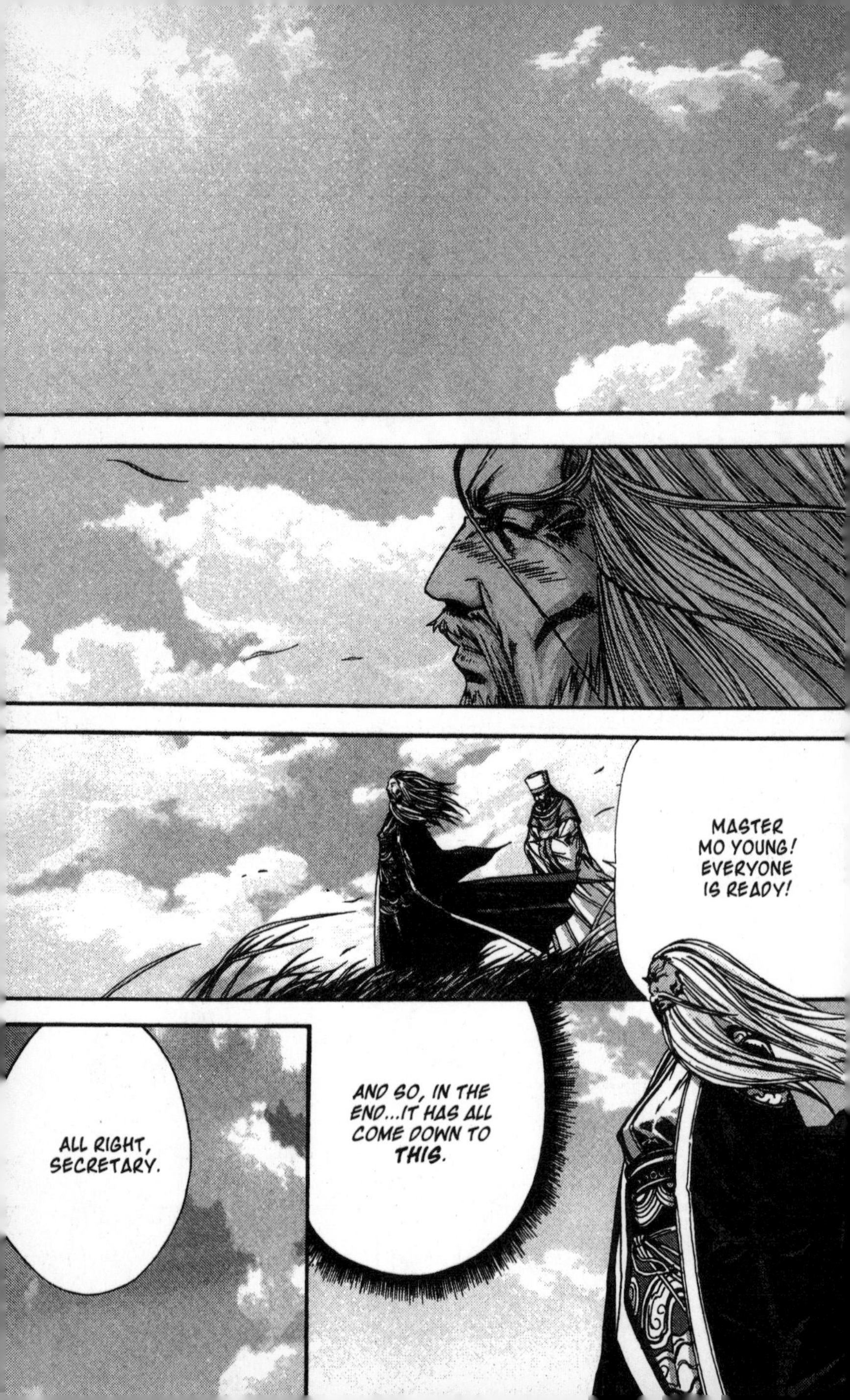
MASTER MO YOUNG! EVERYONE IS READY!
AND SO, IN THE END...IT HAS ALL COME DOWN TO THIS.
ALL RIGHT, SECRETARY.

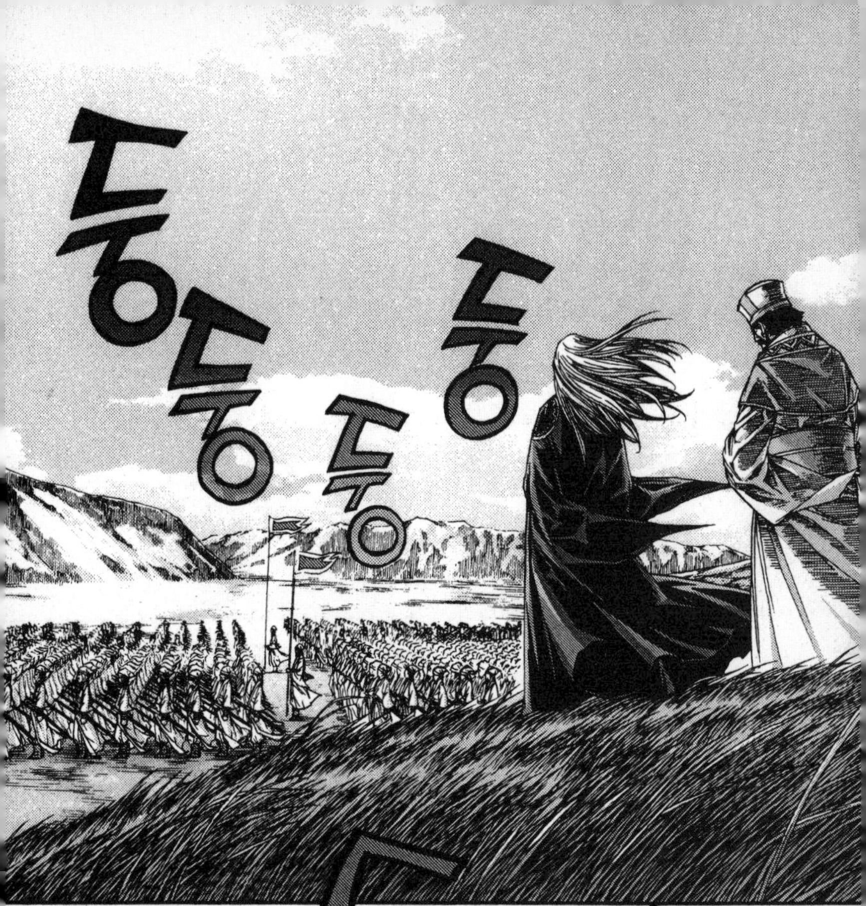
둥
둥
둥
둥

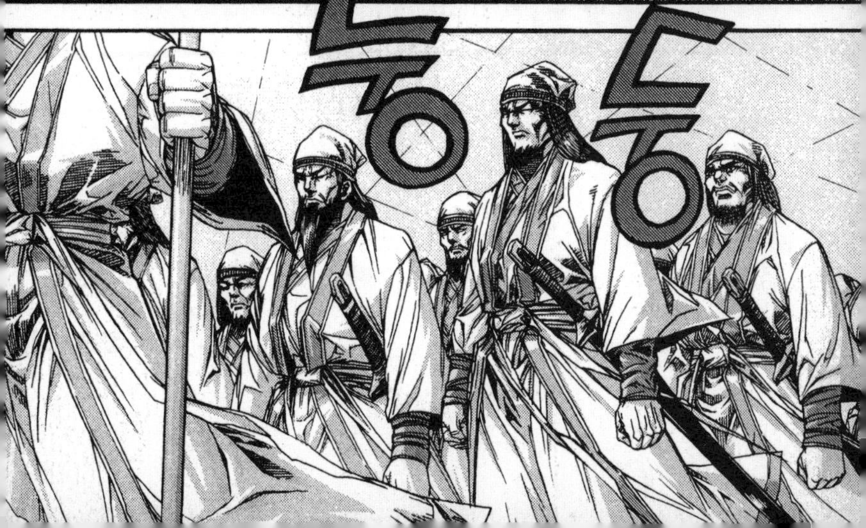
둥
둥

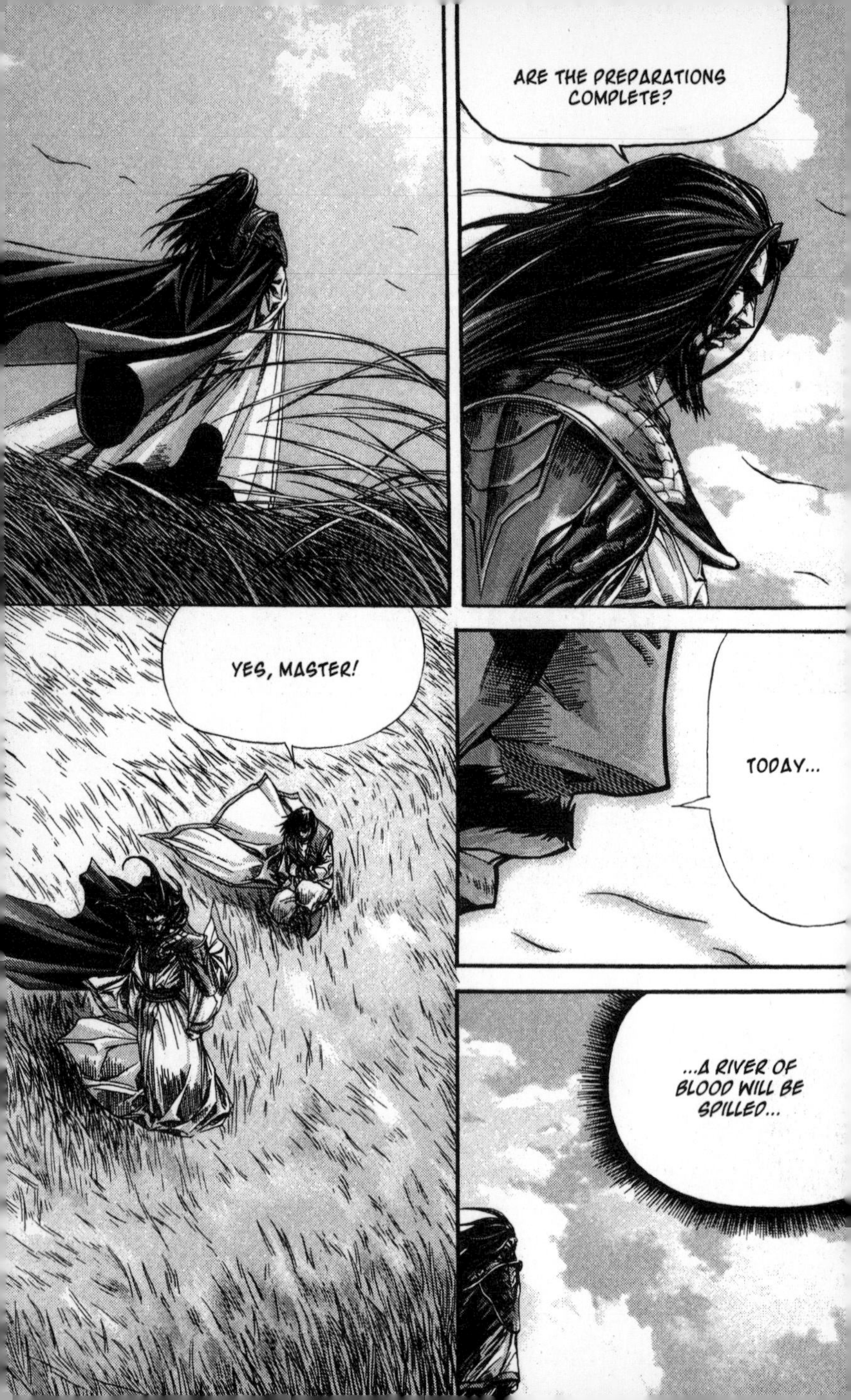
ARE THE PREPARATIONS COMPLETE?
YES, MASTER!
TODAY...
...A RIVER OF BLOOD WILL BE SPILLED...

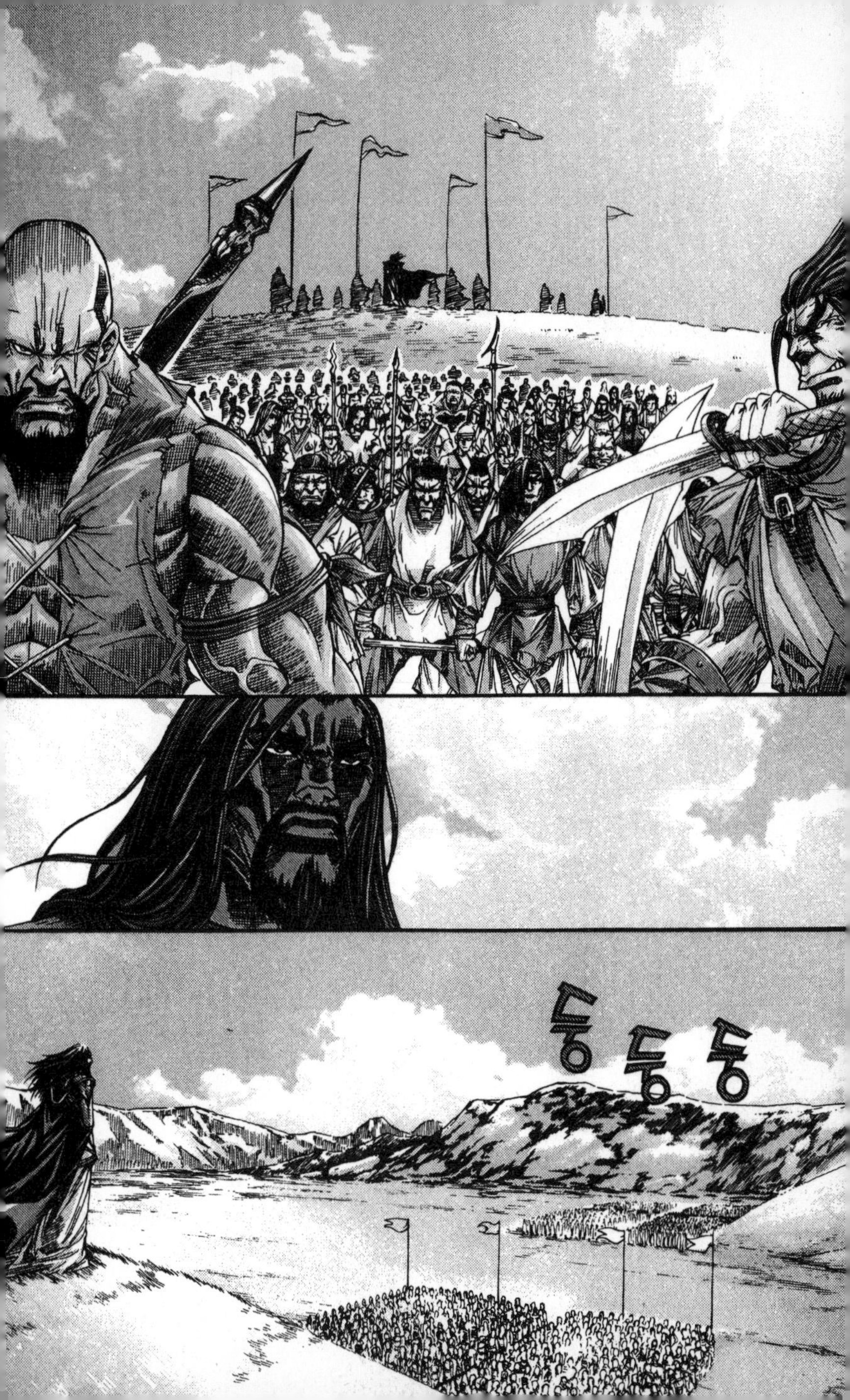
둥
둥
둥

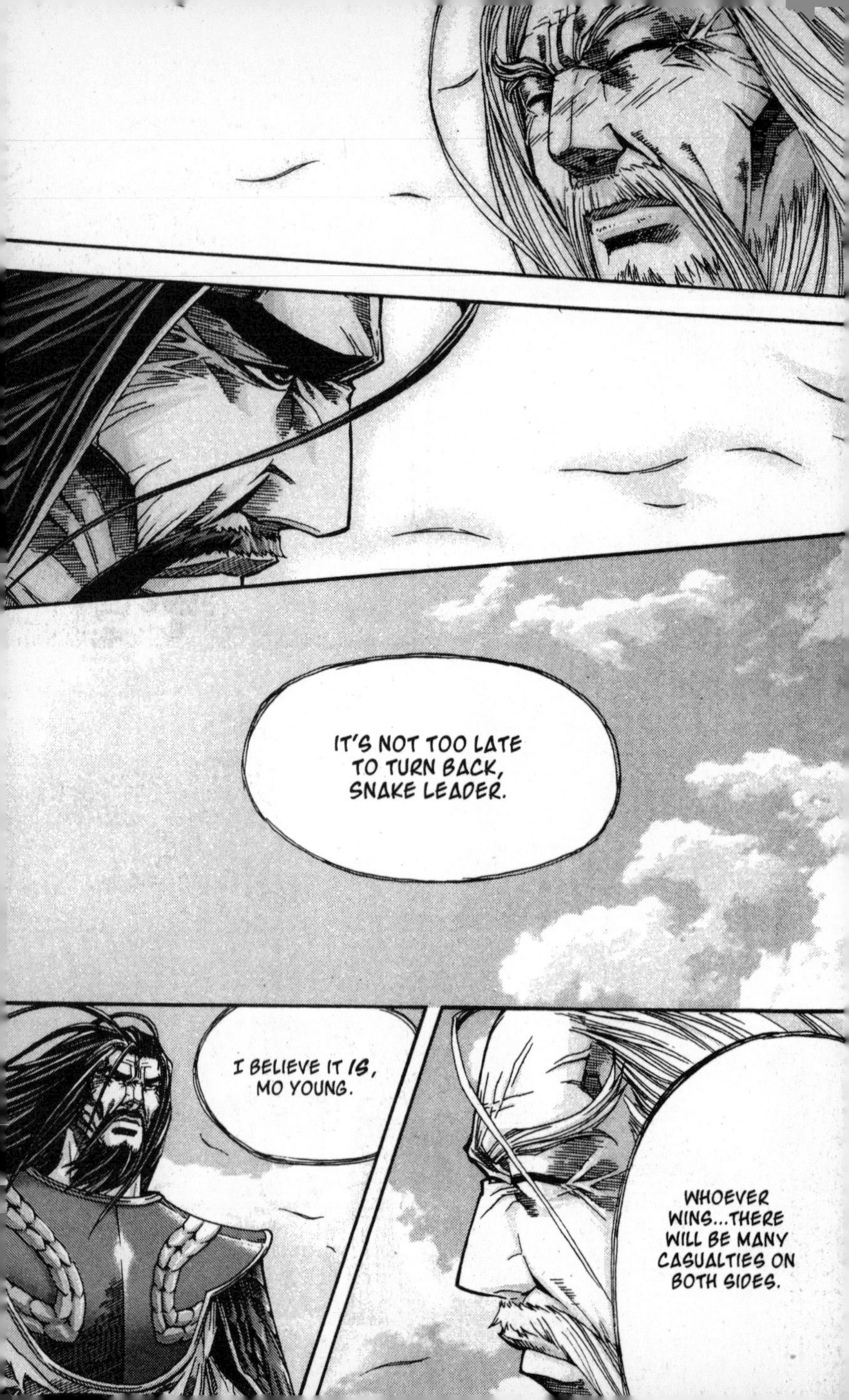
IT'S NOT TOO LATE TO TURN BACK, SNAKE LEADER.
I BELIEVE IT *IS*, MO YOUNG.
WHOEVER WINS...THERE WILL BE MANY CASUALTIES ON BOTH SIDES.

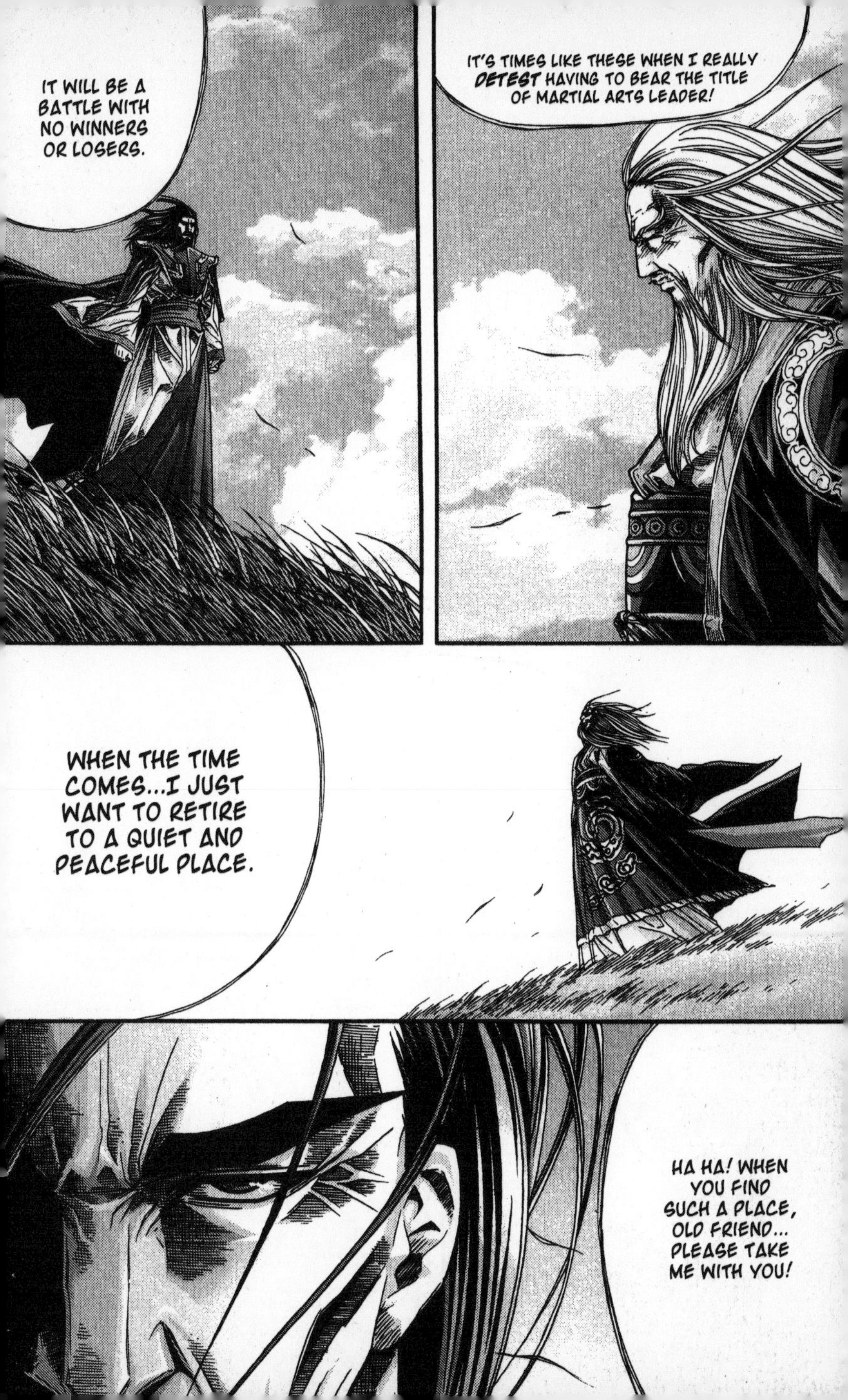
IT WILL BE A BATTLE WITH NO WINNERS OR LOSERS.
IT'S TIMES LIKE THESE WHEN I REALLY DETEST HAVING TO BEAR THE TITLE OF MARTIAL ARTS LEADER!
WHEN THE TIME COMES...I JUST WANT TO RETIRE TO A QUIET AND PEACEFUL PLACE.
HA HA! WHEN YOU FIND SUCH A PLACE, OLD FRIEND... PLEASE TAKE ME WITH YOU!

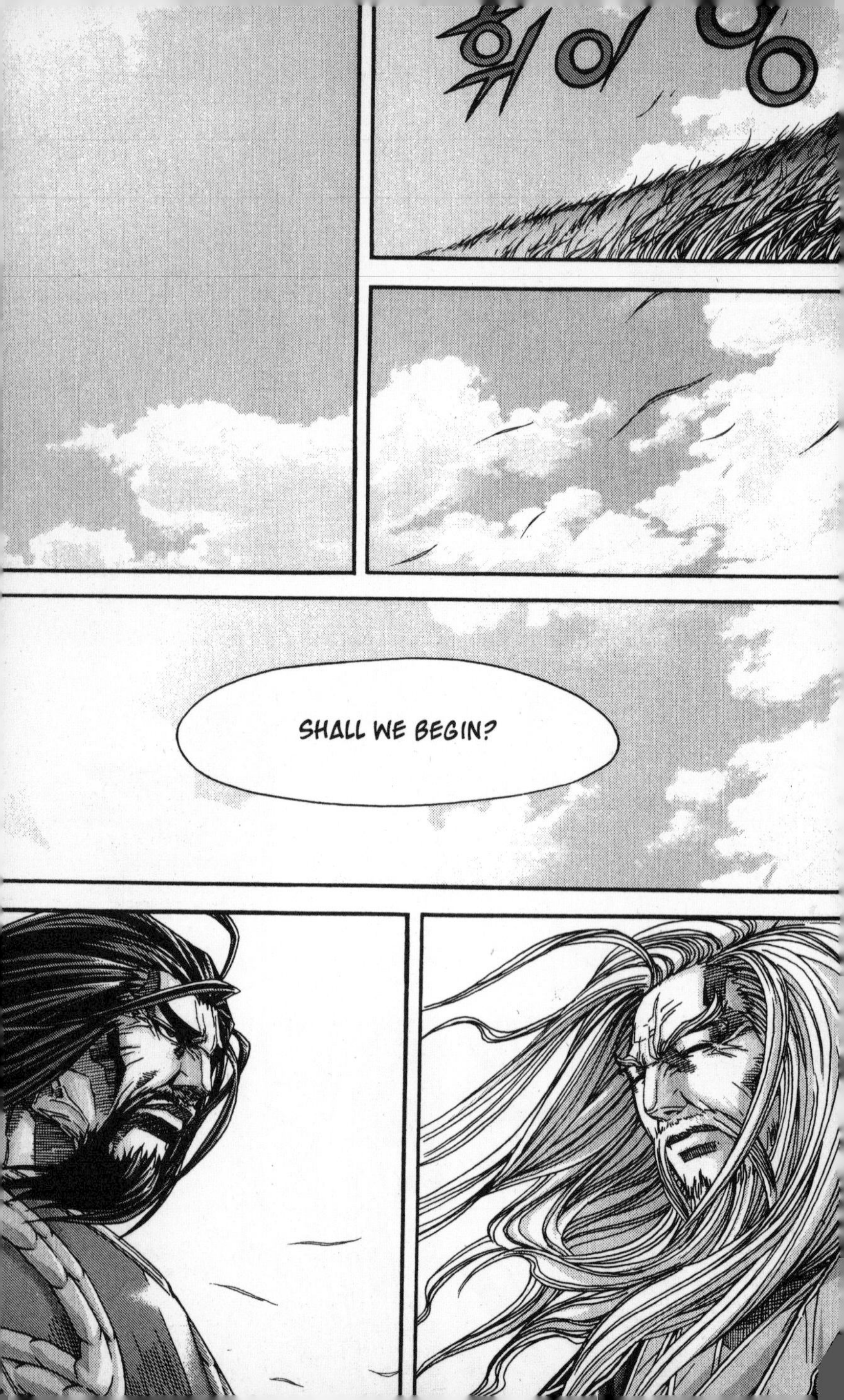
SHALL WE BEGIN?

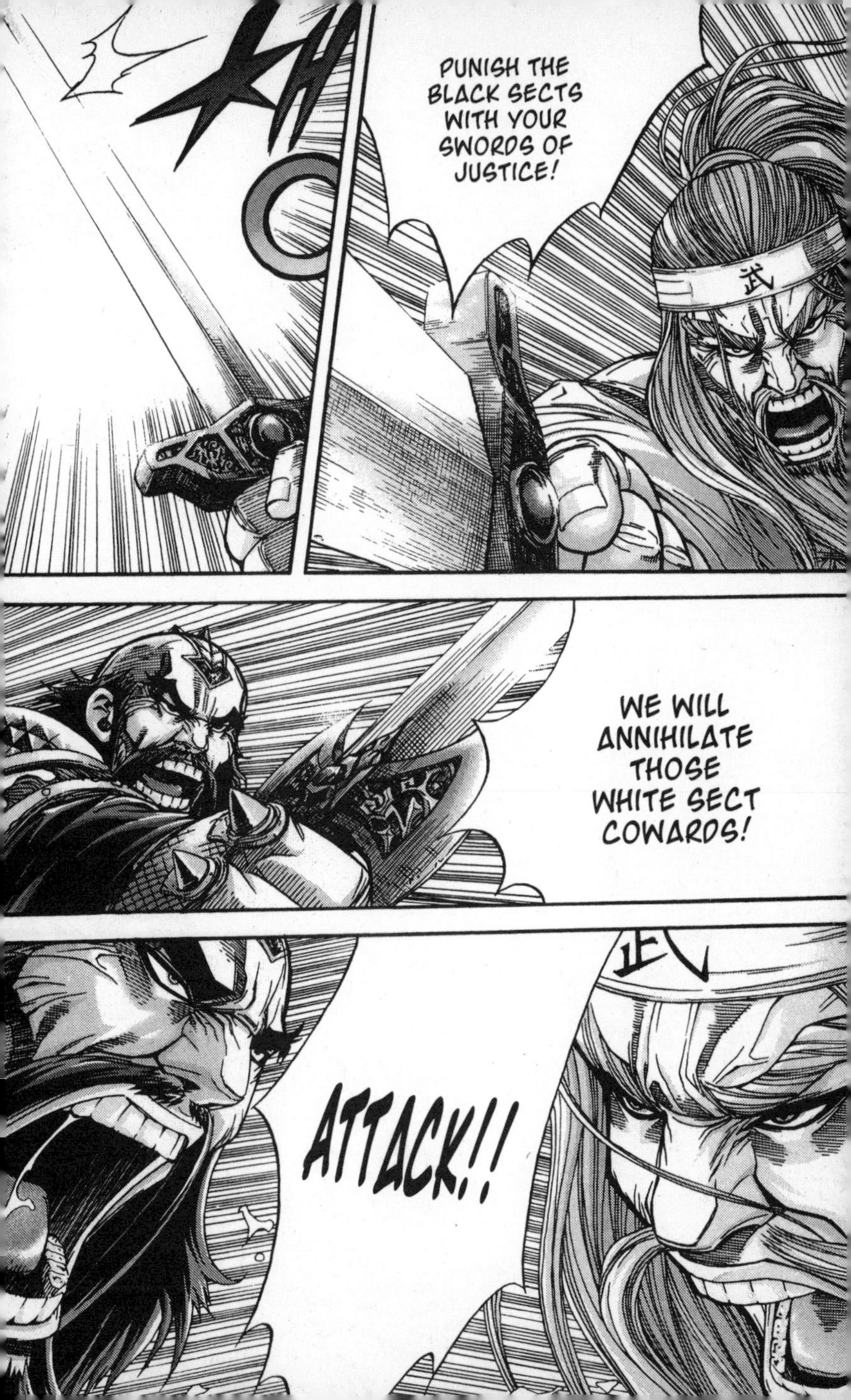
PUNISH THE BLACK SECTS WITH YOUR SWORDS OF JUSTICE!
WE WILL ANNIHILATE THOSE WHITE SECT COWARDS!
ATTACK!!

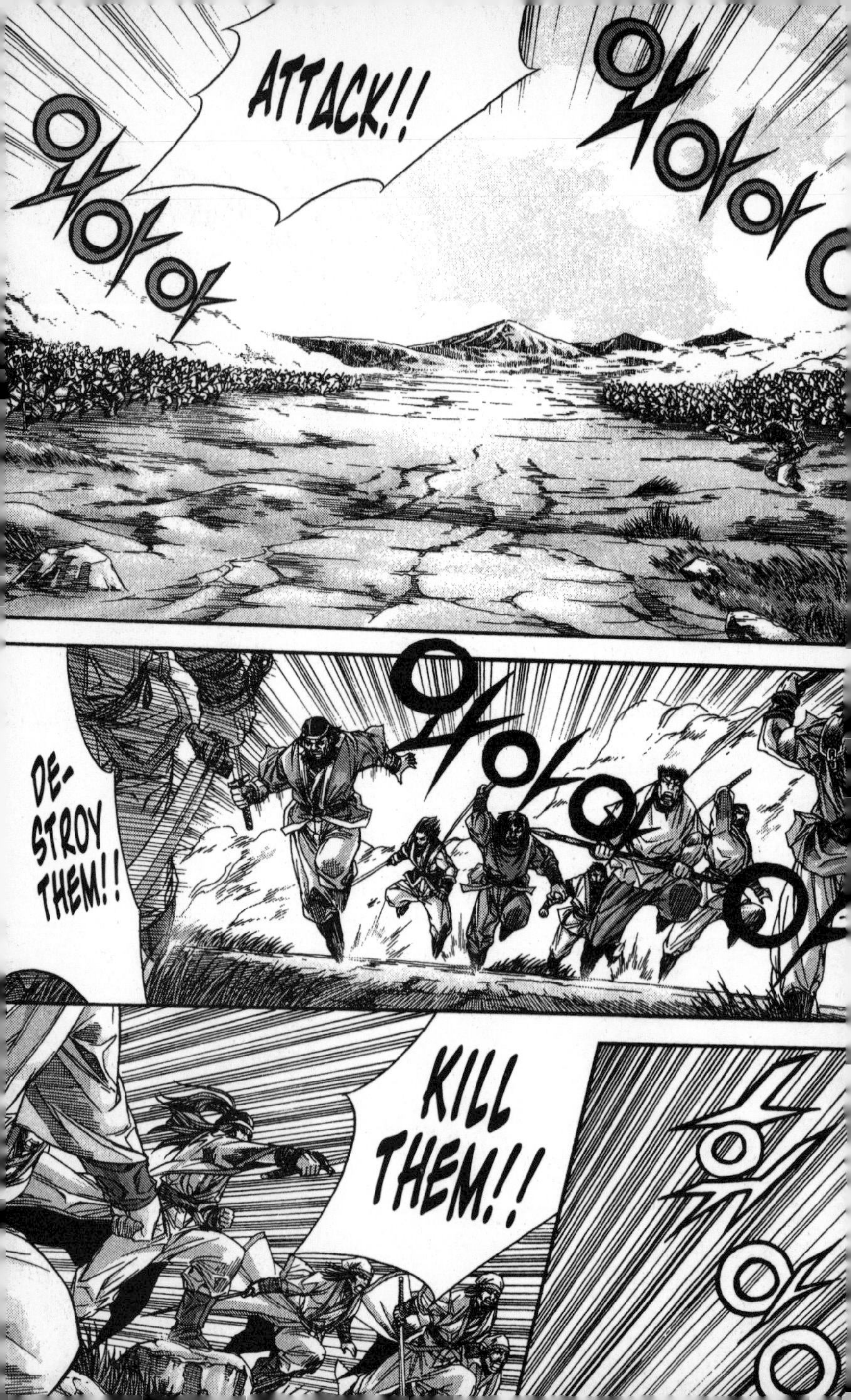
ATTACK!!
DE-
STROY
THEM!!
KILL
THEM!!

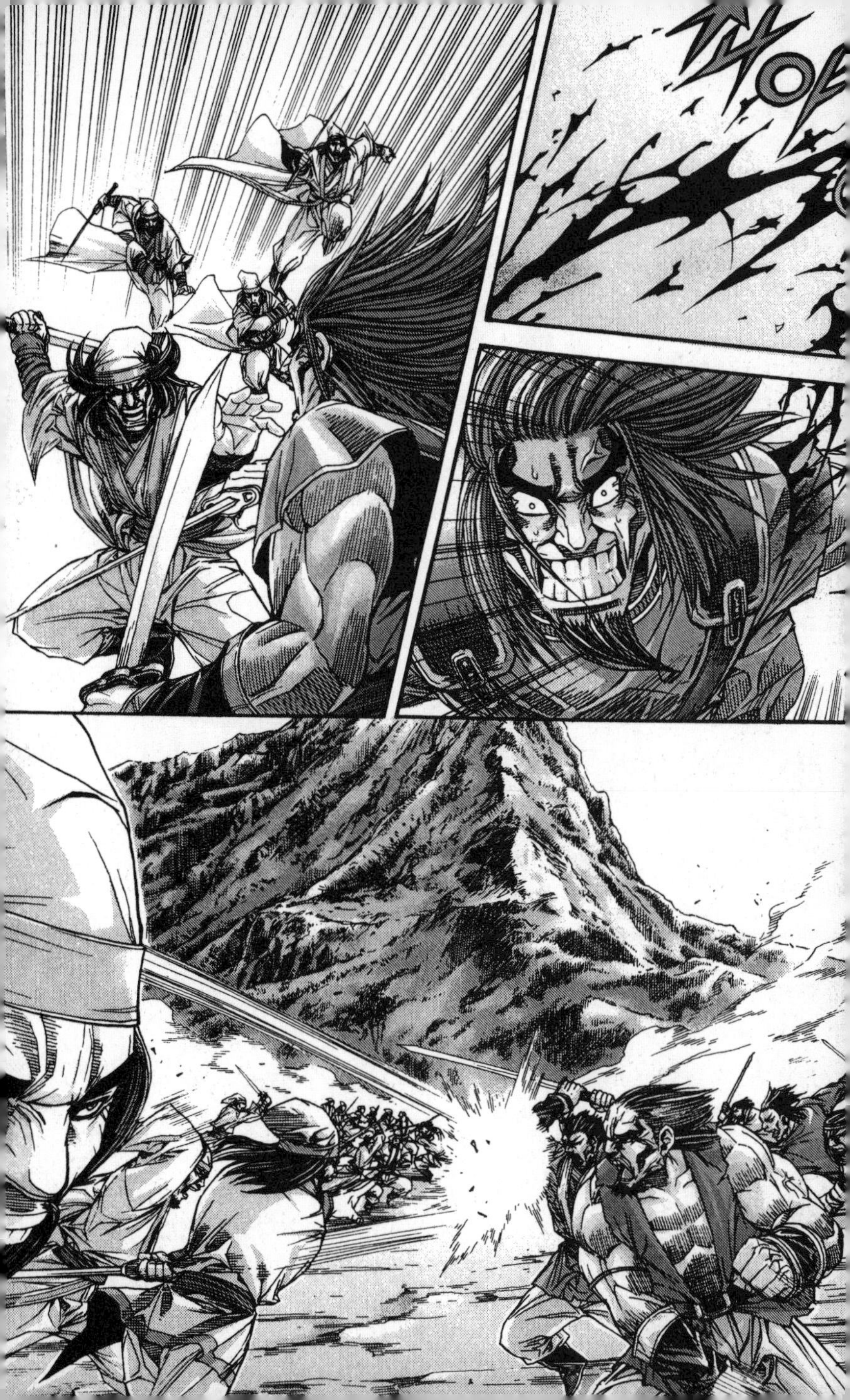
THOK

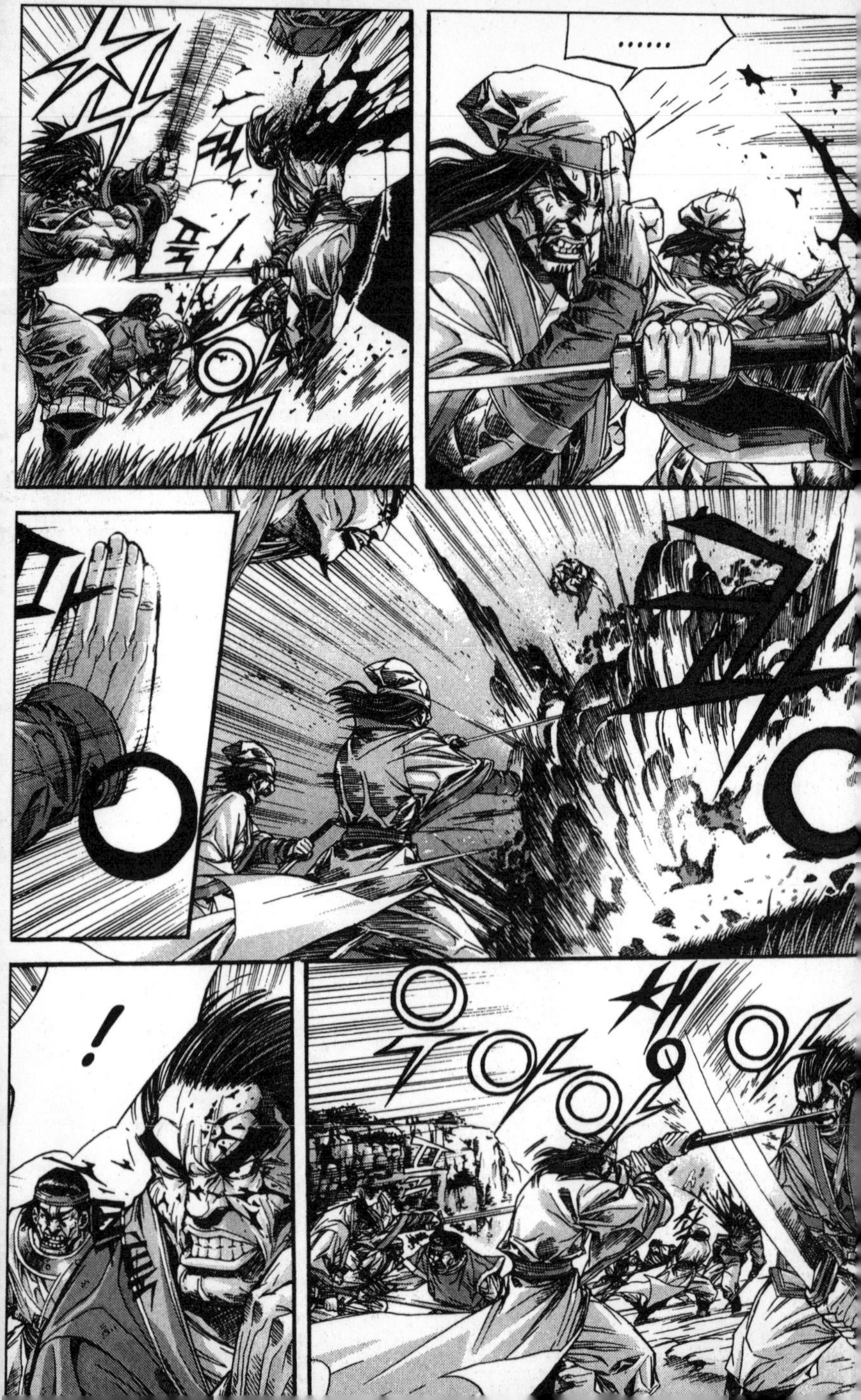
......
푹
!
챙

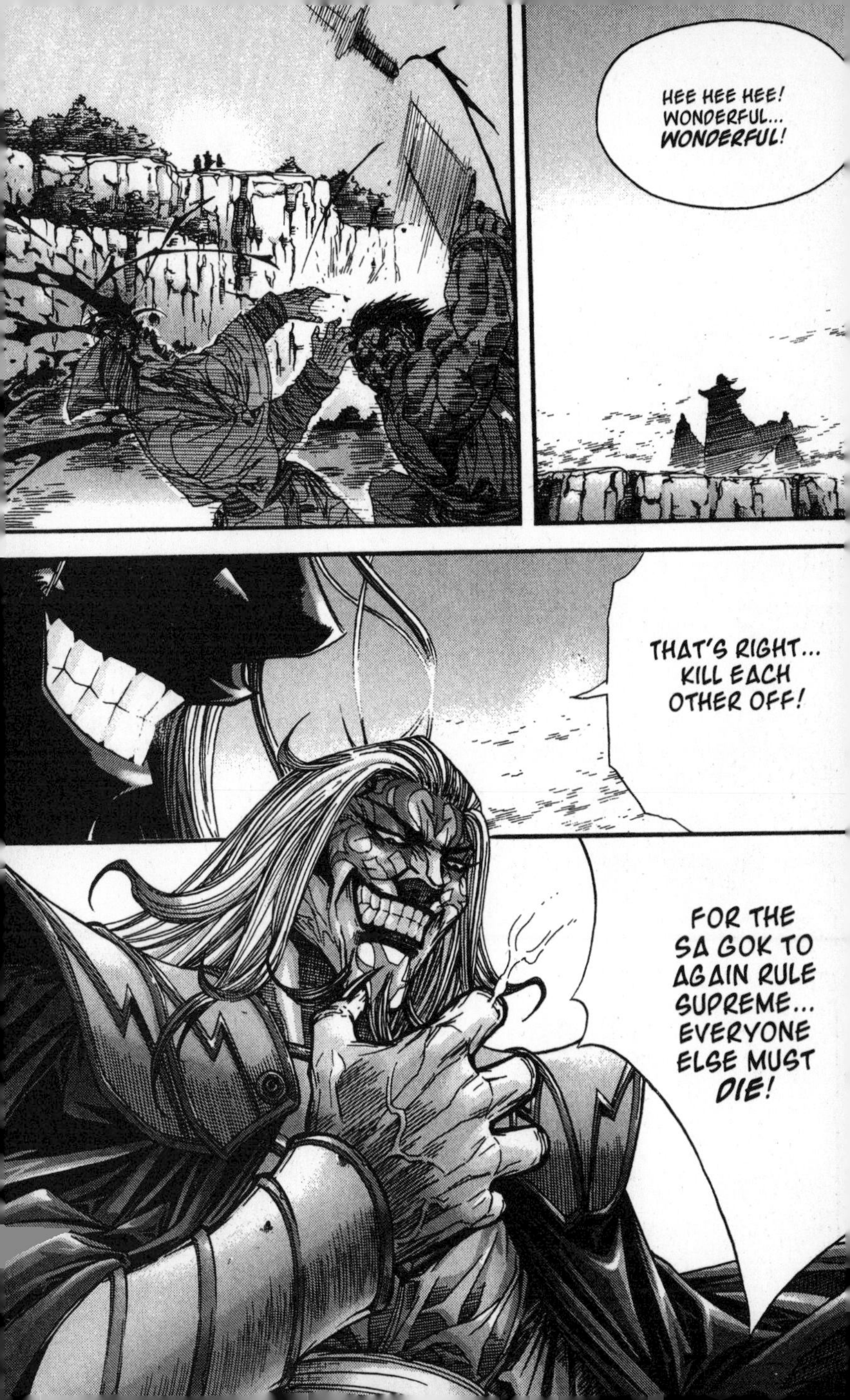
HEE HEE HEE! WONDERFUL... WONDERFUL!
THAT'S RIGHT... KILL EACH OTHER OFF!
FOR THE SA GOK TO AGAIN RULE SUPREME... EVERYONE ELSE MUST DIE!

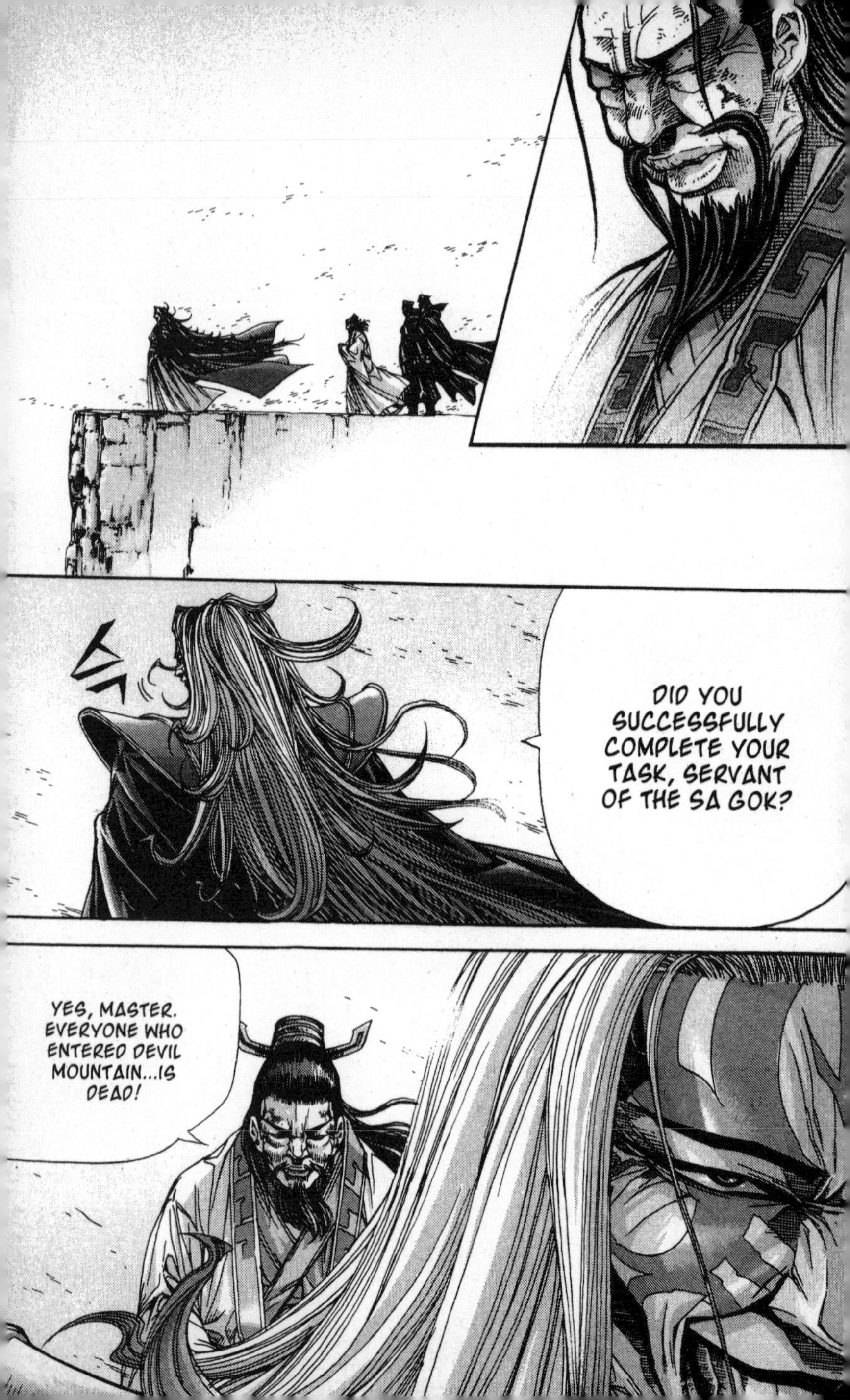
DID YOU SUCCESSFULLY COMPLETE YOUR TASK, SERVANT OF THE SA GOK?
YES, MASTER. EVERYONE WHO ENTERED DEVIL MOUNTAIN...IS DEAD!

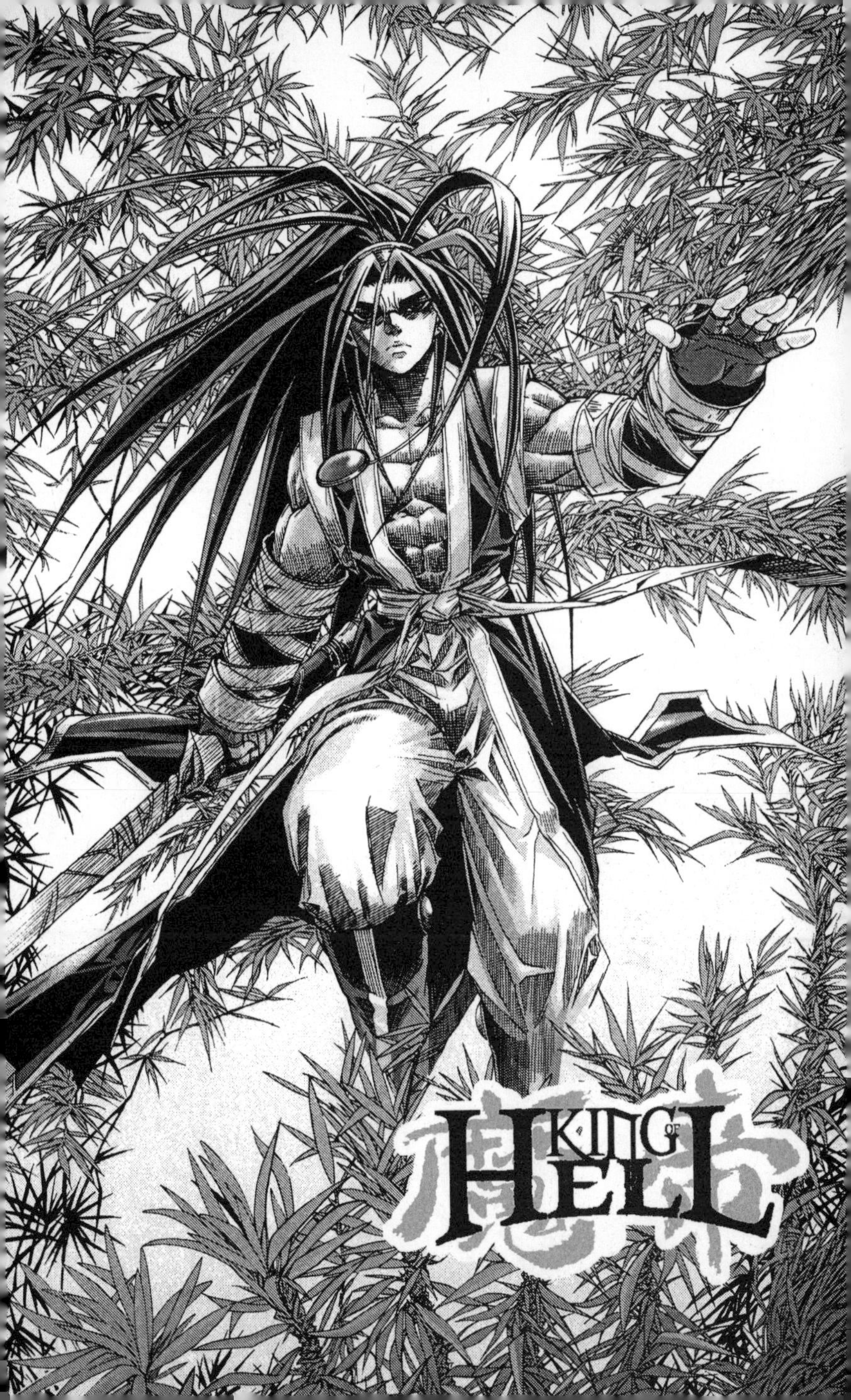
KING OF HELL

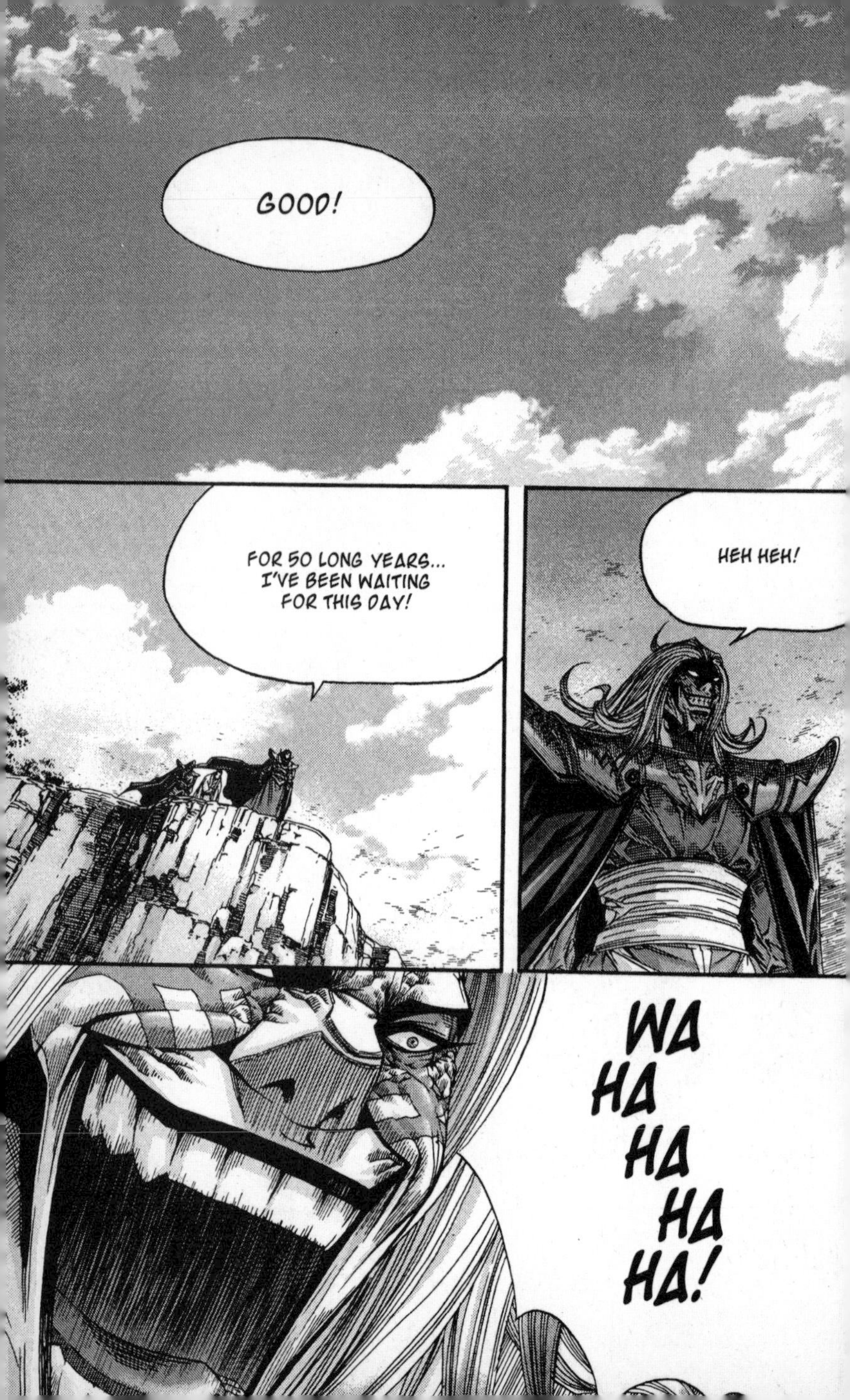
GOOD!
FOR 50 LONG YEARS... I'VE BEEN WAITING FOR THIS DAY!
HEH HEH!
WA HA HA HA HA HA!

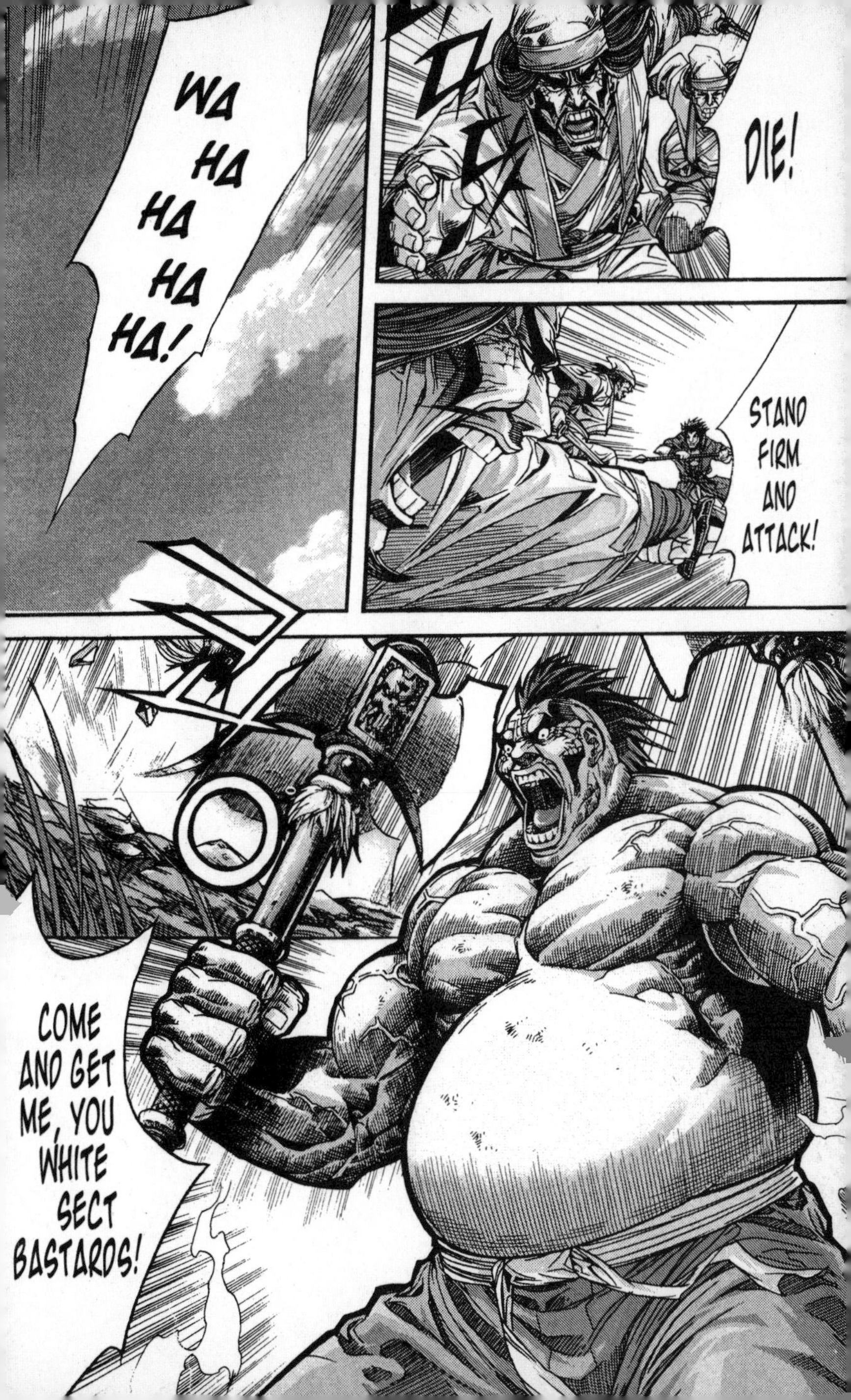
DIE!
STAND FIRM AND ATTACK!
WA HA HA HA HA HA!
COME AND GET ME, YOU WHITE SECT BASTARDS!

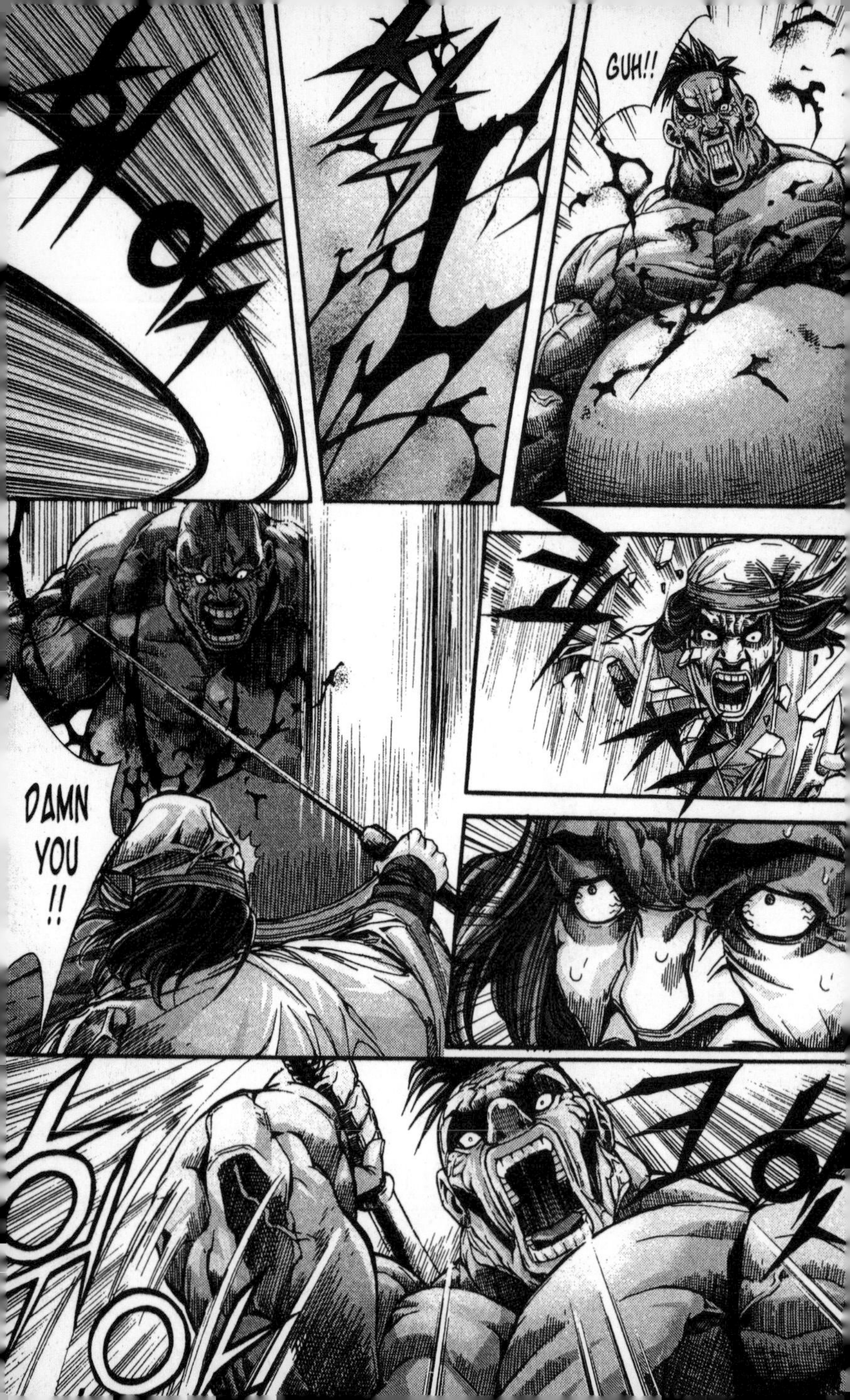
GUH!!
DAMN YOU !!

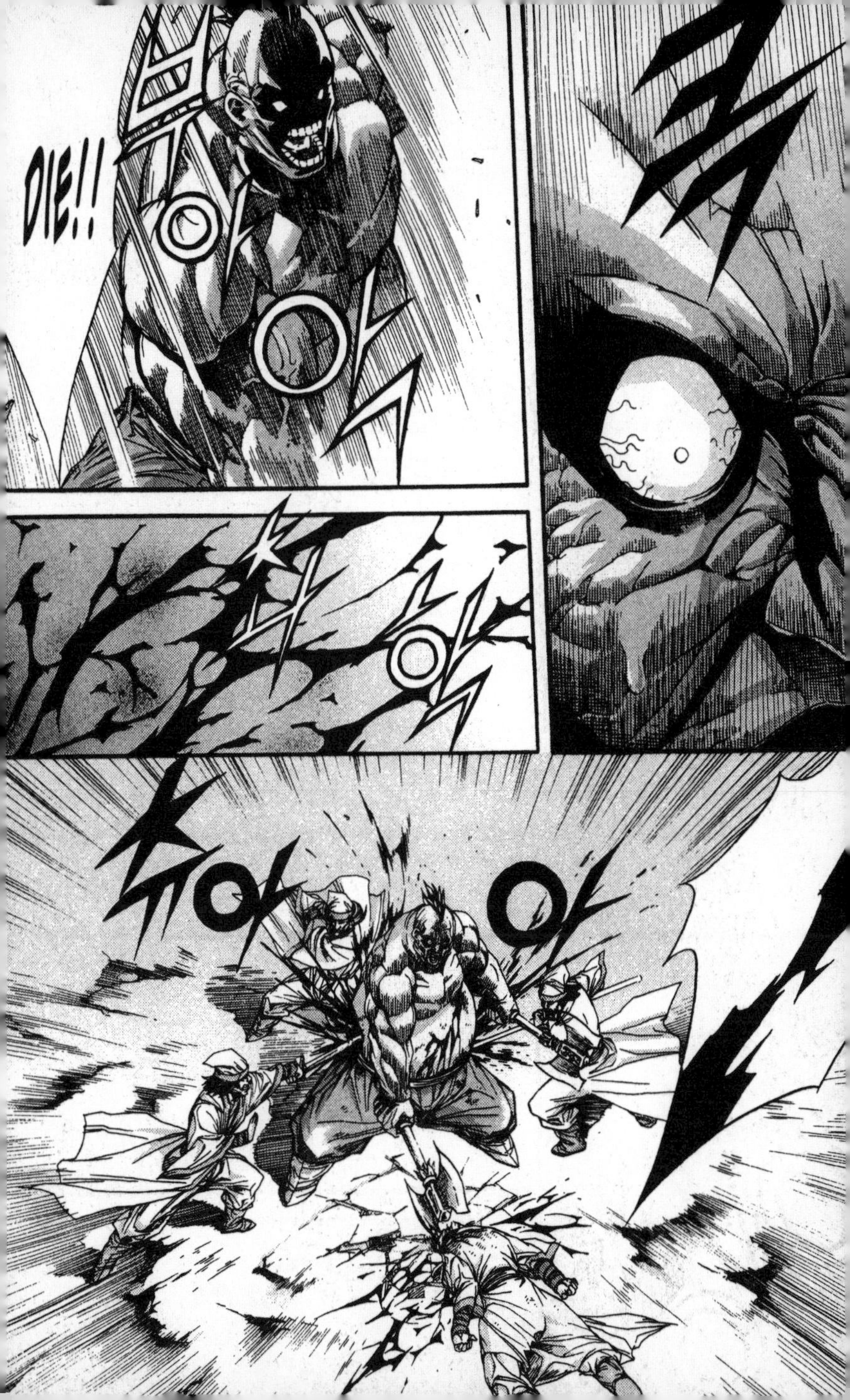
DIE!!

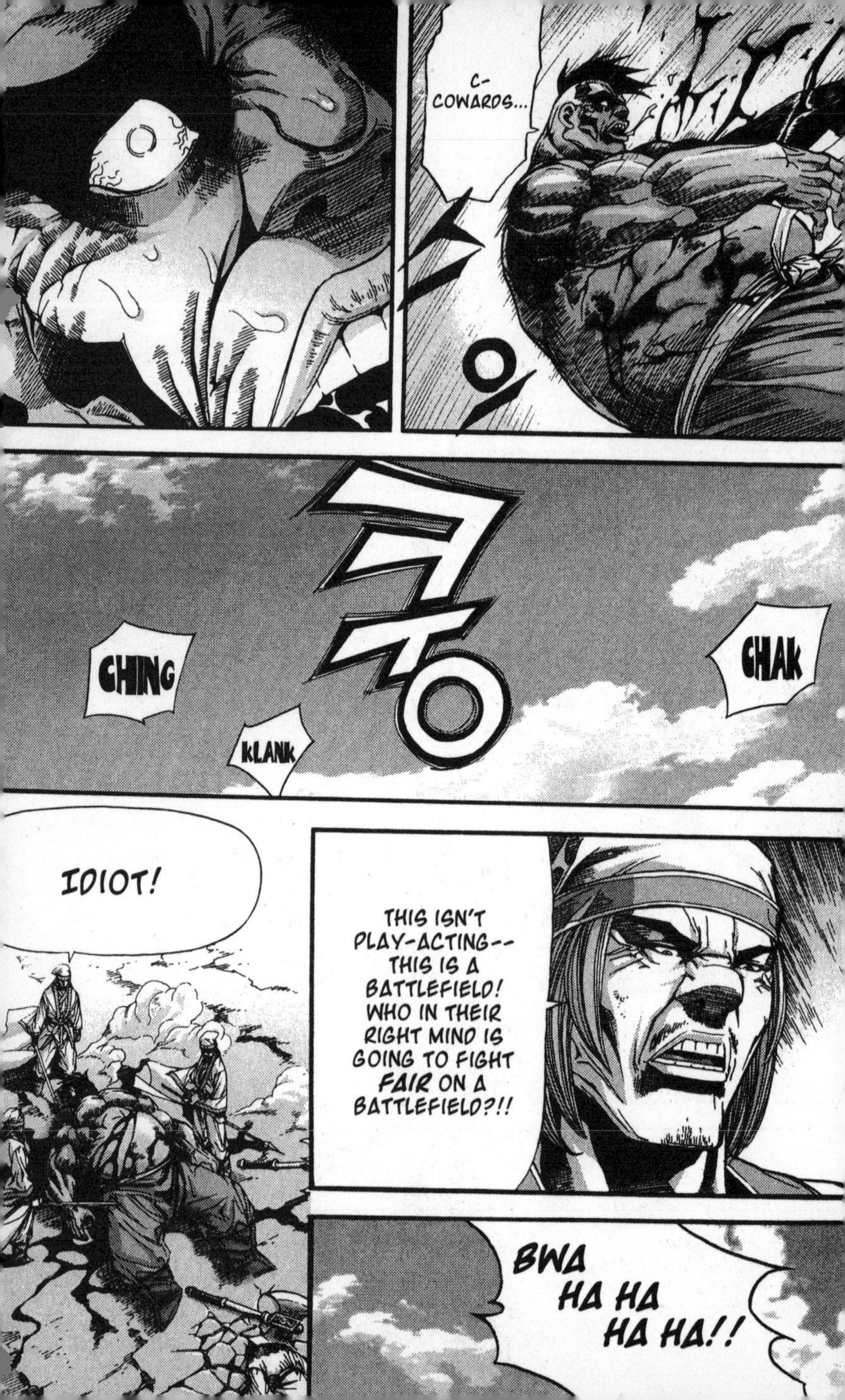
C-
COWARDS...
CHING
KLANK
CHAK
IDIOT!
THIS ISN'T PLAY-ACTING-- THIS IS A BATTLEFIELD! WHO IN THEIR RIGHT MIND IS GOING TO FIGHT *FAIR* ON A BATTLEFIELD?!!
BWA HA HA HA HA!!

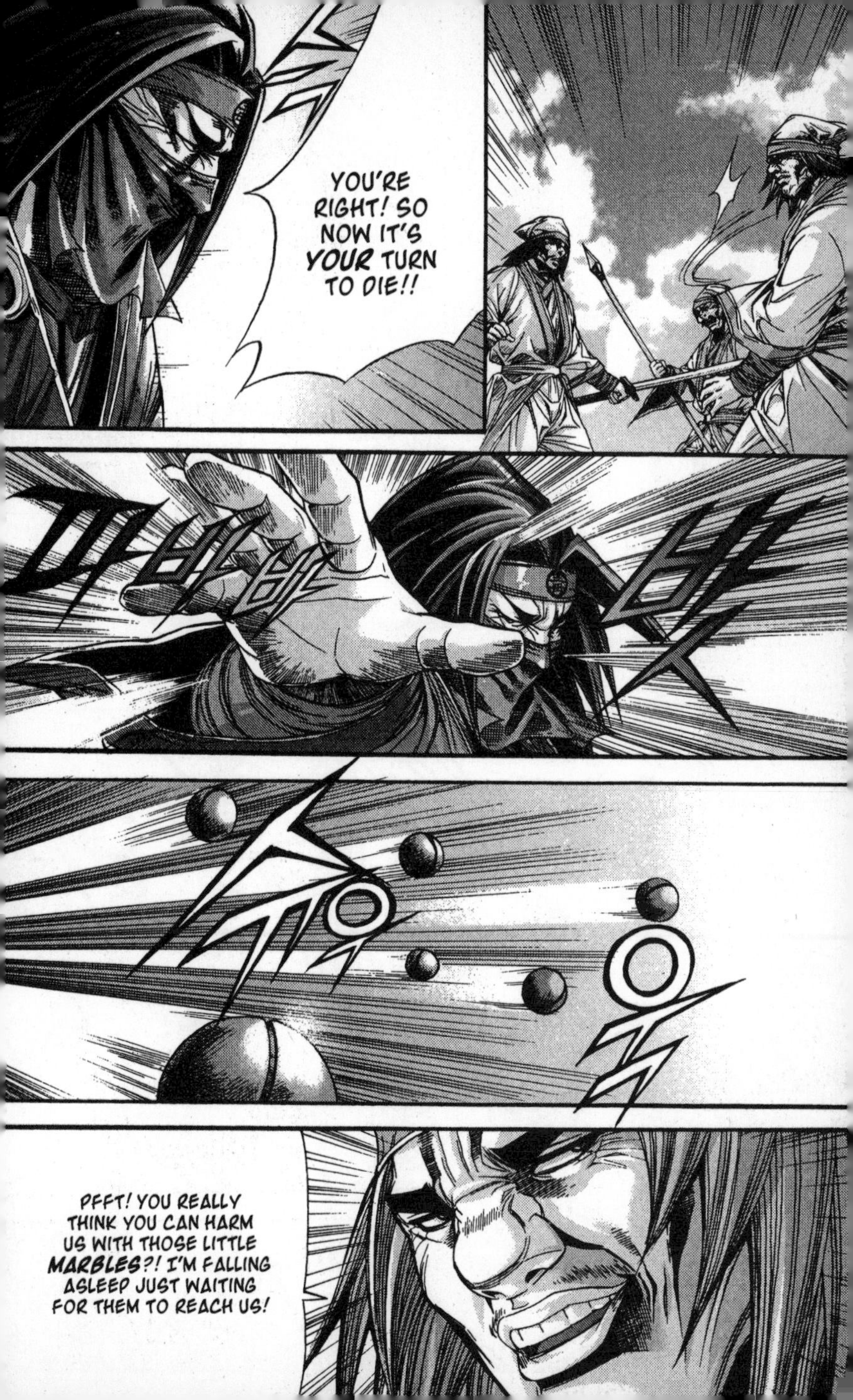
YOU'RE RIGHT! SO NOW IT'S *YOUR* TURN TO DIE!!
PFFT! YOU REALLY THINK YOU CAN HARM US WITH THOSE LITTLE *MARBLES*?! I'M FALLING ASLEEP JUST WAITING FOR THEM TO REACH US!

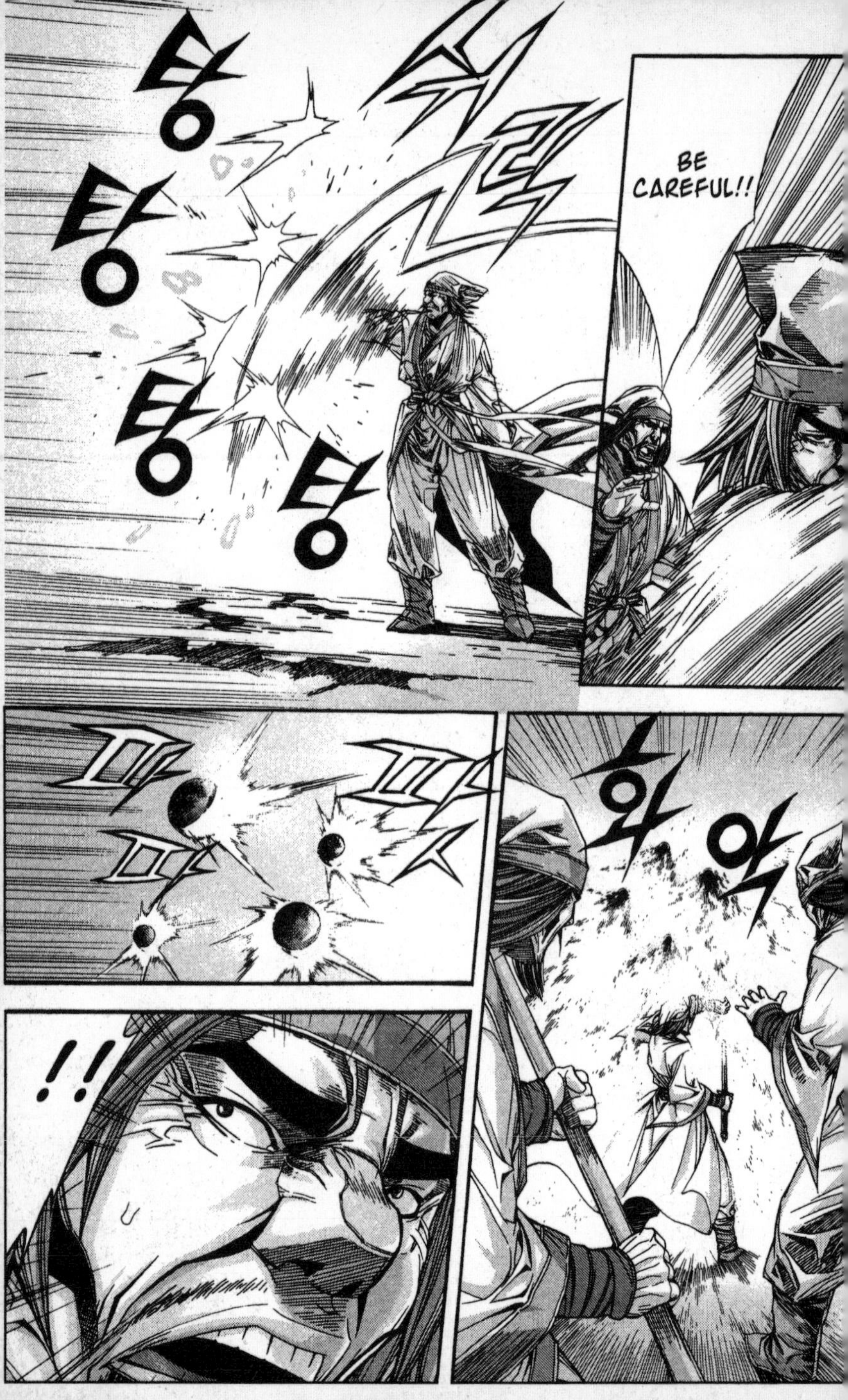
탕
탕
탕
탕
BE CAREFUL!!
!!

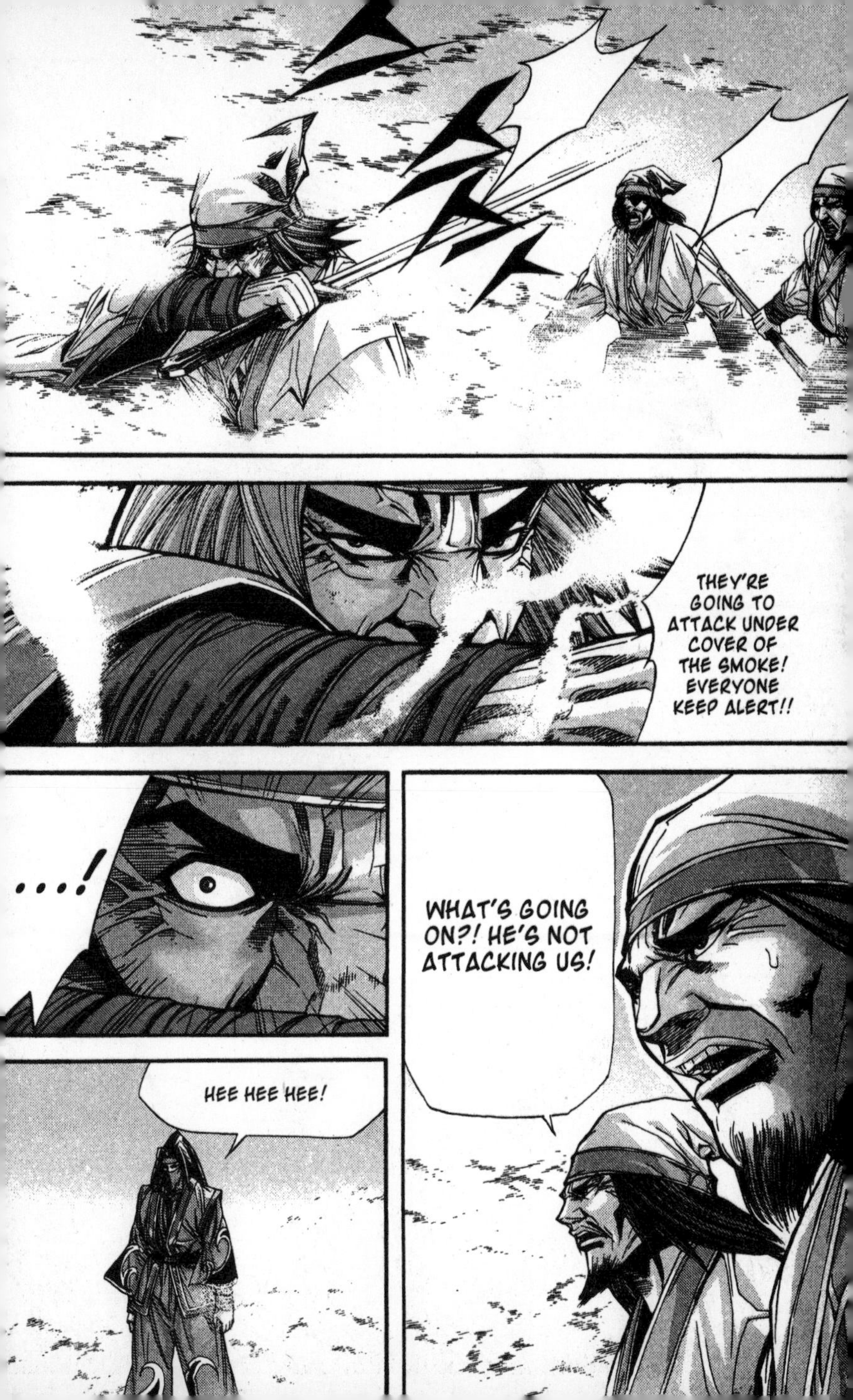
THEY'RE GOING TO ATTACK UNDER COVER OF THE SMOKE! EVERYONE KEEP ALERT!!
WHAT'S GOING ON?! HE'S NOT ATTACKING US!
...!
HEE HEE HEE!

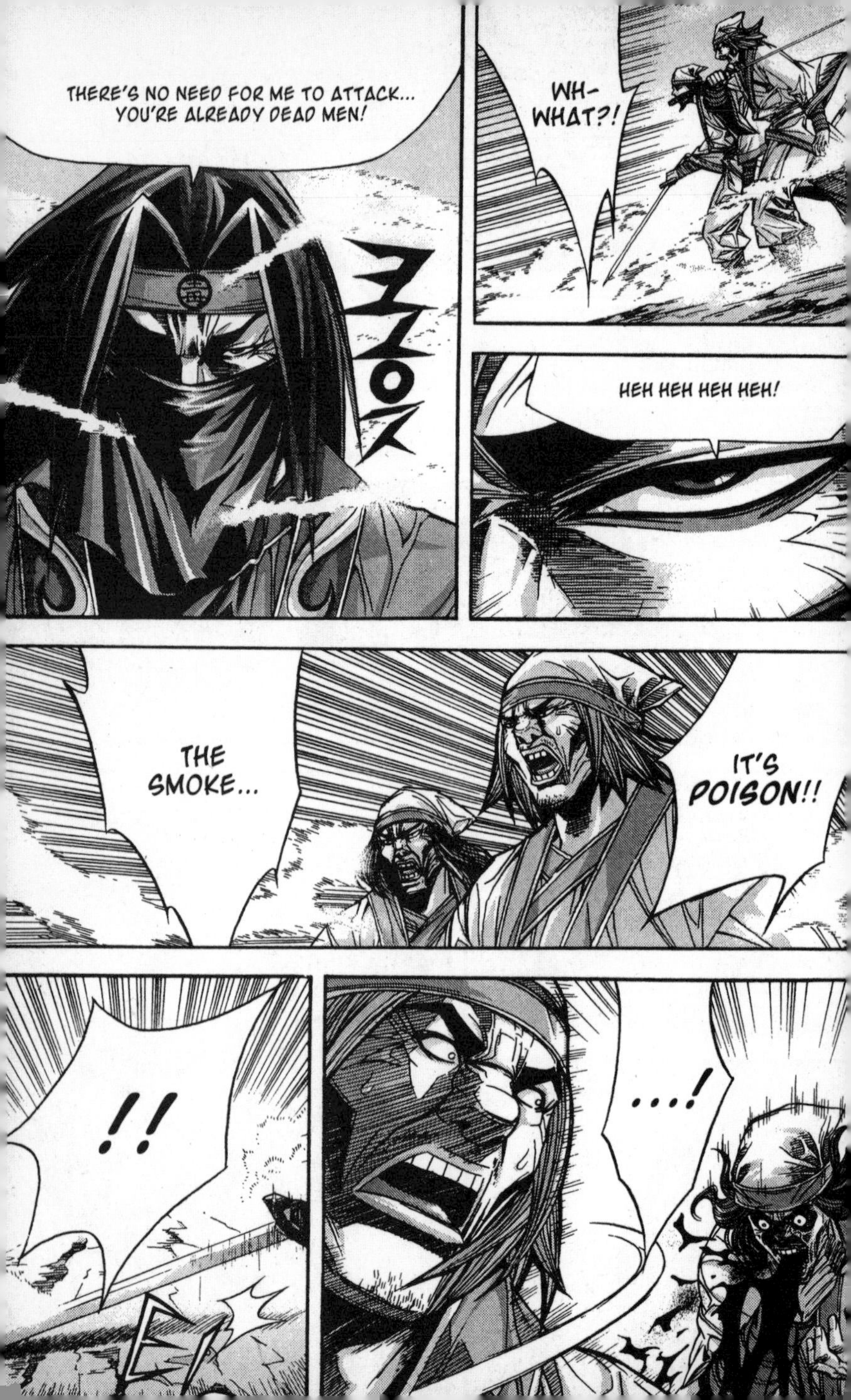
THERE'S NO NEED FOR ME TO ATTACK... YOU'RE ALREADY DEAD MEN!
WH- WHAT?!
HEH HEH HEH HEH!
THE SMOKE...
IT'S POISON!!
!!
...!

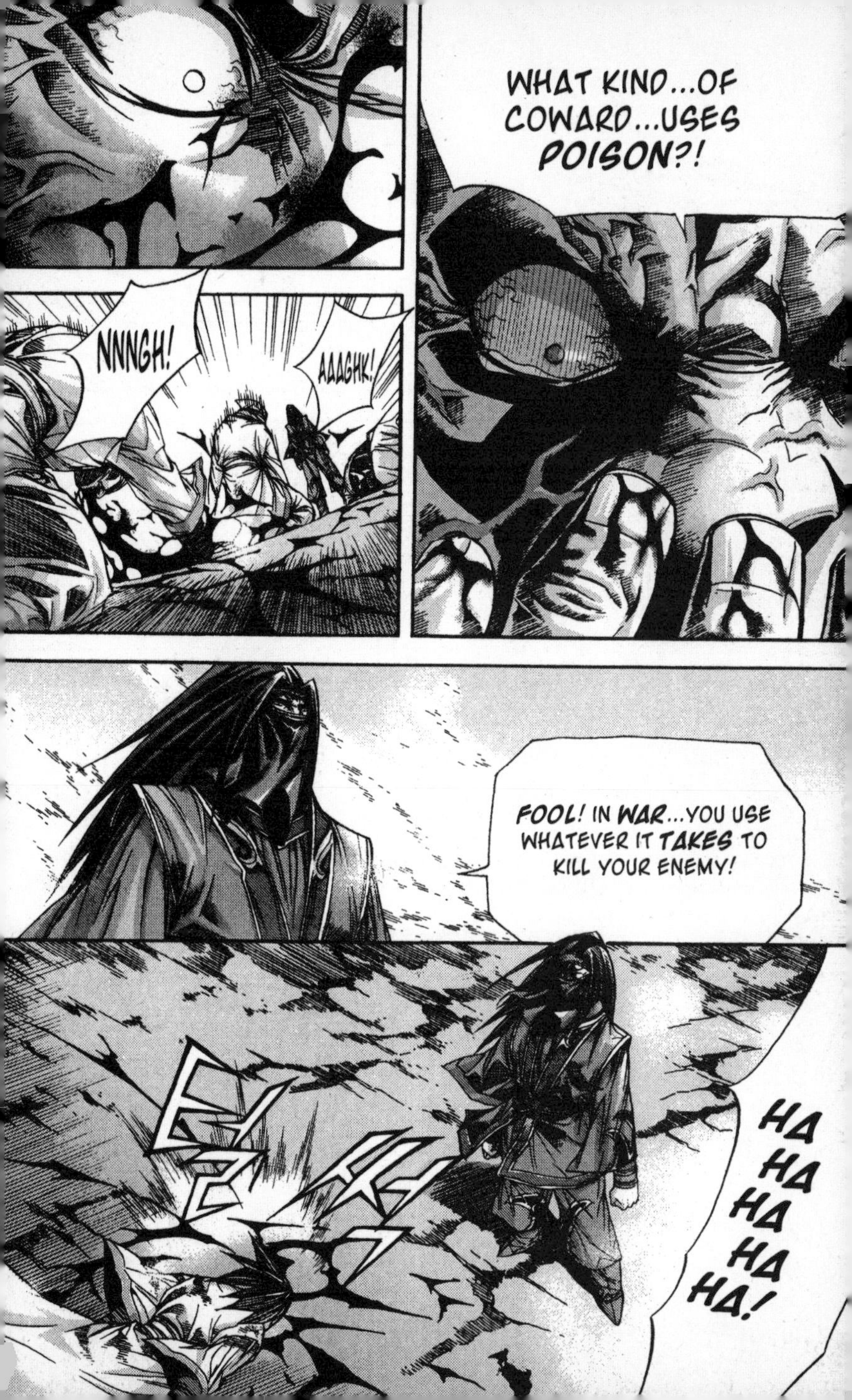
WHAT KIND...OF COWARD...USES POISON?!
NNNGH!
AAAGHK!
FOOL! IN WAR...YOU USE WHATEVER IT TAKES TO KILL YOUR ENEMY!
HA HA HA HA HA HA HA!

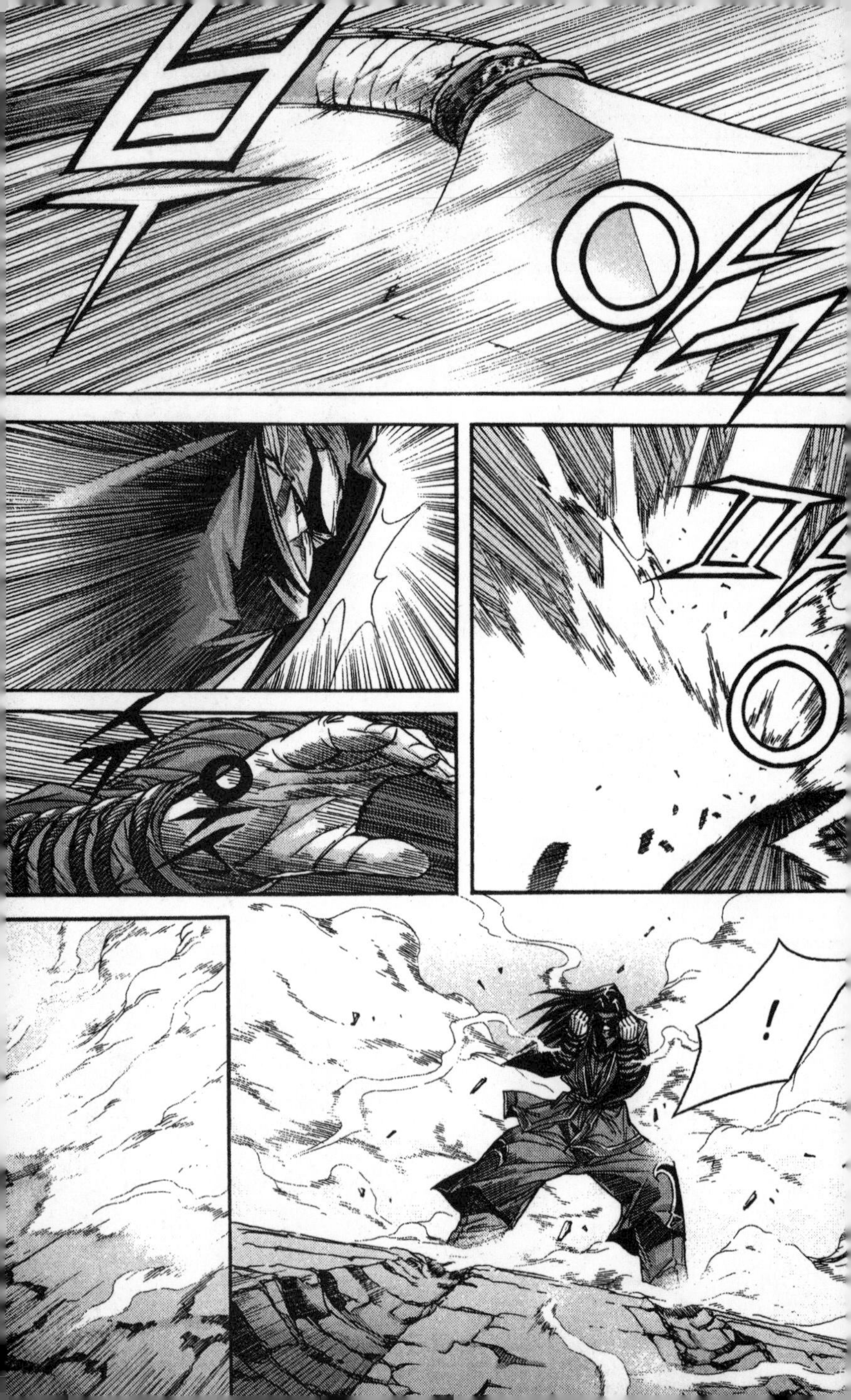
!

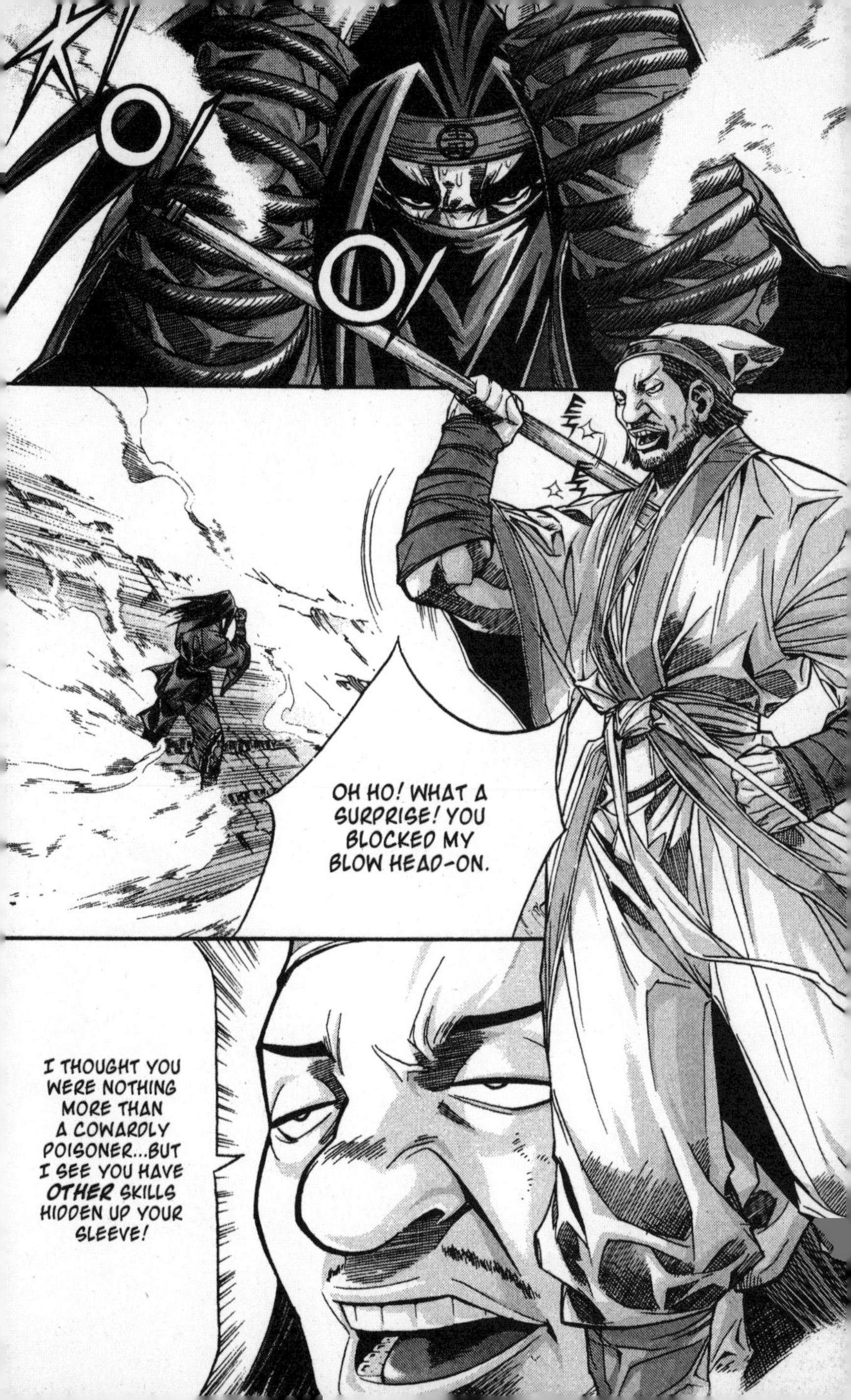

OH HO! WHAT A SURPRISE! YOU BLOCKED MY BLOW HEAD-ON.
I THOUGHT YOU WERE NOTHING MORE THAN A COWARDLY POISONER...BUT I SEE YOU HAVE OTHER SKILLS HIDDEN UP YOUR SLEEVE!

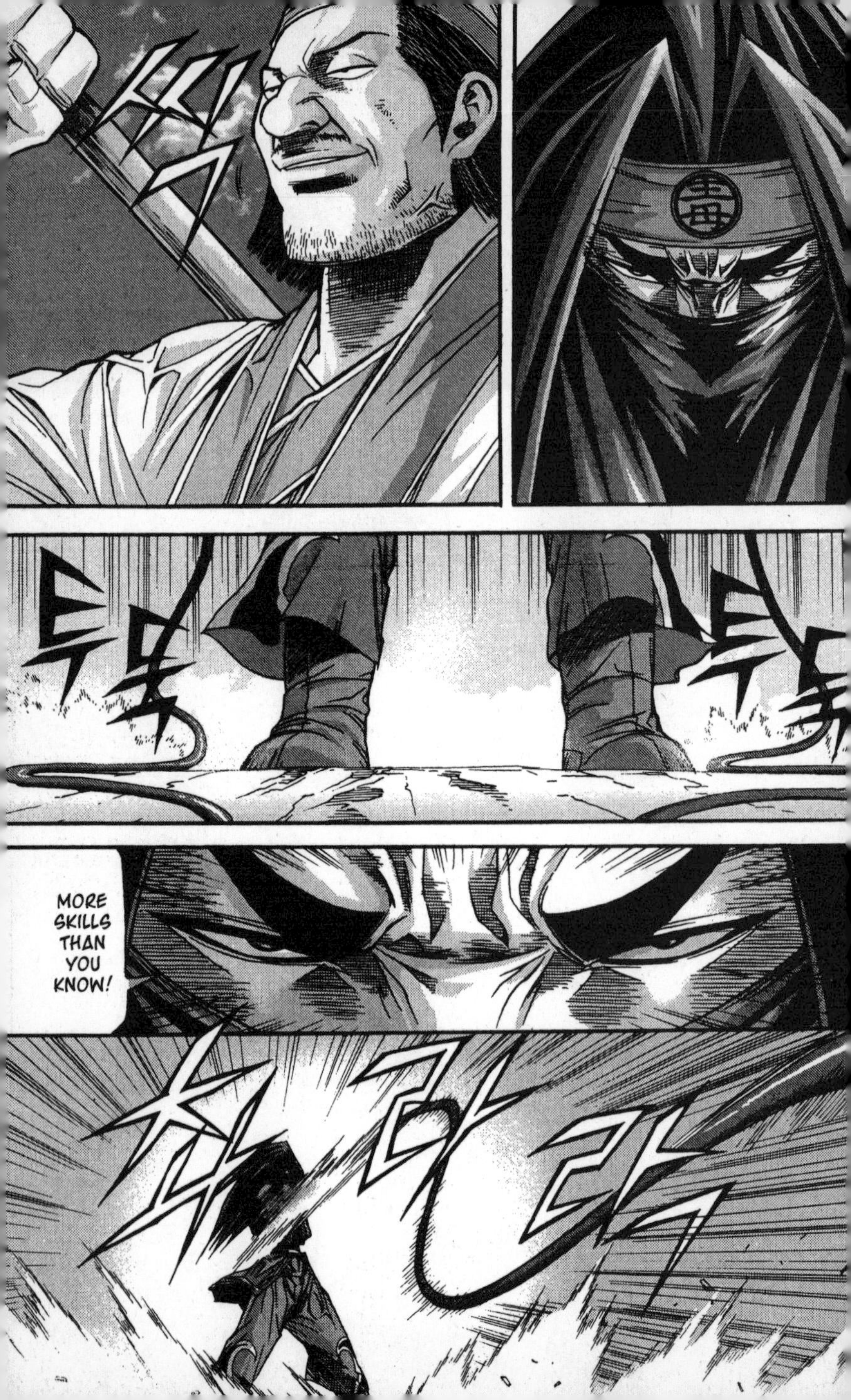
MORE SKILLS THAN YOU KNOW!

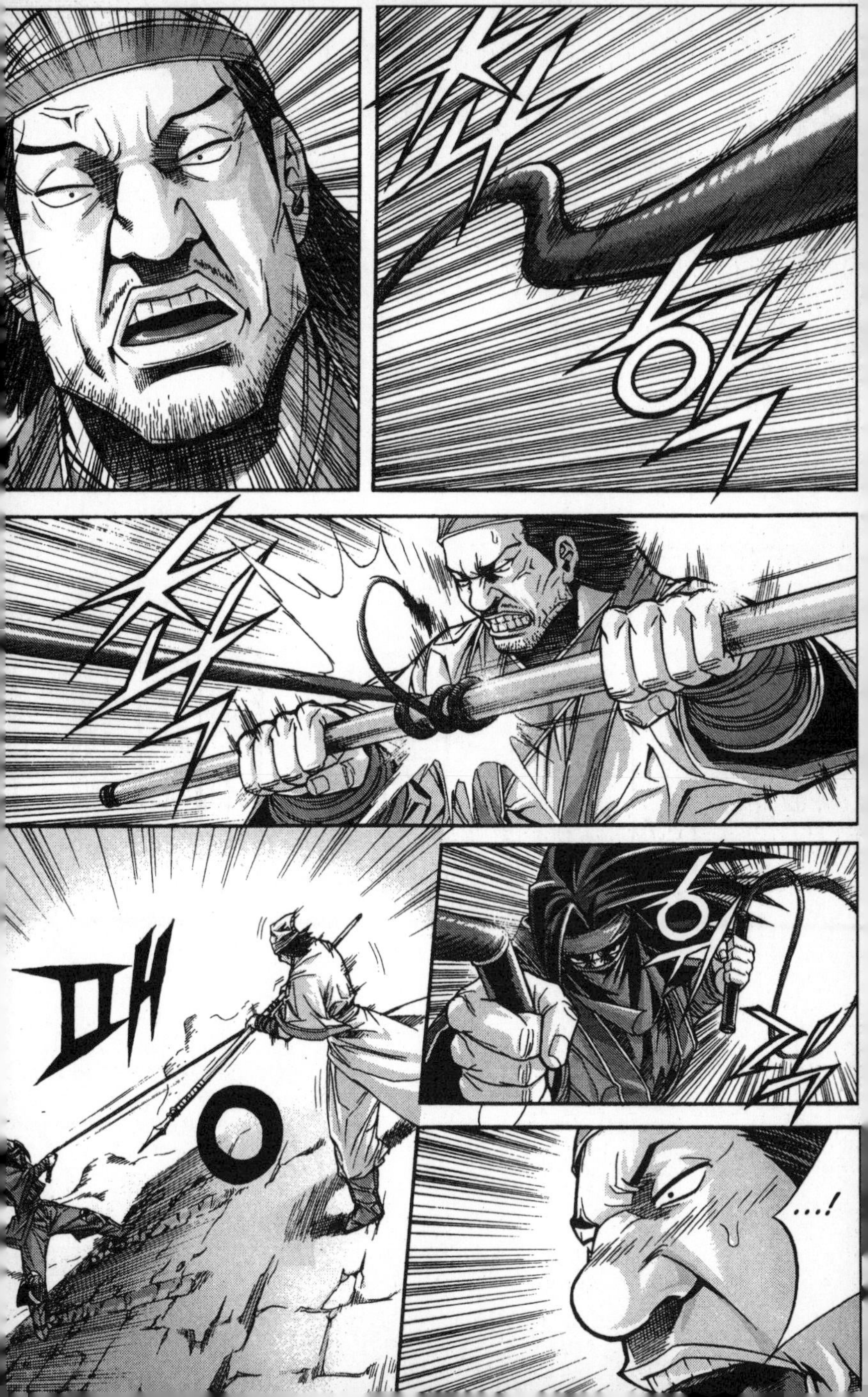
...!

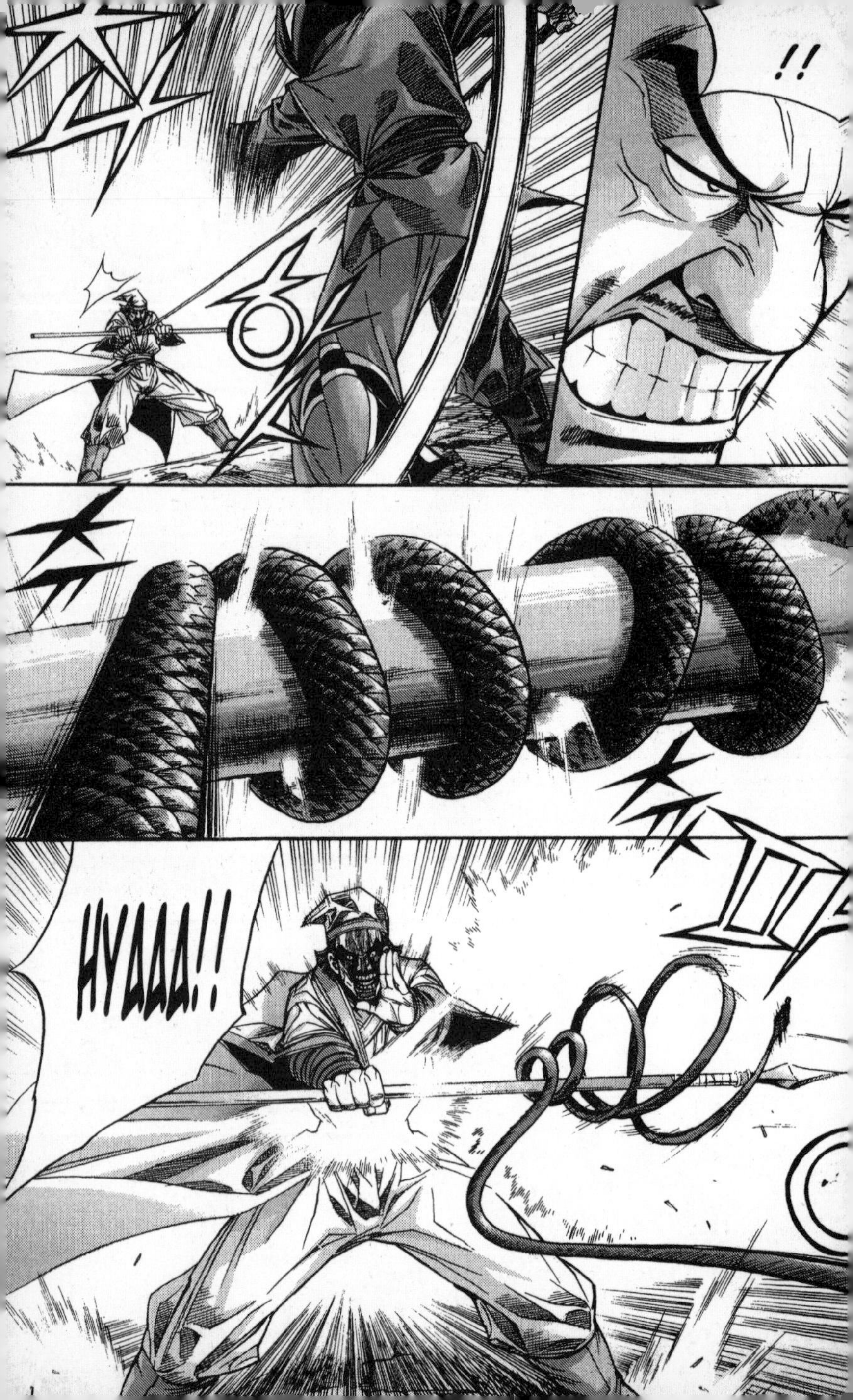
!!
HYAAA!!

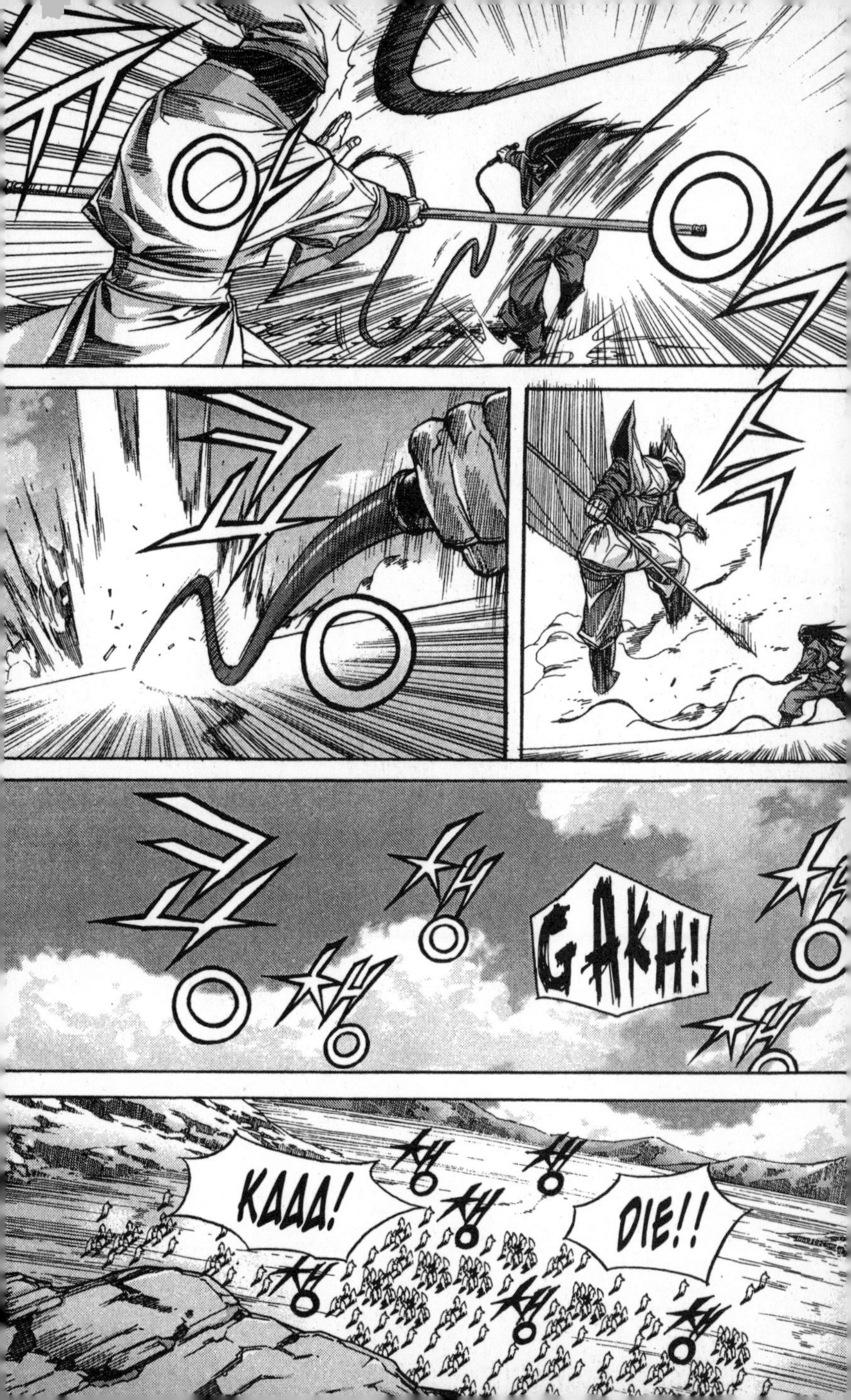
GAKH!
KAAA!
DIE!!

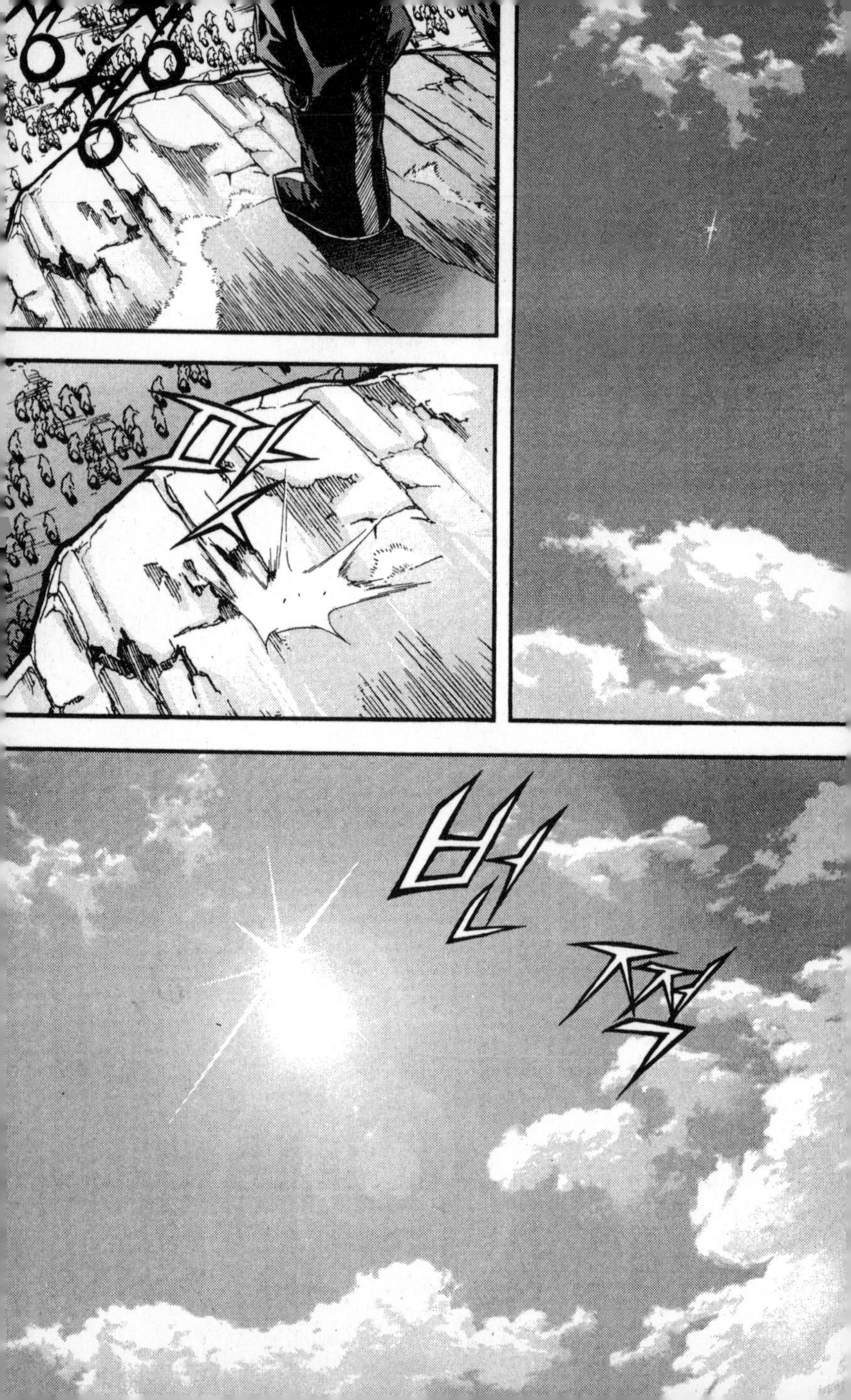
팟
번쩍

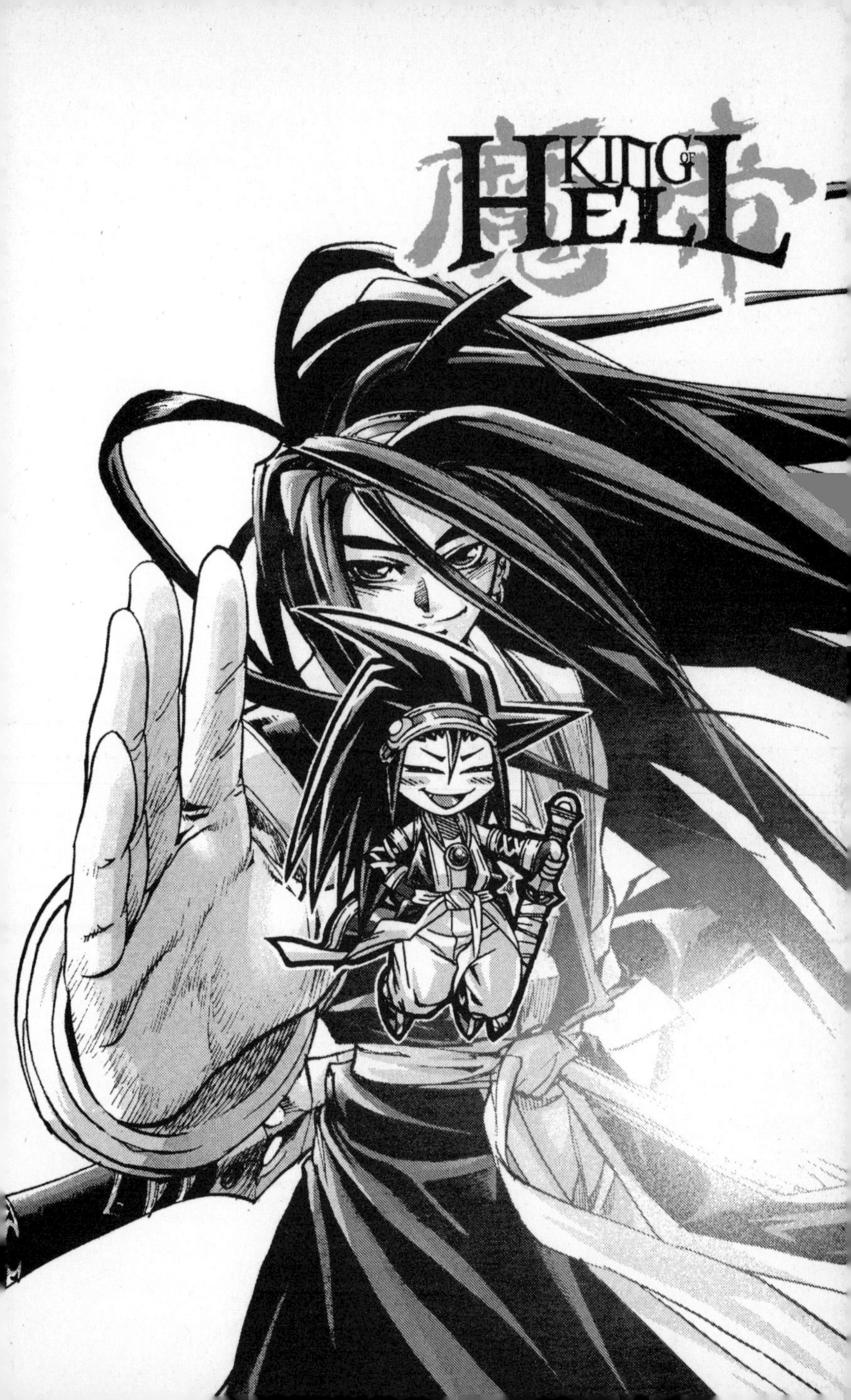
KING OF HELL

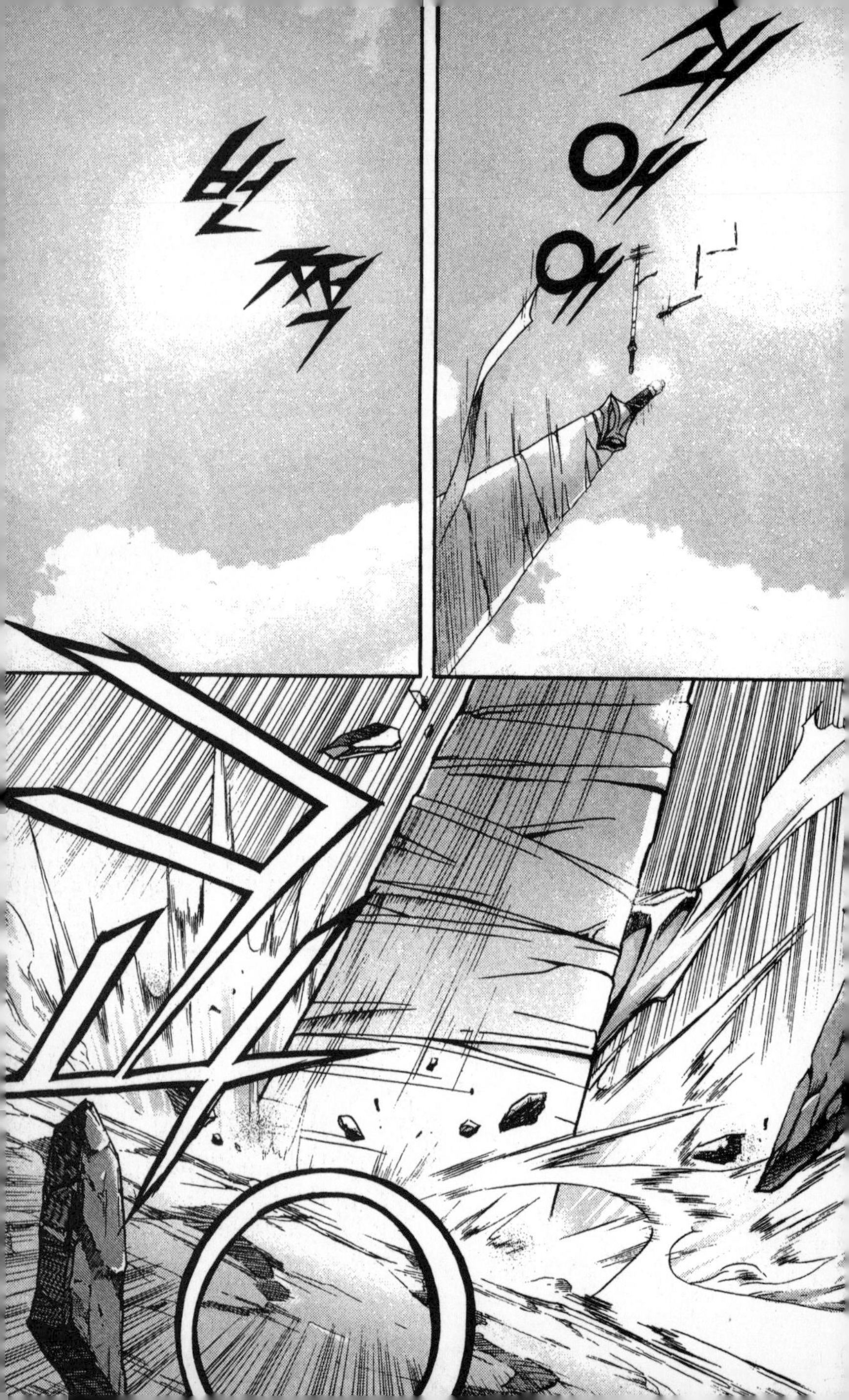
처어어
번쩍

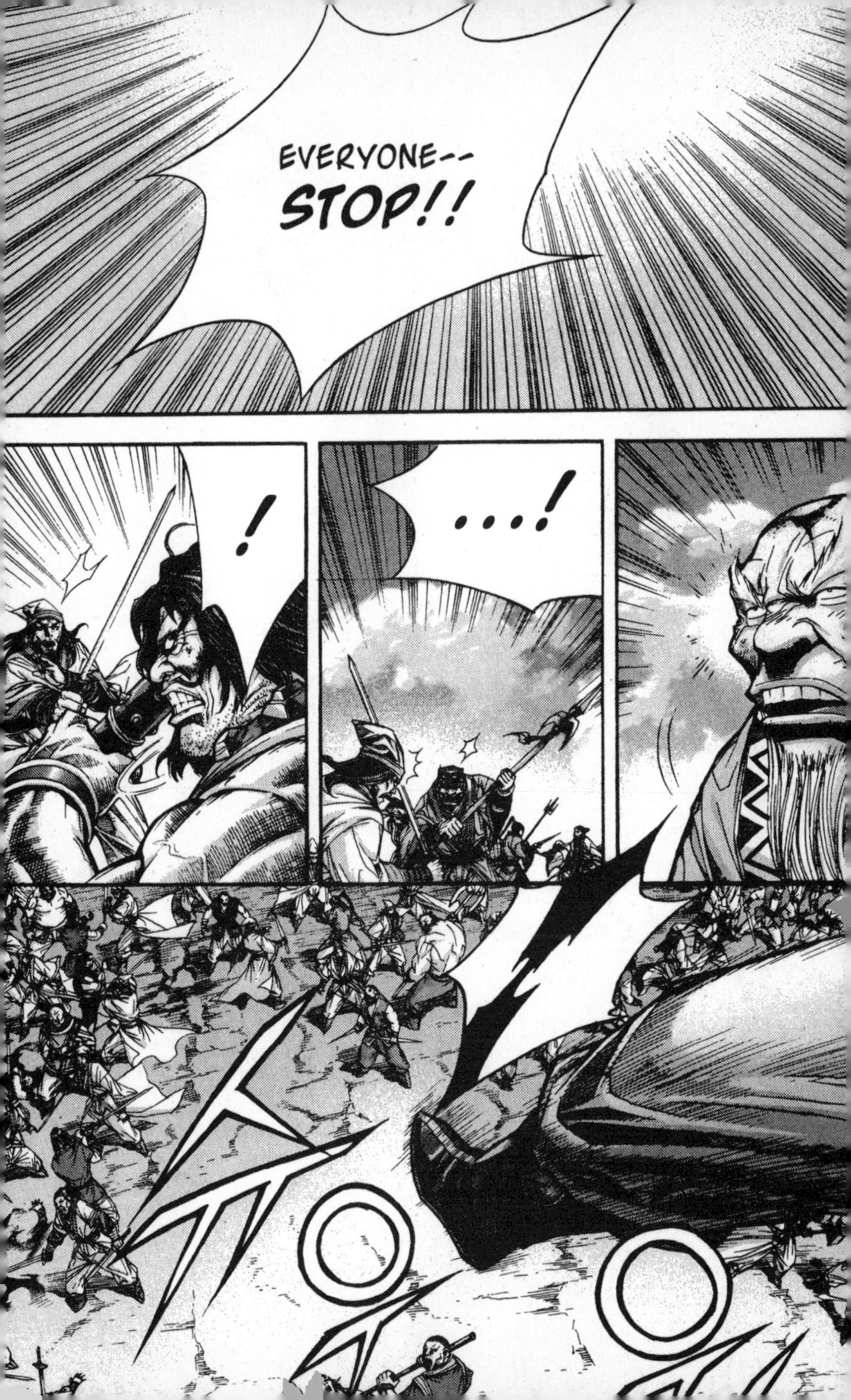
EVERYONE--
STOP!!
!
...!

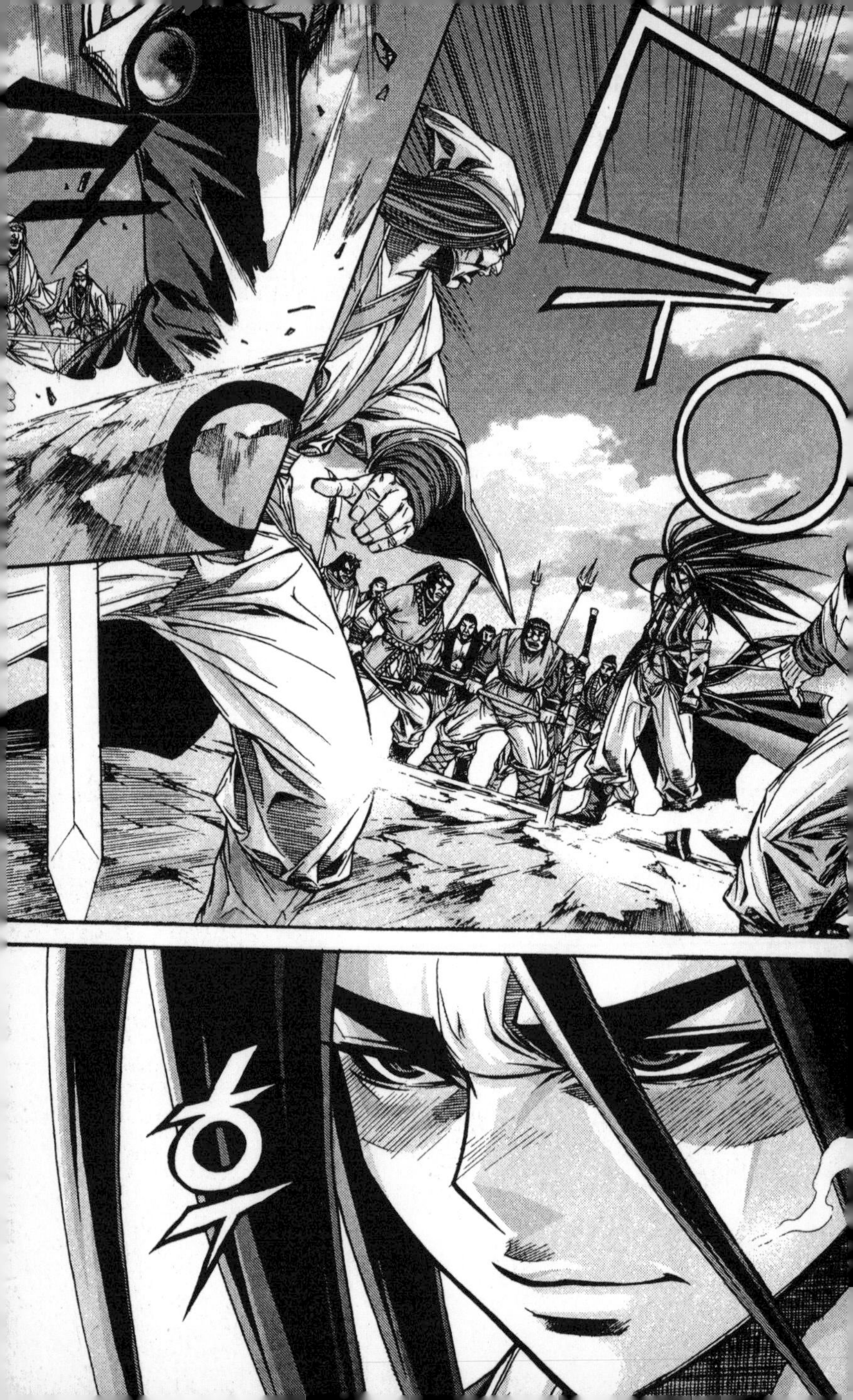

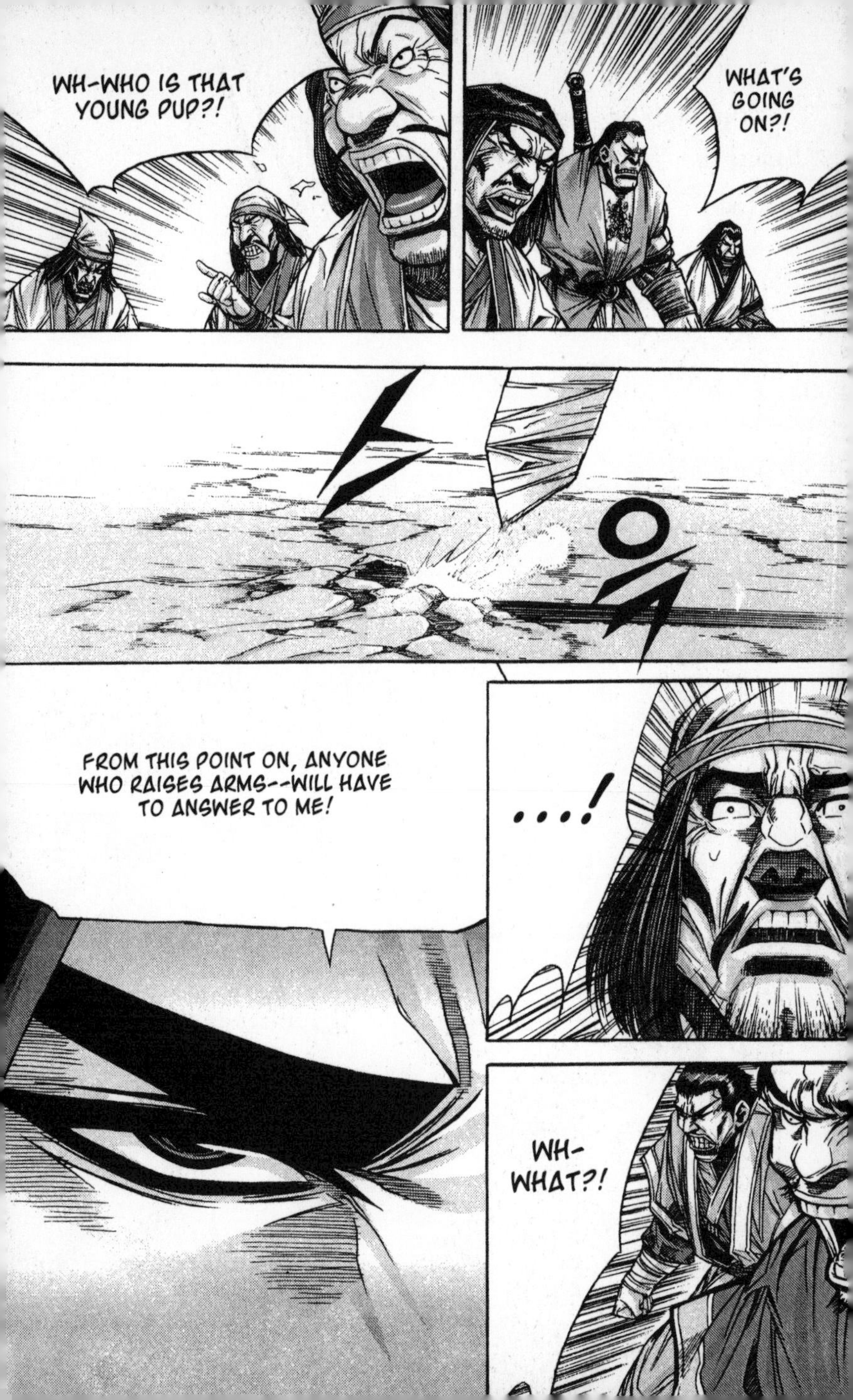
WHAT'S GOING ON?!
WH-WHO IS THAT YOUNG PUP?!
FROM THIS POINT ON, ANYONE WHO RAISES ARMS--WILL HAVE TO ANSWER TO ME!
...!
WH-WHAT?!

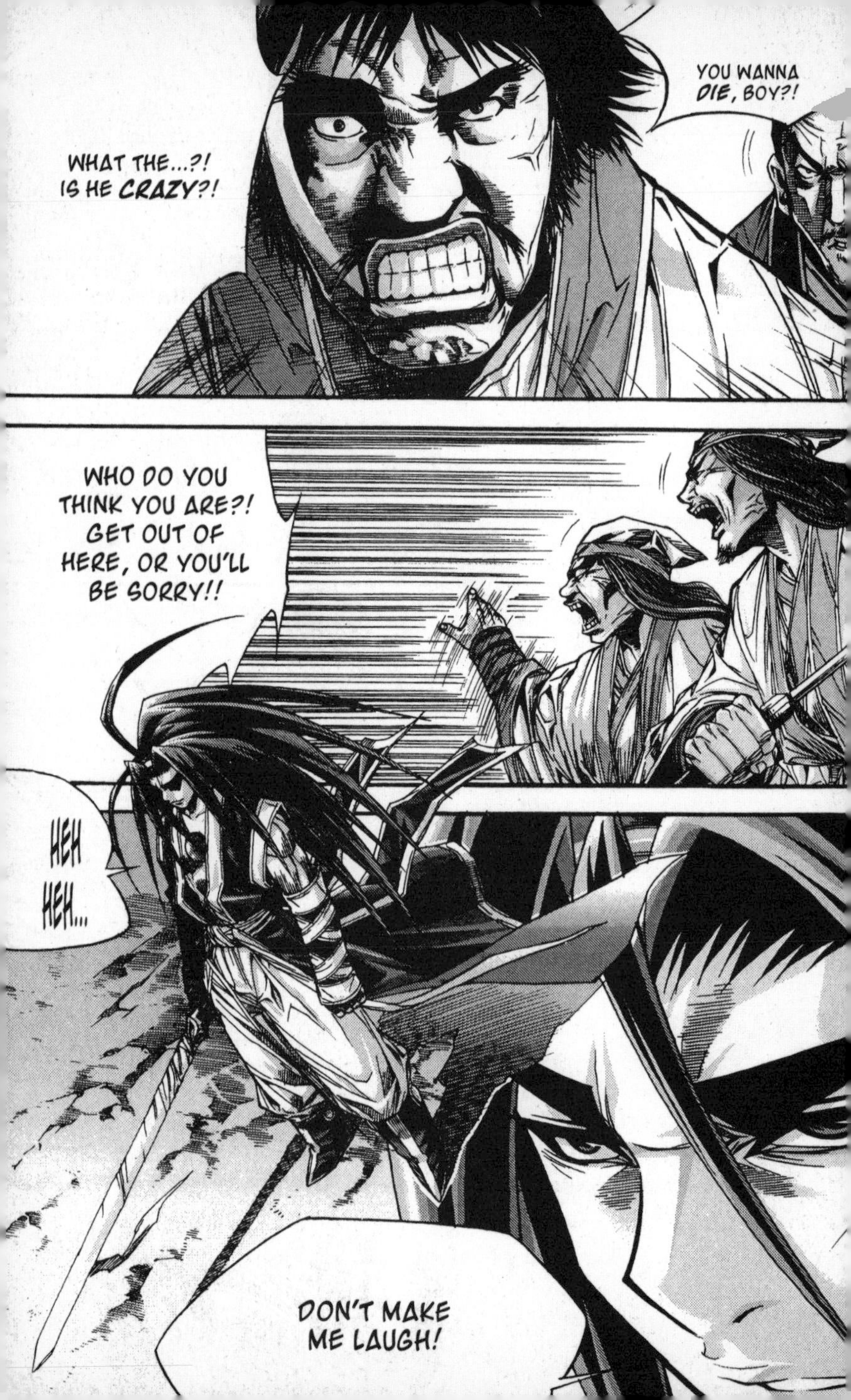
WHAT THE...?! IS HE CRAZY?!
YOU WANNA DIE, BOY?!
WHO DO YOU THINK YOU ARE?! GET OUT OF HERE, OR YOU'LL BE SORRY!!
HEH HEH...
DON'T MAKE ME LAUGH!

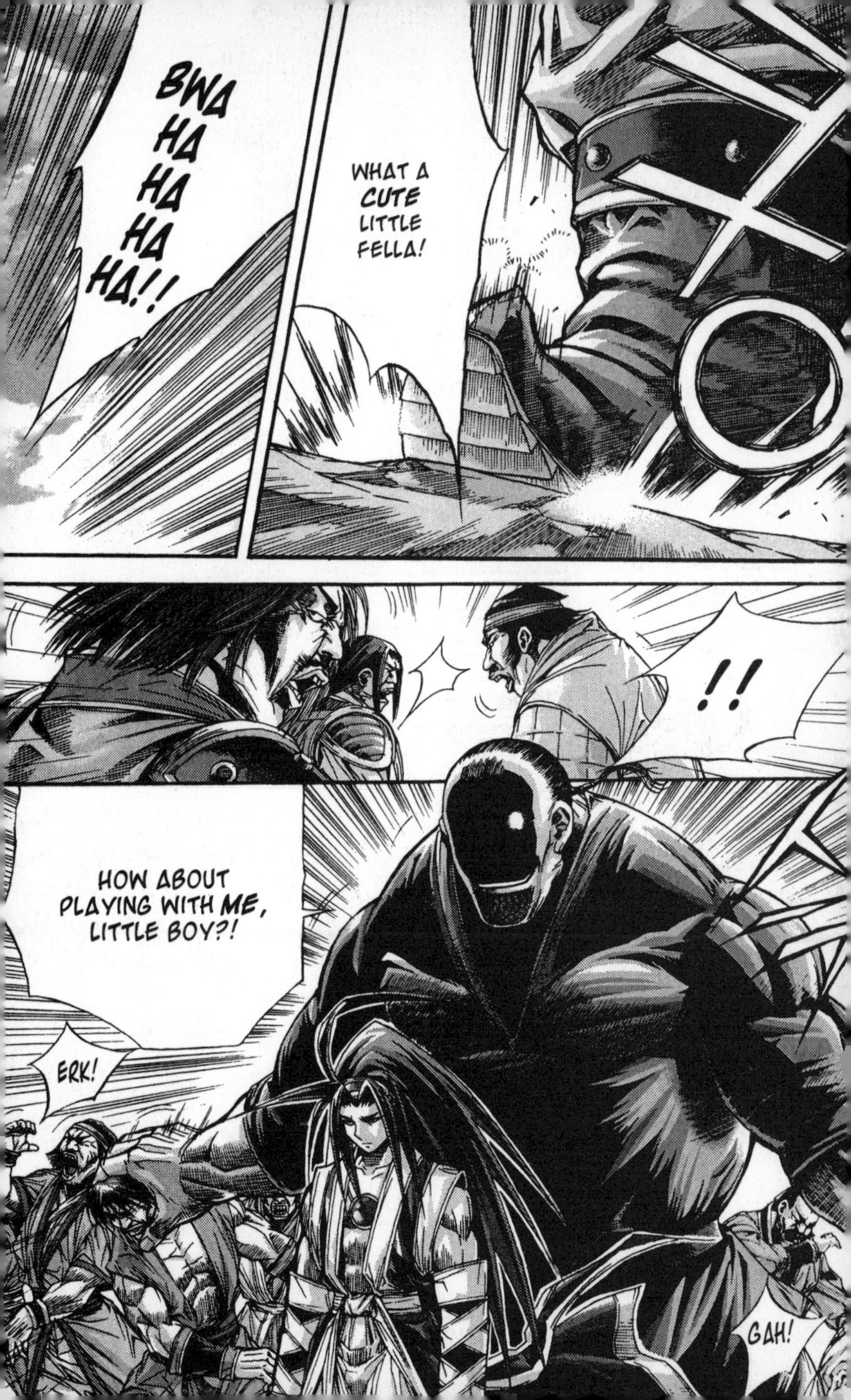
WHAT A CUTE LITTLE FELLA!
BWA HA HA HA HA HA!!
!!
HOW ABOUT PLAYING WITH ME, LITTLE BOY?!
GAH!
ERK!

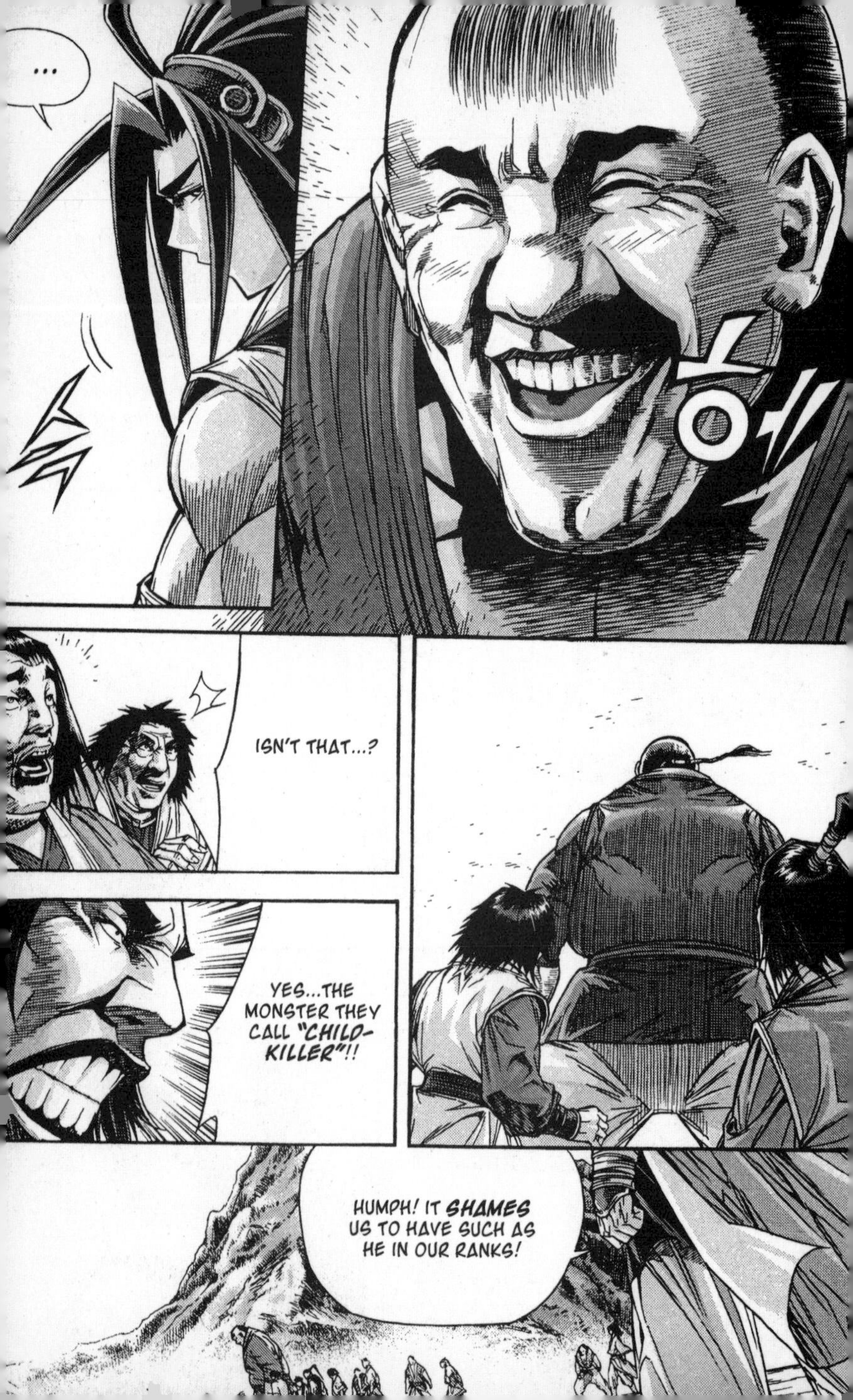
...
ISN'T THAT...?
YES...THE MONSTER THEY CALL "CHILD-KILLER"!!
HUMPH! IT SHAMES US TO HAVE SUCH AS HE IN OUR RANKS!

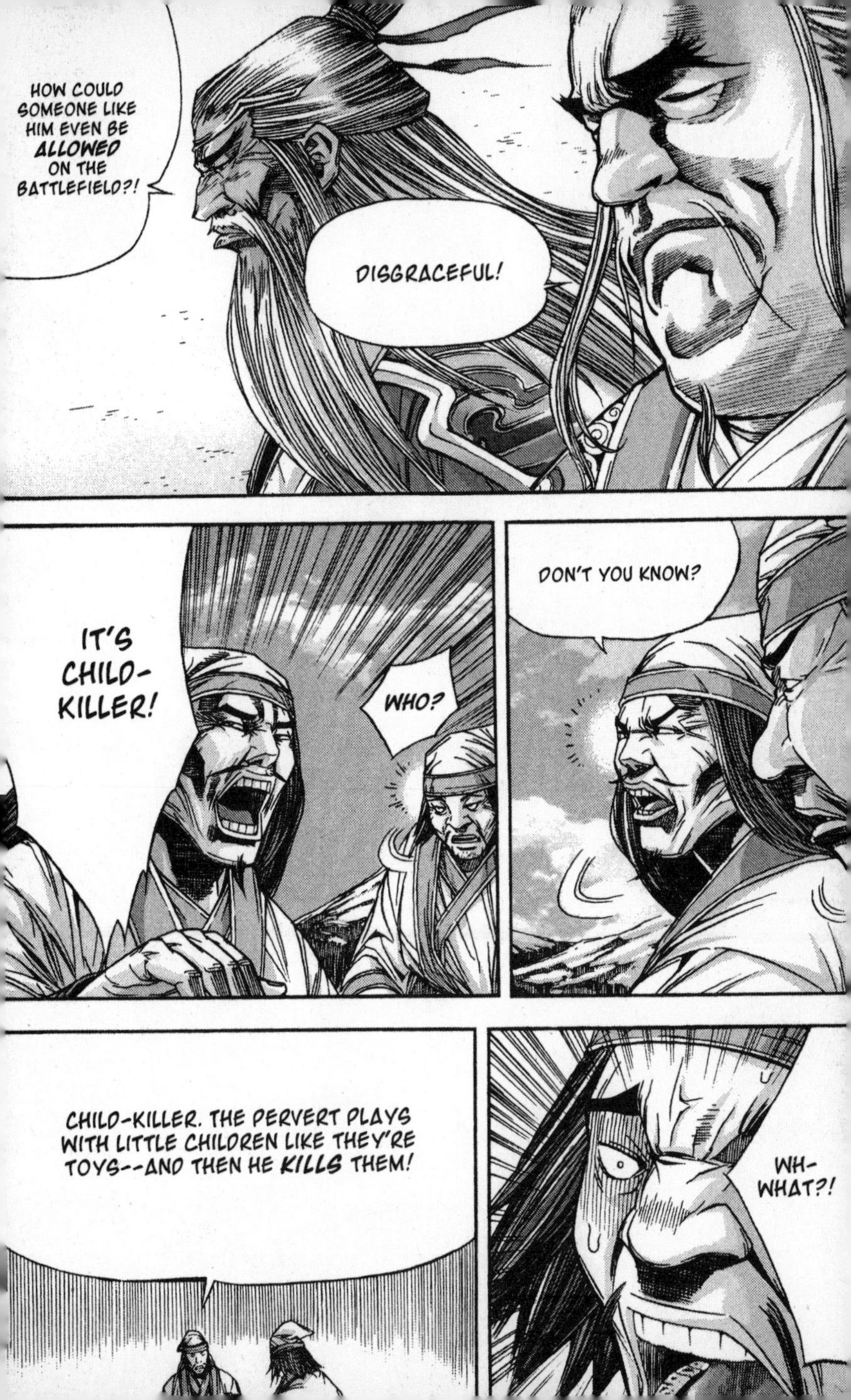
HOW COULD SOMEONE LIKE HIM EVEN BE ALLOWED ON THE BATTLEFIELD?!
DISGRACEFUL!
IT'S CHILD-KILLER!
WHO?
DON'T YOU KNOW?
CHILD-KILLER. THE PERVERT PLAYS WITH LITTLE CHILDREN LIKE THEY'RE TOYS--AND THEN HE KILLS THEM!
WH-WHAT?!

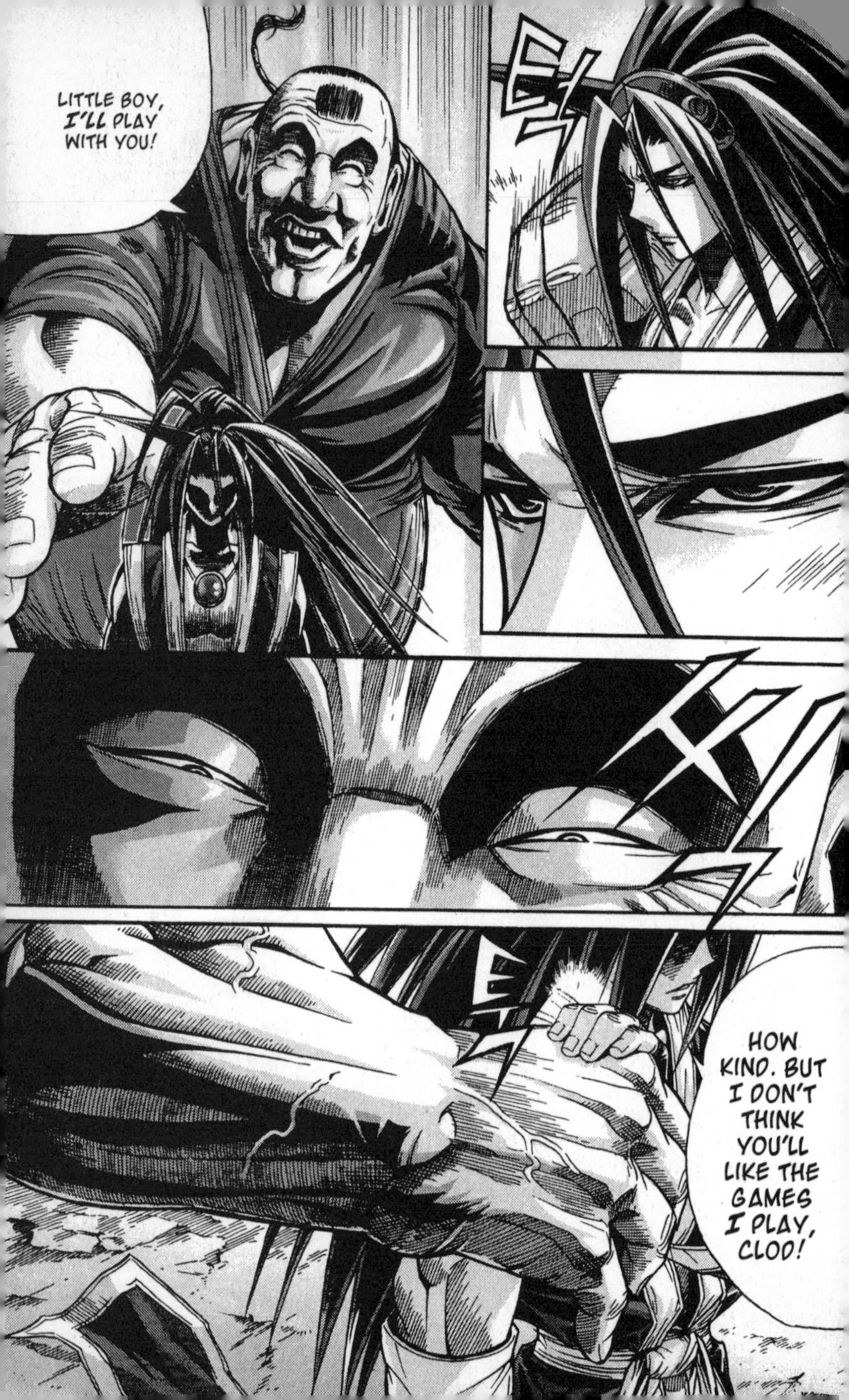
LITTLE BOY, I'LL PLAY WITH YOU!
HOW KIND. BUT I DON'T THINK YOU'LL LIKE THE GAMES I PLAY, CLOD!

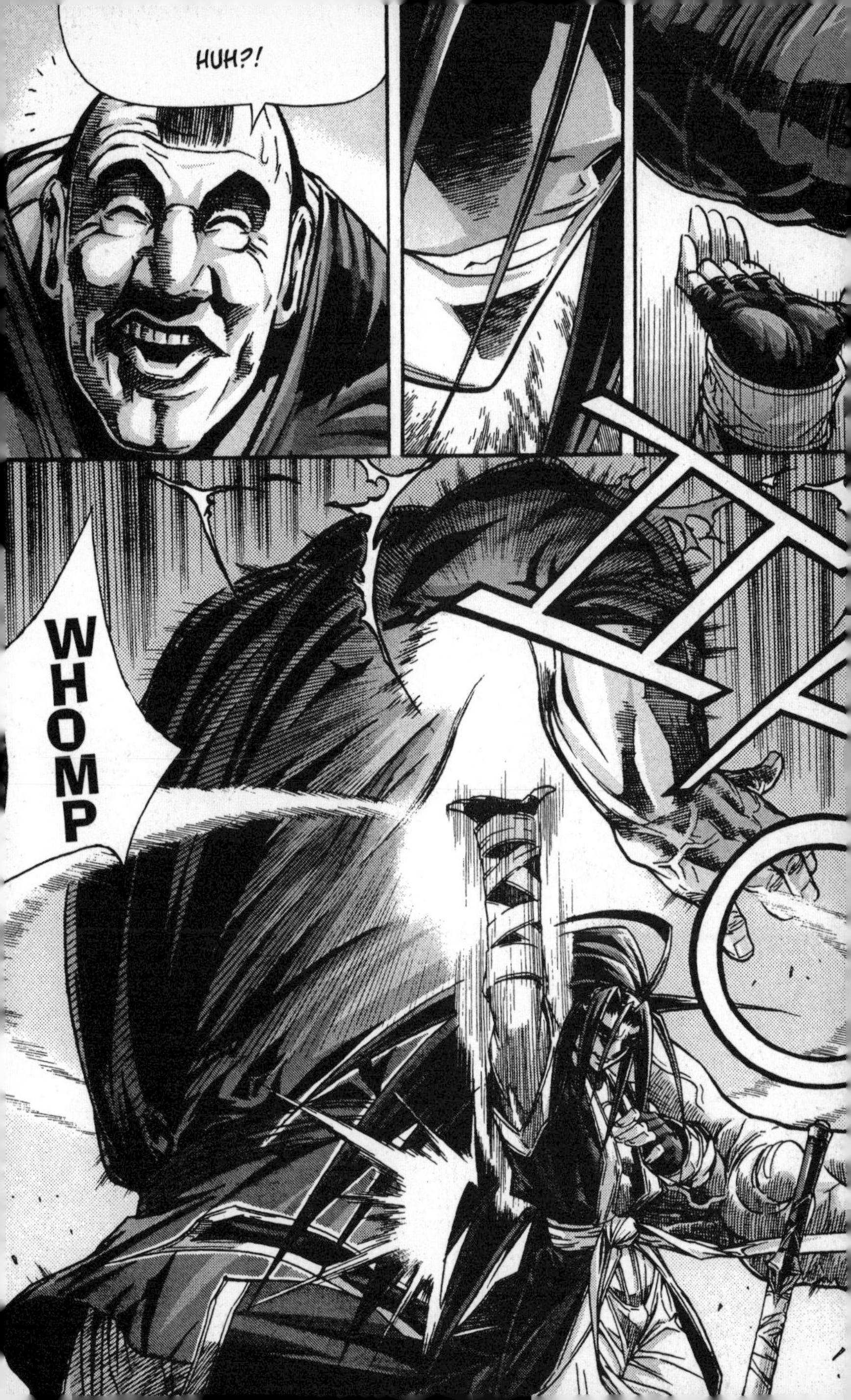
HUH?!
WHOMP

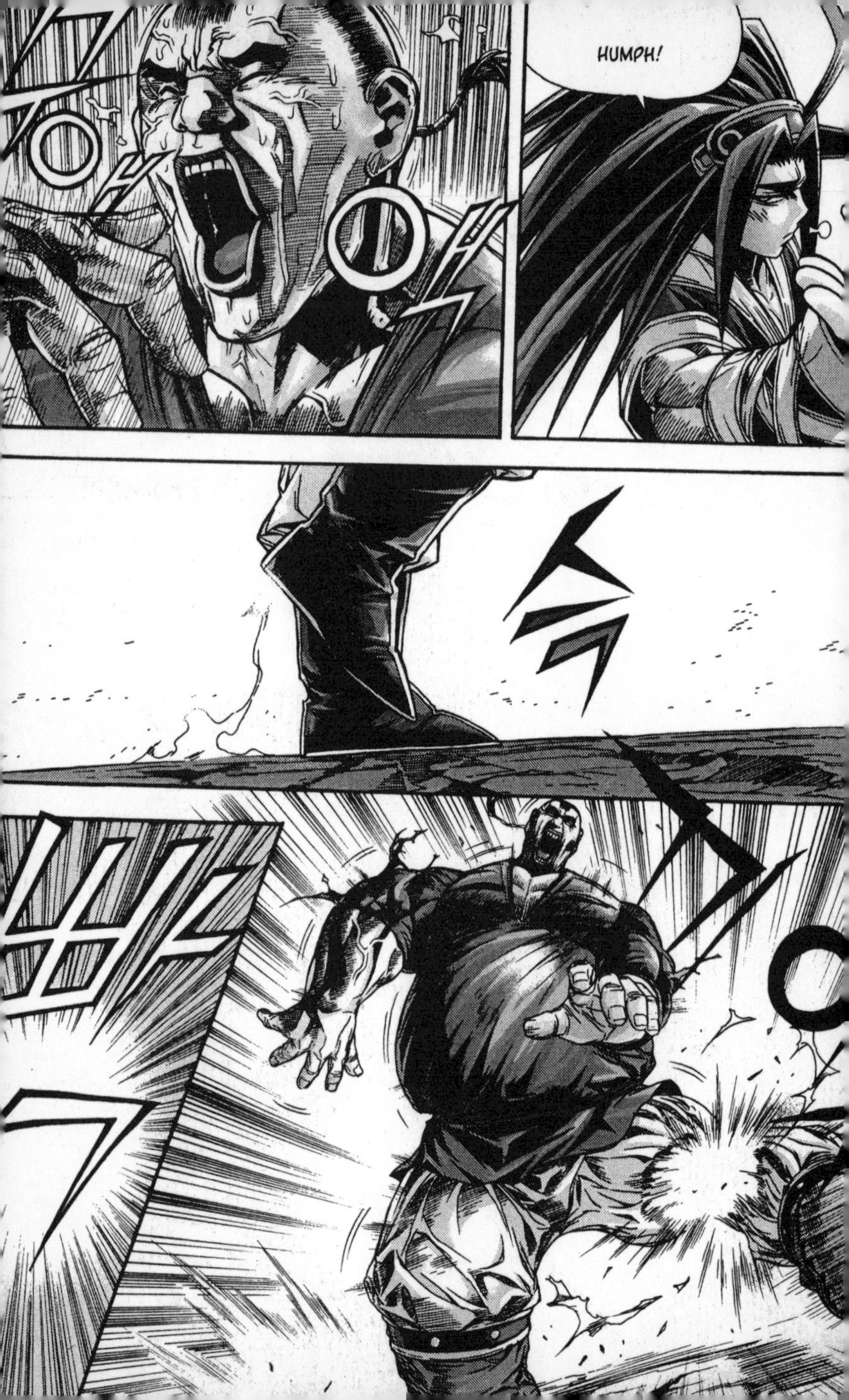
HUMPH!

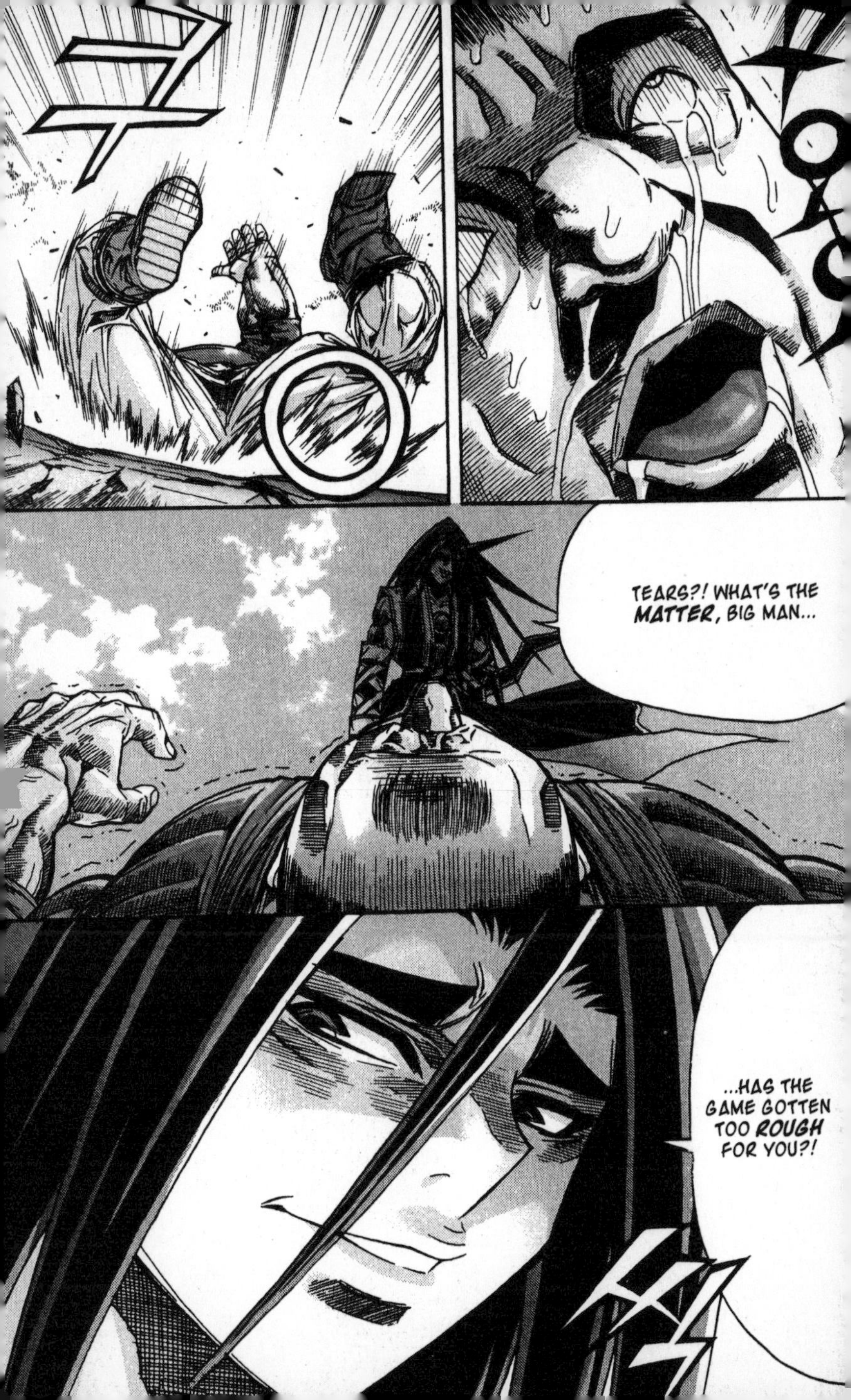
TEARS?! WHAT'S THE MATTER, BIG MAN...
...HAS THE GAME GOTTEN TOO ROUGH FOR YOU?!

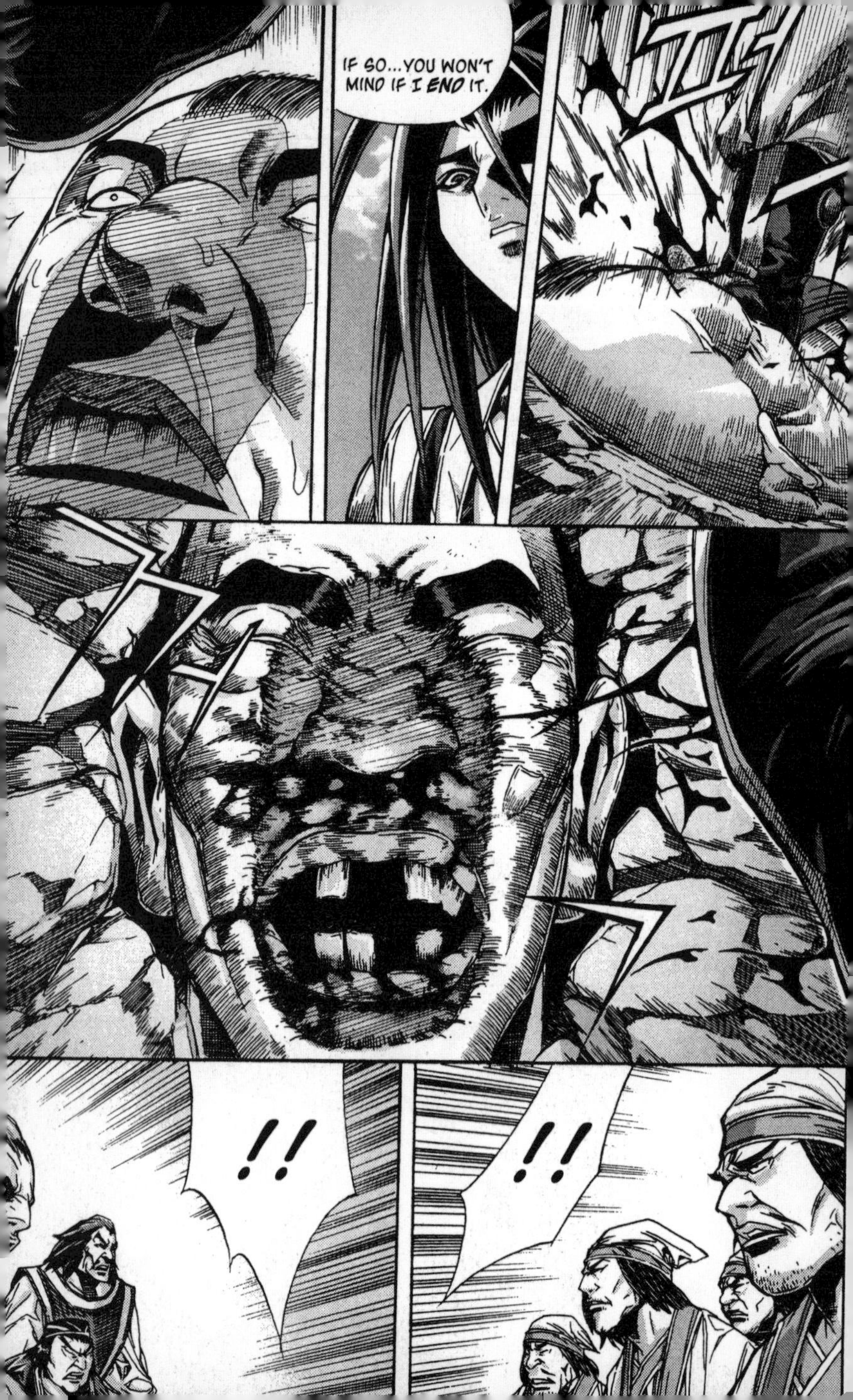
IF SO...YOU WON'T MIND IF I END IT.
!!
!!

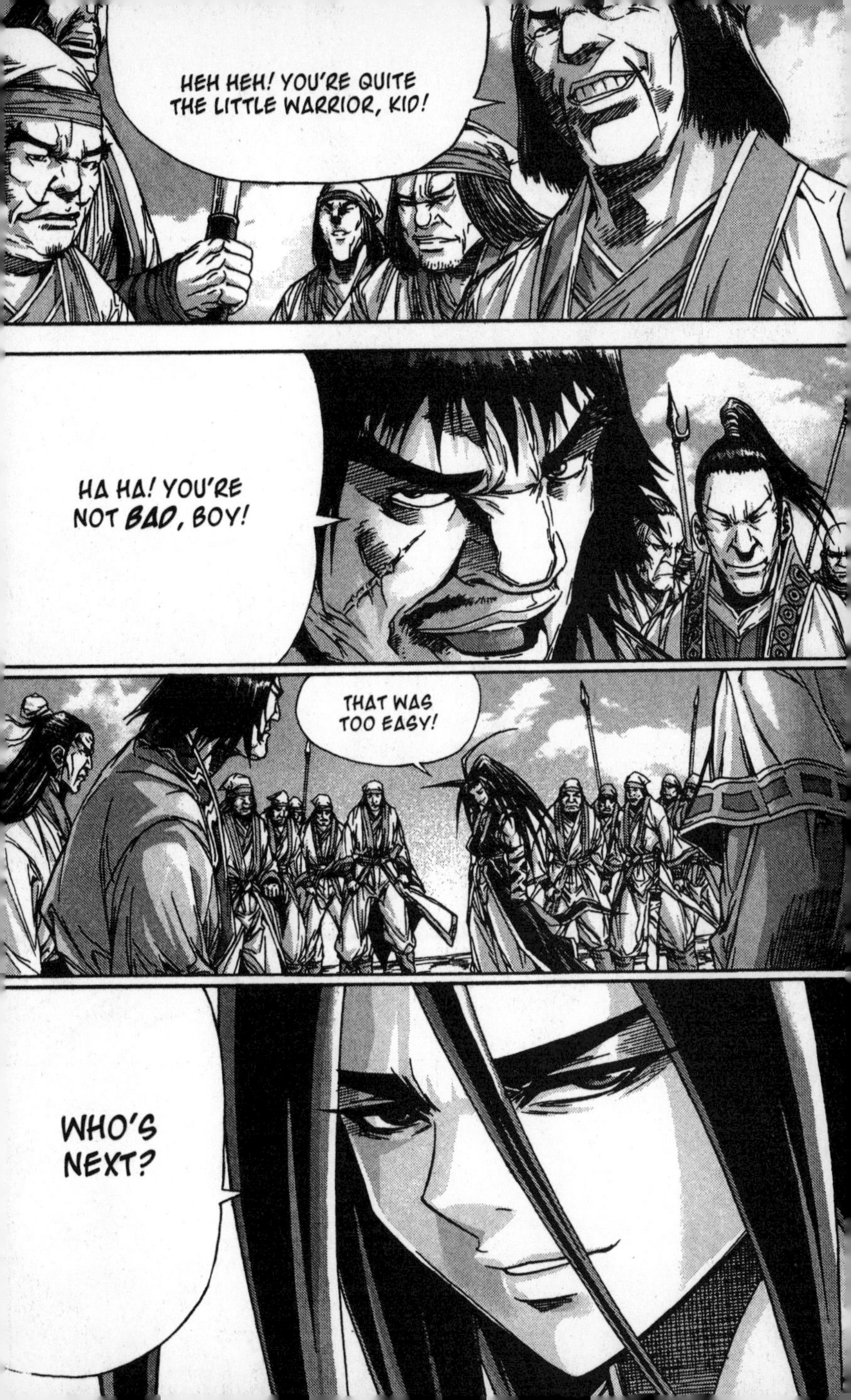
HEH HEH! YOU'RE QUITE THE LITTLE WARRIOR, KID!
HA HA! YOU'RE NOT BAD, BOY!
THAT WAS TOO EASY!
WHO'S NEXT?

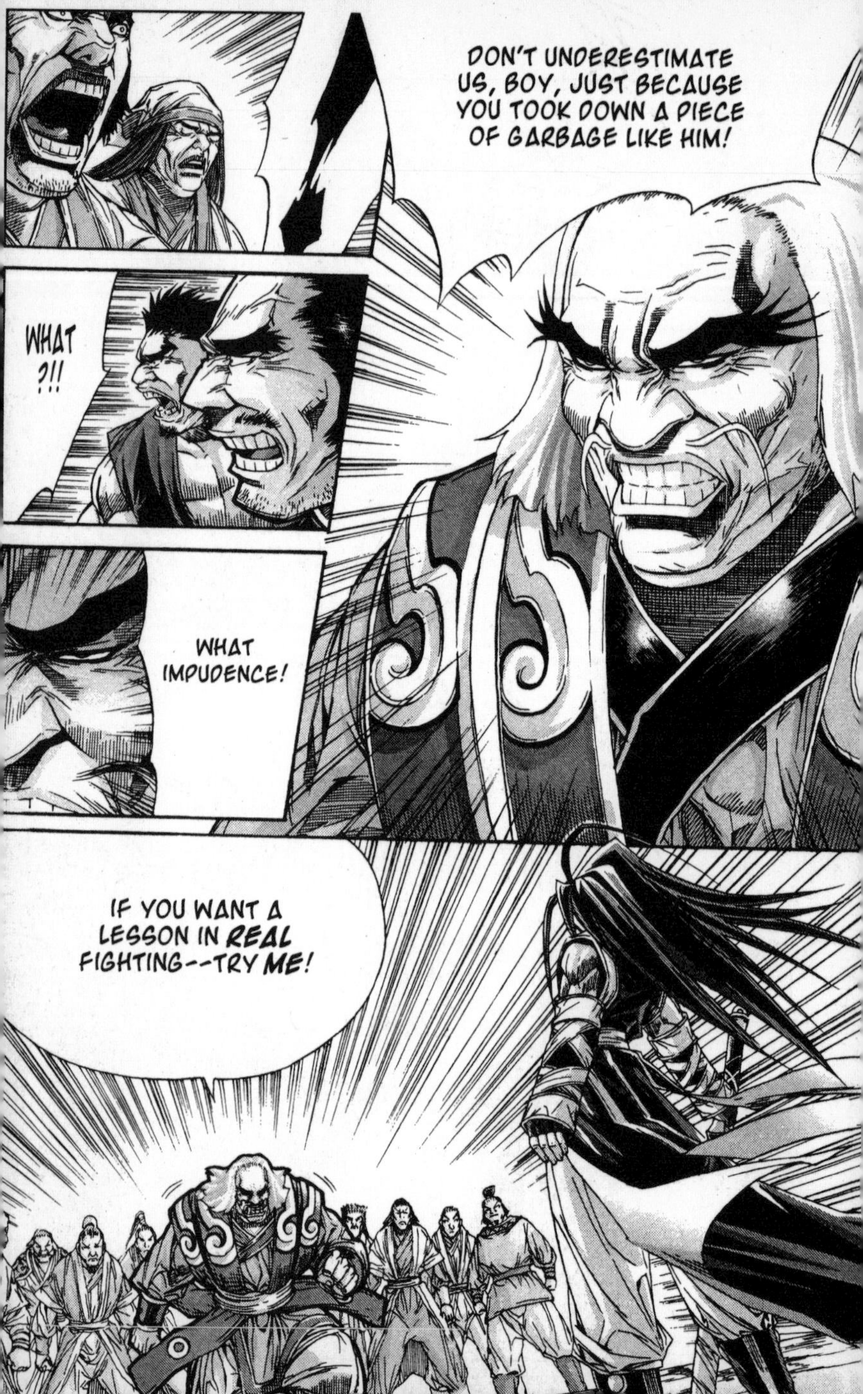
DON'T UNDERESTIMATE US, BOY, JUST BECAUSE YOU TOOK DOWN A PIECE OF GARBAGE LIKE HIM!
WHAT ?!!
WHAT IMPUDENCE!
IF YOU WANT A LESSON IN REAL FIGHTING--TRY ME!

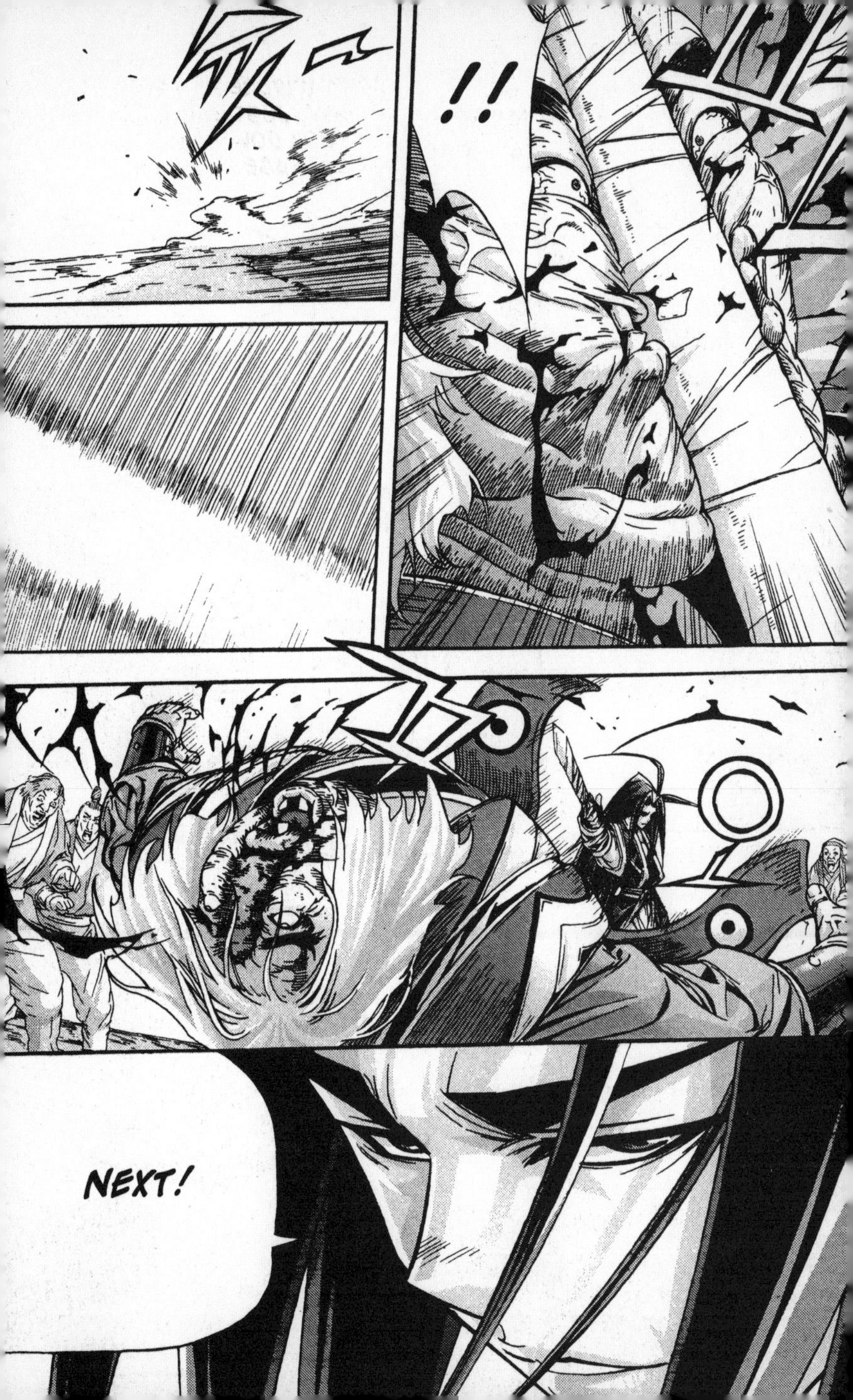
!!
NEXT!

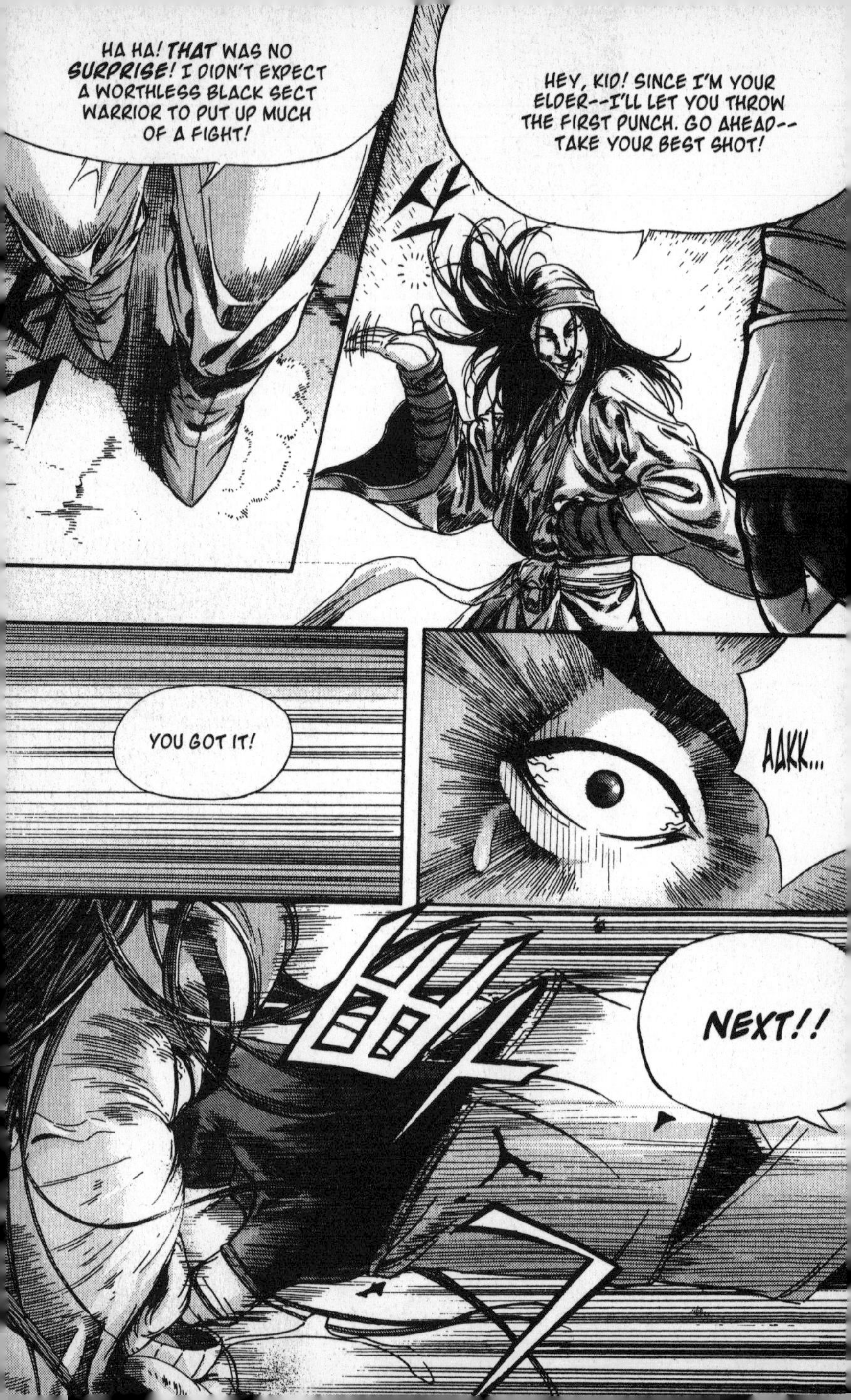
HA HA! THAT WAS NO SURPRISE! I DIDN'T EXPECT A WORTHLESS BLACK SECT WARRIOR TO PUT UP MUCH OF A FIGHT!
HEY, KID! SINCE I'M YOUR ELDER--I'LL LET YOU THROW THE FIRST PUNCH. GO AHEAD--TAKE YOUR BEST SHOT!
YOU GOT IT!
AAKK...
NEXT!!

TO BE CONTINUED...

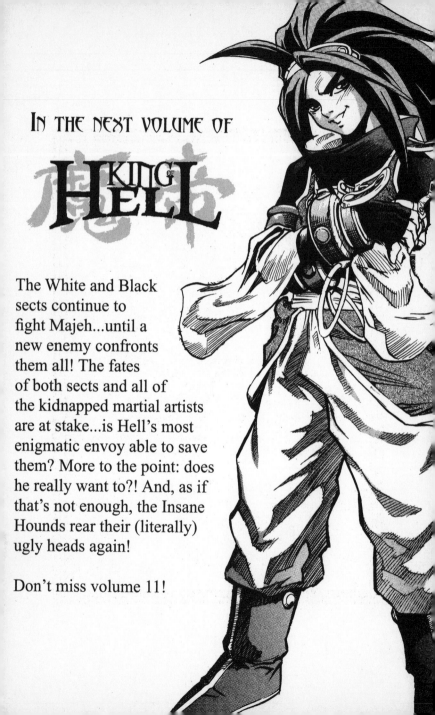

IN THE NEXT VOLUME OF

KING OF HELL

The White and Black
sects continue to
fight Majeh...until a
new enemy confronts
them all! The fates
of both sects and all of
the kidnapped martial artists
are at stake...is Hell's most
enigmatic envoy able to save
them? More to the point: does
he really want to?! And, as if
that's not enough, the Insane
Hounds rear their (literally)
ugly heads again!

Don't miss volume 11!

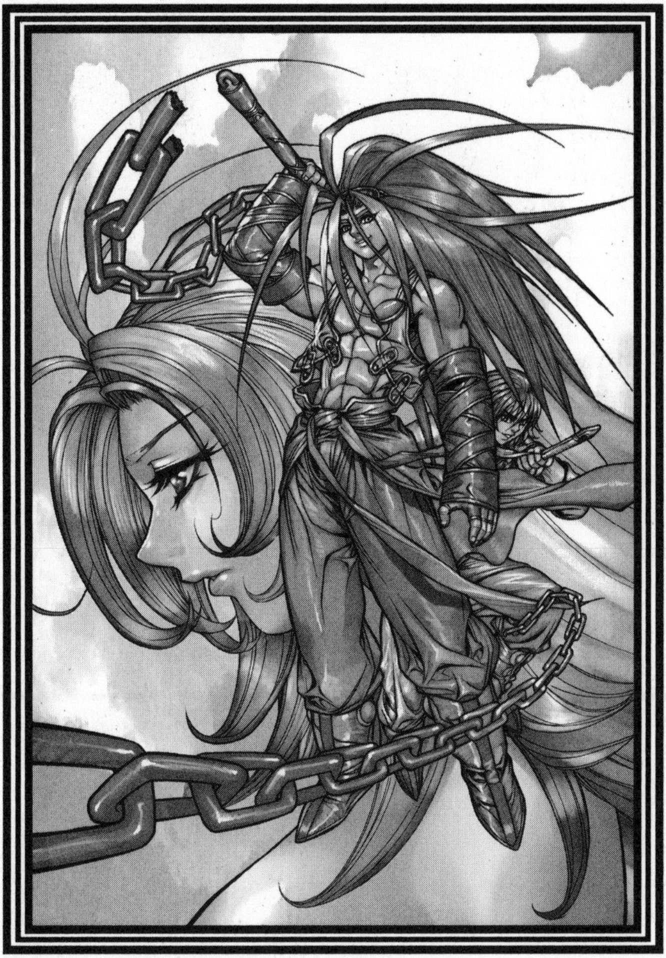

TOKYOPOP SHOP

WWW.TOKYOPOP.COM/SHOP

HOT NEWS!

Check out the TOKYOPOP SHOP! The world's best collection of manga in English is now available online in one place!

SAKURA TAISEN

BECK: MONGOLIAN CHOP SQUAD

Princess Ai and other hot titles are available at the store that never closes!

PRINCESS AI VOL. 2: LUMINATION

- LOOK FOR SPECIAL OFFERS
- PRE-ORDER UPCOMING RELEASES
- COMPLETE YOUR COLLECTIONS

SPOTLIGHT
TOKYOPOP MANGA SUPPLEMENT

SAKURA TAISEN
BY OHJI HIROI & IKKU MASA

SOLDIERS, STEAM ROBOTS, SAMURAI GIRLS... OH, MY!

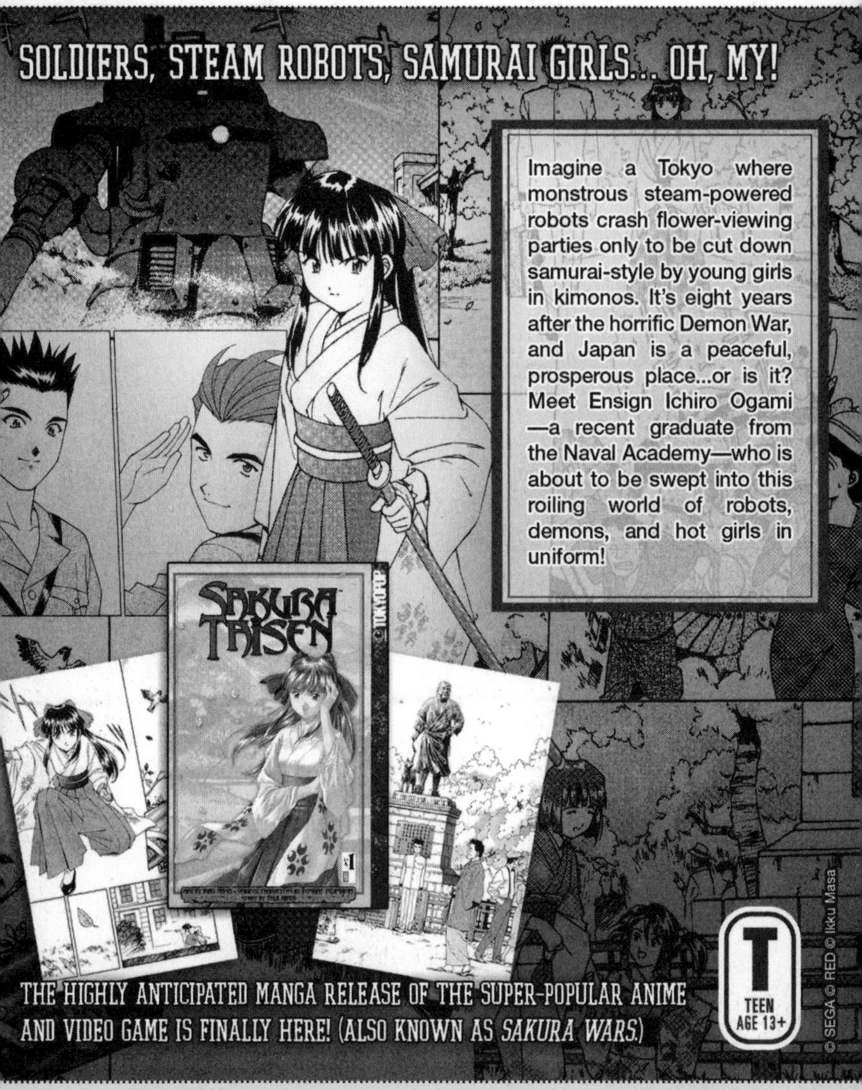

SAKURA TAISEN
TOKYOPOP
T
TEEN
AGE 13+
© SEGA © RED © Ikku Masa

Imagine a Tokyo where monstrous steam-powered robots crash flower-viewing parties only to be cut down samurai-style by young girls in kimonos. It's eight years after the horrific Demon War, and Japan is a peaceful, prosperous place...or is it? Meet Ensign Ichiro Ogami —a recent graduate from the Naval Academy—who is about to be swept into this roiling world of robots, demons, and hot girls in uniform!

THE HIGHLY ANTICIPATED MANGA RELEASE OF THE SUPER-POPULAR ANIME AND VIDEO GAME IS FINALLY HERE! (ALSO KNOWN AS *SAKURA WARS*.)

FOR MORE INFORMATION VISIT: WWW.TOKYOPOP.COM

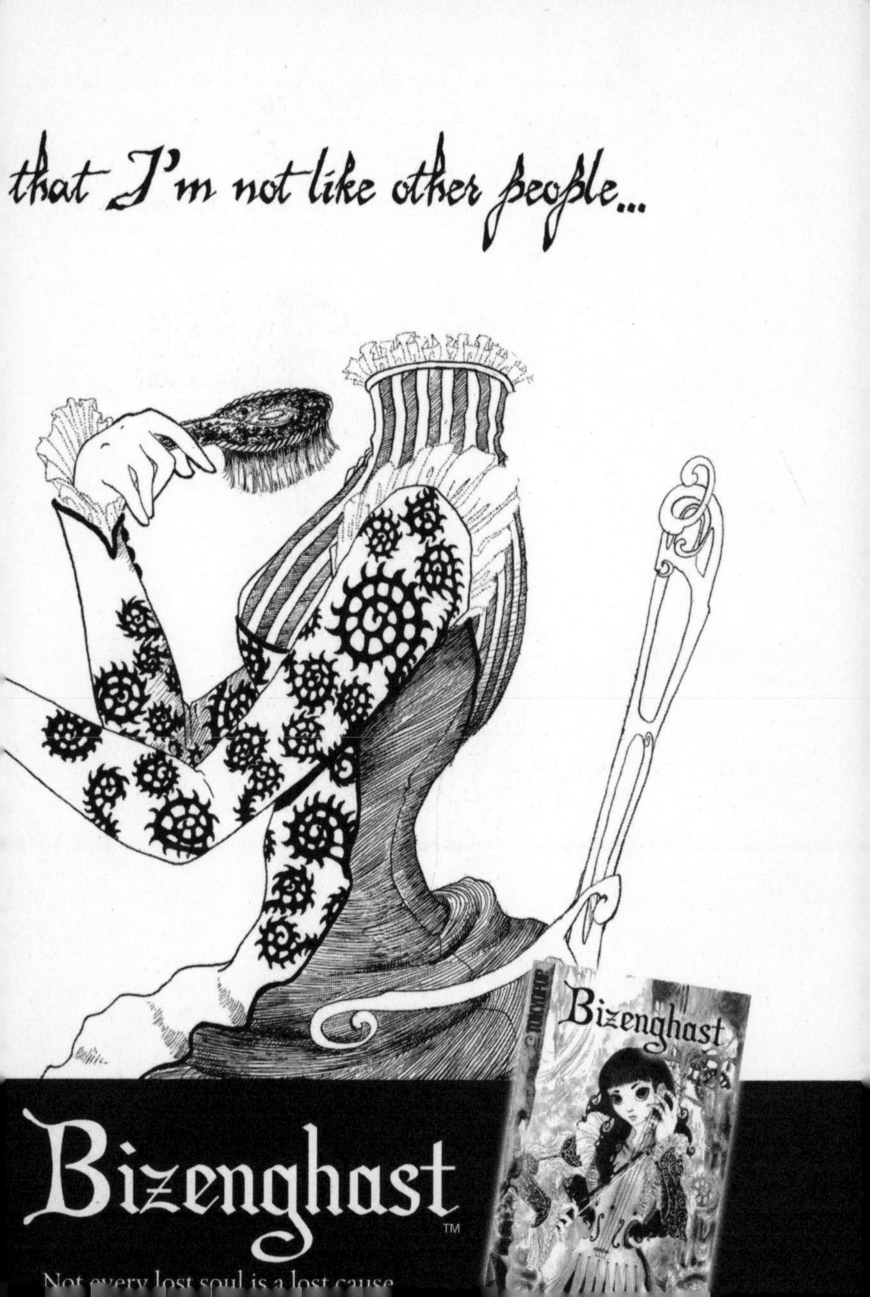
that I'm not like other people...
Bizenghast
Bizenghast™
Not every lost soul is a lost cause.

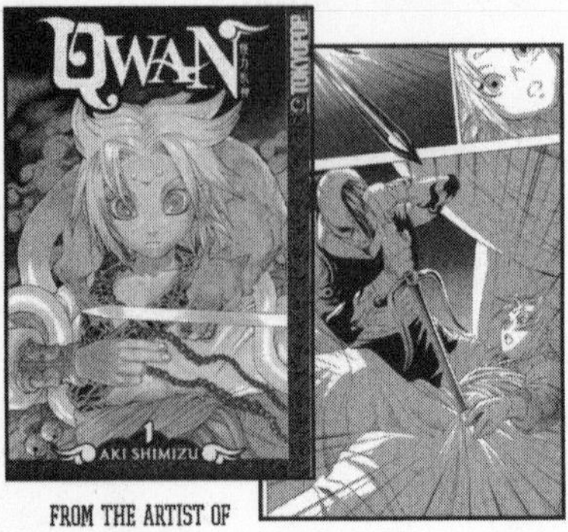
QWAN
1
AKI SHIMIZU
TOKYOPOP

FROM THE ARTIST OF SUIKODEN III

BY AKI SHIMIZU

QWAN

Qwan is a series that refuses to be pigeonholed. Aki Shimizu combines Chinese history, mythology, fantasy and humor to create a world that is familiar yet truly unique. Her creature designs are particularly brilliant—from mascots to monsters. And Qwan himself is great—fallen to Earth, he's like a little kid, complete with the loud questions, yet he eats demons for breakfast. In short, *Qwan* is a solid story with great character dynamics, amazing art and some kick-ass battle scenes. What's not to like?

~Carol Fox, Editor

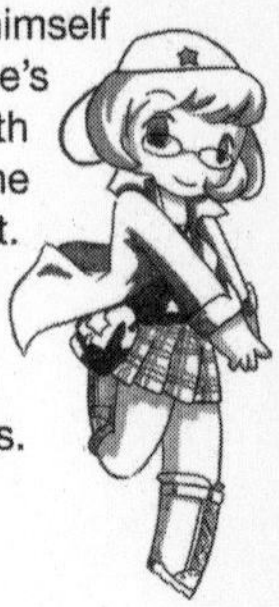

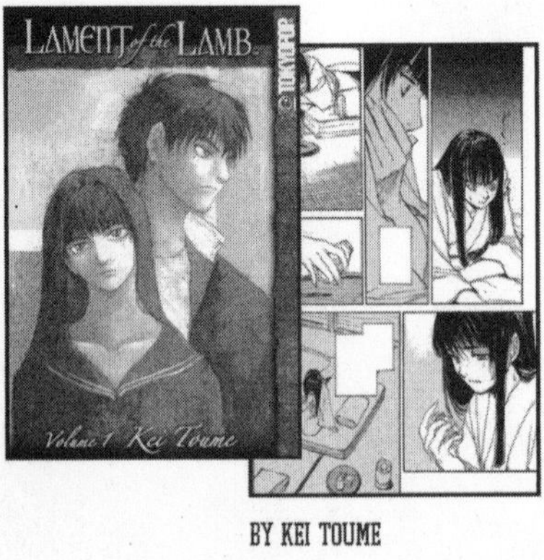
LAMENT of the LAMB
Volume 1 Kei Toume
TOKYOPOP

BY KEI TOUME

LAMENT OF THE LAMB

Kei Toume's *Lament of the Lamb* follows the physical and mental torment of Kazuna Takashiro, who discovers that he's cursed with a hereditary disease that makes him crave blood. *Lament* is psychological horror at its best—it's gloomy, foreboding and emotionally wrenching. Toume brilliantly treats the story's vampirism in a realistic, subdued way, and it becomes a metaphor for teenage alienation, twisted sexual desire and insanity. While reading each volume, I get goose bumps, I feel uneasy, and I become increasingly depressed. Quite a compliment for a horror series!

~Paul Morrissey, Editor

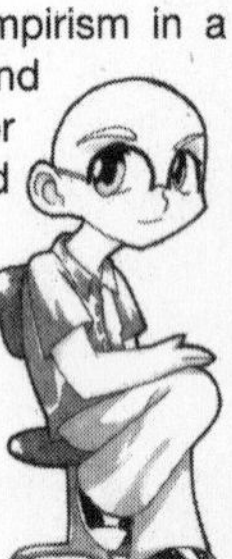